ALIGARH'S FIRST GENERATION

This book explores the nature of Muslim cultural identity, and the changes it underwent in nineteenth-century colonial India, by examining the history of the Muhammadan Anglo-Oriental College (Aligarh Muslim University). It focuses on the first twenty-five years of the college's existence, the period when the first generation of Muslims educated in English graduated from the college to confront the ideological and institutional challenges of colonialism and nationalism. One of the most authoritative works on education and the transformation of Muslim identity in India, David Lelyveld's pioneering study continues to be read by scholars and students of modern Indian history, sociology, and politics, as well as lay readers interested in Indian colonial history and the Muslim experience. An introduction by Mushirul Hasan places the work in its academic context.

David Lelyveld is Professor in the Department of History and Associate Dean of the College of the Humanities and Social Sciences, William Paterson University, New Jersey, USA.

ALIGARH'S FIRST GENERATION

Muslim Solidarity in British India

DAVID LELYVELD

With an Introduction by Mushirul Hasan

OXFORD
UNIVERSITY PRESS

OXFORD
UNIVERSITY PRESS

YMCA Library Building, Jai Singh Road, New Delhi 110 001

Oxford University Press is a department of the University of Oxford. It furthers the University's objective of excellence in research, scholarship, and education by publishing worldwide in

Oxford New York

Auckland Bangkok Buenos Aires Cape Town Chennai Dar es Salaam Delhi Hong Kong Istanbul Karachi Kolkata Kuala Lumpur Madrid Melbourne Mexico City Mumbai Nairobi São Paulo Shanghai Taipei Tokyo Toronto

Published in India
By Oxford University Press, New Delhi

First published by Princeton University Press 1978
First published in India 1996 by arrangement with the original publisher
Oxford India Paperbacks 1996
This edition 2003

ISBN 0 19 566667 4

Printed in India at Sai Printopack Pvt. Ltd., New Delhi 110 020
Published by Manzar Khan, Oxford University Press
YMCA Library Building, Jai Singh Road, New Delhi 110 001

DEDICATED TO

MY "FIRST GENERATION" GRANDPARENTS

Isidor Bookholtz

AND

Gussie Sonberg Bookholtz

IN LOVING MEMORY

Preface

THE Muhammadan Anglo-Oriental College, also called the Madrasat ul-ʿulūm Musalmanān, was a residential school and college established by a group of Indian Muslims under the leadership of Sayyid Ahmad Khan in 1875. Located in the district town of Aligarh, about eighty miles south and a little east of Delhi, it drew students from throughout the heartland of what was once the Mughal empire, stretching from Lahore to Patna, as well as from the Mughal outpost of Hyderabad in the south. Partly financed by a British government subsidy, the college was an affiliate of Calcutta University until 1887, when it joined the newly founded Allahabad University. But, in addition to the prescribed curriculum of these government-sponsored examining establishments, Aligarh College attempted to provide a milieu supportive of Muslim religious concerns and other indigenous cultural values. This book studies the college during its first twenty-five years, 1875-1900, when it was under the leadership of Sayyid Ahmad Khan and a remarkable English principal, Theodore Beck. The students of this period represent a "first generation" of English-educated Muslims in north India.

More generally, the present study attempts to understand what it meant to be an "Indian Muslim" in the nineteenth century, and how that cultural identity may have changed meaning in the context of a colonial restucturing of political institutions. The major concern here will be, then, to ask how a specific group of people—the founders and first students of an Indian college—mediated such changes in their own lives. I am by no means attempting to study all the Muslims of South Asia, and it is not my purpose to account for the statistical representativeness of the people I have studied. Instead, I want to understand the relationship between institutional innovation and changing cultural configurations in a particular Indian milieu. I assume that a concept only has meaning within a context, in this case the context of a cultural system, that is, the ordering of symbols and categories into a paradigm for interpreting experience and guiding action. The kind of cultural system that concerns me here is ideology. I define ideology as a set of assumptions that serves as a model for interpreting the relations of people in groups —what binds people together or separates them, and according to what kinds of principles, such as authority, deference, and loyalty.[1]

New institutions and power relationships call for new ways of thinking. If circumstances change, old perspectives may no longer be successful in interpreting what goes on in the world and guiding a person's actions. Then it becomes necessary to change the world or to change one's values and assumptions —or to work out a compromise. To understand what it meant to be a Muslim in British India, it is useful to ask how social identity was articulated with the political institutions of colonial rule. It would not be surprising to find that as the political system shifted from Mughal to British patterns, the cultural meaning of a group identity might change too. But one might also expect people to take action to transform the institutions of society into something more compatible with their beliefs.

From this point of view it would be a mistake to take up a given identity tag, such as "Muslim," and treat it as a "thing" in itself without regard to the total social map that guided people's perceptions at a given time or place. Instead, it is more useful to ask how a particular concept is learned, at what point in a person's life, and in the history of a society.[2]

[1] My understanding of ideology as a cultural system derives from an article with that title by Clifford Geertz in David E. Apter, ed., *Ideology and Discontent* (London: Free Press of Glencoe, 1964), pp. 47-73; also Louis Dumont, *Homo Hierarchicus*, 2d ed. of English translation (London: Paladin, 1972).

[2] For an abstract theoretical statement that I find sufficiently congenial for present purposes, see Peter L. Berger and Thomas Luckmann, *The Social Construction of Reality*, 2d ed. (Garden City, N.Y.: Anchor Books, 1967).

This perspective on the social context of personal identity may be helpful in interpreting some of the underlying logic behind the creation of an educational establishment like Aligarh College in late nineteenth-century India. One body of contemporary social theory seeks to establish a relationship between the functional needs of a social system and the transition in a person's emotional relationships and self-definitions as he or she moves from childhood to adult life. In the ideology of an industrial society, for example, the participation of any individual in the social system is supposedly determined by particular skills in fulfilling specialized roles. Ideally, a person can compete and cooperate with others according to criteria posited on individual actions, not inherent attributes defined by birth. This kind of social interaction is radically different from the world of childhood, in which the dominant mode is authority and nurturing love on the part of an older person, and obedience and dependent love from the younger. The need for transition from the childhood mode to the adult in this type of society is mediated by membership in "age groups," in which one's most important relationships are defined by one's abilities and actions among people who are otherwise in a similar position in life.[3]

In contrast, the ideal Mughal social structure emphasized asymmetrical kinship-like alliances, which linked separate groups with the imperial dynasty, but discouraged horizontal solidarity among these groups. There existed shared skills and styles among members of the Mughal ruling class, but these did not generate a sense of political community cutting across the great variety of birth-defined identities. To a great extent birth and genealogical position dictated a person's social roles. This Mughal ideological paradigm offered more continuity with the modes of family relationship. According to the "age-group" theory, an absence of non-kin consolidations among the young could be correlated to the

[3] S. N. Eisenstadt, *From Generation to Generation* (Glencoe: Free Press, 1956).

absence of a truly bureaucratic state in Mughal India.[4] But in nineteenth-century India, the British colonial regime offered new incentives for developing social ties that emphasized voluntary participation, personal achievement, and nonfamilial cooperation: hence the creation of institutions that would temporarily isolate the young from the rest of society in order to prepare them for later life.

Such institutions were a special kind of age grouping, a formally organized, self-consciously created social establishment with the defined goal of carrying out transitions of identity and loyalty suitable to the special circumstances of British India. Aligarh College was an especially clear-cut instance of this deliberateness: as a residential establishment it sought a total divorce from family life, a world of its own bound by the walls of the college quadrangle. Every aspect of life would be regulated according to well-articulated educational strategies. Aligarh was a "total institution," a place where boys and young men found themselves locked into a shared situation, enclosed within the physical and psychological boundaries of a formally administered social establishment.[5] Here they were expected to render up their old self-definitions in exchange for new ones as determined by certain controlling personnel, the "managers" and "staff." Such an institution represents a strategy of simplifying the complex overlapping of roles and identities and undermining "ordinary" assumptions about love and work—all to implant a new set of moral commitments. But as a living institution, the contradictions between overall social goals, exigencies of maintaining the institution, and defensive measures among the student "inmates"—all created a social world that was in many respects at odds with the public intentions of its sponsors.

[4] S. N. Eisenstadt, *The Political System of Empires*, paperback ed. (New York: Free Press, 1969), does not examine this idea suggested by his earlier work.

[5] Erving Goffman, *Asylums* (Garden City: Anchor Books, 1961), pp. 1-124.

Such theoretical orientations, useful for writing research proposals, have been in the back of my mind as I have pursued what I take to be the historian's task of narrative and description in an effort to evoke the lives of actual people in concrete situations. My major effort has been to communicate perceptions of people at the time, not what later observers might want to read into them. The relevance of these prefatory theoretical remarks is that they articulate ideas that have guided me, not always consciously, in my choice of what data to present and what interpretations to make. It is proper to give fair warning.

The history of Aligarh College has usually been studied in terms of the rise of political "separatism" among South Asian Muslims. A somewhat different body of historical literature has concentrated on the role of some of Aligarh's leaders, particularly Sayyid Ahmad Khan, in adapting Islamic theological ideas to the assumptions of nineteenth-century European empiricism. There has also been a certain amount of literature, typical of an educational institution, that can be described as commemorative. The Aligarh College and the intellectual and political movement that surrounded it have been historically self-conscious, and this has stimulated a good deal of published writing by participants.

In 1967, when I embarked on the study of the early history of the college, there had been, in addition to a number of pamphlets, three book-length works written on the subject, but the only one that had been published Iftikhar Alam's *Muhammadan College History* in Urdu, dated back to 1900 and had no pretentions of scholarly purpose; it was a compendium of information, pictures, and high praise for the enjoyment of well-wishers of the college. Sometime in the 1930s and 1940s, Muhammad Amin Zuberi wrote an uncompleted history of Aligarh as college and (after 1920) university, which still exists in Urdu manuscript at the Pakistan Historical Society in Karachi. I am indebted to Dr. S. Moinuddin Ahmad for allowing me to read the earlier sections of this work. I am also very much indebted to Shri

S. K. Bhatnagar, who allowed me to read the manuscript of his English history of the college, 1875-1920, which he completed in 1962. Ultimately, that work was published in 1969, after editing by Professor K. A. Nizami of Aligarh Muslim University. It stands now as the standard history of the college, rich in detail although somewhat lacking in analytic purpose.

Unfortunately, Shri Bhatnagar did not have access to the recently established Aligarh University Archives, except when somebody happened to show him a document on the sly. As far as I know the present work is the first monograph devoted to the history of the college to use this valuable collection. I am greatly indebted to Dr. Abdul Aleem, late Vice Chancellor of the university, for granting me permission to use the archives in 1968-1969, and to Professor Nizami and Professor S. Bashiruddin, then University Librarian, for making the necessary arrangements. Before my own explorations into the archives, a volume of selected documents had been published under the university's auspices and has been quite useful to me, despite a number of editorial flaws. But the major documents I used were the docket correspondence of the Honorary Secretary's office, including copies of the letters sent out. These documents I arranged myself according to the old register books by which they are numbered. I have used the numbers, when available, in my references below.

There is also a good deal of primary published literature available in the Maulana Azad Library of the Aligarh University, which I was able to use thanks to Professor Bashiruddin and Mr. Faruq Jalali, curator of the Sir Syed Room. The most important of this kind is an almost full run of the *Aligarh Institute Gazette*, the major publication that came out of the Aligarh establishment. I have also read through much of *Tahẕīb ul-Akhlāq*, the *Muhammadan Anglo-Oriental College Magazine*, the *Aligarh Monthly*, and the *'Alīgaṛh Megzīn*, all publications of the college or university available in the Azad Library. In addition to these journals, I have used published annual reports of the college, proceedings of the Board of Trustees, reports of the boarding house, and various occasional publications. I was also able to read through the published proceedings of the Old Boys' Association, available in the Old Boys' Lodge.

Many of these published materials have already been used by writers who do not deal specifically with the college history as such, but incorporate it in political and biographical studies. The most important single book that has been written on the Aligarh movement is the biography of Sayyid Ahmad Khan, *Ḥayāt-i Jāvīd*, by Altaf Husain Hali, published in 1901. This work has been the major source for numerous other writings on Sayyid Ahmad Khan; few of them have anything additional to contribute. An independent biographical source is by G.F.I. Graham, first published while the subject was still alive in 1887. There have been other good biographies by Abdul Haq and Muhammad Amin Zuberi, but the most valuable sources on Sayyid Ahmad are his own writings, including his correspondence, published during his lifetime and later. Most of this has been reprinted in standard editions by Shaikh Muhammad Ismail Panipati in Lahore, Pakistan. There is a good deal of biographical literature on the lives of Sayyid Ahmad's colleagues, especially Sami Ullah Khan, Mushtaq Husain, and Mahdi Ali, and these are often useful for gathering information about the early history of the college. Even more valuable for my purposes are biographies and autobiographies by members of the first generation of Aligarh students, which generally have chapters devoted to their student days, and also provide information on their backgrounds and what became of them in later life.

More information on the life careers of Aligarh students is available in a wide variety of sources, starting with the *Muhammadan College Directory*, compiled in 1895 and again in 1911 by Sayyid Tufail Ahmad, an early student of the college. For further information I have interviewed a number of relatives and descendants of these first students, in what was surely the most interesting and enjoyable part of my research. I am extremely grateful to the many people who took the trouble to talk to me, often over a period of days and months. Such interviews were carried on in Aligarh, Delhi, Lucknow, Azamgarh, Bombay, and Hyderabad in India; and Lahore and Karachi in Pakistan. They are listed in the bibliography, but I must make special mention here of the late Hashim Muhammad Ali of Karachi, son of one of Aligarh's first students and a member of the family of Sayyid Ahmad Khan, who took great trouble to impart to me the family history, of which he was the acknowledged authority. I could only use a small part of the information I gathered in all these interviews in the present work, but they have immensely increased my "feel" for the culture of Aligarh and I hope to return to them in future studies.

Moving further away from Aligarh, I found valuable information in the government archival collections in Delhi, Lucknow, and Hyderabad, the official proceedings of the governments of India, the North-Western Provinces and Oudh, and Hyderabad State, respectively. The government archives often have very useful libraries as well, and it was there that I saw official publications such as the annual reports of the directors of public instruction, the report of the Indian Education Commission of 1882, and *Selections from the Vernacular Newspapers*, which were published in translation for official purposes. I used similar documentary and published materials during a brief stay in London at the Indian Office Library. I was also able to examine a valuable collection of private letters in the National Museum of Pakistan in Karachi.

There is a good deal of secondary literature that touches on the history of Aligarh, but little of it is of much interest after one has examined the primary sources. The best work is in unpublished Ph.D. dissertations, and I have been able to examine some of these at Aligarh, the University of London, and the University of Chicago. I am indebted to Francis Robinson, who allowed me to read a draft of his fellowship dissertation at Trinity College, Cambridge, which ultimately served as the basis for his book, *Separatism among Indian Muslims*. I am also grateful to Gail Minault, now of the University of Texas, who shared with me all her research on the origins of the Khilafat movement and joined me in a narrative article on the campaign to establish Aligarh as an independent Muslim University. Barbara Metcalf of the University of Pennsylvania, whose work on the Deoband movement touches on many matters examined here in relation to Aligarh, has been an extremely helpful critic and guide.

The present study is conceived as a narrative, although not entirely a presentation of facts in chronological sequence. I have tried to interweave analysis with narration, and have frequently relied on anecdotes to communicate a more general understanding of the symbolic vocabulary of Aligarh's cultural history. Instead of presenting introductions, hypotheses, summaries, and conclusions in orderly progression, I have tried to use somewhat more "literary" devices, such as the juxtaposition and development of symbolic motifs and particular life histories in the course of a larger narrative account. The work is, however, interspersed with more general analytic presentations of arguments and evidence as these seemed appropriate. I hope that in writing in this way I have been able to communicate something of the texture of Aligarh's history, and not merely to create yet another document for future students of late twentieth-century American intellectual history.

The first two chapters, by way of introduction, present the cultural and institutional context in which the Aligarh College was founded. The first chapter contrasts four models of Indian society—colonial, liberal, Mughal, and Islamic—in order to interpret the meaning of the word "Muslim" as a group identity within each model. In this chapter I hope to establish the relevance of the colonial situation to the sense of self and group loyalty as encountered in the Aligarh cultural milieu.[6] The second chapter has two major purposes: first, to set out the range of life career patterns in the pre-Aligarh generation, the generation of fathers, grandfathers, and uncles, as well as the early childhood of Aligarh's first generation of students—all by way of establishing the social and cultural circumstances that preceded the creation of the college. Second, the chapter introduces institutional developments under British rule, especially educational requirements for government employment and related occupations, that stimulated Aligarh's founders to seek a new way of raising their children. My argument here is that the older generation had to make adjustments in the education of their sons if they wanted them to achieve under altered circumstances levels of social prestige and occupational achievement analogous to what their elders had been able to experience, or at least aspire to.

Chapter III is an account of the five-year period of design and the public campaign for the establishment of the Aligarh College. Since the college was founded by Indians, I am interested in the choices they made in making plans, and in the social and political constraints under which they had to operate as members of Indian society and subjects of British rule. Chapter IV carries this study of planning and response to circumstances into the actual history of the college during its first twenty-five years. The chapter portrays Aligarh as a planned settlement, and examines the physical layout of the college in its geographical setting as well as the recruit-

[6] See Georges Balandier, "The Colonial Situation," in Immanuel Wallerstein, ed., *Social Change: The Colonial Situation* (New York: John Wiley and Sons, 1966), pp. 34-61; Clifford Geertz, "The Integrative Revolution: Primordial Sentiments and Civil Politics in the New States," in his *Old Societies and New States* (New York: Free Press, 1963), pp. 105-57; Frantz Fanon, *Black Skins, White Masks* (New York: Grove Press, 1967).

ment of the students, teachers, and "managers" that populated the college community.

Chapters V and VI are the heart of the work: an exploration of the educational experience of Aligarh's first generation of students. Chapter V deals with Aligarh as an intellectual institution from the point of view of classrooms and examinations, as well as the extensive extracurricular activity characteristic of the college. I am concerned here with the style of discourse and the mutual accommodation of specific British and Indian forms of intellectual communication. I also point out that the emphasis on personal and familial models of social relations made the particular British intellectual subculture presented at the college congenial to the indigenous sponsors of the institution. Chapter V also tries to develop some of the intellectual and ideological tensions and incompatibilities that characterized the early years of the college.

Chapter VI is concerned with Aligarh as a social milieu. It examines the changing structure of authority in the college, and the development of a student culture that stood in contrast to the parent-child paradigm familiar both in the homes of the indigenous culture and in the college before the 1887 student strike. The chapter explores the basis of student solidarity, as well as the development of student cliques within the isolated community of the college.

The final chapter, like the first two, returns to the world beyond Aligarh in an effort to place the college in a wider context. The chapter begins by discussing the political activities and views associated with the Aligarh movement during the late nineteenth century, particularly Aligarh's response to the rise of Indian nationalism. From there the study spills out of its chronological boundaries in a preliminary attempt to see what the alumni of the college did in later life. Besides presenting statistical data on the occupational distribution of former Aligarh students, I examine the involvement of Aligarh and Aligarh alumni in the rise of anti-British political movements and in Muslim separatism from the mainstream of Indian nationalism in the early twentieth century.

The study of Aligarh's history was initially suggested to me in 1965 by Professor Edward Shils, and I am grateful to him for his thorough reading of the first draft of this study many years later. Before actually going to India to take up my research, I did a number of preliminary studies at the University of Chicago under Dr. Irfan Habib, Dr. Anil Seal, and Professors C. Arnold Anderson, C. M. Naim, McKim Marriott, and the late Marshall Hodgson. My major advisor throughout has been Bernard S. Cohn, whose own intellectual explorations have been a source of continual inspiration. I am also grateful to Professors Philip Calkins, Ronald Inden, and Leonard Binder for reading all or part of my dissertation and offering valuable criticisms. Professor Joseph Schwartzberg has very kindly designed or adapted the maps; I am very thankful to him. Also Professor Howard Hirt generously shared his geographical research on Aligarh town.

The research for this study of Aligarh's history was conducted in India, and primarily in Aligarh, from 1967 to 1969 on grants from the Foreign Area Fellowship Program and the University of Chicago's Committee on South and Southeast Asian Studies. My debt to numerous people in India and Pakistan for their friendship, hospitality, and help is overwhelming. A great deal of my exposition of cultural matters relies on these personal contacts, and my commitment to the whole enterprise would have died long ago but for their generous encouragement. In addition to the names mentioned above and numerous other friends whom there is no space to name, I must thank Professor A. A. Suroor and reiterate my tremendous sense of obligation to Professor S. Bashiruddin, both now retired from the faculty of the Aligarh Muslim University. Mr. Iftikhar Azmi of Lucknow and Asad ur-Rahman, now of Brooklyn, were good teachers and friends. Dr. Irfan Habib, my teacher when he was a visiting professor at Chicago, was also my supervisor at Aligarh, and I am grateful to him for putting up with me under trying circumstances.

My mother, Dr. Toby Lelyveld, and my brother, Michael Lelyveld, were good enough to read and edit the manuscript in its early stages; Joseph Lelyveld and Carolyn Lelyveld provided frequent intervals of hospitality in Delhi while I was living in Aligarh. My father, Rabbi Arthur Lelyveld, has been a constant encourager of my work. Finally, I want to express my gratitude to Professor Gerda Lerner and the late Carl Lerner for persuading me to complete this work when I was inclined to throw it all in the ocean.

On transliteration of proper names and Urdu words: I have generally confined the full array of diacriticals and italics to the first appearance in the text and to footnote references, although I have sometimes used diacriticals elsewhere to prevent gross mispronunciation. The spelling adopted is a slightly modified version of the Library of Congress system ("c" is to be pronounced as an unaspirated "ch"). Words assimilated into English have not been transliterated from Urdu except when they appear in book titles. I have attempted to standardize the spelling of proper names, despite the fact that the possessors of these names often used non-standardized forms when writing in English; but I have only used diacriticals to clarify ambiguities. Thus I have written Muhammad Ali, not Muḥammad ʿAlī or Mohamed Ali, except in the footnotes and the index. Sara Suleri and Fawzia Mustafa have put in many long hours helping me with transliteration, proofreading, and preparing the index.

Where translations into English have been available to me (for example, in the bilingual *Aligarh Institute Gazette*), I have used them, although I have tried to check them against the Urdu. I am indebted to Dr. Moaziz Ali Beg and Bashir Ahmad Badr for helping me work with Urdu sources in Aligarh. I also read some relevant texts with Professor Muhammad Barker, a good teacher, colleągue and mentor. For me the fount of Urdu has always been C. M. Naim of Chicago, my *ustād* in every sense of the term. I am, of course, responsible for all errors of translation or transliteration; I hope they are few.

Table of Contents

List of Illustrations

List of Maps and Tables

MAPS

TABLES

Abbreviations

AA	Aligarh Archives
AIG	*Aligarh Institute Gazette*
BH Report	*Rīporṭ-i sālānah kāravā'ī borḍing haus Madrasat ul-'ulūm Musalmānān*
DNB	*Dictionary of National Biography*
EC/NWP	Education Commission. *Report of the North-Western Provinces and Oudh Provincial Committee*
GNWP	Government of the North-Western Provinces and Oudh
GOI	Government of India
IOL	India Office Library
MAOCM	*Muhammadan Anglo-Oriental College Magazine*
MEC	Muhammadan Educational Conference
NAI	National Archives of India
RDPI/NWP	*Report of the Director of Public Instruction, North-Western Provinces*
RMAOC	*Report on the Progress of Education at the Muhammadan Anglo-Oriental College, Aligarh*
SDAA	*Selected Documents from the Aligarh Archives*, ed. Yusuf Husain
SVN	*Selections from the Vernacular Newspapers*
TA	*Tahẕīb ul-Akhlāq*

Introduction

Mushirul Hasan

WHEN David Lelyveld started researching at Aligarh in 1967 I was an undergraduate at the university's History department, listening to lectures on medieval Indian polity, economy and culture. Here a whole new world was being thrown open by scholars with exceptional skills and insights. But alas, we were not acquainted with late-nineteenth-century movements in north India, some of which had left an indelible stamp on Aligarh's Mohammaden Anglo-Oriental College. We were not introduced to its founder, Syed Ahmad Khan, nor to the intellectual energy released by his companions at Aligarh and Delhi. Shibli Nomani, Altaf Husain Hali and Maulvi Zakaullah were hazy and distant figures: they did not figure in an otherwise elaborate curriculum. We read the *Babur-Nama* but not the *Asar ul-Sanadid*. We read the great Hindi poets Kabir, Rahim and Raskhan, but not Mir Taqi Mir and Ghalib. The seminar library was stocked with numerous scholarly monographs authored by members of the department, but none on Aligarh's more recent history. Nobody tried to replicate, in the context of the Aligarh Movement, the seminal work of Susobhan Sarkar on the Bengal Renaissance. I wondered why this was so. I did not ask. I merely sensed that the history of Islam during the colonial period was forbidden territory.

Delhi's Jamia Millia Islamia, which I joined in 1978, had an equally poor record. The papers of its two illustrious founders – Mohamed Ali and M.A. Ansari – had for decades gathered dust in a basement. A serious history of the institution, described by the country's first prime minister as 'a lusty child of the Non-Co-operation [Movement]', did not exist. There was no scholarly assessment of those 'self-sacrificing workers' who were, in the words of Gandhi, 'staunch Muslims and equally staunch nationalists'. Mohamed Ali's speeches and writings were first compiled by a retired Pakistani diplomat and published in Lahore. Consequently Mohamed Ali was promptly appropriated by the protagonists of the two-nation theory. The only readable accounts of Ansari were by the Turkish author Halide Edib (who lived in the Ansari household in 1935 and delivered lectures at the Jamia Millia Islamia), and by Jawaharlal Nehru in his autobiography, published in 1936. Nothing much has appeared since.

This scholarly inertia has gripped traditional centres of learning as well. The fortunes of Lucknow's Firangi Mahal, which was once home to the erudite religious thinkers of Awadh, have not improved since independence and partition. And though the Dar-al-ulum at Deoband is still a major theological seminary with a powerful ideological base and an extensive network of schools and colleges in South Asia, no Deobandi *alim* has produced a scholarly history of that institution which has, for well over a century, influenced the intellectual and religious life of many Muslims in the Indian subcontinent. The same is true of Lucknow's Nadwat al-ulama. The venerable Syed A. H. Ali Nadwi is the sole figure to comment, analyse and interpret the political, intellectual and religious currents with some rigour and sensitivity.

It is important to alert the scholarly community to such neglect of an important component of north India's political, cultural and intellectual past. It is equally important to remind the Muslim intelligentsia that scholarly interventions are essential if we want to unfold the variety and diversity in Indian Islam, examine the mixed experiences of its adherents, and reveal deep internal divides and schisms, as well as tangible areas of interaction with castes and communities. Such research would enrich our understanding of inter- and intra-community relationships, and thereby remove many misleading and stereotyped ideas associated with the nature and character of Indian Islam and the structure of Muslim communities in South Asia.

The task is awesome, for several reasons. For one, India's partition had a curiously mixed intellectual impact. Scores of writers connected with formal groups and organizations, notably the Dar al-ulum at Deoband and the Jamiyat al-ulama, dwelt on their nationalist past and highlighted their contribution to the freedom struggle. But serious scholars were reluctant to study the lives of 'defeated' men and 'lost' causes. The ideals and activities of 'nationalist Muslims' were either not taken into account or submerged within rationalizations of the 'victors'. Syed Ahmad Khan — whose contribution to education and reform matched the intellectual stride of Bengal's early reformers and their contemporaries in Egypt and Syria — was an embarrassment because he was widely regarded as the progenitor of Muslim nationalism. The movement he generated among 'Aligarh's First

Generation' was virtually written off because it stimulated communitarian ('communal' in common parlance) and pan-Islamic consciousness among Muslims. The Khilafat upsurge, which began in 1918–19, was regarded as a mere pan-Islamic outburst which reinforced the image of a 'community' with extra-territorial loyalties. The rise of Muslim 'separatism' and the Muslim League clamour for a separate nation were underlined to illustrate a specifically 'Muslim tendency' to organize separately as a religious collective.

The intellectual milieu after independence also influenced the choice of, and preference for, certain themes. A good number of historians, mostly Marxists, enriched the historical explorations into India's past. Seminal work on the colonial economy, economic nationalism, and peasant as well as working-class movements, provided a rich diet to a generation tutored in Marxism-Leninism. At the same time, the dominant historiographical trends until the 1970s allowed little space for research on religion, culture and intellectual life. In fact such themes, especially those perceived as being outside the framework of 'medieval India', were not seen as part of the historian's agenda. This may explain why Kunwar Mohammad Ashraf, endowed with a sharp analytical mind, never completed his projected study on Indian Muslims, or that a generation of scholars, especially at Aligarh and Allahabad, were lured into studying the economic, agrarian and institutional history of medieval India to the exclusion of other themes.

The academic and intellectual impact of these exclusive concerns was profoundly retrogressive. India's partition had raised the most fundamental historical and sociological issues, but these were very inadequately treated within studies on nationalism. Aziz Ahmad and Mohammad Mujeeb opened up, for the first time after independence, new areas of research on ideas and movements among Muslims. Yet academic circles in India were neither prepared nor intellectually equipped (most have no knowledge of Persian and Urdu) for a serious engagement on issues underlined in their remarkably perceptive writings.

The result exists for everybody to see. Indian Islam and its dynamic interaction with local, indigenous traditions is a peripheral area of research in the country, outside the college or university curriculum. One turns to David Lelyveld and C. W. Troll to renew acquaintance with 'Aligarh's First Generation'; to Barbara Metcalf and Francis Robinson to uncover the histories of Deoband and Firangi Mahal, respectively; and to Gail Minault for highlighting reformist trends and movements among north Indian Muslims towards the end of the nineteenth century. Significant related areas have been explored by Paul Brass, Asim Roy, Rafiuddin Ahmad, Susan Bayly, Stephen Dale, Ayesha Jalal, Farzana Shaikh, David Gilmartin, Ian Talbot, Sandria Frietag — all based in universities outside India. David Lelyveld's researches resulted in the finely crafted, broadly erudite and innovative work reprinted within these covers: yet, not a single scholar at the Aligarh Muslim University has pursued the themes that Lelyveld outlined nearly two decades ago.

II

Lelyveld's principal concern is to understand what it meant to be an Indian Muslim in the nineteenth century, how that cultural/social identity changed meaning in British India, and how it was articulated in a colonial context. The Aligarh College serves as his focal point because it was a 'formally organised, self-consciously created social establishment', created 'with the defined goal of carrying out transitions of identity and loyalty suitable to the special circumstances of British India.' But much more than this, *Aligarh's First Generation* analyses an important group whose role in the nationalist movement has been condemned instead of being understood.

Lelyveld's book is firmly rooted in history and sociology. His chief interest is social history, though he has skilfully integrated (as in the last chapter) political themes within his narrative. How completely has he succeeded in his objectives? Not all his conclusions command equal assent; nor is his delineation of situations and problems free from the obscurities of sociological jargon. Yet most readers will find that major aspects of his area of study are better explained than ever before. Many writers have followed his methodology and framework of analysis; many have studied much the same issues in other contexts; some have acknowledged their debt to him; some have not. But all discerning readers are likely to be impressed by Lelyveld's contribution to the ongoing debates, some of which have most recently been underlined in the writings of Sandria Frietag.

There is no doubt that several important publications on South Asian Islam have appeared since 1978, the year in which Lelyveld's book was published. Yet the unexplored areas remain. For instance, we know enough about Aligarh's 'First Generation' involvement in the

Muslim League and the reasons why it came to be described by Mohammad Ali Jinnah as the 'arsenal of Muslim India'. But we are hugely ignorant of other groups, the 'Second Generation', which was deeply committed to liberal, secular and socialist values. I believe it is important to explore the lives, mentalities and activities of men like Mohammed Habib, Hamza Alavi, Rashid Ahmad Siddiqi, Zakir Husain, Moonis Raza and scores of poets and writers who repudiated the polemical two-nation theory and opposed the clamour for a separate Muslim nation.

To what extent have recent historical writings led to a reappraisal of existing approaches and interpretations? In other words, where does one situate them within the vast corpus of historical and sociological literature on Indian politics, culture and religion generally? Or, is it still the case that Indian Muslims are treated as a special category for historical exploration?

Social science scholarship and historiography since the 1970s have generated new approaches and offered new insights into different aspects of Indian society: change, variety, and difference have been highlighted in researches on India's recent past, conducted under Marxist, New Historical, post-Modernist and Subaltern approaches. But research on Muslims is still mired within traditional frameworks, still dominated by widely accepted stereotypes. Colonial categories of knowledge, as applied to them, have been questioned but not changed. Consequently, ideas and movements associated with Muslims are categorized as revivalist rather than reformist, communal rather than secular, separatist rather than nationalist, and finally reactionary rather than progressive. In this scheme, the ideas and actions of Syed Ahmad Khan and his associates — the central theme of Lelyveld's narrative — are placed within the same binary oppositions. They are either marginalized or condemned as separatist. The stereotypical figure of Syed Ahmed Khan as the architect of Muslim separatism, mesmerised by the British, remains unaffected by the knowledge of his role in introducing rationalist ideas and English education in the last quarter of the nineteenth century. As a result his reformist endeavours, which were of far-reaching significance, are obscured and neglected.

Similarly the pioneering ideas of men like Altaf Husain Hali, Maulvi Nazir Ahmed and Sheikh Abdullah, who were all engaged in a project of 'reforming' Muslim women, find little mention in either conventional or unconventional histories and critiques of nationalism and separatism. The old explanations are presumed to unravel and delineate their conduct; it is all too readily assumed that their activities were imbued with 'reactionary' or 'communal' tendencies. There is still talk of a 'Muslim mind', a 'Muslim outlook', and an inclination to construe a 'Muslim identity' around Islam, which is invariably on the wrong side of the binary divide. A sense of Otherness continues to be conveyed in such images and polarities.

Notice, for example, how an inappropriate expression — 'nationalist Muslims' — is widely used to describe the activities of those Muslims who were wedded to a broadly secular polity and to the ideal of composite nationality. Its inappropriateness lies in the majoritarian view of nationalism, a view which assumes that patriotism/nationalism comes 'naturally' to the vast majority of non-Muslims and not to others. If others, such as 'nationalist Muslims', are seen to share the sentiment, this is regarded as the exception rather than the rule. Thus Badruddin Tyabji, Hakim Ajmal Khan, Saifuddin Kitchlew, M.A. Ansari, Abul Kalam Azad, Khan Abdul Ghaffar Khan and Rafi Ahmad Kidwai are treated as exceptional individuals, placed within a separate domain of enquiry which often lies outside nationalist discourse. When the Indian state commemorates their memory to advertise its secular credentials, it draws upon the intellectual resources of Muslim organizations and institutions to organize seminars and conferences. In this way the partition of the nation's heritage proceeds unabashedly.

If Ajmal Khan, Ansari and Azad were 'nationalist Muslims', surely we should say that Gandhi, Nehru and Patel were 'nationalist Hindus'. If religion is the criterion for categorizing an individual or a group, how do we categorize a kisan or a trade union leader? Was Muzaffar Ahmad a 'nationalist Muslim' and P.C. Joshi a 'nationalist Hindu'?

There are other misguided yet widely-held beliefs and assumptions reflected in certain popular and scholarly writings: for instance, the oft-repeated view that orthodoxy represents 'true' Islam whereas liberal and modernist currents are secondary or peripheral to the more dominant 'separatist', 'communal' and 'neo-fundamentalist' paradigms. The focus has been on traditional revival, on religious revivalism, and on fundamentalist stirrings. When it comes to Muslims, the dominant 'orthodox' paradigms are suddenly underlined. Contrariwise, 'heterodox' trends which contest the definition of a 'Muslim identity' in purely religious terms (in the context of imperial institutions), and which refute the popular notion that Islamic values and symbols provide a key to the understanding of the 'Muslim world view', are not.

Consider another area where, despite the wide range of a rich secondary literature, certain views continue to influence our perceptions. Time and again we are reminded of the pervasive impact of Islam on its adherents, their concern to defend values enshrined in the Quran and the *hadith*, their trans-national links with a Muslim fraternity. Time and again we are led to believe that the major preoccupation of a Muslim is praying, going on pilgrimage, observing religious rituals. Time and again we are told that Muslims, more than any other religious entity, attach importance and value to religio-cultural habits and institutions, and therefore that they are more prone to the hegemony and exhortations of Islamic rhetoric.

It is hard to deny that the solidarity of the *umma* was invoked to cultivate pan-Islamism, religio-revivalism and Muslim nationalism. Notice, moreover, how Kanpur Muslims took to the streets when a portion of a mosque in the city was demolished in 1913. Notice, too, how a threat to the Khilafat and the holy places outraged most Muslims. Or consider their stout resistance to interference in Muslim family law, exemplified in the opposition to the Sarda Marriage Bill of 1929, and more recently to the Indian Supreme Court's judgement on Shah Bano.

These are important facets, but their significance should not be overstated in order to construct a unified Muslim structure of consciousness or a singular Muslim community acting in unison to achieve common goals. What should not be assumed is a teleology dictating their actions or a general acquiescence in the actions of a few. Why is it *exceptional* if some Muslims, falling prey to colonial enumerations and definitions and their own fanciful theories, regarded themselves as an indivisible component of a religious collectivity? Other communities have had similar self-images. Else how shall we explain the Hindu Mahasabha, the RSS and numerous Hindu caste associations? What does one make of nineteenth-century religio-revival movements in Bengal, Maharashtra and Punjab, and their deepening anxieties over the future of, or the evangelical threat to, their 'Hindu identity'? The historian Susobhan Sarkar commented on 'the obsession with Hindu traditions which helped to keep the men of our [Bengal] renaissance aloof from the masses': this requires elaboration.

At the heart of the Arya Samaj's brand of reconstruction and reform was the object of restoring the supposedly pristine purity of Vedic culture and civilization. The 'Tilak school' in Maharashtra and the leading architects of the Swadeshi movement in Bengal, including

Aurobindo Ghose and B. C. Pal, were constructively re-thinking their Hindu heritage and meeting the challenges of modern thought by assimilative-creative processes. The Cow question was nothing but an evocative symbol of Hindu resurgence in northern and western India. The crusade for Hindi *in opposition to Urdu* was as much linked with government employment as with a widely perceived symbol of Hinduized identity. And finally, Romila Thapar shows how the emergent national consciousness appropriated an Orientalist construction of Hinduism as well as what this had constructed as the heritage of Hindu culture. The need for formulating a Hindu community became a requirement for political mobilization, when representation by religious community gave access to political power and economic resources.

I concur with Romila Thapar's argument. It makes equal sense in the case of Muslim elites who appropriated certain elements from Islam to legitimize their claim to a greater share in the existing power structures. My own argument flows from a set of fairly simple formulations. First, it was all very well to invoke pan-Islamic ideas or to create the image of a homogenized community. In reality, mobilization along these lines failed to obliterate internal differentiations among Muslims. Religious ties endowed them with a semblance of unity, but they were remarkably fragile and unable to override other forms of identity. The links that bound Muslim groups with other social classes, though occasionally strained, proved in the end to be demonstrably more powerful and enduring. There may have been much Hindu–Muslim ill-will in the nineteen-forties, but it did not undermine traditional cross-communal associations.

Second, it must be borne in mind that a Muslim, like his counterpart in any other community, has many acts to perform, diverse roles to play. He is not genetically or culturally cast in the role of a religious crusader or a relentless defender of the faith. Besides being a follower of Islam by birth and training, a Muslim, or for that matter a Hindu or a Sikh, is a peasant or a landlord, an agricultural worker or a landless labourer, a worker or an industrialist, a student or a teacher, a litigant or a lawyer, a Shia or a Sunni, a Deobandi or a Barelwi. Should we then harp on his Muslim and Islamic identity to the exclusion of everything else, including the secular terms in which he relates to more immediate and pressing socio-economic needs, and to the exclusion of his wide-ranging interactions with his class and not just with his brethren?

The depth and nature of this interaction remain a matter of dispute, but they do not justify an absolute Muslim/Islamic consciousness. If, as we are told, centuries of common living and shared experiences could not create composite solidarities, how could a specifically Muslim self-consciousness emerge out of such multiple and diverse experiences?

Mohammad Ali Jinnah believed he had all the answers. So did the Jamaat-i Islami. But there were other explanations as well, boldly constructed around secular and pluralist conceptions. These were counterposed to an essentialist view of Indian Islam. Though the tenability of some of those theories and assumptions were questioned after partition, the basic tenor and thrust of liberal-left arguments were neither reversed nor substantially modified. Scholars, artists and creative writers, in particular, continued to contest the two-nation theory; they unfolded the past to discover elements of unity, cohesion and integration, and they provided historical legitimation for multi-culturalism and religious plurality. Prominent amongst these were people with pronounced socialist and Marxist leanings. Some *Muslim* intellectuals, both independently and as part of liberal-left formations, did much the same. They carried forth the inconclusive debates of the post-1857 decades, when the *ulama* and the liberal intelligentsia, being confronted with the external political and religio-cultural threat of colonialism, were constrained to sketch out a role for themselves and reflect on the internal weaknesses within a religious tradition that had strong revivalist precedences as well as liberal and reformist tendencies. They did this because certain key aspects in those debates bore contemporary relevance and pertained to how Muslims situated themselves in a world that was brutally shattered by partition. The nature of this engagement in pre- and post-independence India must be explored for a rounded view of the political and intellectual currents that embraced different sections of Muslim society.

Contemporary politics in India is characterized by a preoccupation with communitarian identities, with chauvinistic ideologies, and with movements that divide religious communities and exacerbate differences. Much more attention needs to be given to ideologies and movements that have, in the past or in the present, tried to unite Hindus and Muslims and thereby furthered the post-colonial agenda of social transformation. Furthermore, social scientists need to locate the social norms, cultural patterns and political responses of Muslim groups in relation to what Aziz Ahmad has described as an 'Indian environment', which means not in a specifically religious or Islamic framework. They need to situate prominent political and religious figures within a perspective that would enlarge our appreciation of their role as well as prevent their appropriation by denominational groups. This is surely how the role of people like Ajmal Khan, Ansari and Azad can be evaluated. This is surely how a nation, desperately in search of unifying symbols to withstand a Hindutva wave and a Muslim fundamentalist upsurge, can pay tribute to men and women who nursed the vision of a secular and democratic society.

It is for all these reasons that David Lelyveld's book is relevant. It generates a lively debate which has considerable historical and contemporary importance for scholars and students of India's cultural and social past.

ALIGARH'S FIRST GENERATION

I

The Identification of Indian Muslims

TEN years after suppressing the "Mutiny" of 1857 in north India and ending the Mughal empire once and for all even as a legal fiction, the British government completed the construction of a new imperial seat, located on King Charles Street, Whitehall. Along with the Foreign Office and the still unbuilt Home and Colonial Offices, this imposing bulk of polished granite, marble, and Portland stone was part of a new government complex provided for the expanding administrative activity of the British empire. There was no attempt to make the India Office Indian; its architectural style was Victorian-Palladian, a nineteenth-century English version of something out of Italy. Nevertheless, the building was to become an important resource for the study and analysis of Indian history and culture, for in addition to government records it housed one of the world's great collections of "Oriental" books and manuscripts. The India Office Library was the result of the efforts of generations of Englishmen, mostly scholar-officials, to learn about India.

When Sayyid Ahmad Khan of Delhi, a judge in the subordinate judicial administration of the North-Western Provinces, traveled to London in 1869, one of his major purposes was to consult books and manuscripts not available in India. His project was to prepare a refutation of British attacks on the history of Islam by using the wide range of sources available to his adversaries. Little remained of the manuscript collections that once existed in north India; they had been destroyed, scattered, carried off to Europe. Like the remnants of the Delhi court, many of these libraries were casualties of the 1857 Revolt. Nor were European studies of the non-European world readily accessible in India. But at the India Office Library Sayyid Ahmad found a veritable "city of books."[1] Even with the assistance of his two sons, who knew English, the task of working through the relevant material was overwhelming.

Sayyid Ahmad was then fifty-two years old, separated by over thirty years from the Delhi court in which his father had been an honorary official. Strongly built, his plentiful white beard spreading out over his great barrel chest, everything about this man seemed large and powerful. Though he was familiar enough with the subtle manners of Delhi, his personal style was blunt and straightforward. At the India Office it may not have been immediately clear to a casual onlooker what country he came from (Figure 1). His skin was pale copper; his clothes were modern Turkish—European boots and trousers, knee-length black coat not very different from the European style except that it buttoned at the neck, red brimless hat. A white scarf around his neck assisted the beard in concealing a large goiter. The two young men with him, aged nineteen and twenty, were obviously his sons.

The visitors were shown a recent publication of the India Office, *The People of India*, printed in limited edition by order of the Secretary of State in Council. So far four of the ten gold-edged folio volumes had come out, each an album of striking photographs of individual Indians, accompanied by brief texts, and grouped together vaguely by district or some other territorial unit. Each specimen was labeled "Hindoo," "Mahomedan," or "Aboriginal," and further subdivided by some rough and ready ethnic or occupational category. The first, for example, was a Santhal of the Bhagalpur Hills; he was followed by a Dome of Bihar, a Korewah of Chota Nagpur, a Naga, Manipuri, Sikkimese, and Tibetan.

[1] Sayyid Ahmad to Mahdi Ali, June 4, 1869, *Maktūbāt-i Sir Sayyid*, ed. Shaikh Muḥammad Ismā'īl Pānīpatī (Lahore: Majlis-i Taraqqī-i Adab, 1959), p. 43. Cited hereafter as *Maktūbāt*.

Figure 1. Sayyid Ahmad Khan

Sayyid Mahmud, younger son of Sayyid Ahmad, turned over the pages looking at photographs of nearly naked men or people in unfamiliar dress. If he had looked further into the later volumes he would have seen portraits of named individuals, some of them acquaintances of his father, Muslims accused of practicing "Hindoo rites in secret," an Aligarh District landholder described as having "features [that] are peculiarly Mahomedan, of the centralasian [*sic*] type; and while they vouch for the purity of his descent, exemplify in a strong manner the obstinacy, sensuality, ignorance, and bigotry of his class. It is hardly possible, perhaps, to conceive features more essentially repulsive."[2] But before Sayyid Mahmud reached this part he was approached by a young Englishman, perhaps a future Indian Civil Servant who might have studied the same pictures of scantily dressed hill people and menial laborers that filled the first two volumes of *The People of India.*

"Are you a Hindustani?"

Sayyid Mahmud looked up from the book, blushed, stuttered out a yes, then corrected himself: he was not an "aborigine," his ancestors had come to India from a foreign country.[3]

British rulers were asking their South Asian subjects to identify themselves. The question was not just academic; the official analysis of Indian society was bound up with the formulation of policy, the allocation of resources, the response to Indian political demands. It played a major part in determining rights to agricultural produce, in deciding cases of civil law, in recruiting members of the army. As representative institutions were gradually introduced, the official analysis helped define constituencies. For in all these

[2] J. Forbes Watson and John Wilson Kaye, eds., *The People of India* (London: India Museum, 1868-1875), III, No. 139.

[3] G.F.I. Graham, *The Life and Work of Syed Ahmed Khan, C. S. I.* (Edinburgh: William Blackwood and Sons, 1885), p. 189.

cases British administrators abandoned any commitment they may have had to the idea of society as an aggregation of individuals; they accepted as axiomatic that India was composed of separate collectivities. It was the business of ethnographers, census takers, writers on Indian history and society to demarcate these groups as a guide for the exercise of British power.

But there were many ways to construe group identity among the people of India. Labels existed on many levels of generality and cut across each other in complicated ways. Those based on birth might involve a wide range of identities, from household to property holding group, to lineage, to endogamous group, to a far-flung cultural category supposedly indicating shared status. A person might also be labeled by locality—a section of a village, a village, a cluster of villages, an old administrative unit, a large geographic region. Language identification was similarly ambiguous, because most Indians had command of a whole continuum of linguistic styles and dialects. Religious designations were often unclear; below the surface of the well-known scriptural religions one might detect an immense variety of ritual practices and objects of worship, some purely local, others amalgamating widely different great traditions.

What is more, many of these labels were outsiders' constructs, unfamiliar to the people they purported to describe. The Persian word "Hindu" designated a great religious civilization at the highest level of generalization, comparable to the complex of Middle Eastern religions that included Judaism, Christianity, and Islam; but it did not become a familar category of religious identity until British interpretation standardized its usage. The Linguistic Survey of India was plagued by villagers who would not simply name the language they spoke and had to be told—like Molière's bourgeois gentleman learning that he spoke in prose.[4] The census takers were often hard pressed to get an informant to align

[4] George Abraham Grierson, *The Linguistic Survey of India* (Calcutta: Government of India, 1927), I, Part I, 19.

himself comfortably in the proper column under caste or religion; there had to be special keys for converting unsuitable responses into officially formulated census categories.[5]

All this data collecting by the British was an effort to understand Indian society as it was, not to change it. Most of the labels were of Indian origin, related, if sometimes loosely, to the great proliferation of labels that Indians themselves used to distinguish one group from another. The most serious shortcoming of the British analysis was the failure to see how such group designations were related to each other in any Indian cultural model. By making a list of categories, duly appended with numbers and descriptive phrases, British observers tended to see Indian society as an atomistic collection of isolated corporate groups. In the Indian model social labels were guides to a complex system of social relationships. Indians were capable of grouping and regrouping themselves depending on the situation, be it ritual, business, or war. There was little isolation in Indian society.

But since the British model was bound up with the exercise of British power in a colonial situation, Indians who wished to influence policy had to take account of it. Despite shortcomings, the British analysis had a way of becoming self-fulfilling, by freezing identities, chopping off ambiguities, and eventually providing the mold for associational activities. In the context of British power, old social designations took on new meanings. For example, they could be used for voluntary associations, political pressure groups, the whole apparatus of party interest involved in the British style of doing politics. Would-be Indian politicians would have to declare whom they represented, and do so in terms the British could understand. Not only in answering the census taker but in organizing themselves to use, get around, or overthrow the new institutional system, Indians would have to

[5] For example, see W. C. Plowden, "Report," *Census of India, 1872: North-Western Provinces* (Calcutta: Superintendent of Government Printing, 1873), I, xix-xx.

make conscious decisions about what groups they belonged to and to which loyalties they should give priority.

Sayyid Ahmad Khan's trip to England was above all an effort to see himself and the people with whom he identified through an outsider's perspective. Since the outsider was rich and powerful, and had by now virtually unassailable political dominance over his homeland, this was no casual enterprise. What he discovered was profoundly upsetting. His response was to return to India with the purpose of gathering together a following under a banner marked "Indian Muslim."

MUSLIMS IN THE OFFICIAL ANALYSIS OF INDIAN SOCIETY

There was a variety of British interpretations of the political significance of the term "Muslim." One strain of official thinking saw Muslims as a united body permanently antagonistic to imperial rule. In this view the 1857 rebellion was part of a consistent pattern of Muslim subversion aimed at restoring Mughal rule. In the 1860s there were conspiracy trials against so-called "Wahabi" leaders in Patna, military expeditions across the north-west frontier, and much talk of alleged anti-Muslim bias in recruiting Indians for government employment.[6] Some suspected that the assassination of the Viceroy in 1871 by a Muslim was part of a widespread underground movement; Muslims might some day rise against British rule under "a Mussulman Cromwell." In London, Lord Salisbury subscribed to a domino theory of Muslim expansion throughout the world; not only Kabul but also Constantinople and Cairo were bound up with the political ambitions of Indian Muslims.[7] And all this was none

[6] See P. Hardy, *The Muslims of British India* (Cambridge: Cambridge University Press, 1972), pp. 70-91.

[7] S. Gopal, *British Policy in India, 1858-1905* (Cambridge: Cambridge University Press, 1965), p. 101; see also K. K. Aziz, *Britain and Muslim India, 1857-1947* (London: Heinemann, 1963), pp. 24-25.

other than a continuation of the age-old struggle between Christianity and Islam.

The *locus classicus* for this view was a powerfully written tract by W. W. Hunter—*The Indian Musalmans: Are They Bound in Conscience to Rebel Against the Queen?* Published in 1871, parts of it had already appeared in newspapers, where they were read by Sayyid Ahmad during his London trip.[8] The year the book came out, Hunter became India's first Director General of Statistics, and thus the guiding force behind the extensive *Statistical Survey* and *Imperial Gazeteer.* But *The Indian Musalmans* is not a shining example of rigorous analysis; Hunter is not at all clear who he is talking about. The question posed in the title assumes an identity based on religion, but Hunter also refers to Muslims as a "class," a "community," a "people," a "nationality," and a "race." Indian Muslims are part of the "Muhammadan world," which is united from Constantinople to China.[9] Hindus are "the real natives of the country"; Muslims, "their deadliest enemies." "The Hindu has unquestionably the higher order of intellect," but before the British came the Muslims were "a superior race" on account of their "stoutness of heart" and "power of political organization."

Hunter opens the book by stating, "The whole Muhammadan community has been openly deliberating on their obligation to rebel." It would be a violation of Islam for the thirty million Muslims of British India to accept British rule. The account moves on to a dramatic picture of the Pathan "Rebel Camp on our frontier," which Hunter associates with the revivalist movement of Sayyid Ahmad of Bareilly in the early part of the century. But from there he slips by a tenuous association into a discussion of the Muslims of eastern Bengal, where he claims Islam had become "overgrown with the superstitious accretions . . . borrowed during centuries of contact with the Hindus." And just as the religion had

[8] Sayyid Ahmad to Mahdi Ali, August 20, 1869, *Maktūbāt*, p. 63.

[9] W. W. Hunter, *The Indian Musalmans: Are They Bound in Conscience to Rebel Against the Queen?* (London: Trübner & Co., 1871).

changed, the physical appearance of the people had changed, too: they now had "the unmistakable dark, sallow complexion which is imparted by the steamy swamps of lower Bengal." Later, however, Hunter states that most Bengali Muslims are converts from aboriginal, non-Brahmanical religions. These are the main supporters of the "Wahabis" of north India; in 1851 they rose up like "Communists and Red Republicans" against both Hindu and Muslim landlords.

Though Hunter identifies the threat of rebellion with the general body of Muslim peasants and artisans, he associates the grievances with a Muslim aristocracy, "the haughty foreigner," "the descendant of some line of princes." These are the people who have lost their supposed monopoly on lands and official positions as a result of British conquest. The benefits of British rule, such as Bengali-language schools, are opposed by these upper classes, since Bengali is "the language of idolatry." Therefore such schools are unsuitable for "the illiterate and fanatical peasantry of Muhammadan Bengal"—who, by the way, did not know anything but Bengali. Toward the end of the book, however, he identifies these same people with the Urdu-speaking students at the Calcutta Madrasah. The danger to British rule comes from "the fanatical masses," who take their religion seriously, unlike "the well-to-do Musalmans," who contrive to evade the clear prescription of the Qur'an to flee or rebel. The best policy for the British is to encourage this kind of upper-class compromise with true Islam.

Reviewing Hunter's book, Alfred Lyall, soon to be Lieutenant Governor of the North-Western Provinces, charges his colleagues with being "sorely vexed by a hyperbolic fiend." Hunter had erred in using "European metaphors and phrases for Asiatic events and institutions." Like Hunter an author of gazetteers, histories, and statistical accounts, Lyall complains that Hunter makes unwarranted generalizations from his observations of the Muslims of Bengal. He also warns that what Hunter has said will be overheard by Indian Muslims themselves; they will be encouraged to think of themselves as "an oppressed people or a persecuted sect." But these criticisms notwithstanding, Lyall agrees with Hunter's idea of Muslims as a discrete group, "a community bound together . . . not by nationality, but by their faith." These are the people who made "that last desperate spring after the shadow of a lost empire" in 1857; the presence of Muslims was a permanent obstacle to the creation of an Indian nation.[10]

Written at the Viceroy's request, Hunter's book was part of a British effort to formulate a Muslim policy. First the Government of India called on provincial governments to submit statistics and evaluations of the relative positions with regard to government employment and education of "the Muslims" as opposed to "the Hindus."[11] From then on recruitment policy and curriculum planning had to take Muslim concerns into consideration. In 1882 Hunter headed an Education Commission that made the educational position of Indian Muslims a matter of special enquiry.[12] After that, every annual report of a director of public instruction had to contain a separate chapter on the education of Muslims; there was no comparable chapter on Hindus. Government policies did not necessarily meet the desires of Muslim leaders, but at least the issue had entered the realm of public discourse and the relevant information was always at hand.

There was, however, an alternative, more complicated, and politically less influential view on the significance of Muslim identity. This view, developed in the course of ethnographic surveys and census enumerations, tended to emphasize the general fragmentation of Indian society. The standard Hindu-Muslim division continued to be the major motif of most of these investigations, but at least from the 1840s some

[10] Alfred C. Lyall, *Asiatic Studies, Religious and Social*, 2d ed. (London: J. Murray, 1884), pp. 228-257.

[11] "Encouragement of Muhammadan Education in India," Government of India [GOI], Home Department, Education (A), June 1873, Nos. 74-111 (National Archives of India [NAI]).

[12] *Report of the Indian Education Commission* (Calcutta: Government of India, 1883), pp. 483-507.

official writers were beginning to notice subdivisions and overlaps. In 1846 Henry M. Elliot, an early historian, philologist, and ethnographer, compiled a "Supplement to the Glossary of Indian Terms" from information submitted to him by local officials. According to this work Bhangis, for example, "cannot be said to be of any particular religion, but they are, perhaps, more Muslim than Hindú. . . . They generally, nevertheless, profess to be Hindús." The Rajput "race" of Badgujars included Muslim clans, who, nevertheless, maintained Rajput titles, marriage customs, and the celebration of Holi. Among Jats there were Muslims, Hindus, and Sikhs. The Ghazi Miyan cult was an example of a religious sect that included both Hindu and Muslim adherents. An 1869 revision of Elliot's *Glossary* by John Beames subdivided Muslims as Sayyids, Shaikhs, Mughals, Pathans, and a variety of artisan and service castes such as Jullahas, Nais, Bihistis, and Dhobis. Each of the artisan and service groups had Hindu counterparts—or Hindu members.[13] Similar cases were noted in *The People of India*, the book that had so embarrassed Sayyid Mahmud.[14]

A more thorough and well-organized effort to establish the overlap of Hindus and Muslims in Indian society came out in the 1870s with Dr. James Wise's researches on the Muslims of eastern Bengal. Civil Surgeon of Dacca, Wise travelled to scattered villages interviewing headmen and others, as a result of which he concluded that Muslims were not "an united body, as is generally assumed." "If we examine a crowd of Bengali villagers at the present day, one, and only one type of features, of complexion, and of physique pervades them all." The only difference was in dress, hair style, and beards. Wise proved this to his satisfaction by comparing fifty Muslims and fifty Hindus in the Dacca jail as to age, height, weight, and girth of chest; there was no significant

[13] H. M. Elliot, *Memoirs on the History, Folk-Lore, and Distribution of the Races of the North-Western Provinces of India*, revised by John Beames (London: Trübner & Co., 1869), I, 50, 139, 185, 284.

[14] Watson and Kaye, *The People of India*, I, No. 4; II, Nos. 79, 109; III, Nos., 178, 180, 181, 187, 221; V, No. 228; VII, No. 349.

variation by religion. On the other hand, Muslims were divided among themselves by caste: clean and unclean. He noted that there were twenty-two Muslim *qaums* in Dacca, each under a *pancāyat*, and some included Hindus. He conceded that there had been a recent tendency for Muslims to override these divisions; "the Muhammadan revival of the nineteenth century is one of the most momentous events in the modern history of India . . . uniting under the banner of a common faith millions of the population." But he was generally confident that existing divisions would prevail "unless injudicious interference on the part of the Government causes it to unite against a common enemy."[15]

The first major census in 1872 had construed Indian society as composed of four major "ethnical" divisions: Aborigines, Aryans, Mixed, and Muslims. In the 1881 census, Aryans (defined as Brahmins and Rajputs) and Muslims remained separate, but the Aborigines and those of mixed aborigine-Aryan descent were considered as a single category. Each might then be further subdivided by caste categories, but enumerations for such things as age, marital status, fertility, literacy, and occupation were usually available only by the broad categories of religion rather than by caste or occupation. The *Statistical Survey* and tables in official education reports tended to place much greater emphasis on Hindu subdivisions than on Muslim ones. A commonly used heading was "Caste if Hindu, otherwise religion."[16]

Out of all this data gathering there emerged a census portrait of the Muslims of India. The 1881 census thus revealed that there were over fifty million Muslims, about one-fifth of

[15] James Wise, "The Muhammadans of Eastern Bengal," *The Journal of the Asiatic Society of Bengal*, LXIII (1894), Part III, No. 1 28-63.

[16] For a general discussion on the relation between British census operations and Indian self-perceptions, see Bernard S. Cohn, "The Census, Social Structure and Objectification in South Asia," paper delivered at the Second European Conference on Modern South Asia, Elsinore, Denmark, June 1970.

the Indian population. Over forty percent of these Muslims lived in Bengal, where they were half the Bengali population. One-fifth lived in Punjab, and there, too, they were half the population. In the great Gangetic plain between Bengal to the east and Punjab to the west—the old Mughal heartland known as Hindustan proper—Muslims were fewer than six million, and less than fourteen percent of the population of the North-Western Provinces and Oudh. Most Muslims of Bengal spoke Bengali; of the Punjab, Punjabi; but particularly among the literate Muslims throughout the subcontinent, the Indian Muslim language *par excellence* was becoming Urdu, also called Hindustani, the urban standard of Hindustan that succeeded Persian at the same time that the British were succeeding the Mughals. A second language for many, it was often declared for census purposes as the first. Punjabi and Bengali Muslims were overwhelmingly poor, illiterate peasants; in fact, over two-thirds of the Muslims of the North-Western Provinces and Oudh (later known as the United Provinces) were the same, and most of the rest were equally poor and illiterate urban laborers. Estimated literacy for North-Western Provinces and Oudh Muslims was something on the order of three percent. This and similar information was available in the census: it presented an aggregate view of a population that its members would never otherwise have known.

Denzil Ibbetson, director of the Punjab Census in 1881, cast grave doubts on this emphasis of religious categories. He perceived two different Punjabi social structures east and west of Lahore: in the west even Hindus were very loose about rules of endogamy and caste identification, while in the east a Muslim Rajput, Gujar, or Jat was no different from "his Hindu brother" as to social customs, rules of marriage, and inheritance. Many Muslims retained Brahmin priests; in fact, there were even Muslim Brahmins. A Muslim Jat in Delhi was more rigid in caste rules of purity and matrimony than a Hindu Jat in the north-west. "The difference is national rather than religious," that is, people fit into the social structure of their surroundings.[17] The Punjab recognized this interpretation in the law courts by enforcing a "customary" code of civil law based on region and caste as opposed to the classical systems of Hindu and Muslim law used elsewhere in British India.[18]

Whether based on regional, religious, or racial divisions, most of the official analysis proceeded from a theory of history that saw Indian society as a museum of evolutionary layers, each composed of separate, birth-defined social groups that were unable to relate to each other as constituents of a larger whole. If the differences were based on region, as with Ibbetson, education and improved communication might eventually override them. If they were based on race, as with Wise, the only possible consolidation would be a uniformly inferior "breed" permanently subjected to foreign rule. And finally, if they were based on adherence to one of the great world religions, as with most common understandings of Indian society, consolidations would tend to separate Hindus from Muslims.

VICTORIAN SOCIETY: THE LIBERAL PARADIGM

Although official analysis attempted to distinguish indigenous social groups, it interpreted their social and political relations in terms of British preconceptions. These ideas, however, were not all of one piece; the very task of building and maintaining a colonial regime engendered important modifications. More important, the nineteenth century was a pe-

[17] Denzil Charles Jelf Ibbetson, *Report on the Census of the Punjab, 1881* (Calcutta: Superintendent of Government Printing, 1883), I, 178. See also pp. 100-103.

[18] William Henry Rattigan, *A Digest of Civil Law for the Punjab*, ed. H.A.B. Rattigan, 7th ed. (Lahore: Civil and Military Gazette, 1909); see also J.N.D. Anderson, "The Anglo-Muhammadan Law," *Contributions to the Study of Indian Law and Society* (Philadelphia: South Asia Seminar, University of Pennsylvania, 1966-1967), pp. 137-172.

riod of fundamental ideological transformation in Britain itself. One of the problems for Indians seeking access to government was to figure out the rules of the game—especially when many British officials thought the game they were playing was really an Indian one. Special ideologies, intended for colonial consumption only, interpreted Indian society and justified British rule according to some theory of benevolent despotism.[19] But eventually Indians learned that they could outflank imperialist ideology by appealing to Britain's own domestic parliamentary model, and using it to organize in the direction of anticipated institutional changes. Most British rulers argued that this was inappropriate to Indian circumstances, but it was difficult to sustain a view so radically at odds with the dominant ideology of Britain's own political life. Thus the political history of India after 1857 is usually interpreted as a series of British concessions to the model of representative government in response to Indian demands.[20]

In Great Britain itself people realized clearly enough that they were all on the same playing field, engaged in the same contest. More than that, they shared a safe common denominator of symbolic identification with the nation as a whole: being British was something primarily defined by birth of British parents, an ultimate association with the geographical territory of Great Britain proper, and an allegiance to the British constitution as embodied by "the Queen in Parliament." Nationality consisted not only of knowledge of rules and skill in manipulating them, it meant an inner belief that these rules defined the right way to act, and were a component of one's sense of belonging, one's loyalty to "Queen and Country."

[19] See Raghavan Iyer, "Utilitarianism and All That—The Political Theory of British Imperialism in India," in his *South Asian Affairs*, No. 1 (1960); *St. Antony's Papers*, No. 8 (Carbondale: Southern Illinois University Press, 1960), pp. 9-71.

[20] A good statement of this interpretation is Bruce Tiebout McCully, *English Education and the Origins of Indian Nationalism* (Gloucester, Mass.: Peter Smith, 1966).

Great Britain harbored within it powerful social divisions, but they existed within the bounds of this shared language of political symbolism. When Disraeli spoke of England's "Two Nations," the rich and the poor, he was saying that class antagonism was becoming incompatible with everyone's fundamental assumptions about what a "nation" was.[21] The great task of nineteenth-century constitutional reform was to take account of increasing economic and social differentiation and the increasingly direct relevance in people's lives of government power, without overthrowing the basic symbolic parameters of British nationality.

The controversies of British politics usually referred to the definition of legitimate interests and the allocation among them of opportunities to influence government action. In preindustrial Britain, with its predominantly agrarian society of local communities, the important interests had been the monarch, the church, and the landed magnates. In the limited realm of government policy formulation Parliament had developed as the major formal apparatus for political participation; beneath that parliamentary surface was an informal web of kinship and patron-client ties that served as channels for competition and cooperation among interested groups. In the nineteenth century these channels became inadequate for the growing differentiation of interests, and eventually they were gathered up into the mechanism of Parliament. The alternative would have been for excluded interests to establish themselves as disruptive rivals to parliamentary dominance; Chartist and Irish agitations showed the cost of ignoring a mobilized segment of the public. Such interests might define themselves by a variety of criteria, such as region, religion, social status, or economic class, all of which might overlap and thus provide valuable links for political maneuver. Representation was now awarded by extending the franchise and making the voting criteria uniform throughout the various local constituencies. This meant new or increased representa-

[21] Benjamin Disraeli, *Sybil, or The Two Nations* (London: World Classics Edition, 1956).

tion to the recently populated industrial regions of the north, areas of separate "national" identity (Scotland, Wales, and, less clearly, Ireland), nonconformist churches, Catholics and Jews, commercial firms and industrialists, and finally the urban and rural (male) working classes.

But for all this widening of the vote, it was, nevertheless, possible for the landed classes to dominate government, not only in the House of Lords, but even as the elected representatives of the newly enfranchised. The belief that a man was qualified for government trust by a certain social position and cultural style served to moderate many potential conflicts; all politicians spoke the same language. The same effect was achieved by the increasing standardization of the executive functions of government through the creation of an orderly bureaucracy. To keep administrative posts from being vehicles of political competition, the old system of patronage was replaced by increasingly impersonal and rationalized rules of recruitment, hierarchy, procedure, and reward. In theory, an individual found his place in the system as a result of his own personal talents and achievements, but here too the values associated with the aristocracy and gentry continued to prevail because of the educational requirements of the civil service examinations.

The goals of special interests, then, had to be filtered through the ceremony of public debate in Parliament and the ministrations of a disinterested bureaucracy. But before entering the temple, one had to win and demonstrate a substantial measure of public backing by securing the election to Parliament of members willing to support such goals. In order to achieve any single purpose, it became necessary to combine it with more or less compatible ones, often in the context of some overarching ideological point of view. This required considerable knowledge of the system as a whole and the formulation of opinions on a great variety of subjects. The widening of the franchise and the multiplication of matters of public controversy finally called for the development of a special technique of organization, the political party, which based itself on a cluster of clearly articulated policy positions. The heart of party organization was the ability of individuals and groups to cooperate in a disciplined, organized effort to convince the general public that the party's program and candidates deserved support.

This whole process of mobilizing public support, getting elected to Parliament, conducting debates, and submitting to the regular procedures of a bureaucracy became, in the course of the nineteenth century, part and parcel of the British constitution, that core symbol of British nationality. In fact, the British came to think that such procedures were defining criteria for nationality in general. One might accord recognition to a political activity or group only insofar as it approached this ideal type. To justify the continued need for British bureaucratic despotism in India, then, it was sufficient to point out the absence among the various corporate groups of any shared sense of birth, territory, or constitution. In the British analysis, each Indian group existed as a fossil in its own separate geological layer; each was graded according to its ability to rise above segmentary loyalties and statuses into some more universalistic consolidation and the acceptance of generalized institutions. To the extent that a particular group was able to dress itself up as a British-style interest, however, that group might eventually hope to win government patronage and participate in consultation with the British on the formulation of policy. A category construed by the official analysis of Indian society could serve, like the nucleus of a thunder cloud, as a gathering point for the mobilization of support.

INDIAN SOCIETY: THE MUGHAL PARADIGM

The Mughal empire was also based on well-articulated principles, but they were grounded in different symbols and institutions. Brought to maturity during the reign of the Emperor Akbar (1556-1605), the dominant Mughal concept of society vested authority in a network of kin-like units bound in a system of asymmetrical exchanges that reflected their hierarchical relationships. Not that the culture had failed to develop beyond family loyalties, as British writers contended; on the contrary, kin relations often seem dominated by the bureaucratic and military metaphors of the Mughal regime.[22] Descent was an explanation for the possession of certain moral attributes that determined a group's position in the social order. The dichotomy of kinship and state was a piece of British culture that had no clear Indian translation.

The Mughal empire has been described as "feudal," even "tribal"; it has also been labeled "cosmopolitan" and "bureaucratic." But it is more useful to refrain from evolutionary name calling, and simply observe the differences in political symbols and institutions as they developed in the transition from Mughal society to the society of British India.

The basic principle of Mughal political structure was that society consisted of a great multiplicity of conflicting segments that could only be brought into harmony by virtue of their subordination to the apex of the system, namely, the ruling dynasty. For the most part, these segments were defined by some concept of common ancestry, but they were not simple, separate units; there was a wide array of concentric and overlapping circles of social identity that came into focus according to the occasion. Ancestry at various levels of generality was primarily conceived as a matter of fathers, brothers, and sons, sometimes reaching back to a mythical past, sometimes no more than a generation deep.

The major social categories among north Indian Hindus were the *birādarī*, an exogamous patrilineage, and the *jātī*, the outer network of potential marriages. Jati was a loose category that often subsumed subdivisions of unequal status, and served in the society at large as a vehicle for the attribution of moral qualities and therefore status. Among Muslims the principles of exogamy and endogamy were weaker. There was often a strong preference for marrying *within* the close patrilineal unit, also called biradari, but there was no outer

[22] Below, pp. 37, 40.

boundary beyond which a Muslim male could not make a legitimate marriage. Rarely referred to in matrimonial exchanges, the Muslim equivalent of jati, usually called a *qaum*, was a weaker social bond. A Muslim biradari, on the other hand, probably had less tendency to become fragmented than its Hindu counterpart—and also had less power to proliferate. In making a marriage of equal status (*kufū'*) outside the biradari, common ancestry was one important consideration, but friendship, fame, wealth, power, and sanctity were also valid indications of social equivalence.[23]

Hindu or Muslim, marriage was important as an uneven exchange between groups, an exchange involving a woman and her child-bearing capacity, wealth, social influence, and symbols of prestige. Although ancestry was predominantly through the male line, the mother also made a genetic contribution and had herself to be of suitable ancestry, variously defined as similar, complementary, or equivalent. Hindu and Muslim ceremonies of marriage, remarkably alike, demonstrated the subordination of the family giving the wife to the family taking her; marriage was an alliance between groups, not individuals.

The ability of a family or lineage to maintain its internal cohesion while extending both its membership and influence was the index of its political importance. Whether or not biradari exogamy or endogamy was an advantage depended on the size of the biradari and the relative opportunities for alliance in particular situations. Under either Hindu or Muslim rules it was possible for lineages to develop fairly sizable populations and to establish dominance over a locality. Eventually a large lineage would contain subgroups of varying power, wealth, and status, depending on their separate population histories and genealogical positions. The senior line descended from the lineage founder in the locality or the

[23] M. C. Pradhan, *The Political System of the Jats of Northern India* (Bombay: Oxford University Press, 1966); Richard G. Fox, *Kin, Clan, Raja and Rule* (Berkeley and Los Angeles: University of California Press, 1971); Cora Vreede-de Stuers, *Parda* (Assen, The Netherlands: Van Gorcum, 1968).

lineage branch luckiest or most successful in manipulating its procreation, control of property, or use of force, usually provided the locality with a raja or navab, who in Mughal terminology would be called a *zamīndār*, a land controller. Local dominance entailed economic and status control over subordinate groups outside the lineage—including, of course, the groups that provided the productive labor of the society. As in marriage, the relation of service groups to dominant lineages was mediated through rituals of exchange.

The Mughal dynasty attempted to establish ritual ties of loyalty, analogous to kinship relations, with strategically significant lineage groups. As Abul Fazl wrote in the late sixteenth century, "The world, as a bride, betrothes herself to the King."[24] And just as a bride's ultimate bond is to her spouse's family rather than her father's, the members of the ruling class had to swear that their allegiance to the emperor took precedence over all other loyalties. The bond was forged in a ceremonial exchange—a cash offering from the dependent, who in turn received an imperial robe and turban from the emperor, thus binding his lineage in permanent subordination to the lineage of the emperor. In special cases the offering from a dependent lineage such as the Kachvaha Rajputs also included brides, the wives and mothers of Mughal emperors.[25]

Along with ritual, power relations between the Mughal dynasty and a biradari served to discourage larger solidarities. A deliberate attempt was made to disperse potentially cohesive groups, such as the large Afghan lineages, that might undermine the imperial bond. The qaum composition of a military contingent was supposed to be mixed according to set formulas, and the staff of officials in a locality was supposed to be similarly diverse.[26] In the ideal model these people were bound to the emperor, not to each other.

[24] Abū'l-Faẓl 'Allāmı, *The Ā'īn-i Akbarī*, tr. H. Blochmann (Delhi: Aadiesh Book Depot, 1965), p. 2.

[25] M. Athar Ali, *The Mughal Nobility under Aurangzeb* (Bombay: Asia Publishing House, 1966), pp. 136-144.

[26] *Ibid.*, p. 15.

Place as a category of group identity did not necessarily locate one's political allegiance. The term *vaṭan* or ancestral home could sometimes refer to a remote past, a distant city like Bukhara in Central Asia or an Indian village like Bilgram in the Gangetic plain. Often the vatan provided a surname and communicated abroad a series of stereotypes. But when the term denoted the town or village where a person actually lived or to which he continually returned, it could serve to identify a corporate group, a unit of social, economic, and political action. Mughal administrative categories construed territorial units with a fair degree of precision. A territory under the political domination of a biradari was called an *ʿilāqah*; the entire geographic area subject to the Mughal regime was its *mulk*. But loyalty to the imperial dynasty was personal; it did not, in theory, depend on the particular territory that the dynasty controlled.[27]

The Mughals frequently attempted to convert local land-controlling biradaris or their rajas into creatures of the imperial regime as zamindars. Zamindari, control over territory, was conferred by an imperial grant and involved a number of specific obligations with regard to administration, taxation, and military manpower.[28] The zamindar class was the crucial link between the imperial regime and the rural society at large; if the Mughal dynasty could command the loyalty of zamindars, and zamindars, the loyalty of client lineages, the system would hold together. But the attempt to convert zamindars into officials was at most a remote aspiration of Mughal policy.

Superimposed over the zamindar class as direct agents of imperial power were the soldiers, officials, and nobility of the empire. Mughal administration tried to assign officials to areas outside their own vatans, not a difficult task at the height of the empire, when the overwhelming majority of these officials were from Central Asia and Iran. As free-floating "foreigners," their allegiance was more closely bound to

[27] Cf. Fox, *Kin, Clan, Raja and Rule*, pp. 26-27.
[28] Athar Ali, *Mughal Nobility*, pp. 78-89, 100.

their Mughal patrons than to the indigenous society. The rewards for such loyalty were overwhelming: the Mughal ruling class, in particular its highest members, the *umarā* ("nobility"), about five hundred individuals, disposed of well over half the revenue of the empire, and at least a quarter of the total economic output.[29] The ruling class was recruited from a multifarious array of foreign and indigenous peoples: "various classes and groups of persons from every race and people have sought asylum in the Imperial Court, and various Indians, men possessed of knowledge and skill as well as men of the sword . . . have obtained the privilege of kissing the threshold of the Imperial Court," wrote the great Hindu master of seventeenth-century Persian prose, Chandrabhan Brahman.[30] Like the indigenous population, this ruling class had no ties of unity except through the ruling dynasty. Until Mughal authority began to weaken in the eighteenth century, every effort was made to shift members of the ruling class from place to place every few years to prevent them from building up a territorial base.

Just as the Mughal dynasty attempted to grasp the separate strands of kinship and territorial loyalties, it also tried to become the focal point for all the great diversity of religious beliefs in India. The celebrated religious tolerance of Akbar may be interpreted as an effort to bring the various Indian communities of belief under his patronage and make them dependent on his good will. This enabled the emperor to draw on differentiated symbols of legitimacy, to be a Hindu Raja and a Padshah-i Islam at the same time. The zamindar class was mostly Hindu; the official and military class, especially at the highest levels, mostly Muslim. Imperial rule could be justified to different people on the basis of different ideologies. The emperor was above such divisions; he was, in the words of Abul Fazl, "spiritual guide" to the whole realm. Religious communities in India, both Hindu and Muslim, tended to

[29] Irfan Habib, "The Social Distribution of Landed Property in Pre-British India," *Enquiry*, New Series II, No. 3 (Winter 1965), 62-64.
[30] Translated and quoted in Athar Ali, *Mughal Nobility*, p. 15.

cluster around a *gūrū* or *pīr* in a system of spiritual kinship. Akbar made himself the object of religious devotion by dispensing *darshan* to Hindus and establishing his own little Sufi *ṭarīqah*. As a Muslim ruler he claimed to override sectarian differences within Islam, to be the final authority in disputed interpretations of God's revelation. He would also summon the representatives of non-Islamic faiths to dispute or discourse, commission the translation of Hindu scriptures into Persian—and commit well-calculated acts of religious persecution when they served his political purposes.[31]

But this highly integrated vision of imperial control was difficult to realize or sustain within the great complexity of Indian society and culture. India's religions continued to generate counterideologies as rallying points for resistance to Mughal authority. A remarkable indication of the success of Akbar's political system is that so many movements of resistance—and even the British conquerors of India in the late eighteenth century—felt it necessary to use Mughal symbols and to act in the name of the Mughal dynasty. Others, however, did not. The use of Sanskritic symbols by some of the Marathas, and the rise of such populist sects as the Sikhs and Satnamis represented a direct challenge to Mughal ideology. There was in Indian culture a deeply rooted bifurcation of religious authority and political power that Akbar was not able to overcome. And perhaps the most sustained religious challenge of all came from the spokesmen of Islam.

MUSLIMS AS A RULING CLASS

In contrast to Mughal principles of society, the ideology of Islam set forth a clear concept of a united political community, the *ummah*, consisting of true believers, people committed to conducting every aspect of their personal and social lives according to the specific instructions that God had

[31] See Iqtidar Alam Khan, "The Nobility under Akbar and the Development of His Religious Policy, 1560-80," *Journal of the Royal Asiatic Society of Great Britain and Ireland* (1968), pp. 29-36.

revealed to man through the Prophet Muhammad. Interpretation of these instructions rested with those who were intellectually and spiritually qualified, the *'ulamā*. As for the exercise of the community's political power and enforcement of its laws, this was to be vested in the rightful successor to Muhammad's political leadership, the Caliph. Sunni and Shī'ah Muslims differed over the concept of the caliphate, but both tended to agree that worldly power over Muslims was, in fact, no longer in the hands of Muhammad's successors.

For most of the history of Islam political authority had been located in the *sulṭanat*, an institution extraneous to the revealed law (the *shar'īah*). Kings (sultans, padshahs) were acceptable only by necessity; they were not quite legitimate, but the only alternative was such social chaos that the autonomous institutions of the Muslim community under the leadership of the 'ulama would not be able to function. In this view, political authority and the Muslim community were by no means congruent: the ummah was the worldwide community of believers, while there were many dynasties of sultans, rising and falling, shifting their rule back and forth over different pieces of territory and different populations. The Muslim polity did not exist by virtue of territorial location or common government; it cut across such boundaries to wherever the institutions of the shar'iah were theoretically in force. A Muslim had the right to move freely throughout the entire *dār ul-Islām* (that part of the world where political power was in the hands of Muslim rulers), and many had entered India from other lands to take service in new Muslim courts or to accept their patronage and protection. Non-Muslims existed in such Muslim realms as protected clients, *ẕimmīs*, subordinate to the political dominance of Muslim rulers and Muslim institutions.

Although the Prophet Muhammad may have originally offered the message of God to a particular Arab qaum (usually translated as "tribe"), there had been a marked transition in the Qur'an itself to the concept of community, the ummah, defined by religious belief rather than birth. An individual's submission (*islām*) to God's will was to override bonds of kinship; an ultimate equality of believers would undercut old patron-client ties among Arab kin-defined groups. But in some respects the ummah itself could operate as an Arab qaum: "All Muslims are brothers," Muhammad said. As in an Arab qaum, early Muslim converts, at first "adopted" into Arab kin groups, occupied second-class status. But as Islam spread beyond Arabia, this explicit system of qaum adoption gave way to the ideal of individual adherence to an egalitarian community of believers. The old Arab patron-client concept survived only in relation to non-Muslim communities, the zimmis.[32] A kin-based model of social loyalty also survived in the attribution of special religious prestige along genealogical lines, particularly to descendants of Muhammad, who in Arabic Islam had exclusive claim to the honorific title *sharīf*, literally "exalted." Hereditary sanctity, however, was less important than the religious knowledge, *'ilm*, of the 'ulama that determined leadership in society in the light of the shar'iah, although there was some expectation that such knowledge would be handed down from father to son. There were no grounds in the shar'iah for allotting political rule to a hereditary dynasty of sultans—almost never sacred in its origins—or basing the social order on a hierarchical alliance of kinship groups. The sultanat challenged the equality of believers as well as the supremacy of the 'ulama as interpreters of God's revelation; it agreed with the principles of the shar'iah, however, in assigning non-Muslims to a position of political subordination.[33]

A state ruled by Muslims, a state ruled according to Islam as interpreted by the 'ulama—Islamic history was full of efforts to fudge over the distinction. A "pious sultan" might attempt to give proper deference to the 'ulama and act within the shar'iah, but this meant foregoing the absolute power and

32 W. Montgomery Watt, *Islam and the Integration of Society* (London: Routledge and Kegan Paul, 1961), pp. 145-160.

33 G. E. von Grunebaum, *Medieval Islam* (Chicago: University of Chicago Press, 1953), pp. 199-220.

symbols of legitimacy characteristic of the sultanat itself, and in India writing off the non-Muslim majority as full participants in the regime. In advancing claims to legitimacy, most rulers had to make a political calculation based on the strategic importance of different cultural groups. It would be nice if political calculation and personal conviction turned out to coincide, but that required a level of consensus totally at odds with the facts of Indian pluralism.

The compromise between shar'iah and sultanat was sorely tried by Akbar's efforts to absorb the indigenous lineages of India, largely non-Muslim, into the Mughal power structure. Hindus, especially rajas of the Rajasthan region, were drawn out of their vatan territories and given governorships and military command all over the subcontinent. Other Hindus, generally belonging to a few broad jati designations—Kayasth, Khatri, and certain categories of Brahmin—were the backbone of local administration. The secret of Akbar's success was his ability to attract members of the indigenous population and blend indigenous themes into what became an increasingly distinct variant of the international Islamic culture. In fact, the culture could hardly be called "Islamic" with reference to God's revelations or Muhammad's exemplary life. Centered on the Persian language and taking inspiration from courtly styles of Saffavid Iran, it was a culture that had no religious prerequisites for membership; it included many Hindus, and excluded most Muslims. Numerical data is available only for the very highest officials, the umara, who remained predominantly Muslim, almost eighty percent.[34] But lower levels of the regime probably included an increasing number of Hindus who identified with Mughal styles of dress, manners, architecture, painting, literature, athletic skills, and amusements—the whole complex of cultural forms that established the dominant patterns of communication and ambition.

The class of people who moved in this cultural milieu

[34] Athar Ali, *Mughal Nobility*, pp. 7-33.

were sometimes called sharīf, a word of unmistakable religious connotation in the rest of the Islamic world, but in Mughal India indicating respectability in terms of cosmopolitan Mughal criteria. Mughal respectability included consideration of a person's ancestry, but it would be a mistake to define the *ashrāf* (people who are sharīf) in terms of birth. It was better to be progenitor of a great lineage than an unworthy descendant; and though some people treasured genealogies taking them back to Adam or, at least, Muhammad, other genealogies were content to start with more recent historical figures who achieved eminence out of obscurity.[35] One usually acquired *sharāfat* by birth, however; if acquired in some other way, one's identity was quickly redefined in the vocabulary of honorable descent, which implied new bonds of kinship. Sharāfat also defined character: a sharīf man was one of dignified temperament, self-confident but not overly aggressive, appreciative of good literature, music, and art, but not flamboyant, familiar with mystical experience, but hardly immersed in it. Sharīf social relations involved a pose of deference, but were above all a matter of virtuosity within the highly restricted bounds of etiquette.

The Mughal administrative system rested on an ability to move such people around from place to place, just as it required uniformity in handling the Persian documents that flowed between the center and the various levels of local jurisdiction. Above the village level, Persian literacy was a prerequisite for any nonmilitary role—and not only Persian language, but all those sharīf styles of behavior generated by the Mughal court. When Akbar's Hindu Finance Minister Todar Mal introduced Persian as the uniform language of administration in 1582, the aim was to strengthen the bureaucracy at the expense of the local zamindars. The reform

[35] There is extensive discussion in ethnographic literature on the meaning of sharīf status, but nobody has paid attention to how the word is used in ordinary language. Cf. Imtiaz Ahmad, "The Ashrāf-Ajlāf Distinction in Muslim Social Structure in India," *Indian Economic and Social History Review*, III (September 1966), 268-278.

assumed, however, the possibility of recruiting reliable personnel who would be able to deal with local people as well as carry out the office routines of a large-scale government. There was a complex system of double-checking accounts required of low-level revenue officials and their staffs, all based on standardized procedures and interchangeable personnel throughout the administrative system.[36] For such a system to work, there had to be a substantial reservoir of people literate in Persian and able to participate in Mughal culture, a reservoir far in excess of the restricted numbers of the ruling class.

The presence of Hindus in the Mughal ruling class provoked severe criticism from some contemporary spokesmen of religious piety, for whom it was axiomatic that Hindus were a subject people. Abdul Qadir Badayuni, the historian, and Shaikh Ahmad Sirhindi, founder of a religious movement, expressed outrage at a system of rule they equated with apostacy.[37] Aurangzeb, Akbar's great-grandson and emperor from 1658-1707, made some significant symbolic moves to dismantle Akbar's cultural politics in the name of Islamic piety. Although he never really dismantled the system of Hindu participation in the ruling class—in fact, he strengthened it by adding Hindus from the south—he was able to acquire an international reputation as a true *amīr ul-mūminīn*, commander of the faithful.[38] Members of the ʿulama were recruited into strategic administrative posts, the *jizyah* poll tax on non-Muslims was reimposed—Akbar had abolished it—for the benefit of its ʿulama collectors, temples were torn down, and the laws of the sharʿiah as codified in the famous *Fatāvā-i ʿĀlamgīrī* were given greater govern-

[36] Jadunath Sarkar, *The Mughal Administration* (Calcutta: M. C. Sarkar, 1920); P. Saran, *The Provincial Government of the Mughals* (Allahabad: Kitabistan, 1941); Sh. Abdur Rashid, "The Duties and Functions of the Amin," *Indian Historical Congress* (1950), pp. 193-196.

[37] William Theodore de Bary, ed., *Sources of Indian Tradition* (New York: Columbia University Press, 1970), I, 432-435, 447-448.

[38] H.A.R. Gibb, "Some Considerations on the Sunni Theory of the Caliphate," *Archives d'histoire du droit oriental*, III (1947), 404.

mental attention. But this assertion of Islamic principle was short lived; in the eighteenth century, Hindus became so powerful both as independent rulers and as powers behind the weakened Mughal throne that some sharʿiah-minded Muslims called for foreign Muslim invasion or religious rebellion (*jihād*). By the end of the century the famous religious leader of Delhi, Shah Abdul Aziz, declared that India was no longer dār ul-Islām; it was now *dār ul-ḥarb*, the abode of war.[39] One might interpret that as a call for jihad, or simply as an acceptance of the fact that Muslims were now a minority people in a land not under the rule of Muslims. But there remained an abiding belief that God had revealed to man how society should be organized and that a society under non-Muslim rule could never be a legitimate one.

Despite the opposition of a sharʿiah-minded ideology, however, Mughal political values managed to survive even the demise of Mughal power. The period of imperial unity had not erased India's heterogeneity even within the ruling class, but it did create a level of communication and interaction relevant to the political aspect of Indian culture. Movements on behalf of Islam do not seem overwhelming in the history of the Mughal empire, although later generations have drawn inspiration from them. The tiny ruling class identified itself in terms of ancestral lineages, and there were always ʿulama to serve as willing clients of the forces of wealth and power. The Muslim population in general hardly participated in all this: India was ruled by Muslims, but "the Muslims" did not rule India.

But if an outsider can doubt the identification of Muslims with political authority, it is by no means clear that participants in the culture perceived the distinction. In 1844 W. H. Sleeman reported that Muslims in general identified with the Mughal dynasty, longed for its restoration, and conceived of themselves as the former ruling class. "Whether they really

[39] Taufiq Ahmad Nizami, *Moslem Political Thought and Activity in India during the First Half of the 19th Century* (Aligarh: Three Men's Publications, 1969), pp. 23-24.

were so matters not; they persuade themselves or their children that they were."[40] To such people Mughal rule was Muslim rule, either by virtue of religious doctrine or theories of descent. So long as political power continued to keep up Mughal appearances, it was possible on the whole for non-Muslims to exercise it within legitimate bounds. First Marathas, then Englishmen dominated the vestiges of Mughal government, but the continued presence of an emperor in Delhi until 1857 allowed such people to act in his name. So long as India could be considered Mughal, there were many people, Muslim and non-Muslim, who assumed that being Muslim entailed a special relationship to the ruling power.

Although Mughal legitimacy became increasingly irrelevant in the coastal regions of India, the reality of British power in Hindustan, the Gangetic plain, only dropped the Mughal disguise after 1857. Until that time the old reservoir of people literate in Persian and able to participate in sharīf culture continued to preside over most of the courts and government offices, even of the British Raj. Although the British were making significant changes in land tenure and judicial institutions, they generally had to operate through these people. It was not necessary for a judge like Sayyid Ahmad Khan to know English. Persian, dropped as the official language in 1837, was replaced in north India by Urdu, a Persianized version of the urban vernacular written in the same script. In the early years of British rule, lower-level institutions were sufficiently similar to their Mughal predecessors so that the political education of the early generation of Indian participants followed earlier patterns: learning manners in the *mardānah* (men's section) of one's home from one's father, uncles, and their friends; learning to read and write Persian in a *maktab* (school); learning the details of office work by sitting next to an adult relative as he went about his tasks. Sayyid Ahmad, like his father and grandfathers, was a mo-

[40] W. H. Sleeman, *Rambles and Reflections of an Indian Official* (London: J. Hatchard and Son, 1884), I, 284.

bile civil servant, well educated in Persian literature, able to quote an apt verse on the right occasion, able to keep accounts in the complex Persian style, a man who knew how to be polite, witty, and when appropriate, pious. But in 1857 he supported his British employers against what was clearly a losing cause; when the war was over he was among the first to realize that the next generation would have to be different.

II

Sharīf Culture and British Rule

As if in a cage a captive bird
still gathered twigs for its nest . . .
Ghalib

GROWING UP SHARĪF

ONE part of a child's initiation into the social categories and relationships of nineteenth century sharīf culture was the architecture that surrounded him or, rather differently, her. In a royal establishment, a city ward, an old fortress town, or a peasant village, the living places of the rich and even the relatively poor shared, with varying degrees of elaboration, a common paradigm of rooms and open places, walls and curtains, rooftops and doorways. Learning who might go where and under what circumstances provided a whole structure of assumptions about authority and subordination, group bonds and exclusions. Learning how you yourself fit into this living space had a good deal to do with defining who you were.[1]

One grew up into a life contained, centered on a courtyard that was open to the sky but blocked on all four sides from any opening to the world beyond. The courtyard might be large or small, crowded or lonely, squalid or luxurious; the ground might be covered with marble, brick, or a mixture of earth and dung. Often there was a tree in the center and,

[1] I have used a fairly wide range of sources in this attempt to explore the general outlines of sharīf culture. These sources include general accounts of manners and customs, biographical literature, fiction, and interviews of descendants of Aligarh's first student generation. The references given below are intended to be illustrative rather than comprehensive. Other sources will be found in the bibliography.

sometimes, a well. On the margins could be broad, handsome verandahs set off with richly decorated columns and delicately scalloped arches; or dingy, sunless rooms made of earthen blocks. The structure rising above the courtyard could be one, two, even three stories high. But in all cases the building was a fortress, closed off and protected from the outside world by blank, windowless walls and a substantial, well-secured entrance way.

Within these boundaries one discovered flexible arrangements for channeling the movement of people so as to prevent some of them from being seen by others—a heavy cloth curtain, the *pardah*, hung from the archways, or light bamboo blinds that let in air but shut off light; rooms with doors on three sides so that different sorts of people might come and go without crossing paths; readily moveable bedsteads and cushions to transform the function of a given space; passageways in the walls or over the rooftops leading to a whole network of connected houses within the same *muḥallah* (neighborhood).

Such was the *maḥal k͟hānah*, the palace, as it was called even in modest homes, or more commonly the *zanānah*, the women's place. It was a layout that clearly embodied an "inner space" image of womanhood, something to be protected because it was vulnerable, and also because it was valuable: like food, jewelry, children, and what they all signified—honor, *'izzat*. For it was in terms of these possessions that groups interacted and status or moral worth was assigned. Within these walls a hierarchy of women passed their lives, arrayed in expensive ornaments, the senior wife and mother seated on a *masnad*, a carpeted throne. Women often spoke special dialects, and sometimes adhered to different sects from the male members of their family.[2] Poor women and

[2] 'Abdul Ḥalīm Sharar, *Guzashtah Lakhnau* [Olden Lucknow] (Lucknow: Nasīm Book Depot, 1965 [first published in 1914-1916]), p. 119; for a fictional attempt to reproduce the women's dialect of Agra see 'Iṣmat Cag͟htā'ī, "Cauthī kā Jauṛā," *Readings in Urdu: Prose and Poetry*, ed. C. M. Naim (Honolulu: East-West Center Press, 1965), pp. 1-17. The families of Khvajah Altaf Husain Hali

female servants might have to go out from time to time, covered from head to foot in great white tent-like sheets; others were carried by covered palanquin or bullock cart for formal visits on special occasions. But the ideal was to stay at home from marriage to death, visited, not visiting, carried in, as the saying went, in a bridal palanquin, carried out in a coffin.

Men lived in a different world, a big, bad world that required strength and cunning for survival. In contrast to the purported innocence of female life, men stood constantly on the brink of violence and their own evil impulses. Or perhaps women were not so innocent after all; perhaps it was the men who had to be protected from the overwhelming sensuality of feminine sexuality—such at least was the constant lament of male poets and the admonition of male moralists. Women were the occasion for a man's weakness; they were avoided and frequently resented. Specific rules of female separation, also called pardah, differed from family to family; but the general principle was that a woman might not be seen by any potential mate. That might limit her to fathers, brothers, husband, and sons; in some families even the husband's father and brothers were out of bounds.

But if women were secluded in the mahal, men were excluded from it, permitted to enter only with due warning and required to leave when their presence was inappropriate.[3] If wealthy, a man might have his own *dīvān k͟hānah*, a hall of audience suggestive of a royal court, in a separate section of the building complex or even in a totally different building, across the road.[4] Or it might be a tiny room off the side of

---

of Panipat and the Sayyids of Marehra are well-known examples of Sunni-Shi'ah division by sex.

[3] Vreede-de Stuers, *Parda*, p. 43, though the author is quick to add that the burden of isolation remains on the women; see also Hanna Papanek, "Purdah: Separate Worlds and Symbolic Shelter," *Comparative Studies in Society and History*, XV (1973), 289-325.

[4] Diagram of the family home of Sayyid Ahmad Khan prepared for me by his great-grandson, Hashim Muhammad Ali of Karachi (September 1969); see also Mohamed Ali, *My Life: A Fragment* (Lahore: Sh. Muhammad Ashraf, 1942), pp. 11-12.

the entrance way. A poorer man would have to take a bamboo stool out into the street, one of those narrow lanes of blank walls that snaked through any city or town, and there join the ranks of hawkers, beggars, and, at least in poetry, forlorn lovers who continually passed by. The alternative was to go off to a mosque, shop, government office, or brothel to engage in prayer, work, entertainment, or the rich art of conversation, according to the decorum of the time and place.[5]

A young boy did not learn about that separate men's world until he was old enough to join it, a gradual transition somewhere between the ages of five and ten, well after acquiring all the preliminary skills of walking, talking, and eating. These he learned primarily in the world of women. And in later years the zananah would remain for him an image of refuge and nurture as well as of childish impulsiveness, often little more than a memory after he had lost his right to be there all the time and was forced to deal with the life outside and sometimes far away.

But the zananah was hardly isolated. It is difficult to fix a concept of "household composition" on the rambling network of courtyards and rooftops within which woman's society operated, but there was certainly a great variety of people coming and going throughout the day.[6] Eating, sleeping, playing, cooking, sewing, and praying were all activities that could go on in one of a number of courtyards, rooms, rooftops, or verandahs, depending on the day-to-day relationships of the people involved. These people included an array of relatives, each set off in an elaborate and well-calibrated system of status positions. In all but the poorest homes there were usually servants, often quite a number of them. Long-term guests and poor but "respectable" personages with

[5] Sharar, *Lakhnau*, p. 301; see also Ralph Russell and Khurshidul Islam, *Three Mughal Poets* (Cambridge: Harvard University Press, 1968); Mirza Mohammad Hadi Ruswa, *Umrao Jan Ada*, tr. Khushwant Singh and M. A. Husaini (Bombay: Orient Longmans, 1961).

[6] British census takers were hard pressed to deal with the category of household composition (Ibbetson, pp. 40-42).

no place else to go were often put up in a spirit of almost limitless hospitality.[7] A child growing up into this world would have to learn to make intricate distinctions in the hierarchy of people around him; even the language embodied these distinctions in terms of address, verb forms, and formulas of politeness. The variety of configurations possible in this web of domestic relations would probably go some way to explaining the considerable differences of individual personality encountered in this milieu.

Sayyid Ahmad Khan was raised in the house of his maternal grandfather, Khvajah Fariduddin Ahmad, at the southern edge of old Delhi. Such an arrangement was slightly uncommon in a culture where women normally married into their husband's paternal household and wife-giving indicated lower status than wife-taking. In this case, however, Khvajah Farīd was able to compensate for relatively lower status—he was not a Sayyid (descendant of the Prophet) and his grandfather had come to Delhi as a Kashmiri trader—by wealth, prominence in the Mughal court and Delhi intellectual circles, and especially, a Sufi bond with the father of his daughter's husband. His son-in-law, Mir Muttaqi, was apparently happy to marry into a well-established household in return for freedom to pursue an unconventional life as courtier, mystic, swimmer, and master archer. For Khvajah Farīd the arrangement not only meant a little bit of social climbing, it was also a way to keep his favorite daughter at home.[8]

That home was not a single building, but a complex of houses, some connected, some separated by a narrow lane.

[7] Sarvar ul-Mulk [Agha Mirza Beg], *Kārnāmah-i Sarvarī* (Aligarh: Muslim University, 1933), pp. 2-5; the English version is Nawab Serverul-Mulk, *My Life*, tr. Niwab Jivan Yar Jung Bahadur (London: Arthur H. Stockwell, n.d.), pp. 12-15; see also E. M. Forster, *Abinger Harvest* (New York: Harcourt, Brace and World, n.d.), pp. 315-318.

[8] Khvājah Alṭāf Ḥusain Ḥālī, *Ḥayāt-ī jāvīd* (Lahore: Ā'inah-i Adab, 1966 [originally published in 1901]), pp. 65-85; Hali's discussion of Sayyid Ahmad's childhood draws largely from Sayyid Ahmad's own biography of Khvajah Farīd, *Sīrat-i Farīdiyah* (Karachi: Pāk Academy, 1964 [originally published in 1896]); I am also indebted to Hashim Muhammad Ali for discussing the family history with me.

Khvajah Farīd would come to the mahal for his morning meal when the whole family—his two sons and three daughters, their wives and husbands and their numerous children—ate together, each getting personal attention from the patriarch. In the evening his daughters would serve him separately in the divan k͟hanah. Then he would hear his grandchildren recite their lessons and correct them on their manners and dress.[9]

Such a household was well stocked with servants: nursemaids, cooks, grooms, bearers, sweepers, water carriers, washermen, palanquin carriers, a barber; such servants were likely to be attached to the family on a relatively exclusive and long-term basis. Sharāfat as opposed to mere wealth entailed treating servants according to rank—often the terminology was borrowed from coveted positions among the Mughal nobility—with the proper modulation of authority and consideration. Once when Sayyid Ahmad was eleven or twelve he struck an old family servant; his mother had him turned out of the house. An aunt (his mother's sister) hid him in another house for three days, then interceded on his behalf: he was allowed back only after begging forgiveness from the servant.[10]

Sayyid Ahmad grew up in a well-populated world; his maternal grandfather, his mother, his mother's brothers, his older brother, some of the servants and, more distantly, his father, all represented various levels of authority over him. His status among the children of the house is not clear: normally a child visiting his maternal grandfather's house is treated as a privileged guest. His mother is in her own home and does not have to deal with the hostile authority of a mother-in-law.[11] On the other hand, the absence of a household in the paternal line may have represented some kind of

[9] Sayyid Aḥmad, *Sīrat-i Farīdiyah*, pp. 124-125.

[10] *Ibid.*, pp. 136-137; cf. Muḥammad Z̲akā' Ullāh, *Savāniḥ-i 'umrī Ḥājī Maulvī Muḥammad Samī' Ullāh K͟hān Bahādur* (Hyderabad: Nūr ul-Islām, 1909), pp. 20-21.

[11] See Sayyid Riẓā 'Alī, *A'māl nāmah* (Delhi: Hindustan Publishers, 1943), pp. 21-22.

deprivation, a sense that one's father's line lacked authority and security. Such a background may have something to do with why Sayyid Ahmad sought his career outside Delhi, raising his own children in a whole string of north Indian towns where he was posted for three- and four-year terms.

Such speculations are the stuff of full-blown biography, but the data for interpreting the general cultural patterns of family life for a significant population are sparse and difficult to come by. Even among the handful of available biographical sources, however, there is a wide range of variation with regard to the kinds of people a child would have to deal with as "significant others." Mushtaq Husain, Sayyid Ahmad's co-worker from Amroha, was also raised in his maternal grandfather's house, an only child after his father's early death.[12] Altaf Husain Hali of Panipat, poet of the Aligarh movement, lost his parents at an early age, one to death and the other to insanity, and was raised by his considerably older brother, who was married to his mother's sister's daughter. The same elder brother was "father" to Hali's eldest son; Hali even called the child "nephew" (brother's son).[13] Agha Mirza of Delhi spent his earliest years in the house of his father's sister. When he died, the family shifted to the house of his father's elder brother, his *baṛē abbā* (big father); but the boy's mother, a granddaughter of Khvajah Farīd, spent much of her time with her own side of the family. The uncle was indeed a magnified father: once when Agha Mirza was hit for disturbing some of his father's work, the uncle came to his defense, brandishing a stick. In 1857, when Agha Mirza was nine, the British captured Delhi; his uncle was shot as a rebel and died a Muslim martyr. The family fled in confusion to the protection, first of the mother's sister's husband in Alwar State, then to another father's brother, a pro-British official in Oudh.[14]

12 Muḥammad Ikrāmullāh Khān, *Viqār-i Ḥayāt* (Aligarh: Muslim University, 1925), p. 2.

13 Ṣālḥah ʿĀbid Ḥusain, *Yādgār-i Ḥālī*, 2d ed (Aligarh: Anjūman-i Taraqqī-i Urdū, [1955]), pp. 26-27, 33.

14 Sarvar ul-Mulk, *Kārnāmah*, pp. 5-6, 11. The English translation

One is hard pressed to find cases of children raised simply by father and mother, either in this older generation of the first half of the nineteenth century or in the first generation of Aligarh students. Shaikh Masud Ali was one of the first students at Aligarh College. His uncle (father's younger brother), who had two sons of his own, took responsibility for him when his father died during his infancy. Both father and uncle had been in British service in Delhi, but also had some small property and numerous kinsmen in the town of Fatehpur, near Lucknow. For some years Masud Ali's mother stayed in the household of her brother-in-law; she too was from the Fatehpur lineage. But when Masud Ali was six, his maternal grandfather came to get mother and son and bring them back to the vatan for an extended visit. For several years the boy traveled with his mother from one rural relative to another, then rejoined his uncle, who was then in service in Dujanna, a small princely state in the Punjab.[15]

Sayyid Riza Ali, another student of Aligarh's first generation, was born in 1880 in his paternal grandfather's house, a small two-story building in the *qaṣbah* of Kandarkhi, near Moradabad. Apart from that house, there was also a mardanah, a separate building for men. Riza Ali's father was the only child of the grandfather's first wife, who died young, but that wife's mother still lived in a little *kaccā* (unfinished) house next door. When his second wife died, the mother of eight children, the grandfather married a third time. Like the grandfather, all three wives belonged to the lineage of Sayyids that had settled in the qasbah two hundred years before and now lived side by side, visiting each other, sharing meals, intermarrying, and sometimes engaging in bitter disputes. Most of them were cultivators, religious teachers, and sol-

---

omits reference to the martyrdom. A Muslim martyr goes directly to Paradise without waiting for the Day of Judgment.

15 Mas'ūd 'Alī Maḥvī, *Kitāb-i makhdūm zādgān-i Fateḥpūr* ([Hyderabad? 1946?]), II, 143-158. I am indebted to Mashfiq Khwaja of the Anjuman-i Taraqqi-i Urdu, Karachi, and Brigadier Kirmani, also of Karachi, for loaning me copies of this privately printed family history.

diers, but the grandfather had managed to achieve relative wealth by establishing a modest sugar-processing operation. There is no information about other marriages in the grandfather's household, but Riza Ali's mother came from a previously unrelated family of Sayyids in a distant village near Bareilly. An outsider, she somehow communicated to her son an unwillingness to accept food from anybody but herself, and used that as an excuse not to attend weddings and celebrations or otherwise accept hospitality from her husband's relatives; she had to stay home to feed him. When Riza Ali was six she took him off for a long visit to her native village. The grandfather died two years later, and shortly after that the brothers quarreled, divided the property—houses, land, and sugar business—and established separate households. The family of the grandfather's young widow, who was childless, instituted a litigation that lasted for twenty years.[16]

Particularly in rural areas, where agricultural land and political consolidation hung in the balance, social bonds based on a shared genealogical identity could be extensive and deeply rooted. In many cases, however, such unity was more an historical memory—or fabrication—than a resource to be summoned up in the interests of mutual security and ambition. Aftab Ahmad Khan belonged to a cadet lineage of Yusufzai Pathans, attached to the Navabs of Kunjpura, a defunct little kingdom north of Delhi, dating back to the early eighteenth century. Although living close beside their wealthier kinsmen, Aftab's own branch of the family was landless and derived its income from service outside the qasbah. Aftab's grandfather had been a courtier in Kapurthala State; Aftab's father's elder brother was a sepoy who rebelled and disappeared in 1857. Ghulam Ahmad Khan, Aftab's father, ultimately received high office in Gwalior. He left two younger brothers, wife, and two sons in Kunjpura.[17] Fakhruddin Ahmad Khan also came from a large rural line-

16 Riẓa 'Alī, *A'māl nāmah*, pp. 7-12, 30-32.

17 Ḥabībullāh Khān, *Ḥayāt-i Aftāb* (Allahabad: Asrār Karīmī Press, [1947]), pp. 1-5.

age, Lodi Pathans of Jullundhur District, and also had a father named Ghulam Ahmad Khan who held important official posts far away from home, as a Punjab Revenue officer and later an official in Kashmir. But in this case wife and children tagged along on the father's peripatetic career. There was one other difference between the family backgrounds of Aftab Ahmad and Fakhruddin: Aftab's mother came from an unrelated family in Muzzafarnagar District; Fakhruddin's was a cousin (her husband's father's brother's daughter).[18]

From these few examples one discovers numerous variations in household type that were possible within the same culture: the sibling position of one's father; whether or not the paternal grandparents are alive and on the scene; whether one's mother is a close relative on the paternal or maternal side, or had no previous relation with her husband; the proximity of other related households, and the extent to which they share social and economic activities; the presence of elder brothers and their wives and children; the career of the household head, and whether he is absent or present; whether the family wealth can support a large household and many servants. Some of these variations are linked to birth and mortality; others to the economic resources available to a kinship unit. There was room for disagreement about how widely economic resources should be spread and at what point a joint holding in house or land should be divided. One also comes across strong statements for and against marrying cousins.[19] Such controversies were possible within the bounds of sharāfat. In the absence of data on the frequency of particular patterns, one can only note scattered biographical variation, and suggest that such variation was itself a characteristic of the culture. Individuals did not grow up in

[18] Mushtāq Aḥmad K͟hān, *Ḥayāt-i Fak͟hr* (Lahore: Nuqūsh Press, 1966), pp. 4-12.

[19] For an argument in favor of marrying outside the family see Naẕīr Ahmad, *The Bride's Mirror or Mir-Ātu l-Arūs*, tr. by G. E. Ward (London: Henry Frowde, 1899), p. 160; for a family dispute on the issue see Mas'ūd 'Ali, *Kitāb-i mak͟hdūm*, II, 123.

identical family contexts. The emergence of significant personality differences in what was supposed to be a group-oriented society may be one reason, among others, for the endemic quarrels and infighting one so frequently encounters.

There was, however, a well-plotted scenario for growing up, designed in the case of male children to lead them from the protection and nurture of the zananah to the battlefield of the outside world of men. "The best time of all in a man's life is that of childhood," wrote Nazir Ahmad of Delhi in 1869. "At that age he has no kind of anxiety."[20] A child was born into a family after nine months of rituals and omens regarding life and death for mother and child and determination that the child would be a boy. For the mother it was a period of pain and sickness—she was often just barely past puberty at the birth of her first child—but the act of giving birth, especially to a boy, was the ultimate fulfillment of her role in life, the ultimate source of her recognition as a person. When a boy was born, the household announced it by shooting off cannons or, at least, an old rifle, by way of expressing proud triumph—and to accustom the child to the sound of gunshot from the start.[21] A midwife brought the infant out to the men, and one of them—a religious teacher, a senior member of the family or, sometimes, a boy—uttered the call to prayer in the baby's left ear and the Islamic credo in the right, this accompanied by a taste of honey.[22]

Loving devotion of mother for child was a hallowed ideal, but the particular weight and manner of that relationship was hardly uniform in the culture. A mother like Riza Ali's, who

[20] Naẕīr Ahmad, *The Bride's Mirror*, p. 20.

[21] This particular practice was terminated after 1857, when the British disarmed the population. But people could still use firecrackers.

[22] For birth customs in different localities, see Mrs. Meer Hasan Ali, *Observations on the Mussulmauns of India* (London: Parbury, Allen, and Co., 1832), II, 1-13; Jaffur Shureef, *Qanoon-e-Islam*, 2d ed. (Madras: J. Higginbotham, 1863), pp. 1-4; Sayyid Aḥmad Dehlvī, *Rasūm-i Dehli* (Rampur: Kitābkār Publications, 1965 [originally published in 1905]), pp. 42-65.

came as a stranger to the house of her father-in-law, had few alternative points of focus for her attention and concern. Sayyid Ahmad's mother, on the other hand, had her father, brothers and sisters, nephews and nieces all about her. Similarly, a mother who was her husband's father's brother's daughter, like the mother of Fakhruddin Ahmad, or who had some other close kinship tie in addition to marriage, would not be so dependent on her role as mother for recognition as a family member. Furthermore, in many households there were other women to take up and diffuse the mother's role: the child's grandmother, aunts, elder sisters. When a mother died or was unable to nurse, another woman was usually available. For example, a child might be nursed by his father's mother, sharing the breast with the father's younger sister, and the two infants would grow up calling each other brother and sister.[23] In wealthier families there was usually a wet nurse to spare the actual mother the burden of total devotion and special diet; such a wet nurse became a permanent member of the family and object of the child's life-long devotion, her own children sometimes growing up in the household as lesser brothers and sisters.[24]

For at least two years the infant had a mother-figure totally available, at least as a source of nourishment. Whether that availability was accompanied by warmth, playfulness, clinging attachment, or some other personal quality was a matter of wide variation. Male biographical literature portrays mothers as paragons of self-sacrifice, loving devotion,

[23] Mushtāq Aḥmad Khān, *Ḥayāt-i Fakhr*, p. 17; see also Sayyid Hāshmī Farīdabādī, "Maulvī 'Abd ul-Ḥaq," *'Alīgaṛh Megzīn*, Aligarh Number, Part II (1954-1955), p. 53.

[24] Mrs. Meer Hasan Ali, *Observations*, II, 11-12; for a fictional account involving a Hindu wet nurse and her son in a Muslim home, see Attiya Hosain, "The Loss," *Phoenix Fled* (London: Chatto and Windus, 1953), pp. 117-133; also complaints about friendships with servant children by Sayyid Husain Bilgrami in *Addresses, Poems, and Other Writings of Nawab Imadul-Mulk Bahadur* (Hyderabad: Government Central Press, 1925), p. 105; I am indebted to Mr. Sajjad Mirza of Hyderabad, son of Aziz Mirza, for discussing these matters with me (Hyderabad, September 1968).

and profound religious piety, but there are occasional hints of callousness and neglect.[25]

For the first three days an infant was fed on a medicinal mixture prepared by the midwife and sometimes laced with opium; nursing started on the fourth day, inaugurated by a crowded, joyful women's party in the zananah when mother and child were put on display. This was followed by a series of similar gatherings in the zananah for bathing the child, shaving its head, placing the baby in a special cradle, or celebrating his first handclaps, his first nonmilk diet (at seven months), his first tooth, and the first time he crawled—all accompanied by music, the presentation of gifts, feasting, processions, and food for the poor.[26]

All such celebration was hedged, however, with the persistent fear of early death and a large repertoire of techniques to prevent it. The infant was the embodiment of vulnerability, and proper care consisted of sparing him pain and responding to his desires. Dressed only in a thin loose shirt, but wrapped warmly in a quilt during cold weather, the infant spent his first few months reclining except when being nursed. To move him around was considered a cruel disturbance.[27] On the other hand, it is likely that no one interfered in the child's exploration of his own powers of movement, making sounds, regulating his bladder and bowels. So while there was protection from pain there was little social constraint on an infant's search for autonomy.

Many children continued to nurse after growing teeth and into the third or fourth year, while gradually developing alternative nourishment such as rice, lentils, and buffalo milk. But at least in Delhi there was a decisive moment of weaning, and even a ceremony in which relatives from both mother and father's families gathered and the child was

[25] For a fictional account of a bad mother, see Naẕīr Ahmad, *The Taubau-n-Nasùh*, tr. by M. Kempson (London: W. H. Allen & Co., 1886); for the more saintly variety, C. F. Andrews, *Zaka Ullah of Delhi* (Cambridge: W. Heffer & Sons, 1929), pp. 53-55.

[26] Jaffur Shureef, *Qanoon-e-Islam*, pp. 15-23.

[27] Mrs. Meer Hasan Ali, *Observations*, p. 7.

offered a dish of dates or date-like candies. If he picked up one, that meant his weaning would go smoothly with only one day of fussing; if he picked up more, the household was in for a long siege. The wet nurse, if there was one, got money and a dress, and there were gifts to the other servants as well. So the painful transition of weaning was accompanied by a reaffirmation of family solidarity. Nevertheless, it was the beginning of adversity; the breast wasn't simply denied but covered with the juice of a bitter plant so the child would learn that what was once a source of pleasure could turn in the end to pain. As Nazir Ahmad of Delhi wrote in 1869:

> So long as the child is very small the mother nurses it, and carries it about with her wherever she goes. She gives up her whole night's rest, while she is patting the baby to sleep. But when the child is old enough to begin eating "khichri," the mother leaves off nursing it altogether, and that milk which she has gone on giving to it so fondly for many years she now withholds from it persistently and sternly. She applies bitter tasting things (to keep the child away), and if the child is pertinacious she slaps and scolds it.[28]

British commentators on Indian society frequently complained about "the enervating and stultifying influence of the Zunana" upon the developing character of Indian males. According to Sleeman, who as a man was not in a position to benefit from direct observation, "The sons are tyrannised over through youth by their mothers, who endeavour to subdue their spirit to the yoke . . . ; and they remain through manhood timid, ignorant, and altogether unfitted for the conduct of public affairs."[29] A contrasting observation was that Indian children were themselves the tyrants, taking advantage

[28] Naẕīr Ahmad, *The Bride's Mirror*, p. 5; interview with Sajjad Mirza; see also Sayyid Ahmad Dehlvi, *Rasūm-i Dehlī*, p. 71; for a critical comment on prolonged breast feeding see the *Aligarh Institute Gazette* (hereafter AIG), July 2, 1892.

[29] Sleeman, *Rambles and Reflections*, I, 332.

of a mother's desire to please them and satisfy their every wish. Thus Margaret Morison, wife of an Aligarh professor, complained that children lacked firm discipline and fixed schedules.[30] Indian critics of contemporary social life, whether influenced by British standards or not, often took up the theme that zananah women were inadequate as raisers of children because of undue leniency aggravated by lack of education.[31] On the other hand, there are accounts of mothers, such as Sayyid Ahmad Khan's and Mushtaq Husain's, who are portrayed as firm and skillful disciplinarians.[32] In both those cases the mothers were in their own father's house, and there is reason to believe that the authority of a woman was a function of her security in the household as a lineal member of the kindred.

Sharīf child-rearing assumed that a child progressed from helpless vulnerability to arrogant willfulness; it was the role of male society to tame and redirect this development by imposing an adult relationship on the child that played down love and affection and emphasized stern authority. A father would often be addressed by a title such as *ḥuẓūr* (literally, "the presence"), and his authority was supposedly absolute.[33] "No boy ever dared leave the compound without the permission of his father." Such was the norm, if not universal practice.[34]

As a young boy began to emerge from the zananah, he

[30] Margaret Morison, "A Conversation," *Aligarh Monthly*, December 1904, pp. 6-12. Englishmen made similar complaints about American children, so these references may tell us more about the English than about either Indians or Americans (Richard L. Rapson, "The American Child as Seen by British Travelers," *The American Family in Social-Historical Perspective*, ed. by Michael Gordon [New York: St. Martin's Press, 1973], pp. 192-208).

[31] Bilgrami, *Addresses*, p. 35.

[32] Sayyid Aḥmad, *Sīrat-i Farīdiyah*, pp. 135-148; Ikrāmullāh K͟hān, *Viqār-i Ḥayāt*, pp. 2-3.

[33] See *The Diary of Sahibzada Aftab Ahmad Khan Ahmadi, 1892-93*, ms. in the Aligarh Muslim University Archives, Maulana Azad Library, Aligarh (hereafter the Aligarh Archives will be referred to as AA).

[34] Bilgrami, *Addresses*, p. 23.

would at the same time begin to experience the competitiveness and rough and tumble excitement of the world of men and boys. Ceremonies marking the steps in this transition were held in the presence of men, although women had separate celebrations. First came the *bi'smi'llāh* ("in the name of God"), preferably at the age of four years, four months, four days and even four hours, when the child was taught the opening words of the Qur'an, often against the background of lavish feasting and entertainment by musicians and dancers. When the child finished reading through the whole of the Qur'an, there was a similar celebration called *ḥidīyah.* In the midst of his schooling, preferably at age seven, or at least before puberty, a Muslim boy would undergo circumcision, honored once again by a great celebration of feasting, gift giving, and procession through the streets.[35] The point of this practice was to place male sexuality within the bounds of God's covenant with the Prophet Ibrahim; circumcision, like discipline and education, was designed to tame a boy's impulses and subject him to divine law.

Teachers, like fathers, were sources of strict discipline and objects of formal respect. But there were different kinds of teachers, designated not only by what they taught, but by their social status in relation to the students. The earliest lessons in Qur'an, the recitation and memorization of the Arabic scriptures without benefit of translation, could be taught at home by a paid employee, called a *miyānjī* or, if female, an *ustānī*. Or the child could be sent out of the house to learn Qur'an from the *qārī ṣāḥib*, the public reciter of a mosque, or to the house of the teacher, who could be doing the work as a living or a philanthropic act. At the hidiyah ceremony the teacher would receive a shawl and money.[36]

[35] Sayyid Aḥmad Dehlvī, *Rasūm-i Dehlī*, pp. 71-73; Jaffur Shureef, *Qanoon-e-Islam*, pp. 27-34.

[36] Sayyid Ahmad was taught by an ustānī (Ḥālī, *Ḥayāt-i jāvīd*, p. 86); Aftab Ahmad Khan was taught by a miyānjī (Ḥabībullāh K͟hān, *Ḥayāt-i Aftāb*, p. 6); Zafar Ali Khan started with his father's father (Ashraf 'Aṯā, *Maulānā Ẕafar 'Alī K͟hān* [Lahore: Caravan, (1962)], p. 22); Masud Ali and Hali started with a qārī ṣāḥib (Mas'ūd

Recitation of Qur'an, often accompanied by chanting and memorization, as well as learning the movements of the body associated with prayer, were all formidable achievements for a young child. He was now able to do what adults could do in this most important aspect of life, and had in his power skills that united him with the great world community of Islam. Interpreting these actions—learning, for example, the meaning of the words he recited—was a matter to be taken up in later life, if at all. But for a child of seven or eight it must have been extremely gratifying to stand side by side with the men of the community and side by side to prostrate himself in prayer. Such a child participated only to the extent of his inclination: the full religious obligation of adulthood came only with puberty, as signaled by a boy's first nocturnal emission.[37]

After going through the Qur'an, the next step was usually some sort of education in Persian, usually with a few other children in a maktab. The maktab was a makeshift arrangement located on the verandah or in the courtyard of the teacher or some benefactor. Often it was in the home of some of the children, but neighboring students, sometimes from among the poor, could attend as well, paying the teacher a separate fee or just allowed to sit in. There was often a mixture of Muslim and Hindu boys, but not of boys and girls. Maulvi Zain ul-Abdin, a founder of Aligarh College, started his maktab education in the house of a Hindu benefactor in Machlishahar. Before entering Aligarh, Masud Ali had frequently shifted from place to place; some of his education was with village relatives, some with Hindu Khatris in Delhi, some with the sons of the Navab of Dujanna. There is little evidence that there was a feeling of solidarity among the students

---

'Alī, *Kitāb-i makhdūm*, II, 144; and Ṣālḥah 'Ābid Ḥusain, *Yādgār*, p. 26); for study in the teacher's home see Mīr Vilāyat Ḥusain, *Āp bītī* (Aligarh: privately published by Sayyid Ḥādi Ḥusain Zaidī, 1970), p. 23; examples of philanthropic teaching are in Zakā' Ullāh, *Savāniḥ*, p. 14.

[37] Jaffur Shureef, *Qanoon-e-Islam*, p. 36.

in a maktab, each of whom proceeded separately at his own pace through the course of study.[38]

The course seems to have been fairly standardized: first learning to recognize the letters of the Persian alphabet by sight and sound, a task essentially accomplished by a Muslim who had already done his Qur'an, then memorization of passages out of S'adi and other Persian classical writers, but without translation. Only after that would a child start writing, spending three to six hours a day at painstaking calligraphy, written first on dirt, then on a wooden slate, finally on paper. Gradually the teacher would introduce the translation of the Persian or, at least, his approximation of it. Next a child would take up Persian composition, imitating models that were often by Indian, even Hindu authors, in formal and informal correspondence, petition writing, old Mughal imperial proclamations, *shikastah* shorthand, and *raqm* accounting, as well as all the elaborate forms of polite address. Wealthier youths had special tutors for etiquette, and the basic maktab education could also be supplemented by study with a master of calligraphy. Arabic grammar and literature was often part of a child's studies, for Hindus as well as Muslims. This system of education always consisted of reading classical texts with one's teacher; rather than grades, classes, or degrees a person's education was signified by the books he had read and the teachers he had read them with. As for written Urdu, it could be extrapolated from the classical languages, that is, using the Persian script to approximate the vernacular, a task that required no formal instruction.[39]

[38] Education Commission. *Report of the North-Western Provinces and Oudh Provincial Committee* (Calcutta: Superintendent of Government Printing, 1884), p. 383 and elsewhere (hereafter EC/NWP); Mas'ūd 'Alī, *Kitāb-i makhdūm*, II, 150; Qamruddīn Aḥmad Badāyūnī, *Maḥfil-i 'Azīz* (Hyderabad: A'jāz Printing Press, 1962), pp. 99-100.

[39] For a general account see G.D.M. Sufi, *Al-Minhāj: Being the Evolution of Curriculum in the Muslim Educational Institutions of India* (Lahore: Shaikh Muhammad Ashraf, 1941); see also EC/NWP; William Adam, *Reports on Vernacular Education in Bengal and Behar* (Calcutta: Home Secretariat Press, 1968 [originally published in 1835, 1838]); Ziaul Haque, "Muslim Religious Education in

Teachers, of course, were of uneven quality, some of them highly learned men, themselves the students of famous teachers; others, sadistic charlatans who knew little beyond the alphabet and the use of a switch.[40] Whether a boy decided to continue with this experience depended partly on the prompting he got from his elders, but also very much on his own inclination or *shauq* for a particular aspect of learning. If he had such an inclination, he would often go in search of an *ustād*, the master of a particular area of knowledge or art, and seek to be accepted as his *shāggird*, or disciple. Such a teacher was considered to be a second father.[41] Sayyid Ahmad Khan got his mother's brother to teach him mathematics; then he went to a famous *ḥakīm* to learn the Arabic tradition of Greek medicine.[42] Hali defied his family and slipped away from Panipat to Delhi to pursue his gift for poetry with the greatest poet of the age, Ghalib.[43] Sami Ullah Khan became a disciple of the famous Delhi *muftī* Sadruddin Azurdah, who taught him Islamic theology and law.[44] A person's intellectual ancestry became as important as his family background in establishing his claim to honor. Honored teachers might be associated with an endowed institution, a madrasah, like Farangi Mahal in Lucknow, but they were often private persons who received no income from their teaching. Often poor students received stipends, called *vazīfahs*.[45]

A religious teacher from among the ʻulama was often revered as a spiritual guide (*pīr* or *murshid*), whose knowledge touched the disciple with a kind of spiritual electricity passed from generation to generation. Sayyid Ahmad's father was

---

Indo-Pakistan: An Annotated Bibliography," Occasional Paper Series, Muslim Studies Subcommittee, Committee on Southern Asian Studies (Chicago: University of Chicago, 1972).

[40] Vilāyat Ḥusain, *Āp bītī*, p. 24; Muḥammad Saʻīd K͟hān [Navāb of Chatārī], *Yād-i ayyām* (Aligarh: Muslim Educational Press, n.d.), I, 22.

[41] Jaffur Shureef, *Qanoon-e-Islam*, p. 33.

[42] Ḥālī, *Ḥayāt-i jāvīd*, p. 86.

[43] Ṣalhah ʻĀbid Ḥusain, *Yādgār*, p. 29.

[44] Z̲akā' Ullāh, *Savāniḥ*, p. 20. [45] EC/NWP, p. 287.

part of such a mystical genealogy, called a *silsilah*. The religious establishment where one entered such a communion and learned its discipline was called a *k͟hānqāh*, and one's murshid, like an ustad, was yet another "father" in a person's life.[46]

The relationship of ustad and shaggird extended from knowledge, *'ilm*, to art or skill, *fan*. The same uncle who taught Sayyid Ahmad mathematics had studied archery with Sayyid Ahmad's father.[47] Swordsmanship, swimming, horseback riding, and exercises with Indian clubs all represented carefully acquired military skills. Wrestling was another art learned from an ustad in a kind of gymnasium or pit called an *akhārā*.[48] In the same category of *fan* were music and painting—Sayyid Ahmad's uncle was a devotee of both—and here, too, a teacher would only take on a disciple who seemed to have the shauq for learning in a spirit of total devotion and painstaking imitation.[49]

In contrast to all this seriously acquired learning, however, there were activities devoted to pure pleasure, in which a man, young or old, could release all those carefully cultivated powers of aggression. A typical pastime was flying kites from the roof of the house: the kite string would be coated with pieces of broken glass and the object of the game was to get your own kite up above competing kites sent up from the other roofs in the neighborhood, then to pull down fast and cut away as many strings as you could. Even this sport could be a serious enterprise: Sayyid Ahmad's uncle, the devotee of music, also wrote a treatise on kite making.[50] Similarly, many people kept pigeons on their roofs and

[46] Jaffur Shureef, *Qanoon-e-Islam*, p. 33; among Hindus there were analogous institutions in the *gurū*, *pāṭhshālā*, and *maṭh*, and a sharīf Hindu, such as the poetic disciples of Ghalib or several witnesses in EC/NWP, would have Sanskrit along with Persian and Arabic as part of his education.

[47] Sayyid Aḥmad, *Sīrat-i Farīdiyah*, p. 133.

[48] Sharar, *Lakhnau*, pp. 153-154; Ḥabībullāh K͟hān, *Ḥayāt-i Aftāb*, p. 6.

[49] Sayyid Aḥmad, *Sīrat-i Farīdiyah*, pp. 129-134.

[50] *Ibid.*, pp. 132-133.

trained them to obey commands: then one would send the pigeons up and try to draw away birds from the neighboring flocks. Board games like chess or parchesi, team games like *kabaḍḍī*, gambling games like cockfighting, all involved intense and aggressive competition. For the puritanical, for whom such pastimes were frivolous, there were equally fierce competitions in poetry, the *mushāʿirah*, and scholastic disputation, the *munāẓarah*. In all these examples it was individual virtuosity that was being asserted as the measure of social worth.[51]

But if this social environment sometimes seethed with rivalry, there were certainly occasions for warm friendship. The favorite pleasures were those of the *maḥfil*, the social gathering, though they tended to be idealized as the glory of an irretrievable past, a time of emperors and navabs. Such gatherings cut across lines of kinship and religion, but were bound together by an identity of cultural style. Sayyid Ahmad recalled occasions when his mother's brother would hold colorful musical entertainments, or would take him along to the home of a wealthy Hindu connoisseur to listen to the amateur performances of the sharīf and the professional singing and dancing of the leading courtesans of the city.[52] Pious Muslims avoided such courtly displays, but still cherished the spirit of the mahfil, a time when friends could be relaxed, sitting together, exchanging witty remarks, philosophic speculations, poetic repartee. The *huqqah* would be passed around, there would be Mughal cuisine, some sweets, *pān*, perhaps a special kind of mango. Each remark was supposed to be like pān, an exquisitely folded betal leaf, to be tasted and savored in a rich "flower-shower of conversation."[53] The spirit of friendship and equality was communicated in a vocabulary of social precedence: one's own house was a hovel,

[51] Mrs. Meer Hasan Ali, *Observations*, II, 14-21; Jaffur Shureef, *Qanoon-e-Islam*, Appendix 8; Sarvar ul-Mulk, *Kārnāmah*, p. 22.

[52] Sayyid Aḥmad, *Sīrat-i Farīdiyah*, pp. 130-132.

[53] A recurring motif, for example, in Ralph Russell and Khurshidul Islam, *Ghalib: Life and Letters* (London: George Allen and Unwin, 1969).

the house of another was a palace; one's own remarks were humble submissions, one's partner in conversation issued only commands. But these formulas of politeness were mutual, and a young boy sitting quietly in the midst of such a gathering would only gradually learn the intricate subtleties of social precedence.[54]

THE KACAHRĪ MILIEU

In 1869, "Deputy" Nazir Ahmad described in his novel *The Bride's Mirror* circumstances under which a young man might seek employment. Newly married and living in Delhi with his mother, wife, younger sister, and a servant, Muhammad Kāmil gets bored with his life of leisure and desultory study. His father lives in Lahore as steward to a wealthy landowner, and visits his family once every few years for very special occasions. Out of a salary of fifty rupees a month the father sends down twenty for the maintenance of his family, sufficient for them to eat plentifully, dress well, employ a servant (at the "high" wage of two rupees a month plus food) and provide for ceremonial obligations and kinship responsibilities.[55] A didactic guide to young wives, the novel demonstrates the dangers of bad household management—namely, the accumulation of debts—and the benefits of careful budgeting; but in either case the family manages to live in sharīf style on an income equal to about two percent of the lowest-grade British civil servant. That income was, at the same time, twenty or even forty times the wage of a laborer.[56] Economic calculations are not, then, Muhammad Kāmil's primary motive in seeking a job; it is more a matter of rest-

[54] Sharar, *Lakhnau*, pp. 300, 314-322.

[55] For a family budget see Naẕīr Ahmad, *The Bride's Mirror*, pp. 105-106; I am indebted to Justice Sharfuddin Ahmad of Hyderabad for showing me the account book for 1887 of his grandfather Shaikh Ali Ahmad of Delhi, the uncle of Masud Ali.

[56] This, of course, is a very approximate statement; biweekly wage data were reported in the official *North-Western Provinces and Oudh Gazette*, which can be found in the NAI.

lessness. His exemplary wife, however, realizes the practical issues: that her father-in-law is old and his income will not always be available, that her husband has a younger sister to be married off and will require a *jahez*, or trousseau. But she is also aware of the moral perils of an idle life.

Muhammad Kāmil's first thought is to enlist the assistance of his wife's father, who holds the lofty post of tahsildar, revenue administrator for a subdistrict. His wife, however, points out that it would be socially disgraceful for him to be under an obligation to his father-in-law; instead he must find his way by his own efforts. And she proceeds to tell him how—this being Nazir Ahmad's advice to young women on how to guide their husbands' careers. The trick is to befriend people who work in government offices and get their help in gaining access to one of the "rulers"—that is, an Englishman.

Taking this good advice, Muhammad Kāmil starts hanging around the *kacahrī*, the complex of courts and government offices that marked any administrative center, and soon he is paying visits to such important figures among the Indian staff as the sarishtadar and tahsildar.[57] Everyone realizes, of course, what he is after, but since he is a well-brought-up young man, he knows the proper mixture of deference and self-assertion appropriate to his position. Finally a deposition writer in one of the courts takes a liking to him, and offers to take him on as a kind of apprentice, showing him the office procedures in return for a little free assistance. People get to know him; he presents papers to some of the British officials for signature, he substitutes—for a fraction of the salary—when some of the clerks are absent. Then a vacancy occurs and he gets a permanent position as log-keeper at ten rupees a month.

From there on up, the road is smooth. Again acting on his

[57] Nazīr Ahmad, *The Bride's Mirror*, ch. 23-24; but the translation is misleading here: for example, there is nothing in the Urdu about "paying court" to "personages," and the word *naukar* is rendered as "official" rather than "servant" (cf. Urdu reprint ed.; Delhi: Kutb Khānah Naẕariyah, n.d., where the equivalent chapters are 26-27). A sarishtadar is an office supervisor or head clerk.

wife's advice, Muhammad Kāmil goes to bid farewell to a departing Englishman who is being transferred to Sialkot in western Punjab. Maybe he can get a chit, a certificate attesting to his worthy service. But as luck would have it, the Englishman offers to take the young man with him as a personal assistant at fifteen rupees a month. With this opportunity in hand, Muhammad Kāmil's wife proceeds to orchestrate a meeting between the Englishman and her father-in-law's employer in Lahore, in which Muhammad Kāmil gets a casual recommendation from a man who happens to own several villages in Sialkot. Thus armed with a sharīf background, an adequate education, and good connections, the young man becomes assistant or naib-sarishtadar at fifty rupees and, within a year, sarishtadar at a hundred.

Nazir Ahmad's account, though fictional, recapitulates the early careers of Indians in government during the first three-quarters of the nineteenth century. Sayyid Ahmad Khan decided to enter the British service in 1838, just after his father's death. In order to learn the system of work, he made himself useful at the court of the Delhi Ṣadr Amīn, who happened to be his mother's sister's husband. After a few months he was sarishtadar of that court. He became acquainted with an English judge, who took him along the following year as naib-munshi (assistant Persian or Urdu secretary) in the Commissioner's Office at Agra. In Agra, Sayyid Ahmad prepared a guide on land revenue procedures and a summary of the Civil Code, thus demonstrating his ability and ambition. His British patron recommended his promotion to the post of munsif, a lower-level judge. The government just then introduced a qualification examination for the post, but Sayyid Ahmad passed it easily on the basis of two years' experience and a good educational background. Briefly posted to Mainpuri, he then spent a four-year stint as munsif of the Emperor Akbar's short-lived capital, Fatehpur Sikri. In 1846, shortly after his elder brother's death, he got himself transferred to Delhi to be with his mother; he spent the next eight years there, his longest tenure in any one place. In 1854 he moved up to the next rung in the judiciary, Ṣadr Amin, and was sent to Bijnor. He continued as Small Cause and Subordinate Judge in Moradabad, Ghazipur, Aligarh, and Benares, finally retiring in 1877.[58]

The Sadr Amin who started Sayyid Ahmad on his career had a nephew (brother's son), Sami Ullah Khan, the young man who had studied Islamic law and theology with the famous mufti Sadruddin Azurdah. In 1856 Sami Ullah, then about twenty-two years old, decided to take up British law and leave aside a potential life as a member of the ʿulama. He therefore went to Sayyid Ahmad's court in Bijnor to help with the paper work and serve an unofficial apprenticeship in the Anglo-Indian judicial system. He passed the examination for munsif, and in 1858 was posted to Kanpur. Four years later he passed the examination for pleader at the High Court (Ṣadr Dīvān ʿAdālat) in Agra and embarked on a private legal practice, moving to Allahabad when the High Court was shifted there in 1865. His knowledge of Islamic jurisprudence made him particularly useful in Muslim inheritance cases. In 1873 he returned to the bench as Subordinate Judge of Aligarh, Sayyid Ahmad's old post; later he was transferred to Allahabad, Moradabad, and Fatehgarh. Because of his learning in Islamic studies he was chosen to accompany the former Viceroy of India, Lord Northbrook, to Egypt in 1884 to help the extension of the British empire to yet another country. On his return he was raised to District and Sessions Judge, on a salary of one thousand rupees a month, a post once limited to I.C.S. Englishmen and previously assigned only to a handful of Indians, all educated in the English language.[59]

Mushtaq Husain entered government service in 1860 by means of similar connections: his father's sister's husband, tahsildar in Moradabad, not only took him on for initiation into government office work but also married off a daughter to

[58] Ḥālī, *Ḥayāt-i jāvīd*, ch. 2-3, cover, among other things, his official career; the initial phase is on pp. 91-93.

[59] Ẕakā' Ullāh, *Savāniḥ*, p. 23.

him. At the time, Sayyid Ahmad was Sadr Amin in Moradabad, John Strachey was Collector, and Mushtaq Husain managed to impress both of them during a brief tenure as clerk dealing with income taxes and famine relief. Armed with a Persian letter of recommendation from Strachey, he got his first regular appointment as a document writer in the tahsil office of his home town of Amroha at fifteen rupees a month. Since it was his home town, however, he was soon shifted to Bijnor, where he remained for three years, then to Badaun, where he rose to sarishtadar. In 1865 he became sarishtadar under Sayyid Ahmad in Aligarh. He spent most of the next ten years in Aligarh, serving in various capacities and establishing close relationships with a variety of government officials, including Sami Ullah. In 1874 Strachey, now Lieutenant Governor of the North-Western Provinces, appointed him to work on famine relief in the eastern part of the region. Advancement in the judicial department was blocked by new requirements for knowledge of English, so in 1872 Mushtaq Husain switched back to the revenue administration, where he qualified as a tahsildar. The following year Salar Jang I, Prime Minister of Hyderabad State, asked Sayyid Ahmad to recommend capable government servants, and Mushtaq Husain, along with another protégé of Sayyid Ahmad, Mahdi Ali of Etawah, received enthusiastic nominations. Both men rose to the very highest positions in Hyderabad State Government, becoming rich and famous as Navab Viqar ul-Mulk and Navab Muhsin ul-Mulk respectively—and both were ignominiously dismissed in the early 1890s, thus enabling them to rise to further fame as Sayyid Ahmad's successors to leadership in the Aligarh movement.[60]

This, then, was the model of success in government service through most of the nineteenth century, at least in north India and the princely states: a good maktab education in Persian,

[60] Ikrāmullāh Khān, *Viqār-i Ḥayāt*, pp. 6-16; Muḥammad Amīn Zuberī, *Ḥayāt-i Muḥsin* (Aligarh: Muslim University Press, 1934); interviews with Mushtaq Ahmad, son of Mushtaq Husain, Aligarh, 1968-1969; and Dr. Jafar Hasan, nephew of Mahdi Ali, Hyderabad, July 1969.

informal apprenticeship in some government office, usually with a relative, and the establishment of personal ties with Indians and Englishmen farther up the hierarchy.[61] In the Punjab it was possible to start a successful government career in the army. Sardar Muhammad Hayat Khan, for example, rose through the army to high judicial and revenue posts.[62] But this route was not available elsewhere in India; after 1857, Hindustanis, authors of the "sepoy mutiny," were particularly unwelcome in the army.[63]

Ambition to rise in the governmental hierarchy was hardly the only motivation for entering government service in some low-paid clerical post. Even if one failed to take advantage of the numerous opportunities for bribes, gratuities, and selling protection, a small salary and an official position was a matter of relatively comfortable security in an insecure world.[64] Still, for the ambitious there were further economic opportunities: one was acquainted with laws and litigations, one had access to records; in time of revenue settlements or tax default such information could be used to advantage either on one's own account or on behalf of a client. A number of major zamindari families got their start as petty government officials; still others were rewarded for acts of "loyalty" to the British, particularly after 1857.[65]

[61] Sources for careers are the provincial *History of the Service* volumes, which give postings and salaries of each official above the level of naib-tahsildar; Niẓāmī Badāyūnī, *Qāmūs al-mushāhīr* (2 vols.; Badaun, Niẓāmī Press, 1926); Pānipatī has included brief sketches of Sayyid Ahmad's correspondents in *Maktūbāt.*

[62] Anvār Aḥmad Zuberī, *Khuṭbāt-i 'ālīyah* (Aligarh: Muslim University Press, 1927), I, 44-46.

[63] Discrimination in the recruiting of Hindustanis was justified on the theory that they had degenerated as a result of the benefits of British rule: not enough adversity (Lord Roberts, *Forty-One Years in India* [London: Richard Bentley and Son, 1897], II, 441-442).

[64] For a British parody on the possibilities of corruption by low-level kacahri personnel, see Paunchkouree Khan (pseud.), *Revelations of an Orderly* (Benares: E. J. Lazarus & Co., 1866).

[65] See Bernard S. Cohn, "The Initial British Impact on India: A Case Study of the Benares Region," *Journal of Asian Studies,* XIX (1960), 418-431; R. N. Nagar, "The Tahsildar in the Ceded and Conquered Provinces (1801-1833)," *Journal of the Uttar Pradesh His-*

A family with landed interests would be well advised to have one or two of its members connected with the government, familiar with the regulations, and friendly with the men in power. There was always the danger of litigation among kinsmen or peasant resistance against the collection of rent. So if there were adult males able and available to spend their time in some capacity at the kacahri, then the police, courts, and revenue administrators might be available for necessary protection. But there were noneconomic motivations as well: perhaps a wish to escape a boring or quarrelsome domestic situation by being posted to far-off places, a positive excitement at the intellectual complexities of government and law, a desire to come in contact with wielders of power and maybe become one of them, to intimidate lesser personages and ingratiate greater ones who came seeking to benefit or protect themselves from the institutions of British rule. And bound up with this exercise of power were the pleasures of collegiality and the excitement of rivalry among government servants that, with their frequent transfers from station to station, might extend over a wide geographic expanse. Membership in the kacahri meant belonging to a wider world.

Aside from this array of orderlies, document writers, copyists, record keepers, accountants, policemen, administrators, and judges employed by government in the business of the kacahri, there was also a hierarchy of agents and legal practitioners retained by private parties to represent their interests. *Mukhtārs*, *vakīls*, and pleaders of "lower" and "upper" grades were admitted to practice before specified jurisdictions, after passing relevant examinations.[66] Often they were

---

torical Society, New Series, II (1954), 26-34. Sayyid Ahmad's friend Raja Jaikishan Das received a large zamindari in Moradabad District for his brother's pro-British actions in 1857 (AIG, February 17, 1871), but Sayyid Ahmad refused to accept such a grant and took a pension instead (Ḥālī, *Ḥayāt-i jāvīd*, pp. 116-117).

[66] See below, pp. 95-96; for biographical examples of the legal profession as a social milieu see A. M. Khwaja, *The Early Life of the First Student of the M.A.O. College* (Allahabad: Allahabad Law Jour-

former government officials who now saw ways to use their knowledge of kacahri law and procedure to develop some private mine of local good will and promising circumstance. Such legal practice, especially when it involved protracted litigation over zamindari holdings, could be extremely profitable. As permanent residents, legal practitioners had the benefit of connections and information denied to the frequently transferred government officials. At the same time, it was crucially important for them to maintain good ties with members of the government establishment and with professional colleagues practicing at other courts, particularly the central courts of appeal.

The kacahri was not the only arena of power; there was power in owning large amounts of land, in leading a lineage, in lending money or otherwise engaging in commerce, and in religious leadership. But after 1857 it was clear that the only way to participate in political decisions about the allocation and control of social resources was to make some accommodation with the ruling power. Men holding zamindari titles needed government assistance to collect rents; they were no longer permitted to have their own armed retainers. Tenants hoped for some measure of government assistance in resisting encroachments from zamindars or money-lenders. Commerce and manufacturing took place under government regulation that specified the nature of property and rights, and that could be enforced by police power. Transference and inheritance found their ultimate sanction in the courts. Religious leaders relied on the government to protect charitable endowments and other forms of patronage that came their way as a result of economic enterprise. Sacred personal law touching on issues of marriage and family required government enforcement. Revenue administrators, policemen, and judges presided over the security and distribution of all kinds

---

nal Press, 1916), pp. 1-3; B. R. Nanda, *The Nehrus* (New York: John Day Company, 1963), pp. 26-33.

of wealth and property and even the physical safety of individuals.

An individual was truly powerful when he or his family could hold on to several of these strands simultaneously; then he was called a *ra'īs*, a notable. In Aligarh town Khvajah Muhammad Yusuf was a prominent vakil, an owner of bazaars and other urban property, a zamindar holding near-by agricultural land, a dealer and processor of indigo, and a man known for his religious learning, piety, and charitable interests. He had also married into the same Delhi family that linked Sayyid Ahmad and Sami Ullah.[67] In Azamgarh, Shaikh Habibullah was a vakil, a substantial rural zamindar, a leader of a long-established lineage of Muslim Rajputs, the founder of a school, and owner of an ice factory. His sons became lawyers and government officials except for one, the eldest, who was Shibli Numani, the famous religious leader and literary figure.[68]

The kacahri, then, was a nexus for a variety of interests, some divergent, some interlocked. As a social milieu it included people with no prior connection to each other, from different geographic localities, different religious and ethnic backgrounds. What these people shared was the common vocabulary of sharīf culture; all those rich resources of etiquette, ceremony, hospitality, aesthetic tastes, and kinship alliance—fictive or made palpable through marriage—were ready at hand to maintain and manipulate social relations.

Sayyid Ahmad, for example, established a set of warm and abiding relationships with people throughout northern India in the wake of his transfer from station to station. The collections of his letters reveal the diversity of these friendships and their tendency to express themselves in the vocabulary of kinship. Maulvi Zain ul-Abdin, a fellow Sadr Amin from an ʿulama family of Machlishahar, was buried by Sayyid Ahmad's

[67] Interviews with Khwaja Muhammad Yunus and Khwaja Muhammad Masud, Aligarh, April 1969.

[68] Sayyid Sulaimān Nadvī, *Ḥayāt-i Shiblī* (Azamgarh Maṯbūʿah Maʿārif, 1943), pp. 62-63; interview with Shaukat Sultan, husband of Shibli's granddaughter, Azamgarh, February 1969.

side; so was Mahdi Ali, who had a well-developed uncle-nephew relation with Sayyid Mahmud. At the *bi'smi'īllah* ceremony of Sayyid Ahmad's only grandson it was a Brahmin Deputy Collector from Moradabad, Raja Jaikishan Das, who held the child in his lap.[69] Even some Englishmen, such as John Strachey and G.F.I. Graham, were familiar enough with the culture to establish mutually meaningful bonds of loyalty with Sayyid Ahmad.[70]

There was also the possibility of long-standing rivalry as kacahri alliances tended to inspire counter alliances. Sayyid Ahmad left behind a trail of rival Indian officials who competed with him, not so much in terms of government activity as in their extramural concerns as intellectuals and public leaders. An official might also be drawn into local family feuds, as when Sayyid Ahmad's family rivalry with Sami Ullah got entangled with more large-scale lineage divisions among the Shervanis of Aligarh District, and spilled over into a whole set of public activities.[71] But for better or worse, the course of Sayyid Ahmad's life revolved around these kacahri relationships.

Success in the kacahri milieu, however, was by no means the object of universal ambition: for some it gave off a distinctly bad odor. Muhammad had grounded his religious vision in an explicitly political order, but throughout the history of Islam it had been a special mark of piety to shun worldly power not exercised according to God's revelation. And if shar'iah-minded Muslims had remained aloof from impious sultans within the dar ul-Islam, it was doubly impious to serve a government of Christian usurpers.[72] Alterna-

[69] *Maktūbāt*, pp. 39, 94-97, 495; Sayyid Badruddīn, "Rājah Jaikishan Dās Bahādur Sī Es Āī [C.S.I.]," *'Alīgaṛh Megzīn*, XVI, No. 4 (January 1939), 79.

[70] Sayyid Ahmad to Graham, November 24, 1885; G.F.I. Graham, *The Life and Work of Sayed Ahmed Khan, C. S. I.*, 2d ed. (London: Hodder Stoughton, 1909), p. 268; AIG, September 7, 1886; Sayyid Ahmad to John Strachey, May 2, 1888 (88B, AA).

[71] Interview with Professor Haroon Khan Sherwani, Hyderabad, August 1968; see below, pp. 270-272.

[72] See above, pp. 27-29; also M. Kempson, "Report on the Ver-

tively, from the point of view of Mughal political values, British rule in India had little claim to legitimacy once the East India Company had cast off its guise of subordination to the emperor; among Hindus as well as Muslims the foreign regime had demonstrated its profound unpopularity in 1857. Sayyid Ahmad Khan had resisted severe family objections when he left to serve the British in 1838; some of his relatives later died as Muslim "martyrs" while he was steadfastly standing by his employers.[73] But even aside from British rule or high Islamic beliefs, government service could smack of something disreputable. Persian-educated clerks, the so-called "amlah class," were widely assumed to be corrupt exploiters, who used their secret shorthand techniques to mystify and defraud the helpless public. "The native officials are all corrupt, be they Hindoos or Mussalmans," said the subahdar Sita Ram in 1861.[74] Nor was it easy to maintain one's self-respect in the face of frequent demands for humble deference toward a British superior.[75]

But however widespread these anti-British attitudes may have been, there were plenty of people who considered government service to be honorable as well as advantageous; positions in the kacahri were always matters of intense competition. The number of these positions was very small. In the North-Western Provinces, an area with over forty million people, there were only about a thousand Indians earning over seventy-five rupees a month in government service in 1867. The number increased only slightly over the following decades; by 1903 it was just a little over 1,500.[76] Even count-

---

nacular Press, N.-W.P." [1870], *Selections from the Records of the Government of North-Western Provinces*, 2d Series (Allahabad: Government Press, 1871), IV, 371-372.

[73] See above, p. 41.

[74] [Sita Ram], *From Sepoy to Subahdar*, tr. from Hindi by Lieutenant Colonel Norgate, ed. D. C. Phillott, 8th ed. (Calcutta: Thacker Spink & Co., 1933), p. 143; also EC/NWP, pp. 164, 245.

[75] For examples of British insults see Ḥālī, *Ḥayāt-i jāvīd*, pp. 352-354; Ikrāmullāh K͟hān, *Viqār-i Ḥayāt*, pp. 10-13.

[76] GOI, Home Department, Establishment (A), June 1904, No. 103, p. 139 (NAI).

ing less significant jobs in government offices and courts, about 16,000 in 1881, the total makes a very slight dent in the population—even the literate population of slightly over one million. Entrance into the various grades of the legal profession was controlled by similar government examinations and personal connections. In 1881 the N.W.P. had 1,662 lawyers, ranging from a few London-trained barristers, mostly British, to old-style vakils who knew no English at all. There were about 3,000 mukhtars, agents with power of attorney but no right to plead in court, and another 3,000 law clerks and deed writers.[77] In any one district, kacahri government servants and legal practitioners formed a fairly compact group, usually fewer than 250 people.[78]

After the failure of violent rebellion in 1857, British policy affecting recruitment and qualification of government employees and legal practitioners became the focus of a new style of politics. Seeking out areas of competitive advantage, kacahri people began to organize themselves around a set of public issues in the hope of attracting local support and influencing certain government decisions. Some of these issues, as well as the methods used to deal with them, could be found not only in other parts of India, but also in Britain itself. There was, for one thing, the matter of whether government posts should be filled by personal patronage or by open competitive examination. Britain's own first foray in the direction of examinations had been with the Indian Civil Service as recently as 1856. Closely bound up with any such shift in methods of recruitment were the educational criteria for appointment, and this raised in India as well as in Britain the whole matter of what part the state should play in the organization and content of education. In north India, moreover, there was the special problem of the languages of instruction and administration—Persian, Urdu, Hindi, or Eng-

[77] *Report on the Census of British India, 1881* (London: Eyre and Spottiswoode, 1883), III, 71-72.

[78] *Report on an Enquiry, District Establishments, N.-W.P. and Oudh, 1892* (title page missing, title written on spine: located in the Uttar Pradesh Secretariat Library, Lucknow).

lish—that had much to do with determining access to public office. And finally all these debates summoned up newly articulated definitions of status and of ethnic groups as competing party interests.

The issues of kacahri politics were to have far-reaching cultural implications: a challenge to the continuity between family modes of personal relationship and the institutions of education and political power. So long as the requisite literary training for public office was a matter of private domestic arrangement, and success in one's official career depended on personal, kin-like alliances, the dominance of sharīf cultural styles and the hereditary advantage of sharīf families were assured. But even if alternative means for training and recruiting public servants did not necessarily shift or extend the access of social groups to positions of power, the change reached into areas of cultural self-definition communicated to an individual in the experience of growing up. For what was being suggested for any potential participant in the political process was not merely the substitution of one set of intellectual competences for another. Childhood and family life, language, ideology, and religion all came into question, were threatened with fundamental revision and an altered place in the total context of a person's life. Many sponsors of change, Indian as well as British, were quite explicit in making this connection: they did not approve of Indian family life or of the beliefs and practices that it tended to promote. But because the implications were so fundamental, institutional transformations came in driblets, adjusted and reinterpreted to suit indigenous cultural expectations.

THE INTRODUCTION OF ENGLISH-STYLE EDUCATION

The well-rehearsed early history of English-style education in northern India is interesting as a piece of British intellectual history, but is largely peripheral to a social and cultural analysis of the region in the period before 1857.[79] Only in the latter part of the century did these debates and institutional experiments of the initial period become relevant from an indigenous point of view. By that time there existed a sizable literature of educational opinions, based on experience in other regions of India, especially Bengal, and a ready-made superstructure for adaptation into new regions of the empire. But in large measure the task of making this adaptation was left to Indians belonging to the sharīf culture and the kacahri milieu. Although there were certainly Englishmen committed to establishing an extensive educational system and coordinating it to the allocation of political participation, the government was extremely parsimonious in providing financial support or employment incentives, let alone any suggestion of compulsion, for making schools a fundamental part of the social system. Indians had to come up with their own motivations for creating or taking advantage of educational establishments. They did not have a great deal to go on. For while the British government believed in private enterprise, it imposed severe limitations on the form and content of those schools it did choose to support or recognize.

It took a good deal of imagination to see possible benefits from English-style education. In the coastal cities of the subcontinent there were significant British enclaves and commercial activities, even something in the way of British intellectual life to stimulate self-interest or curiosity outside the spheres of government recruitment. And the courts and offices of these areas conducted a great deal of their business in English. But in north India for most of the nineteenth century, all that sponsors of a new educational arrangement had to offer was what they called enlightenment—often in the

79 See EC/NWP and EC for Punjab; also Moti Lal Bhargava, *History of Secondary Education in Uttar Pradesh* (Lucknow: Superintendent, Printing and Stationery, Uttar Pradesh, 1958), pp. 1-48; H. R. Mehta, *A History of the Growth and Development of Western Education in the Punjab (1846-1884)*, Punjab Government Records Office Publications, Monograph No. 5 (Lahore, 1929).

form of Christianity—and it was difficult to see the advantage of this unless you had it. To find any takers for such an education, it had to be laced with stipends and directed to segments of society excluded from the benefits of the dominant sharīf culture.

That culture was, in fact, so dominant that some of the most active British sponsors of government patronage to education devoted their efforts to the encouragement of classical learning in Sanskrit, Arabic, and Persian. The Sanskrit College at Benares in 1791, the Delhi College in 1792, even Punjab University College at Lahore in 1870, were all cast initially in the classical mold. Nazir Ahmad and Zaka Ullah attended Delhi College without departing from the mainstream of sharīf cultural life; Zain ul-Abdin spent three years in the Arabic Section of Benares College, which probably did not differ significantly from any other madrasah.[80] These establishments eventually developed English sections—Delhi was the first in 1828—but were often unable to attract sufficiently high enrollment to sustain much in the way of British official attention. In the 1850s James Thomason, Lieutenant Governor of North-Western Provinces, shifted the government's modest efforts, establishing a small-scale, experimental program of rural primary schools in Hindi or Urdu, not Persian, which were staffed by old-style teachers, who used reading, writing, and arithmetic books provided by the government. Primary school teachers got paid four rupees a month out of a special educational cess on zamindars. Although such schools introduced a slight modification in subject matter, they were intentionally as close as possible to the existing system of indigenous education. Above these schools

[80] Sayyid Iftikhār ʻĀlam Bilgrāmī, *Ḥayāt un-Nazīr* (Delhi: Shamsi Press, 1912), pp. 19-20; Andrews, *Zaka Ullah*, pp. 59-66; EC/NWP, p. 383; see also ʻAbd ul-Ḥaq, *Marḥūm Dehlī Kālij* (Delhi: Anjūman-i Taraqqī-i Urdū, n.d.); Sayyid Ahmad Khan, *Causes of the Indian Revolt* [tr. Auckland Colvin and G.F.I. Graham in 1873], published as an appendix in Hafeez Malik and Morris Dembo, eds., *Sir Sayyid Ahmad Khan's History of the Bijnor Rebellion*, South Asia Series, Occasional Paper No. 17 (East Lansing: Asian Studies Center, Michigan State University, [1972]), p. 127.

the government maintained a handful of slightly more advanced vernacular institutions at tahsil headquarters, again with teachers of the old school, though slightly better paid.[81]

In 1854 somewhat fewer than 2,000 students were studying English at the six "Anglo-Vernacular" government schools and colleges, and about 1,000 in missionary ones. The whole system taken together reached fewer than 50,000. That year, pursuant to the Educational Despatch from London, the government created an all-India system of inspection and departmental regulation, as well as grants to private—that is, mostly missionary—schools. The establishment of Calcutta University in 1857 was supposed to inaugurate a coordinated system of affiliated schools and colleges preparing for matriculation, First Arts, and B.A. examinations. In north India, however, there was no immediate expansion of English education, the major financial commitment, such as it was, going to vernacular primary education. In 1860 government expenditure on education came to about one rupee for every hundred people in the province, and that was two and one-half times as much as in 1854; almost none of the increase went for English education.[82] The rebellion slowed down the implementation of the new educational system, but during the 1860s it at last began to attract some public attention in north India. By that time Punjab and Oudh had been incorporated in the area of direct British rule —in 1849 and 1856 respectively—and were ready to enter the educational arena.

Sayyid Ahmad Khan's interest in the government's educational efforts started in Moradabad just after the 1857 Revolt. A pamphlet he wrote in 1858 on the causes of the rebellion discussed popular antipathy to British-run schools.[83] There had been no objection so long as the schools were ma-

[81] EC/NWP, pp. 2-18; Bhargava, *History of Secondary Education*, pp. 5-24.

[82] EC/NWP, pp. 18, 20.

[83] *Causes of the Indian Revolt*, pp. 126-127.

drasahs with a little English thrown in, as in the case of the early Delhi College. But missionaries and British civil servants were talking too openly about using schools as instruments of Christian conversion for these schools to be easily accepted into the culture. Thomason's rural schools, a few forays into educating women, and proposals to favor students of the new schools for government employment, all created discontent as direct cultural challenges. Sayyid Ahmad complained in another pamphlet at about the same time that shifting education to Hindi and Urdu effectively blocked off access to original sources of knowledge as well as to the languages of political power. He called for more education in English, and at the same time set up a Persian madrasah in Moradabad. The Persian school, however, was soon absorbed into a government establishment started by Strachey.[84] Sayyid Ahmad's own sons, who had already started English at home, studied in this new school.[85]

Although Sayyid Ahmad had worked for the British government for twenty years, his intellectual activity, which was considerable, had remained consistent with the genres and interests of the Delhi literati. It was after the death of his older brother and during his long tenure as munsif in Delhi, from 1846 to 1854, that Sayyid Ahmad took up in earnest his long and prolific literary career, returning to his studies as a disciple of the theological and mystical tradition of the great eighteenth-century figure, Shah Vali Ullah and his grandson, Shah Abdul Aziz. Under the guidance of a descendant of the same family and other prominent Delhi ʿulama, he wrote a few treatises and a translation of the life of Muhammad, the proper approach to mysticism, and errors of the Shīʿahs.[86]

[84] Ḥālī, *Ḥayāt-i jāvīd*, pp. 120-121.

[85] Muḥammad Amīn Zuberī, *Taẕkirah-i Sayyid Maḥmūd marḥūm*, Bashīr Pāshah Series, Islamia High School, Etawah (Aligarh: Muslim University Press, n.d.), p. 2.

[86] Ḥālī, *Ḥayāt-i jāvīd*, pp. 89, 93-94, 99-100; see also J.M.S. Baljon, Jr., *The Reforms and Religious Ideas of Sir Sayyid Ahmad Khan*, 3d ed. (Lahore: Sh. Muhammad Ashraf, 1964), pp. 71-74.

At the same time, Sayyid Ahmad turned with great energy to the history of Delhi itself in his *Aṣār us-ṣanādīd* (1847), which described in detail the buildings and inscriptions of the Delhi vicinity, as well as providing a section on contemporary religious, literary, and artistic figures of the city. The work, written in an established Persian genre, was an innovation only insofar as it was written in Urdu. It took note of a learned article by James Prinsep on the Mauryan Iron Pillar at the Qutb Minar, but otherwise revealed no consiousness of the British presence except a ready use of the printing press.[87] Soon after, while in Bijnor, Sayyid Ahmad prepared an edition of the great sixteenth-century description of the Mughal empire, Abul Fazl's *Ā'īn-i Akbarī*. This work, like *Aṣār us-ṣanādīd*, was copiously illustrated and produced with impressive thoroughness and clarity.[88]

Before publishing the *Ā'īn-ī Akbarī*, Sayyid Ahmad asked Ghalib, among others, to contribute some poetry by way of preface to the work. Ghalib honored his young friend with a lengthy Persian poem in which he said it was useless to look to the dead past when all around them drawing near were the wonders of the British present. Sayyid Ahmad chose not to print this contribution from the greatest poet of the age. The 1857 Revolt, however, changed his attitude. In Moradabad he pursued some of his old interests, issuing a pamphlet against the sin of religious innovation, and preparing a standard edition of another major historical text, the *Tarīkh-i Firūz Shāhī*. But above all he was caught up in defining his own response to the reality of British rule.[89]

[87] Sayyid Aḥmad Khān, *Āṣār us-ṣanādīd* (Delhi: Central Book Depot, 1965 [first published in 1847]); Ḥālī, *Ḥayāt-i jāvīd*, pp. 95-99; A.B.M. Habibullah, "Historical Writing in Urdu: A Survey of Tendencies," in *Historians of India, Pakistan and Ceylon*, ed. C. H. Philips (London: Oxford University Press, 1961), p. 482.

[88] Ḥālī, *Ḥayāt-i jāvīd*, pp. 102-106; the illustrations were reproduced in the Blochmann translation cited above.

[89] When Ghalib passed through Moradabad in 1860, Sayyid Ahmad prevailed on him to stay over at his house. As usual, the poet arrived with bottle of wine in hand; Sayyid Ahmad quickly hid it so that no one would see wine in a good Muslim home. Ghalib retaliated with an

Sayyid Ahmad's major literary work while in Moradabad consisted of three explicitly political pamphlets on the 1857 Rebellion. Two of them were addressed directly to a British audience: the entire edition of *Asbāb-i Baghāvat-i Hind* (*Causes of the Indian Revolt*) was sent off to England, and *Loyal Muhammadans of India*, a serial publication that reached only two numbers, came out only in its English translation. His discussion of the causes of the revolt was remarkably forthright in setting out Indian dissatisfaction with British rule and calling for greater Indian participation in the creation and communication of government policy. Above all, the pamphlet argued for warm personal relations between Englishmen and Indians as the emotional basis of political stability. While purporting to show that religion was not a cause, Sayyid Ahmad emphasized popular suspicion of missionary efforts. He was anxious to absolve Islam as such from any blame, though he conceded that certain "vagabonds and ill-conditioned men . . . wine drinkers and men who spent their time in debauchery and dissipation" had exploited the slogan of jihad or religious war.[90] In *Loyal Muhammadans* he offered case studies of Muslims who had bravely backed the British and saved British lives, in order to counteract the common British belief that the 1857 Revolt had been a Muslim uprising.[91] And in his third pamphlet, a history of the revolt in Bijnor, he recounted at length his own actions and experiences, ending with an impassioned address to both Hindus and Muslims to learn the lesson of the revolt. By divine providence they could now see what pre-British rule was like: the old Muslim nobility once again terrorizing Hindu zamindar lineages, violent anti-Muslim revenge, and

appropriate couplet from Hafiz, accusing his host of taking a drink on the sly. This is most unlikely, but in any case Sayyid Ahmad was getting ready to come out into the open about the cultural consequences of British rule. Some people considered that equally sinful (Russell and Islam, *Ghalib*, pp. 9-91, 235-236).

[90] *Causes of the Indian Revolt*, p. 119.

[91] Ḥālī, *Ḥayāt-i jāvīd*, pp. 129-134.

the distress of ordinary people, Hindu and Muslim—victims of both ruling elites. Only under the strong and neutral rule of the British could there be justice and security for all.[92] In all this Sayyid Ahmad was expressing classical Indian political theory, Hindu as well as Muslim, that the only alternative to strong government was brutalization of the weak by the strong; there could be unity among the separate sections of the society only in relation to overarching royal authority.

While in Moradabad, Sayyid Ahmad started preparing a commentary on the Christian Bible. He hired two research assistants, one for English and one for Arabic, and set about to discover where the Bible differed from the Qur'an and where they could be reconciled. Before 1857 his attention to Christianity had been completely hostile; now his major concern was to find some reconciliation between the two religions. His effort was apologetic and openly political, addressed in two directions, to Christians and to Muslims, that each might respect the other religion. He continued the work when he was transferred to Ghazipur, this time employing a Jew to go over the Hebrew with him. In Ghazipur he became friends with Inayat Rasul of Ciryakot, a member of an unusual lineage of 'ulama that had always prided itself on its rationalism and cosmopolitan interests. Inayat Rasul had already studied Hebrew in Calcutta and now became in important influence in Sayyid Ahmad's intellectual liberalization.[93] At the same time somebody in Ghazipur, perhaps an Englishman such as G.F.I. Graham, pointed out that the very latest and most radical English Biblical criticism, Bishop

[92] Sayyid Ahmad Khan, in Malik and Dembo, *History of the Bijnor Rebellion*, pp. 1-109.

[93] Interview with Muzammil Abbasi, Azamgarh, March 1969, who also wrote out for me a brief essay on the history of the Abbasi family of Ciryakot; Ḥālī, *Ḥayāt-i jāvīd*, pp. 139-147; see also Sayyid Shāh Naẕīr Hāshmī G͟hāzīpurī, "Maulvī 'Ināyat Rasūl Ciryākōṭī aur 'ilmī zindigī kē rāz," *Aligarh Monthly*, III (1905), 447-448; Rahmān 'Alī, *Taẕkirah-i 'ulamā-i Hind*, tr. [from Persian to Urdu] by Muḥammad Ayyūb Qādrī (Karachi: Pakistan Historical Society, 1961), pp. 358-359.

Colenso's attempts to reconcile Genesis and geology as the difference between metaphor and reality.[94] All this was included in Sayyid Ahmad's commentary.

Beyond this literary enterprise, Sayyid Ahmad sought a new way to combine his intellectual and political concerns, to stand forth as a public leader. As a judge he had long presided over public proceedings, but now he went beyond his official role and started to build a personal following. Along with several leading Muslims of Moradabad town, he organized a public subscription for charity and illuminations in honor of the reestablishment of British rule. There was a great Muslim prayer gathering for the recitation of the *k͟huṭbah*, a prayer-sermon for the rulers of the land, composed by Sayyid Ahmad.[95] Two years later, while active in famine relief programs, he attempted unsuccessfully to establish an orphanage under Indian auspices, Hindu and Muslim, to preempt the field from Christian missionaries.[96] In Ghazipur in 1863-1864, Sayyid Ahmad tried again to gather public commitment and private funding for the establishment of a college and a literary society, both relatively new enterprises in north India. Collecting funds and holding public meetings were not new, but in Ghazipur he established membership lists and published proceedings, and his appeal did not depend on religious charisma.[97] It grew out of the kacahri milieu and reached out to members of all religions.

While Sayyid Ahmad was trying to attract public interest in a private "college" under Indian auspices, a rival judge in Ghazipur, also a Muslim, was engaged in the same enterprise. Both establishments were "a compromise between a first class desi [indigenous] Madrassah for the teaching of logic and literature; and a Government Secondary school for teaching the Vernacular with a modicum of History and

[94] Hardy, *Muslims of British India*, p. 96.

[95] Malik and Dembo, *History of the Bijnor Rebellion*, pp. 157-160.

[96] Ḥālī, *Ḥāyat-i jāvīd*, pp. 137-138.

[97] Compare the large-scale campaign of Sayyid Ahmad of Bareilly (1786-1831) in the 1820s (Qeyyumuddin Ahmad, *The Wahabi Movement in India* [Calcutta: Firma K. L. Mukhopadhyay, 1966]).

Science."[98] Both received government grants. Sayyid Ahmad's Victoria College, soon reduced to Victoria School and incorporated with a new government high school, was about evenly divided between Muslim and Hindu students; the rival school was ninety percent Muslim.[99]

Very much aware of his political weakness as an outsider only temporarily stationed in the town, Sayyid Ahmad did not maintain his association with the school; but the effort provided him with further organizational experience and another step in his gradual intellectual transition toward an interest in English learning. His major concept of education remained literary and linguistic; he described the school in terms of the languages it taught: English, Arabic, Persian, Sanskrit, and Urdu. One of Sayyid Ahmad's first public speeches, given at the school in 1864, emphasized the political significance of the enterprise: an effort to establish "brotherhood" among his "fellow countrymen"—he used the words biradari, vatan, and qaum for what he called the Hindustanis—and a brotherly feeling between them and their British rulers. Noting the recent inclusion of nominated Indians on the Viceregal Legislative Council, he looked forward to the establishment of representation from every district in the government of the country, when there would be Indians sufficiently educated to qualify as spokesmen.[100]

A more sustained effort, also started in Ghazipur, was the Scientific Society, but from the outset it aimed beyond the immediate locality to the whole of northern India. The organization had two announced purposes: one, consistent with Sayyid Ahmad's earlier interests, was to search for and publish rare "oriental" manuscripts, provided they were nonreligious; the other, much more important as an intellectual

[98] EC/NWP, p. 319; *Report of the Director of Public Instruction, North-Western Provinces* (hereafter RDPI/NWP), 1869-1870 (Allahabad: Government Press, N.W.P., 1871), p. 86.

[99] RDPI/NWP, 1874-1875, p. 72.

[100] Sayyid Aḥmad K͟hān, *Mukammal majmū'ah lekcharz o ispīcaz* (hereafter cited as *Lectures and Speeches*), ed. Muḥammad Imāmuddīn Gujrātī (Lahore: Muṣṭafā'ī Press, 1900), pp. 15-22.

departure, was to translate European works on arts and sciences into "such languages as may be in common use among the people," the alternatives being Urdu, Persian, Arabic, and Hindi.[101] In 1863 Sayyid Ahmad issued a pamphlet calling for support in establishing the organization. He also travelled to Calcutta, where he lectured in Persian to a gathering of the Muhammadan Literary Society of Abdul Latif on the need for a new historical understanding of the rise and fall of civilizations, specifically the rise of Europe and the fall of Islam. The lecture is the first indication that Sayyid Ahmad felt there was something to learn from the English besides their language. He spoke about the accessibility of European science and technology, and denied that there was anything in Islam that militated against the study of such subjects. On the contrary, the most glorious period of Islamic history was characterized by a great flowering of rationalism and science; Muslims had declined in the world by ignoring this heritage. Abdul Latif, who was living in the very different milieu of Calcutta, had long argued just these points, but they were unfamiliar ideas in northern India.[102]

The Scientific Society held its first meeting early in 1864, by which time Sayyid Ahmad and his British collaborator, G.F.I. Graham, Ghazipur's Assistant District Superintendent of Police, were able to present a lengthy set of by-laws, a membership list of 109, and a treasury of over Rs. 2,700. Of the members, 22 were British, 37 were Indians in government service. The following year membership was 196, 90 in government service, 20 vakils, 57 described as ra'īs. There were 107 Muslims, 85 Hindus. Five years later the society reached its height with 310 members, after which it rapidly fell into obscurity.[103] Membership was limited by the expense, two

[101] "Bye-laws of the Scientific Society," *Proceedings of the Scientific Society*, No. 1, January 9, 1864 (Ghazeepore: Syud Ahmud's Private Press, 1864).

[102] English translation read by G.F.I. Graham at the opening meeting of the Scientific Society, *ibid.*; the Persian original is in *Lectures and Speeches*, pp. 8-14.

[103] *Proceedings of the Scientific Society*, No. 1; *ibid.*, No. 8 (Ali-

rupees a month, and perhaps by a rule that members had to be elected. But membership was mostly limited by the difficulty in sustaining interest in the society's activities. Sayyid Ahmad was hard pressed to come up with books for translation. The first two were histories of ancient Egypt and Greece, insisted on by Sayyid Ahmad despite advice of a British scholar that they were obsolete. And one of the early books to be translated, again with British opposition, was a portion of Mill's *Political Economy*.[104] Sayyid Ahmad soon decided that the most important work of the society would be in the field of practical technology, especially mechanics and agriculture. Besides publishing elementary texts on these subjects, he initiated model agricultural experiments with new seeds and cultivating techniques.[105] But the majority of the society's output, fifteen of its twenty-five publications, were basic mathematics text books translated by Zaka Ullah.[106]

The initial by-laws of the Scientific Society provided that it ultimately be stationed in Allahabad, which was soon to replace Agra as capital of the province, but that "until the Society be thoroughly set agoing, it shall be wherever Principal Sudder Ameen Syud Ahmud Khan be stationed."[107] Four months after its first meeting Sayyid Ahmad was transferred to the other end of the province at Aligarh, and the society went with him. In Aligarh, a place he had never before seen, he encountered an extremely gratifying reception on the part of wealthy local zamindars as well as the local kacahri society. In particular he joined forces with Deputy Collector Jaikishan Das, whom he had met five years earlier in Moradabad. Soon the society was putting out a weekly newspaper on

---

garh: Institute Press, 1865); RDPI/NWP, 1869-1870, Appendix E; for the decline of the society see AIG, September 28, 1878.

[104] *Proceedings of the Scientific Society*, No. 2 (Ghazeepore: Syud Ahmud's Private Press, 1864), pp. 1-2.

[105] *Selected Documents from the Aligarh Archives* (hereafter cited as SDAA), ed. Yusuf Husain (Bombay: Asia Publishing House, 1967), pp. 71-73, 77-79, 120-124.

[106] For a list of books see Graham (1st ed.), *Life*, p. 83.

[107] SDAA, p. 16.

Sayyid Ahmad's private printing press, and constructing a substantial brick building for its headquarters. The government responded favorably to Sayyid Ahmad's proposal for local education committees for the inspection and management of schools by setting up such a committee on an experimental basis in Aligarh District. In 1866 Sayyid Ahmad founded another organization, the British-Indian Association of the North-Western Provinces—the name was borrowed from an older Calcutta group—with the intention of addressing north Indian political demands to Parliament. This too recruited membership and financial support from Aligarh notables.[108] Within two years, then, Sayyid Ahmad was presiding over a number of exciting enterprises and had become a well-known public figure. The Viceroy even awarded him a gold medal for his "efforts to spread the light of literature and science," along with a set of the works of Macaulay, that eloquent champion of an Anglicized India.[109]

For Sayyid Ahmad and his co-workers, the decade of the 1860s was above all a period of education in new styles of communication. The Scientific Society with its by-laws, President, Secretary, and Treasurer, Executive Council, Directing Council, General Meetings, and various categories of membership, was an exercise in speech making, voting, the whole ritual of British deliberative procedure. The *Aligarh Institute Gazette*, which started coming out weekly in March 1866, not only printed the proceedings of the society's meetings but was a general newspaper printed, like the government gazette, in parallel columns of Urdu and English. There were news items reprinted from English-language papers or reporting local gatherings; there were essays and editorial comments touching on issues as diverse as Indian-British social relations, the need for railway waiting rooms, political activities in Calcutta, a succession dispute in Baroda, or the Franco-Prussian War. In 1872 the journal had the largest circulation in the province: 381. The paper employed an English-

[108] Ḥālī, *Ḥayāt-i jāvīd*, pp. 152-157.
[109] AIG, February 22, 1867.

language editor and an Urdu one under the unpaid supervision alternatively of Sayyid Ahmad and Jaikishan Das.[110]

When Sayyid Ahmad was next transferred, in 1867, this time to Benares, he left the Scientific Society behind in Aligarh under the direction of his friend Jaikishan Das. He continued to write articles for the newspaper, but his interest in arranging translations of European books ceased. In Benares he threw himself into yet another public enterprise, the establishment of an institute for homeopathic medicine. He was now operating over a wide geographical area in a whole array of public activities. The most important was an association to send Indians on visits to England, and a petition for the creation of an Urdu-medium university for north India, independent of the London-style university at Calcutta. His son Sayyid Mahmud was now a student of Queen's College, Benares, and preparing to study in Britain.[111]

Schools, literary societies, newspapers, and political associations—these were not Sayyid Ahmad's work alone, but were cropping up in several of the district towns of northern India. The Scientific Society was the largest and perhaps the best publicized, but it had been preceded by similar organizations in Shahjahanpur and Benares. By 1869 there were fourteen such societies in the North-Western Provinces, some of them run by resident Bengalis.[112] Similar groups had sprung up in the Punjab, ranging from a horticultural association to G. W.

[110] Of the 381 subscriptions, 191 went to private Indians paying twelve rupees a year or belonging to the Scientific Society, 38 were British, 52 were in exchange for other journals, and the rest went to the government, mostly to circulate in the schools (M. Kempson, "Report on the Vernacular Newspapers and Periodicals Published in the North-Western Provinces during 1872," *Selections from the Records of Government, North-Western Provinces* [2d series; Allahabad: Government Press, N.W.P., 1874], VI, 512).

[111] J. A. Venn, *Alumni Cantabrigienses* (Cambridge: Cambridge University Press, 1940), Part II, IV, 291.

[112] RDPI/NWP, 1869-1870, Part II, Appendix E.

Leitner's Anjuman-i Punjab, perhaps the most vigorous of all in its campaign for an autonomous and "oriental" education system.[113] Such organizations were most important as illustrations of a concept, idioms of discourse and organization, and models for future reference; they achieved little in "the diffusion of knowledge" or political influence. North India was hardly swept away by a great tide of voluntary associations; like Sayyid Ahmad's efforts, they all rose with a little flurry of interest, then quickly petered out.

While specific publications did not achieve wide circulation, the press as an institution became increasingly important in the culture, at least for a portion of the 5 percent of the male population that could read. The first Urdu newspaper was started in Calcutta in 1822, and very quickly the idea spread to northern India.[114] Sayyid Ahmad's brother owned a weekly newspaper in Delhi in the late 1830s, and Sayyid Ahmad himself had managed it for a while.[115] In 1848 there were 14 newspapers in the North-West Provinces, 3 in Persian and the rest in Urdu.[116] In the following decade Hindi papers were started, often the same as the Urdu ones except for the script. Circulation, however, was low, generally close to a hundred. In 1870 there were 33 newspapers with a circulation of 7,509.[117] In addition to periodical publications, in 1871 there were 317 books published in over 440,000 copies. A tabulation on language and subject matter showed that 81 were in Urdu, 29 in Persian, 11 in Arabic, 52 in Hindi, and 6 in Sanskrit; 80 of the books were "educational and moral," 48 religious, 36 poetic, with a variety of residual categories to make up the difference.[118]

113 McCully, *English Education*, pp. 155-156.

114 Muḥammad ʿAtīq Ṣiddīqī, *Hindūstānī akhbār navīsī* (Aligarh: Anjūman-i Taraqqī-i Urdū, 1957), p. 160.

115 *Ibid.*, p. 277.

116 "Native Presses," *Selections from the Records of Government, North-Western Provinces* (Allahabad: Government Press, N.W.P., 1868), IV, 1-166.

117 *Ibid.*, 2d series, IV (1871), 315.

118 *Ibid.*, 2d series, VI (1874), 248.

There was undoubtedly an expansion of English education after 1860, though far less than some had expected. Though annual government expenditure tripled over the next ten years, official policy was to offer these sums as a moderate stimulus to what would have to be primarily a matter of private enterprise. Except in the Punjab, such help as did come was confined to English-style education; indigenous learning had to shift for itself.[119] As a matter of fact, the late nineteenth century seems to have been a period of expanding madrasah education, carried out totally without government aid—the most famous institution being Deoband, established in 1867.[120] But up to the mid-1880s, the demand for English education appeared glutted at a very low level. Not content to reduce its financing—the initial spurt in the 1860s was followed by a decade of retrenchment—the government set up minimum tuition and maximum scholarship levels even for private schools. Government colleges were closed in Delhi and Bareilly; a local committee managed to save Agra College by putting it under private auspices; several missionary institutions lost their government grants and had to terminate higher-level classes.[121]

Dropout and failure rates were spectacularly high; from 1864 to 1885 only 272 students managed to make their way all the way through to graduation, nearly half of them in the last five years of the period. Educational statistics are confusing because they do not always use the same criteria, but the table of passing and failing students at university examinations over the twenty-year period gives some idea of the magnitude of an English-educated class in north India as compared with the province of Bengal, all of India, and the total population base (Table 1).

119 EC/NWP, pp. 20-67.

120 Muḥammad Ṭayyib, *Dār ul-ʿulūm Deoband* (Deoband: Daftar-i Ahtimām, Dār ul-ʿulūm Deoband, 1965); Barbara Daly Metcalf, "The Reformist ʿUlamā: Muslim Religious Leadership in India, 1860-1900" (Ph.D. dissertation, University of California, Berkeley, 1974).

121 Bhargava, *History of Secondary Education*, pp. 40-42.

TABLE 1

Examination Results: Matriculation and B.A., 1864-1885

	Matriculation		*B.A.*		*Total population, 1881*[a]
	Pass	*Fail*	*Pass*	*Fail*	
N.W.P. and Oudh	3,200	3,210	272	270	44,849,619
Punjab	1,944	2,614	107	129	22,712,120
Bengal	16,639	21,151	2,153	2,776	69,536,861
All-India	48,251	79,509	5,108	5,853	253,891,821

SOURCE: Tabulated from *Report of the Public Service Commission, 1886-87* (Calcutta, 1888), in Anil Seal, *The Emergence of Indian Nationalism* (Cambridge: Cambridge University Press, 1968), p. 18.

[a] *Report of the Census of British India, 1881*, I, 5. "Bengal" includes Bihar and Orissa.

These unimpressive educational statistics for northern India attracted a fair amount of comment in the press, in the annual reports of the provincial directors of public instruction, and in testimony before the Indian Education Commission, set up in 1882 under the chairmanship of W. W. Hunter to review the state of education in India province by province. Why this sluggish response to the wonders of European enlightenment? Here was a fitting occasion for sociological analysis of Indian society, an opportunity to plug in all those surveys, censuses, ethnographies, and other bits and pieces of data collection in order to find out what categories of people were particularly resistant to the attractions of the exotic West. Most contemporary observers, Indian as well as British, diagnosed the failure of education in terms of Indian culture, not of British policy. Compulsory and universal public education was not part of contemporary discourse. With the burden of initiative on private Indian efforts, so was the blame for failing to take it up.

A glance at educational statistics revealed that one group in particular was lagging far behind in acceptance of the government-sponsored educational system: "the Muslims"—not just in the north but throughout India. Muslims, one-quarter of the subcontinent's population, made up a tiny percentage of the so-called English educated class. In 1865-1866, only 57 Muslims were studying in the colleges of India, out of a total student body of 1,578. In 1882 the number of Muslims had risen to only 197 out of 5,399, the percentage remaining steady at about 3½. The secondary school statistics for that year were better, but not much: 5,433 out of 62,938, or 11 percent.[122] Some writers on the problem of Indian education remembered to combine these statistics with the equally available data on regional differentials, but most of the contemporary literature assumed that one could discuss all India's Muslims as a single aggregate. In Bengal Presidency (including Bihar and Orissa), where Muslims were almost one-third of the population, they contributed less than 5 percent of college students, less than 10 percent of high school students, and only reached their proportion of the general population at the lower primary level.[123] In the Punjab, Muslims were over half the population, but formed only one-fifth of the high school students, and less than 13 percent of college students.[124] But in the North-Western Provinces and Oudh, where Muslims were less than 14 percent of the population, they were just about equal to that proportion in colleges and considerably more—one-fifth—of the secondary school population. When one turned from percentages to absolute numbers, however, even the comforting statistics of North-Western Provinces and Oudh amounted to very few Muslims: in 1882 there were 35 Muslims enrolled in English colleges, 802 in secondary schools. Up to 1886 there were 25 Muslim

122 McCully, *English Education*, pp. 179-180.

123 Anil Seal, *The Emergence of Indian Nationalism* (Cambridge: Cambridge University Press, 1968), p. 59.

124 Memorandum of W.R.M. Holroyd, Director of Public Instruction, Punjab, September 28, 1882, *Correspondence on the Subject of the Education of the Muhammadan Community in British India and Their Employment in the Public Service Generally*, Selections from the Records of the Government of India, Vol. CCV (Calcutta: Superintendent of Government Printing, 1886), p. 300.

college graduates from the North-Western Provinces and Oudh.[125]

The notion that Muslims as a "class" were "backward" received support, then, from well-publicized statistics, and elicited a good deal of official British solicitude. Muslims of the kacahri milieu were probably the first people in India to benefit from such a designation, but at the cost of altering their own estimate of themselves. Muslims now were laggards, all sulking in their tents, dreaming of lost empires and reciting decadent poetry. Some Englishmen who interpreted the 1857 Revolt as an effort to restore Muslim rule felt some urgency in winning over Muslims, drawing them into the system of British rule and British values. An 1859 Educational Despatch from the Secretary of State in London had urged special attention to problems of Muslim access to education. Hunter's polemic in 1871 on the Indian Musalmans, his reiteration of these concerns as chairman of the Education Commission in 1882, and a petition from a Calcutta-based Muslim political association in the same year all prompted full-scale government enquiries and a large literature of diagnosis and prescription for the problems of Muslim education. Muslims required special attention and, some argued, special treatment.[126]

Why were Muslims holding aloof? Some of the reasons given had to do with intellectual styles and commitments. Indians from the old maktab or madrasah sometimes argued that English schools were simply inferior: they did not stimulate independent reasoning and self-expression, did not inspire discipline or mastery in some area of knowledge or skill. English schools seemed to have goals similar to those of the indigenous system—linguistic competence, literary appreciation, the development of reasoning powers—but they achieved them less effectively. The teachers were not respected scholars; students, regardless of shauq, had to follow

[125] Seal, *Indian Nationalism*, p. 306.

[126] See *Correspondence on the Education of the Muhammadan Community*.

a uniform, stereotyped course of study that left them with an imperfect knowledge of the English language and little else. Furthermore, many elders complained that the milieu of government-sponsored schools developed a kind of mannerless arrogance totally at odds with the spirit of sharāfat, or at least failed to communicate a comfortable sense of being sharīf.[127]

But the most common objection of all was that English learning competed with religious learning for time, and perhaps even for spiritual allegiance. A Muslim's first commitment was to learn the Qur'an, if he was to learn anything at all. Afterwards it might be all right to take up a little practical English, arithmetic, useful knowledge for conducting private and public business.[128] But if one were in search of enlightenment—well, after all, Indian and Islamic civilizations had much to offer. The cultural attractions of European learning were not self-evident. Advocates of English education such as Sayyid Ahmad tried to combat such attitudes and to encourage genuine intellectual excitement about European ideas; they may have played an important part in such success as English education did achieve. But their little meetings and publications were not able to overwhelm the existing culture by simple juxtaposition.

Apparent statistical evidence notwithstanding, a few contemporary writers were prepared to deny that Muslims, as such, were behind Hindus, as such, in education or anything else.[129] People were Muslims and Hindus, but they were other things as well. One could just as easily say that poor Bengali cultivators, who were mostly Muslim, were behind the Kay-

[127] *Report of the Select Committee for the Better Diffusion and Advancement of Learning among the Muhammadans of India* (hereafter *Report of the Select Committee*) (Benares: Medical Hall Press, 1873); see also essay on "the moral and mental torpor of Islam in this country" by M. Kempson, Director of Public Instruction, N.W.P., in RDPI/NWP, 1872-1873, Part II, pp. 29-38.

[128] Holroyd memorandum, *Correspondence on the Education of the Muhammadan Community*, p. 311.

[129] See below, p. 121.

asths and Brahmins of Calcutta; that upper India was behind Bengal; that the sons of landlords lagged behind the sons of government employees. But such arguments did not lend themselves to ready statistical analysis. Caste statistics did in fact exist, though not quite so conveniently, and revealed that the Hindu student population in North-Western Provinces and Oudh was overwhelmingly Kayasth and Brahmin. For example, the students who took the 1896 Allahabad University Entrance Examination included 199 Brahmins, 180 Kayasths, and 108 Muslims with all other categories far behind. The great rural lineages of Rajputs and Jats, the merchant communities called Banya—these were barely represented: 3 Rajputs, 1 Jat, 21 Banyas. One could enlarge these statistics only slightly by collapsing the caste designations people wrote down for themselves, grouping the 19 Kshattriyas with the Rajputs, the 2 Seths and 7 Aggarwals with the Banyas.[130] In any case, these people did not choose to make such aggregations, and nobody was saying that the Banyas were lagging behind in education.

Muslims, however, were treated as an aggregate. But even though the Muslim population of the province was just about equal to the combined population of Brahmins and Kayasths, the range of occupational and social status among Muslims was much greater. There were no convenient ascriptive labels to identify Muslim groups who, like Brahmins and Kayasths, had some cultural and occupational stake in literacy and education—as opposed to Muslim butchers, weavers, and cultivators, for example. Perhaps Islamic egalitarianism allowed such people greater mobility than their Hindu counterparts, but usually one acquired sharāfat by belonging to a a sharīf family.

130 Calculated from *Allahabad University Calendar*, 1896-1897; such statistics were not collected regularly. Students registered caste if they were Hindus; if they were Muslims they just wrote their religion. Earlier educational data were compiled for Muslim castes as well—Sayyid, Shaikh, Mughal, and Pathan, with no residual categories (e.g., RDPI/NWP, 1873-1874, Part I, p. 89); this is dropped later on (e.g., RDPI/NWP, 1894-1895, p. 38).

Caste statistics were artifacts of British analysis, but they serve to show how misleading it could be to treat Hindus as an aggregate and suggest what should be obvious from the low absolute numbers in the educational data: that most people, Hindu or Muslim, either had no access to English education or chose not to take advantage of it. Even among Kayasths, just over half a million in the North-Western Provinces and Oudh, the overwhelming majority never got anywhere near an English school or college. While it is safe to say that a student was more likely to be a Brahmin, Kayasth, or Muslim than anything else, the truth is that these categories are much too gross to serve as descriptions of the student population. Large ascriptive designations of caste and religion are important because they were used in the political discourse of the time to express demands of sections of the population that were a good deal more specific. "The actual number of Mahomedan boys at school," said Mathews Kempson, Director of Public Instruction, in 1872, "may be small, but then so is the number of Hindoo boys, and all special pleading on behalf of the Mahomedans alone is out of place. With only one boy in 15 of the whole boy-population at school, *we want more schools and more money to open them.*"[131] Such a statement is remarkable for its rarity in the contemporary literature.

The question of why people did not take to English education is less useful than the question of why they should have done so in the first place. And that was a matter very much tied up with the decision to be involved in the kacahri milieu. That decision, once again, was not simply a desire for employment and a salary, but was bound up with complex family commitments, the distribution of social influence in a particular local situation, and motives of cultural style. Schools and government offices were just two of a variety of institutions relevant to the distribution of wealth, power, and prestige in the society. The operation of these institutions had to

[131] GOI, Home Department, Education (A), September 1873, No. 48 (NAI).

be mediated by some set of mental constructs, an ideology, and it is in this sense that British interpretations of Indian religion and caste may indeed come into play. But even accurate formulations of indigenous cultural groupings would not be sufficient as an analysis of the clientele of English education. It is at this point that one might turn to concepts of class and status, the position of an individual or group in relation to the distribution of wealth, power, prestige, ideas, and symbols. It is around these elusive concepts that an analysis of the place of English education must be made.

Demarcations of class are elusive when one tries to relate them to the data available in contemporary sources. Unlike the labels of caste or religion, class is not something you can pin on a person on the basis of his name or his response to a simple query. There were scattered enquiries into the occupations and even incomes of students' parents or guardians, but even when such information was rendered up without deliberate falsification, it is a very inadequate indication of a student's position in the society. Occupational data did not take into consideration the possibility of multiple institutional attachments, the ability of an individual or kinship group to diversify. But it is just such multiplicity that would indicate class position: the summit of class in the Mughal concept of society would be identical with the summit of status—the image of the Mughal emperor drawing in to himself all the differentiated sources of symbolism, kinship loyalty, religious leadership, and economic resources. In nineteenth-century India, there was no such personage, but some lesser people—Khvajah Yusuf of Aligarh, for example—were operating on many fronts at the same time.

Detailed data relevant to such a question may not be available, but at least one can attempt some impressionistic and preliminary account of what the question might involve. The economic resources available to an individual depended very much on his social relationships, and cannot be reduced to the salary or rents he collected. When education authorities attempted to gather such information—usually for the purpose of establishing financial need for a stipend or a financial guarantee for fee payment—they received, at best, information on cash income.[132] Such information is of doubtful value. An educational inspector reported in 1872 that the fathers of Bareilly College students had an average monthly income of only eight rupees,[133] but one would have to know a good deal more about such a person before one could say much about his class position—his ability to go into debt, to elicit patronage, to rent or sell property, the willingness of his wife or mother to pawn her jewelry, and the value and availability of his relatives' resources. Wealth was part of a family web and relied on family reputation. It was also a matter of occasions. Nazir Ahmad's novel, *The Bride's Mirror*, showed how a low-income family could get together thousands of rupees for a wedding without even going into debt by calling in all the chips of established social obligation in the hour of need. In this case the marriage alliance was a remarkably good investment—Muhamad Kāmil's sister was marrying into a rich and powerful family. A lesser opportunity would not claim such an extensive pooling of social resources.[134]

So what kind of opportunity did English education provide? What considerations would lead a family to invest

[132] For an attempt to use this kind of data see Ellen E. McDonald and Craig M. Stark, *English Education, Nationalist Politics and Elite Groups in Maharashtra, 1885-1915*, Occasional Paper No. 5 (Berkeley: Center for South and Southeast Asia Studies, University of California, 1969); see also Seal, *Indian Nationalism*, pp. 92, 109.

[133] RDPI/NWP, 1871-1872, p. 103; the following year the Education Department compiled statistics on "the profession or occupation of pupils' parents or guardians" at Agra, Bareilly, and Benares colleges, including school-level classes. Of 821 students, 259 had parents or guardians in government service; 85 were in private employment, 49 were professionals, 149 agriculturalists, 120 tradesmen, 56 priests, and small numbers listed as independent means, pensioners, soldiers, merchants, and artisans (RDPI/NWP, 1872-1873, p. 35). For similar data see EC/NWP, pp. 94-95.

[134] Naẕīr Ahmad, *The Bride's Mirror*, pp. 173-174; cf. Tom G. Kessinger, *Vilayatpur, 1848-1968* (Berkeley and Los Angeles: University of California Press, 1974), pp. 130-146.

money and the energies of one of its children, often to send him a significant distance from home for long years before he had much to show for the effort? For it wasn't "the Muslims" or even "the Kayasths" who sent their children to schools, but particular families, and for intelligible reasons. These reasons may be a clue to the class standing of these people, their relations to the institutions of their society.

Two sorts of information are relevant here in any effort to place the government-sponsored schools in some fuller social context: detailed information on particular families, and something that contemporary observers had the good taste not to call "the structure of opportunity." For the present, information on families must rest at a preliminary stage, little more than impressionistic accounts of people like Sayyid Ahmad, Sami Ullah, Khvajah Yusuf, and Shibli Numani. Information on rules of access into the kacahri milieu is available, but requires interpretation in the light of contemporary cultural expectations and social relations.

BACK AT THE KACAHRĪ

Testifying before Hunter's Education Commission in 1882, Sami Ullah Khan commented that respectable Muslims considered it degrading to send their children to government schools, where they would have to mix with "the vulgar people." In the past, he continued, "The Government appointments . . . thought to be obtainable through the medium of the educational Department were regarded by the respectable Musalmans as unbecoming to their position and, at the same time, their sons by means of their private instruction, were generally able to get such handsome employments as were often denied to those brought up in the Government Education Department."[135] In other words, when success in the kacahri milieu depended on one's sharīf attributes, it was better to raise a son in an atmosphere of correct manners

[135] *AIG*, Supplement, October 7, 1882.

and literary attainments not available in English-style schools. The few people who went to such schools usually had weak and subordinate links to the other institutions of the society, and therefore were not able to operate very successfully at the nexus of wealth, power, and prestige. In 1868 Kempson observed that a person who had spent eight years reaching matriculation and managed to learn what the course purported to teach was then "of little use to native Society in its present condition, except as a teacher of what he has learnt himself."[136] Besides being a teacher, such a person could be an English-language clerk, a *kirānī*, which sometimes doubled as a synonym for Christian.[137]

There were some examples of English-educated Indians who were sufficiently sharīf to overcome the stigma of their vulgar associations. Sayyid Husain Bilgrami, member of a prominent family of Oudh, was raised with his father and uncle in Bihar, then part of Bengal province, where they were both in British service. He was one of a small group of English-educated Muslims in Lucknow in the 1860s, who associated themselves with Sayyid Ahmad and later rose to major positions in Hyderabad State; others were Ciragh Ali, Mahdi Hasan, and Agha Mirza.[138] Hindustanis resident in Calcutta, such as Sayyid Amir Ali and many members of the Muhammadan Literary Society, provided other examples of the viability of some cultural compromise, but the examples were not particularly visible or overwhelmingly convincing to those who held negative attitudes to English schools.

Even before 1857, there had been some pressure within the British government to encourage government-sponsored edu-

[136] Quoted in *Report of the Select Committee*, p. 23.

[137] ʻAbd ul-Ḥaq, *Cand Ham ʻAṣr* (Karachi: Urdu Academy, 1959), pp. 14-15; John T. Platts, *A Dictionary of Urdū, Classical Hindī and English* (reprint ed.; Oxford: Oxford University Press, 1965 [first published in 1884]), p. 822.

[138] Edith Boardmann, "Biographical Sketch," in Bilgrami, *Addresses*, pp. vii-xi; ʻAbd ul-Ḥaq, *Cand Ham ʻAṣr*, pp. 13-58; Sarvar ul-Mulk, *Kārnāmah*; Ghulām Samdānī Khān, *Tuzuk-i Maḥbūbiyah* (Hyderabad: Niẓām ul-Muṭābaḥ Press, n.d.), II, 243-244, 319-320, 339.

cation by making it a requirement for government employment. There had been a vague directive to this effect in the North-Western Provinces in 1856, and Sayyid Ahmad had listed rumors on the subject among the causes of the revolt.[139] There were no such rules in Oudh or the Punjab. Most government business was conducted in Urdu; until 1837 it had been Persian, but official terminology and record-keeping symbols and techniques were the same in both languages. Insofar as there was English paper work, it tended to be handled by British, Anglo-Indian, or Bengali members of the uncovenanted civil service. The need for English correspondence and translation increased in the 1860s as more time was spent dealing with the central government, and as the courts paid more attention to statutes and precedents that were accessible only in English. In 1865 education officials complained that their colleagues in other departments were ignoring the 1856 directive about giving preference to former students of government schools, but still 48 of 102 fell into that category.[140] Even among these, however, few had advanced far enough at school to satisfy the advocates of English education that they were more than "half educated," and that estimation did not enhance the reputation of the educational system.[141] Many British officials continued to prefer men of the old school, partly out of a desire to exercise personal influence rather than follow bureaucratic instructions, and also out of sympathy for the ideology of sharāfat as a kind of government by gentlemen. The small upsurge of interest in English in the 1860s had failed to demonstrate the advantages of learning it: "the demand has now reached its limit," said Kempson in 1872. "The small fraction of the population which learns English is more than

[139] A. M. Monteath, "Note on the State of Education in India, 1862," *Selections from the Educational Records of the Government of India* (New Delhi: Government Publications, 1960), I, 100-102; *Causes of the Indian Revolt*, p. 128.

[140] Monteath, "Note . . . 1865-66," *ibid.*, I, 267.

[141] Kempson in RDPI/NWP, 1872-1873, I, 129.

sufficient to meet the requirements of the public service or the bar."[142]

But already by the late 1860s there had begun to be an Indian constituency for changing the rules of recruitment in order to displace the hold of entrenched families on kacahri positions. Some of this demand was a continuation of earlier anti-Muslim sentiment, but a good deal of it was a quest to change the criteria for employment to the disadvantage of the so-called *ʿamlah* class, so long resented for its esoteric shorthand techniques and petty corruptions. It is not clear whether the people making these demands were newcomers to kacahri society or established denizens seeking a competitive advantage. Some were Bengalis; others may have been sons of village accountant families—Kayasths in Hindustan, Khatris in the Punjab—who wanted to get closer to the action. Proposals for changing recruitment rules indicated a plea for alternative cultural models, or at least the beginnings of a different symbolism. One alternative was closely tied to the English language and liberal ideas about recruitment by merit. In 1869 a Lucknow newspaper, the *Oudh Akhbar*, complained that government recruitment still operated by personal favoritism, while those who passed examinations were ignored.[143] And a few months later the *Aligarh Institute Gazette*—in the absence of Sayyid Ahmad Khan—reiterated the complaint and demanded that High Court pleaders, munsifs, and "even" Deputy Collectors should all be university graduates.[144]

After 1865, some knowledge of English was necessary for higher levels in the legal profession or judicial service, but rigorous educational requirements were very slow in coming. The rules for becoming a lower subordinate pleader, as of 1882, called for a certificate from a school principal or in-

[142] RDPI/NWP, 1871-1872, p. 102.

[143] *Oudh Akhbar*, June 22, 1869, as reported in M. Kempson, *Report on the Vernacular Press* (N.W.P., 1869), pp. 305-306 (Uttar Pradesh Secretariat Library, Lucknow).

[144] AIG, September 3, 1869.

spector testifying that a candidate had studied for three years at a governmental-sponsored school. A lower pleader could be upgraded after three years of practice to upper subordinate status, and reach the height of the profession as High Court vakil after another three years. One could short-circuit that procedure by having higher educational qualifications at the outset as a university graduate, but that was not necessarily the best way to build up a successful practice. A vakil, however, had to pass an examination in English, whereas the lower levels still provided an option of Urdu.[145] Qualifying for high-level practice in Allahabad, however, was not necessarily desirable, particularly if one had local interests. The same qualifications applied for analogous levels of the judicial service. Only toward the end of the century did the Allahabad High Court move to close off the old channels of initiation into a legal career. Lower subordinate status was abolished, English was required and, after 1889, one could not start a legal career without a Bachelor of Law degree from an Indian university unless one went to London.[146] By the end of the century it was no longer possible to be a Sami Ullah or a Khvajah Yusuf.

In other departments the transition was even slower. As of 1887, no Indian was to be appointed to a post of over ten rupees a month without having passed the middle-level vernacular or Anglo-vernacular exam. Deputy Collectors were to know English, unless they had risen from lower positions in the revenue administration. But such rules were not observed very seriously: of 77 revenue appointments in Benares and Allahabad Divisions in 1882-1883, only 4 complied with the rules.[147] As of 1886-1887, of the 521 gazetted Indian employees of government in the North-Western Prov-

[145] Circular Order No. 7 of 1882, *North-Western Provinces and Oudh Gazette*, February 11, 1882

[146] Circular Order No. 9 of 1889, *North-Western Provinces and Oudh Gazette*, December 7, 1889.

[147] Government of the North-Western Provinces and Oudh [GNWP], General Department (A), February 1885, Nos. 1-3 (India Office Library [IOL]).

inces and Oudh, there were only 94 who had passed matriculation, only 34 who had graduated. By contrast, Bengal employed 623 Indians in the uncovenanted service; 542 of them had matriculated, 275 were graduates.[148] Even as new regulations were introduced, it would take many decades before there could be a significant turnover in the ranks of Indian officials. At the same time, British officials clung to the prerogative of nomination, maintaining candidate lists of people of "good family" for appointment to higher revenue posts from naib-tahsilder on up to Deputy Collector.[149] But again, by the last decade of the century, it was becoming increasingly difficult to rise to such positions by starting as an apprentice clerk; one would do better to have something in the way of educational qualifications. In 1898 clerks were barred from promotion in the North-Western Provinces and Oudh, and a young man could only enter the higher posts with university qualifications.[150]

There was another cultural alternative that appeared in the 1860s and threatened to dislodge the culture of sharāfat from its hold on government office. This was the demand to change the official language from Urdu to Hindi. In 1868 Sayyid Ahmad's translation projects and proposal for a vernacular university came up against a public dispute about what the vernacular was. Since the 1850s government primary education, particularly in rural areas, had sponsored the development of Hindi textbooks. There were two concepts of Hindi: one that it was the same language as Urdu, written in a different script; the other, that it was a substitution of Indic for Persian and Arabic vocabulary. In either case, both languages aspired to the status of regional standard in an area of great linguistic diversity.

In 1868 a predominantly Bengali organization, the Alla-

[148] Seal, *Indian Nationalism*, p. 118.

[149] Standing Order No. 12, pursuant to Section 9, Punjab Land Revenue Act XVII of 1887.

[150] *Anīs-i Hind* (Meerut), March 9, 1898, as reported in *Selection from the Vernacular Newspapers* (hereafter cited as SVN), North-Western Provinces and Oudh, 1898, p. 171 (IOL).

habad Institute, started a campaign to get Hindi recognized as the language of the courts.[151] Bengali had replaced Persian in Bengal; similarly, they argued, the establishment of Hindi would be more suitable for the dominant Hindu population of north India. Another major advocate of Hindi, Raja Shiva Prasad, had written many textbooks in the Nagri script in his capacity as an official of the Education Department. A proud descendant of Jagat Seth, the famous Marvari banker who sold out the Navab of Bengal to Robert Clive, Shiva Prasad was blatently anti-Muslim both in his textbooks and in other public utterances: the British had come to rescue the Hindu population of India from Muslim persecution.[152]

Sayyid Ahmad's response to the Hindi campaign in 1868 was to argue that Hindi and Urdu were, in fact, the same language, and that good Urdu style avoided heavy use of Persian or Arabic vocabulary. Legal terminology, on the other hand, was inherently technical and might as well be of Persian or Arabic derivation, since those terms were already in use. As for script—Nagri, Persian, or Roman—that was purely a matter of convenience, and should not be changed except for practical reasons.[153] All Sayyid Ahmad's early writings on the issue sought to defuse it of its cultural symbolism, but the issue became increasingly charged as the century wore on.

In 1871, the Lieutenant Governor of Bengal barred Urdu, "that bastard hybrid language," from use in the courts of Bihar, an act that gave encouragement to the champions of Hindi further west.[154] The Hindi-Urdu debate developed a

151 AIG, November 13, 1868.

152 AIG, March 24, 1883; GOI, Home Department, Education (A), September 1873, Nos. 44-56; in later life Sayyid Ahmad blamed Shiva Prasad's promotion of Hindi for the rise of Hindu-Muslim enmity (Ḥālī, *Ḥayāt-i jāvīd*, pp. 163-164; also copy of Urdu letter with English translation from Sayyid Ahmad to Pandit Lakshmi Shankar Misra of Benares, May 10, 1896 [218A, AA]).

153 AIG, November 27, 1868.

154 Minutes of the Lieutenant Governor of Bengal, G. Campbell, December 4, 1871, quoted in AIG, December 29, 1871.

large literature, full of conflicting linguistic claims, but most of all it developed into an issue of public debate suitable to the new institutions: the voluntary association and the newspaper. The heart of the matter was what language was to be used in the kacahri, and therefore what kind of education would prepare people for official employment or the legal profession. Proponents of Hindi argued that Muslims had an advantage in using the same script they studied with their Qur'an, and in drawing on family traditions of Persian learning. In 1873 Sayyid Ahmad became secretary of a short-lived group called the "Central Committee, Allahabad," which maintained simultaneously that Urdu was not inherently Muslim, and that substituting Hindi would put Muslims at a great disadvantage. All the committee members were Muslim.[155] Although Sayyid Husain Bilgrami wrote an article sympathetic to the claims of Hindi, the controversy otherwise divided on clear religious lines.[156] It cropped up from time to time over the next three decades, and in 1900 Hindi won its first victory by being admitted alongside Urdu in the courts.[157]

Hindu-Muslim division was a familiar theme in the new style of political discourse. Among British officialdom, of course, this had long been the case, and provided the terms for the most readily available statistical information. There were certainly Englishmen with pro-Muslim predilections, but the historical assumption that "the Muslims" were the former rulers of India inspired many with a distrust of their "loyalty." This view was particularly widespread after 1857; it was renewed by the "Wahabi" conspiracy trials in Patna during the following decade, and again by Hunter's book in 1870. While some officials argued for a policy of solicitude,

[155] An untitled thirteen-page printed pamphlet in Urdu and English lists the members of the "Central Committee, Allahabad," and recites the group's arguments in favor of Urdu and against Hindi; located in Sir Syed Room, Azad Library, Aligarh Muslim University; see also Ḥālī, *Ḥayāt-i jāvīd*, pp. 162-167.

[156] Bilgrami, *Addresses*, pp. 10, 17.

[157] Hardy, *Muslims of British India*, p. 143.

others felt that, particularly in the region of the rebellion, the power of Muslims was altogether too great. And it was true that before 1857 the proportion of Indian officials who were Muslim was overwhelming in the North-Western Provinces—72 percent of the judiciary, for example, in 1850.[158]

English educational qualifications and the demand for Hindi were openly construed in the political debates of the time as an effort to cut back on Muslim dominance of the kacahri. And, indeed, the proportion did drop in the course of the next decades, though it remained well above 14 percent—the proportion of Muslims in the general population of the province. In the 1880s Muslims were over 45 percent of the gazetted Indian officials, and nearly 30 percent of those earning more than seventy-five rupees a month.[159] Still, as one Muslim political group complained, "the Hindus outnumber the Muhammadans in the Government Offices."[160] The increasing relevance of English education threatened to repeat the statistical fate of Muslim office-holders in Bengal, where Muslims, once dominant, held only 5 percent of the higher posts.

Here, too, however, the figures on government employment take on a different meaning when one thinks of recruitment as a family matter: it is true that members of the same family tended to have the same religion. Public information emphasized the proportions, but the absolute numbers again show that the people in question were very few. In 1867 there were 333 Muslims earning over seventy-five rupees in North-Western Provinces and Oudh; in 1897 the number was 466. Over the same years the number of Hindus had

[158] Thomas R. Metcalf, *The Aftermath of Revolt* (Princeton: Princeton University Press, 1965), p. 303.

[159] Paul R. Brass, "Muslim Separtism in United Provinces: Social Context and Political Strategy before Partition," *Economic and Political Weekly*, V (Annual Number, 1970), 173; Seal, *Indian Nationalism*, p. 305.

[160] Memorial of the National Muhammadan Association, Calcutta, to the Viceroy, Lord Ripon, February 6, 1882, *Correspondence on the Education of the Muhammadan Community*, pp. 237-244.

increased a good deal more, from 692 to 1,069, but not necessarily at the expense of Muslims. Statistics were similar in the Punjab.[161] Everybody plays, everybody wins; at first it was only in terms of political rhetoric that the entrenched Muslim families of the kacahri world had to be worried. But by the late nineteenth century, political rhetoric was becoming increasingly important in the distribution of power.[162]

From the point of view of a man like Sayyid Ahmad in about 1870, there was good reason to believe that the day was coming when the established forms of a sharīf upbringing would no longer qualify a man for participation in the life and benefits of kacahri society. Widespread British antagonism to Muslims as authors of the 1857 Revolt, popular Indian dissatisfaction with the "amlah class" as exploitative, efforts to encourage English educational prerequisites for office, and finally, a new kind of organized political campaign for Hindi as the language of the courts—all this threatened those Muslim families that had an interest in getting official employment for their sons. Some were not perceptive enough to see the danger; others were not willing to sacrifice their religion and cultural commitments. But the incentive both for a new kind of education and a new kind of public life had appeared on the horizon. And it helped if, like Sayyid Ahmad, you also considered the prospect of these changes to be an exciting opportunity for improvement.

[161] GOI, Home Department, Establishment (A), June 1904, No. 103, pp. 137-139.

[162] Whether "the Muslim elite" of the region was "rising" or "falling" is analyzed in detail in two recent studies, which rely heavily on official British concepts and statistical data: Paul R. Brass, *Language, Religion and Politics in North India* (Cambridge: Cambridge University Press, 1974) and Francis Robinson, *Separatism among Indian Muslims* (Cambridge: Cambridge University Press, 1974).

III

The Establishment of the Muhammadan Anglo-Oriental College

IN the early 1870s a small group of North Indian Muslims led by Sayyid Ahmad Khan joined forces to design and establish a private British-style educational institution that would make adequate room for the religion of Islam. The college at Aligarh was a self-consciously planned institution, planned for the most part by people who themselves had never been exposed to English education. It arose out of a dissatisfaction with British-Indian schools, government and missionary, as well as with Islamic madrasahs, which were supposedly giving the wrong kind of education to the wrong kind of people. Instead, Aligarh's founders sought different foreign models, and introduced features of curriculum and social environment designed to attract a new clientele for English education. In magazine articles, committee proceedings, and public meetings over a period of five years, from 1870 to 1875, they articulated goals and worked out institutional mechanisms in response to public criticisms and practical limitations.

This formidable public enterprise reveals a good deal about the ideological matrix into which the new institution was set, how the founders hoped to make it fit into the total situation of their social relationships and ways of thought. Despite deliberate efforts to copy features of a particular type of British education—Oxford, Cambridge, and the "public schools"—the college at Aligarh was to be not a simple transplant of a foreign model, but an indigenous creation. When Sayyid Ahmad and his friends selected bits and pieces of contemporary British education, they often perceived them inaccurately, or deliberately modified them. More important, the borrowed traits were forced into new relationships and took on new meanings. They were made to serve Indian purposes.

Aside from the selection of foreign models, the questions relevant to Aligarh's founding serve only to lay out the initial frame of reference within which the institution was to develop: who were the founders, whom did they hope to reach as prospective students, what kind of intellectual and social environment did they hope to establish, how would the college relate to the existing system of political and educational institutions, and what adult careers did they anticipate for their alumni? The older generation could only imperfectly anticipate the actual workings of the college and its place in the lives of its students. As a living institution, the college had to respond to pressures that were often unanticipated and unwelcome. Twenty-five years later, Sayyid Ahmad was to speak of his life's work as a bitter failure. The fathers of Aligarh's first generation sought change and acted to bring it about, but the changes they got were different from what they had in mind. These departures from the preliminary plan serve to mark off the social and cultural changes of which the college itself was a part.

The founding of Aligarh College also involved the definition and mobilization of a constituency. Fund raising and the effort to win public and governmental approval were political acts, and called for decisions about what categories of people Aligarh might represent and serve. Immersed in a whole new ideology about the history and present status of Indian Muslims, Aligarh was not only a school, it was a political symbol. The rhetoric that developed in these early years was to take on a life of its own. The organizational methods and styles used to win backing for the college were later turned to a new world of Indian party politics.

PRELUDE: SAYYID AHMAD'S TRIP TO ENGLAND (1869-1870)

In the aftermath of the 1857 Revolt, Sayyid Ahmad Khan had been active in seeking an accommodation with British rule in northern India. The schools in Moradabad and Ghazipur, the translations of the Scientific Society, the *Aligarh Institute Gazette*, the local school committees, and the petition for a vernacular university, were all efforts to win a place for Indians within the British political system by drawing on British ideas and organizational techniques. These scattered activities were not original; they had been anticipated a half-century earlier in Bengal, and repeated widely throughout British India. Sayyid Ahmad's efforts in the 1860s tended to be localized in the particular district towns in which he was stationed for stretches of two and three years. He was not the leader of a well-defined constituency, and in general did not reach beyond the government servants and legal practitioners with whom he came into daily contact—men, like himself, belonging to kacahri milieu and educated in Persian. In these days Sayyid Ahmad tended to confine his Muslimness to theological writings, while speaking to educational and political matters as a Hindustani ra'īs.[1] In his speeches and writings he metaphorically extended the usage of the words qaum and biradari, the birth-defined categories of Mughal society, to regional and linguistic designation, such as the Hindustanis, the Bengalis, and the British. For religious groups—the Muslims, the Hindus, and the Christians—he tended to use the Arabic word for "sect," *mazhab*.[2]

A shift in Sayyid Ahmad's thought and vocabulary and consequently the proposal for a separate Muslim educational movement came in the course of his seventeen-month

[1] The major exceptions are his pamphlets, *Loyal Muhammadans of India*.

[2] For example, *Maqālāt-i Sar Sayyid* [hereafter *Maqālāt*], ed. Muḥammad Ismā'īl Pānīpatī (Lahore: Majlis-i Taraqqī-i Adab, 1963), XII, 5.

trip to England in 1869-1870. His younger son, Mahmud, had won a government scholarship for study in England—he was one of the first north Indians to do so—and the old man seized the opportunity to go with him. In his application for leave, Sayyid Ahmad explained that he wanted to see the commerce, factories, and hospitals of Britain.[3] Privately he spoke of gathering material for a refutation of Muir's *Life of Muhammad*, an intention considered unwise by some friends, since Muir was then Lieutenant Governor of the North-Western Provinces.[4] In retrospect, fifteen years later, he claimed his main purpose had been "obtaining an insight into the English system of education."[5] Handicapped by not knowing English, he relied on his sons—the elder Sayyid Hāmid came also—to act as interpreters and research assistants.[6]

By all accounts Sayyid Ahmad's experience of England was a major personal and intellectual crisis. His writings took on a new passionate intensity or *jōsh*, which often expressed itself in terms of shocking self-debasement totally at odds with his usual stance of proud self-respect. Overwhelmed by the accomplishments of British technology, the general level of literacy, the self-confident sense of achievement that he encountered, Sayyid Ahmad was struck for a time with a feeling of powerlessness. The worst British

[3] AIG, February 5, 1869. [4] Ḥālī, *Ḥayāt-i jāvīd*, p. 426.

[5] Sayyid Ahmad's testimony, ED/NWP, reprinted in AIG, Supplement, August 5, 1882.

[6] Sayyid Ahmad had some slight conversational ability in English, but generally relied on Sayyid Mahmud to interpret for him (Sayyid Ahmad to Mahdi Ali, London, August 20, 1869, *Maktūbāt*, p. 63); see also 1889 speech (*Lectures and Speeches*, p. 401), but this must be interpreted in the light of the later dispute over Sayyid Maḥmud's role in running the college (see below, pp. 269-72); in 1883 Wilfred Scawen Blunt wrote in his diary that Sayyid Ahmad "speaks very little English" (*India under Ripon* [London: T. Fisher Unwin, 1909], p. 156); Percy Wallace, a newly arrived professor at Aligarh, was apparently able to converse with Sayyid Ahmad in 1887 (letter to his mother, August 8, 1887, in Duke University Library, Durham, North Carolina; thanks to Harlan Pearson). Sayyid Ahmad wrote out letters in Urdu for translation into English by an assistant (AA).

characterizations of the people of India began to seep into his consciousness. But he was not a man easily immobilized; he had the ability to turn his inner conflicts into public energies, and to use the nightmare images of his private despondency to startle and awaken an Indian public into action. He wrote to the *Aligarh Institute Gazette*: "The natives of India, high and low, merchants and petty shopkeepers, educated and illiterate, when contrasted with the English in education, manners and uprightness, are as like them as a dirty animal is to an able and handsome man." But he went on to say that Indians could overcome their handicaps by deliberate activity.[7]

Such statements inspired angry replies in India, which drove Sayyid Ahmad further into a mood of frustration and isolation. Early in the trip he provoked pious outrage by wearing a "modern" Turkish fez and high-buttoned coat, and by reporting his willingness to eat chicken slaughtered in a manner contrary to Islamic dietary law. His private letters home reveal that he was greatly disturbed by the public attacks against him, especially those made on religious grounds.[8] Throughout his trip he found himself struggling on two fronts—addressing himself to the home audience as radical critic of Indian shortcomings, while attempting to lead Englishmen to a new attitude toward Indian culture and public policy. With orthodox Muslims on one side and English evangelicals on the other, Sayyid Ahmad was provoked into a new level of self-consciousness.

Through the greater part of his stay abroad, Sayyid Ahmad continued to separate religious and political matters. He published two works in England, both translated and addressed to an English audience. The first, a short pamphlet on English education in India, did not concern itself with special

[7] AIG, October 15, 1869.

[8] For example, Sayyid Ahmad to Mahdi Ali, London, January 21, 1870, *Maktūbāt*, pp. 85-87. For the Indian reaction to Sayyid Ahmad's letters, see Kempson, "Report on the Vernacular Press, N.-W.P.," 1870, pp. 417-420.

problems of Muslims. *Essays on the Life of Muhammad*, written in refutation of Muir, did not deal with contemporary India. The long, excited letters to the *Aligarh Institute Gazette* belittled Hindustanis without regard to religion. By the close of his stay, however, Sayyid Ahmad had undergone a change in orientation.

The pamphlet *Strictures on the Present State of English Education in India* came out in the early part of Sayyid Ahmad's sojourn in London. It did not allude to observations made in England, but was of a piece with his earlier ideas and activities. The argument he made was that the government system of schools had failed to achieve either popular mass education or the stimulation of intellectual creativity. Before British rule, India had been notable for men of genuine learning and original thought. "The sum total of all that has been effected by the English Colleges, has been to qualify an insignificant number, as letter-writers, copyists, signal-men, and railway ticket collectors."[9] Compared to the standard of London University, the University of Calcutta had been fobbed off with an inferior curriculum. Nor had elementary education received adequate resources or supervision from the British government.

Sayyid Ahmad believed that Indians of his—the older—generation had been better educated, educated to occupy positions of power. Now the equivalent education was confined to Englishmen in England. He demanded "equality of rights with our European fellow subjects"—an educational system not only to prepare Indians for the Civil Service, but to "direct their thoughts and inclinations to the acquiring such a knowledge of machinery and other mechanical appliances, without which the national products of the country can never be made available to their fullest extent."[10] The British, having "despoiled us of our mother tongue, and our hereditary sciences," must make good the loss by establish-

[9] Sayyid Ahmad, *Strictures on the Present State of English Education in India* (London: n.p., 1869), p. 11.

[10] *Ibid.*, pp. 31-32.

ing a three-tier educational system: a lower level to enable working people to read and write sufficiently to conduct their daily affairs and take advantage of recent technological improvements, a middle level to train teachers and other transmitters of the expanding realm of knowledge, and an upper level for original research. Such an educational system could only succeed in bringing about genuine cultural change if it were conducted in the vernacular, even at the highest level.

Sayyid Ahmad was in search of the foundations of British achievement and British power; he perceived them to lie in the area of technological innovation and the diffusion of knowledge and skills to a wide population. His own education had touched on scientific matters—he had studied mathematics with his uncle and traditional medicine with a well-known hakīm—but these had been, like the literary accomplishments of a sharīf upbringing, a matter of personal cultivation. Now he saw a need to transform society with knowledge, and accepted the notion that for this to happen, knowledge itself would have to be transformed. Although he was not prepared to go very deeply into the intellectual wellsprings of such a transformation, he realized that it involved experimental research and an institutional structure that would rely on something more than shauq, personal inclination, to maintain the enterprise of learning. He also realized that any such advancements would be doomed to dwell on the periphery of Indian culture unless there was some mechanism of reaching out to a wider public; knowledge could not be confined to men of leisure. The Scientific Society had been a step in that direction, but had hardly reached beyond the level of dilettante curiosity. Sayyid Ahmad's trip to England had given him a new sense of urgency.

Sayyid Ahmad closed his pamphlet with an assertion that British officials in India were unsympathetic to demands for quality education despite the benign intentions of the Home Government. In India the *Strictures* provoked angry replies from Muir and Shiva Prasad, antagonists familiar to Sayyid Ahmad.[11] A newspaper accused him of "agitating the subject of Mussulman Education," to which the *Institute Gazette* responded by pointing out that Sayyid Ahmad had not raised any issues peculiar to Muslims: "The Syud's services . . . are of a more catholic character."[12]

Sayyid Ahmad considered madrasah education better than what the British schools had to offer, but unlikely to lead India into a new future. News that Sami Ullah was busy raising funds for an Arabic madrasah in Delhi sent Sayyid Ahmad into diatribes about how the Indian Muslims were drowning in the seas of decadence, with no one competent to save them. "There is no benefit in these ordinary madrasahs. . . . If you came here [to England]," he wrote Mahdi Ali, "you would see how education is carried on and how children are taught, how knowledge is acquired and a qaum receives honor."[13]

In addition to his observations in England, Sayyid Ahmad also became newly aware of Muslims outside of India. He felt the humiliation of Islam at the hands of Christian Europe, as when he saw a mural at Versailles depicting the French conquest of Algeria. On the other hand, he had passed through Egypt and also learned something of the reforms introduced in the Ottoman empire. The Turks and the Egyptians were already moving in much the same direction as Sayyid Ahmad wanted to go. Early in the century they had established European-style schools for the training of military officers and physicians. The Ottoman government had made a significant start in translating European scientific works into Turkish, and in 1846 had initiated an educational program for Muslims in which authority rested with the new Ministry of Education rather than the ʿulama. The schools included religious education, but consciously copied

[11] AIG, February 11 and April 15, 22, 29, 1870.
[12] *Ibid.*, October 22, 1869.
[13] Sayyid Ahmad to Mahdi Ali, London, September 10, 1869, *Maktūbāt*, p. 90.

the French in curriculum and teaching methods. The year before Sayyid Ahmad left India, the Ottomans had opened the Galatasaray Lycée, a French-medium secondary school to train the administrative elite of the empire.[14]

These examples of change under Muslim auspices made an impression on Sayyid Ahmad, but the dominance of European power and culture forced him to think about the place of Islam in world history and "Whether Islam Has Been Beneficial or Injurious to Human Society in General."[15] There is little doubt that the trip to England made Sayyid Ahmad more sensitive to his Muslim identity than he had been before, not so much, perhaps, a change in abstract ideas as in their emotional emphasis in his life. He felt compelled to justify his own piety in the eyes of Indian critics, and to justify Islam in the eyes of English ones.

It was in England that Sayyid Ahmad commenced a prodigious enterprise of reformulating Islamic theology in order to prove the consistency of God's revelation with nineteenth-century European rationalism. There had been hints of this in the past, particularly in his 1862 Bible commentary, but now he turned a full measure of attention to this task, conceiving the idea of a special journal for this purpose, *Tahẕib ul-Akẖlāq*. To Sayyid Ahmad the truth of Islam was always prior: modern scientific ideas were either consistent with Islamic doctrine, or they had to be refuted. On the other hand, he was prepared to simplify received doctrine and to forego transcendental acceptance of the supernatural, for example, by taking great pains to provide naturalistic explanations for specific miracles related in the Qur'an. He nevertheless pointed out that, just as certain features of Greek

[14] See Roderic H. Davison, *Reform in the Ottoman Empire, 1856-1876* (Princeton: Princeton University Press, 1963), pp. 244-250; Bernard Lewis, *The Emergence of Modern Turkey* (London: Oxford University Press, 1961), pp. 82-85, 111-112, 119-121. For Sayyid Ahmad's attention to Ottoman affairs see his letter to Mahdi Ali, London, April 29, 1870, *Maktūbāt*, pp. 104-105.

[15] This is a chapter title in *Essays on the Life of Muhammad*, reprint ed. (Lahore: Premier Book House, 1968).

science had been superceded, the same might be the fate of contemporary science. He was not quite prepared to accept the heliocentric theory, and certainly not the theory of evolution. He had been a student of Shah Vali Ullah's grandson, and could support his arguments by citing the great theologian's own rationalistic interpretation of miracles. Now, however, Sayyid Ahmad broadened this approach by setting down as a basic principle of Qur'anic exegesis that if a passage could be given a naturalistic explanation, that explanation must be accepted. Even Paradise and Hell could be interpreted as "allegories and metaphors," just as some classical commentators had accepted the figurative nature of God's "throne," "hands," and "legs." In his search for a confluence of Christianity and Islam, Sayyid Ahmad made some effort to acquaint himself with modern European theological writings, although here, in his ignorance of English, he was at the mercy of other people's judgments. A major intellectual hero was Joseph Addison, the eighteenth-century Whig essayist and spokesman for "Rational Piety," who was a regular part of the British Indian college curriculum. The citation of non-Islamic theology and a rather decorative use of transliterated English terms in his Urdu writings, such as "word of God" and "supernatural" were particularly insulting to pious Muslims, who gave him the title "*Naicarī*."[16]

Just as he wanted to reinterpret Islam for an Indian audience, he was also concerned with the reputation of his religion in the eyes of the British public. By far his greatest efforts were devoted to the refutation of Muir, who as British, Christian evangelical and, worst of all, Lieutenant Governor of Sayyid Ahmad's own province, embodied the full challenge of the ruling power. Day and night for months he prepared materials, pressing his sons and others into service, writing urgent appeals to friends at home for funds to pay

[16] For Sayyid Ahmad's religious thought see Aziz Ahmad, *Islamic Modernism in India and Pakistan, 1857-1964* (London: Oxford University Press, 1967), pp. 31-56; also Baljon, *Reforms and Religious Ideas*, pp. 71-155.

publication costs.[17] Only when the work was done, translated into English, and published, did he feel released for other concerns.

In addition to religious apologetics and concern for Muslims outside India, other matters further magnified his religious self-consciousness during the trip. He was troubled by the newspaper articles of W. W. Hunter, which portrayed the Muslims of India as a community of former rulers now fallen on evil days, and especially deprived in education and government employment. Generalizing from Bengali experience, Hunter painted a dramatic and alarming picture of a desperate people, and Sayyid Ahmad was one of many who accepted Hunter's line of argument. He did not, however, accept the notion that opposition to British rule was bound up in the religion of Islam, an argument that threatened every one of his political and educational efforts.[18] Shiva Prasad's continued campaign for Hindi was a further threat that worried him during his stay in England.[19] More inwardly, his letters reveal frequent bouts of loneliness as a foreigner unable to speak English. Also, the death of his daughter during his absence may have summoned up special religious needs.[20] So on many levels it became important to him that he was a Muslim.

Sayyid Ahmad could not help believing that there was a correlation between worldly success and cultural superiority. In the past, Muslim political dominance in much of the world had been justified on the basis of such superiority, derived from acceptance of God's revelation. But now Muslims were no longer dominant. Sayyid Ahmad's new religious in-

[17] A recurring theme in his letters to Mahdi Ali, *Maktūbāt*, pp. 40-126.

[18] Sayyid Ahmad to Mahdi Ali, London, August 20, 1869, *ibid.*, p. 63; soon after his return to India, Sayyid Ahmad published a lengthy critique of Hunter's book in the *Pioneer*, AIG, and as a pamphlet (*Review on Dr. Hunter's Indian Musalmans*, reprint ed. [Lahore: Premier Book House, n.d.]).

[19] Sayyid Ahmad to Mahdi Ali, London, April 29, 1870, *Maktūbāt*, pp. 103-104.

[20] Letters of May 10 and 27, 1870, *ibid.*, pp. 107, 112.

tensity was probably provoked most of all by the shattering experience of seeing Britain's strength, wealth, and self-confidence—as if the insults of colonialist bigotry had gained some justification even in his own eyes. The response was to argue that the fault was not basic, in religion or in human potential. If the country of the Mughals had fallen low, it was due to British policy as well as to indigenous error. Hindustanis, like Bengalis and Parsis, had to be convinced of the need for change. But the British public, too, had to realize that there were people in India who were potentially their equals, and one part of the lesson involved learning respect for Muhammad and the Qur'an. Finally, a new public policy, particularly with regard to education, might lead members of the indigenous population to a fair share of the power and prosperity of the British empire.

SEARCH FOR AN EDUCATIONAL PROTOTYPE

There is little specific information as to how closely Sayyid Ahmad looked into the detailed workings of English colleges and schools. He visited Oxford and Cambridge, and provided Sayyid Mahmud with a tutor to prepare him for university admission. He was impressed by the general level of literacy of the British, particularly the women, and observed that widespread education provided England with tremendous human resources for the development of commercial, technological, and even political enterprises. Maid servants were acquainted with the news of the day; workingmen understood complicated machinery. In contrast to India, England seemed to be a society united by shared values, information, and skills.[21]

But Sayyid Ahmad's visit to England happened to coincide with a great national debate on educational policy, and the beginnings of some fundamental changes. If England seemed a land of the learned from an Indian point of view, the truth was, nevertheless, that she fell far short of universal

[21] AIG, February 25, 1870; January 13, 1871.

elementary education. The year of Forster's Education Act, 1870, greatly extended the reach of the state-sponsored school system. Such an act had long been delayed by an intense controversy involving two issues: the role of the state in the education of children, and the inclusion of religious instruction. The compromise of 1870 provided for state financial aid to church schools as well as Bible study in government schools.[22]

Sayyid Ahmad picked up two new ideas from this controversy. Consistently with his earlier efforts to find an opening for Indian participation in the control of the school system, he now fell upon the Victorian doctrines of laissez faire and self-help. He thus chose the very principle that England was at that moment beginning to abandon in the field of education. "As England seems to be the foremost of all other countries in the possession of knowledge and intelligence, civilization and wisdom, so is its Government one that has the least concern and occasion for interference with the matter of public education." Education should be a matter of private, voluntary action.[23] Yet the idea of free enterprise meant something very different in the context of colonial rule: it meant Indians controlling their own institutions.

The second idea Sayyid Ahmad came upon at this time was the inclusion of religious instruction in a system of public education. Although this was a feature of Ottoman education and a familiar enough issue in discussions of Indian education, it had been absent from Sayyid Ahmad's previous statements on the subject. His *Strictures* did not call into question the British effort to stay at arm's length from religious controversy by keeping religion out of the schools. In England, however, he now saw the pervasiveness of religious consciousness in Victorian life, expressed in such things as compulsory chapel in the schools. He began to see religion not merely as a private, theological matter but as a

[22] G. M. Young, *Victorian England: Portrait of an Age* (London: Oxford University Press, 1960), pp. 115-117.

[23] AIG, April 8, 1870.

source of the kind of social discipline he so admired in the English public.

Sayyid Ahmad was now prepared for the confluence of religion and education in his own program of public action. His *Essays on the Life of Muhammad* were completed in late March of 1870. The following month he wrote an article on Forster's Education Act,[24] and soon after, he was writing letters to Mahdi Ali aimed at getting a movement started for Muslim education. On April 22 he asked his friend to establish an association for the improvement and reform of Indian Muslims, suggesting that it would be best if the beginnings of such an organization were not tainted with his own controversial name.[25] A week later he specified that what he had in mind was a separate school for Muslims. "No night goes by here without discussions and proposals for the establishment of such a madrasah."[26] And a month after that he was making plans for a journal, *Tahẕīb ul-A<u>kh</u>lāq or the Muhammadan Social Reformer*, to be a vehicle of the new movement[27]

The specific content of Sayyid Ahmad's program for Muslim education did not emerge until his return to India. Having left the exciting spectacle of industrial Britain behind him, he was once again caught up in dealing with the Britain of colonial bureaucrats. In the search for a prototype of an educational system to adapt to Indian needs as he saw them, Sayyid Ahmad gravitated in the end to the public school-Oxford-Cambridge example. In making this choice he was abandoning the very goals set forth in his previous writings—the encouragement of science, technology, empirical research, and the whole Victorian ethic of dynamic change. For the model he selected represented to its advocates in England a commitment to continuity and permanence, and a very explicit rejection of the whole scientific and techno-

[24] *Ibid.*

[25] Sayyid Ahmad to Mahdi Ali, London, April 22, 1870, *Maktūbāt*, p. 99.

[26] *Ibid.*, April 29, 1870, p. 106. [27] *Ibid.*, May 27, 1870, p. 114.

logical point of view. Oxford, Cambridge, and the public schools were designed for the landed aristocracy and gentry of England—cabinet ministers, members of parliament, upper civil servants, army officers, and clergy—but not for the entrepreneurial, managerial, or technological personnel of the country. The goal was "moral perfection" to qualify men for social leadership.[28]

In the two decades preceeding Sayyid Ahmad's visit to England there had been a considerable expansion of the public-school system to admit a broader clientele of middle-class boys whose parents aspired to the gentry style of life—including many who were to go to India. In the 1860s the seven old endowed public schools and a couple dozen more recent imitations had been subjected to a damning investigation by a Royal Commission, which revealed their educational shortcomings and financial scandals, both the result of institutional inbreeding. It was at the very time that Sayyid Ahmad was turning to these institutions as the glorious progeny of laissez faire that the British government was undertaking for the first time to control them.

As one historian puts it, public-school education conceived of the human mind as "a single weapon to be forged and sharpened."[29] Parsing Greek and Latin sentences, constructing stereotyped hexameters, memorizing conjugations and declensions—such was the day-to-day business of public-school classrooms. They had more in common with the old madrasahs Sayyid Ahmad had rejected than with the cultivation of an experimental mentality. Only recently had teaching shifted to classroom lessons as opposed to madrasah-like exposition and recitation of different subjects in an unpartitioned school building. Public-school authorities tended to condemn science, particularly applied science, as a lower-class attack on the legitimate realms of power; few British

[28] See T. W. Bamford, *The Rise of the Public School* (London: Nelson, 1967); Rupert Wilkenson, *The Prefects* (London: Oxford University Press, 1964); Sheldon Rothblatt, *The Revolution of the Dons* (London: Faber and Faber, 1968).

[29] Bamford, *Public School*, p. 99.

scientists came out of such schools.[30] Room was provided for pure mathematics, but above all it was the discipline of language study that qualified men to be leaders of society. For a man of Sayyid Ahmad's background, the intellectual content and career preparation of the public schools represented the shortest distance one had to move in choosing traits from the ruling culture.

The aspect of the public schools that most appealed to Sayyid Ahmad was the social milieu, the cultivation of "character." He did not have the linguistic equipment to go very deeply into matters of curriculum, but the author of *Aṣār us-Ṣanādīd* knew how to look at a building. The architecture had much in common with the familiar buildings of north India. The quadrangle, its walls and gates shutting out the distractions of ordinary life, offered the hope of raising a generation of Muslims with a new sense of group loyalty. What Sayyid Ahmad saw as the secret of British power were the virtues of cohesiveness and social discipline. At the public schools these virtues were explicitly religious; "good learning" was bound up with "godliness," as expressed in chapel sermons and spiritually improving studies.[31] Thus Sayyid Ahmad found confirmation for his new emphasis on religion. Public-school boys also acted out of a sense of duty to the "historic community." Within the confines of group membership, a civil servant was expected to be a person of individual initiative, one who could be relied on for loyal and intelligent action, not mindless obedience. The duties attached to his role were of a piece with his most deeply felt values. Such was the rationale behind the public-school experience with its games and societies, its etiquette and discipline.[32] For Sayyid Ahmad, who long before had identified the road to political participation for Indians as the development of a social milieu in which they could meet the British as equal members of a shared community, the public school

30 *Ibid.*, pp. 105, 224.

31 David Newsome, *Godliness and Good Learning* (London: Murray, 1961).

32 Wilkenson, *Prefects*, pp. 29-53.

seemed to be the best strategy. This consideration drowned out his attraction to the technological achievements of the industrial revolution. He decided to befriend the gods rather than steal their fire.

PRELIMINARY ORGANIZATION

Soon after his return to India, Sayyid Ahmad set about drawing up a blueprint for action to translate the perceptions and ideas inspired by his trip abroad. The Committee for the Better Diffusion and Advancement of Learning among Muhammadans of India came into being in December 1870 in Benares, where Sayyid Ahmad resumed his post as subjudge. Financed initially on fifty- and hundred-rupee contributions from a dozen donors—including Muir and the Navab of Rampur—its working membership consisted of Sayyid Ahmad's close friends, some associates from previous official posts such as Aligarh, and a large contingent of petty officials and vakils from the kacahri in Benares. The committee included self-confident, independent-minded men like Sami Ullah Khan and Mir Akbar Husain (later famous under his pen-name Akbar Allahabadi for his satires against Sayyid Ahmad and Aligarh). They were prepared to dissent from Sayyid Ahmad and to force through modifications of his program. With parliamentary procedure, published minutes and accounts, the movement was something more than a one-man show. *Tahẕīb ul-Akẖlāq*, the journal associated with Sayyid Ahmad's educational efforts, contained articles by men such as Mahdi Ali and Mushtaq Husain, neither of whom sympathized with Sayyid Ahmad's theology. Although Sayyid Ahmad's was the loudest voice, he learned that he would have to mute it in order to win public acceptance for the new madrasah.

Before advancing his own scheme for Muslim education, Sayyid Ahmad attempted to draw in other participants by initiating a public enquiry in the form of an essay contest. A subcommittee of fourteen reviewed thirty-two essays on the subject: why Muslims have failed to take advantage of English education and what should be done to overcome this failure. The subcommittee tended to rely on its own judgment rather than the arguments of the essayists, and Sayyid Ahmad as secretary was inclined to report his own opinions at length, while making only the briefest reference to the views of other committee members. But in the end there was unanimous agreement on his proposal, presented in April 1872, for the establishment of a private Muslim school system that would give sufficient place to religious practice and instruction.[33] An important ingredient of this plan was an essay that Sayyid Mahmud sent in from Cambridge in February; he proposed the establishment of a residential college "where Muslims alone would be able to obtain an education according to their wishes."[34]

The following month the original committee replaced itself with the Muhammadan Anglo-Oriental College Fund Committee, which survived until 1889 in legal control of the college and its assets. The committee was composed of personal connections of Sayyid Ahmad from the class of the mobile, Persianized literati of Hindustan. Of the original twenty-six members, eighteen were vakils or government servants for the British or princely states. At least fifteen were posted temporarily in places other than their permanent residences. The remainder included some wealthy zamindars from Aligarh and Benares districts. At least one of the vakils was also a large landholder. There was a contingent of seven from Delhi, including Sayyid Ahmad, his two sons, his nephew, and three relatives by marriage. Four of the members were from Benares, and three from Aligarh. Otherwise the members had their permanent residences in a dozen small towns stretching from Patiala in the Punjab to Bhagalpur in Bihar. In July a dozen more members were elected to the committee, including five from Ghazipur and the Navab of

[33] *Report of the Select Committee.*

[34] Sayyid Muḥammad Maḥmūd, "Yūniversitī-i Kaimbrij," *Tahẕīb ul-Akẖlāq* (hereafter TA), 10 Muḥarram, 1289 H.

Pahasu (near Aligarh), who was also Prime Minister of Jaipur.[35] In accordance with the rules framed at the outset, all were Muslims.[36] Membership was for life.

Located in Benares, since that was where its Life Honorary Secretary was posted—according to the rules, committee headquarters would shift with Sayyid Ahmad until the college got started—the job of the committee was to collect at least one million rupees as endowment for the college. The members would establish local organizations, and there would also be subcommittees to perform specific tasks such as the selection of textbooks. Charged with implementing Sayyid Ahmad's proposal for a separate educational system, the Fund Committee had to make basic ideological choices concerning what kind of people to recruit as students and how to arrange the curriculum, social milieu, and governing authority of the college. In 1873 it adopted a revision of Sayyid Ahmad's original scheme, this one drawn up by Sayyid Mahmud upon his return from Cambridge.[37] A further modification came the following year, prepared by a subcommittee chaired by Mirza Rahmatullah Beg, a Benares vakil and ra'īs.[38] The three educational schemes help measure how much the later establishment of a living institution tended to refract the original ideas behind it.

THE IDEOLOGY OF RECRUITMENT

One important part of deciding who the college would serve was already taken care of: it would serve Muslims. The

[35] "Rū'idād-i ijlās-i majlis-i khazānat ul-bazā't li tāsīs Madrasat ul-'ulūm Musalmānān" (July 31, 1872), TA, 15 Jamādī us-Ṣānī, 1289 H.

[36] "Rū'idād-i ijlās-i ṣadr kamiṭī khvāstgār-i ta'līm-i Musalmānān-i Hindūstān" (May 12, 1872), TA, 15 Rabī' us-Ṣānī, 1289 H.

[37] Sayyid Mahmud, "A Scheme for the Proposed Mohammedan Anglo-Oriental College," included in the proceedings of the M.A.O. College Fund Committee, February 10, 1873, SDAA, pp. 222-237.

[38] *Ṭarīqah-i intiẓām o silsilah-i ta'līm o tarbiyat jō mujvazah-i Madrasat ul-'ulūm Musalmānān kē liyē tajvīz hūā* ([Lucknow?]: Naval Kishore, 1873). I am indebted to Faruq Jalali for calling this to my attention.

assumption behind the whole enterprise was that there existed a definable entity, the Muslims of India, and that they were "behind" the non-Muslims in acquiring English education. When a few essay writers in Sayyid Ahmad's contest pointed out that the percentage of Muslims in educational institutions as well as in government jobs in the North-Western Provinces was well in excess of the Muslim proportion of the population, their arguments were dismissed as irrelevant.[39] The issue was one of ideology, not statistics—how the founders of Aligarh perceived their society and the categories of people they chose to portray as competitive entities. The proportion of English-educated Muslims in terms of the total population was beside the point, not only because the actual number was so infinitesimal, but simply because there were fewer Muslims than Hindus. True, Muslims of the North-Western Provinces were less than fifteen percent of the population, and only one-third even of the urban population; nevertheless, it was reasonable to expect Muslims to make up at least half of the school population.

> India is originally the native Country of the Hindoos; in India as, in other countries, there are several low tribes, such as Bhangís, Chamars, Bheels, Pharsias, Kanjars, Barbarias; these tribes being the inhabitants of India, are all reckoned among the Hindoos. Now the Muhammadans are not the original inhabitants of this Country. People of the higher and middle Classes, having emigrated from their fatherland, came to settle in India, and their descendants occupied a large portion of the country, adding to their number many Hindoos such as Rajpoots &c., not of the lowest class, who became Muhammadans. . . . If the proportions between the Hindoos and Muhammadans of equal ranks be ascertained a correct conclusion might perhaps be arrived at, but the members [of the committee] still doubt whether the inference thus drawn will be altogether correct, as amongst the Muhammadans who came to reside

[39] *Report of the Select Committee*, p. 4.

> in this country, the number of families whose profession was learning was large, and thus the proportion of learned Muhammadans was larger than that of Hindoos of the same class.[40]

Against this statement one could point out that the Muslims of the North-Western Provinces and Oudh were overwhelmingly poor cultivators, petty traders, and artisans of indigenous descent; that only some six percent were literate, or about twenty percent of males over the age of five.[41] But it is more useful to consider the statement as a genuine expression of the self-view of Sayyid Ahmad and his colleagues, a self-view projected on to the entire Muslim population of India. It had been suggested by some essay writers that one objection to attendance at English schools was that they tended to mix children of sharīf families with those of the people (*lōg*). The members of the committee admitted such a view was widespread, although many spoke out against it as contrary to Islamic principles. The truth was that the idea of social hierarchy by birth existed strongly among the founders of Aligarh; they all counted themselves among the sharīf. Sayyid Ahmad spoke sarcastically about Muslims who were willing to pay the same respect to men of wealth as to men of respectable ancestry. Drawing on the style of W. W. Hunter, he depicted with great pathos the fate of the grass cutters of Tughluqabad, supposedly descendants of the emperors who built that old Delhi city.[42] Once again, the way to resolve the conflict between Islamic egalitarianism and Indian ideas about hierarchy was to assume that Muslims were by definition a ruling class; they were all descendants of the former rulers of India.[43]

Sayyid Ahmad's awareness of Muslim peasants, shop-

[40] *Ibid.*, pp. 4-5.

[41] D. C. Baillie, *The North-Western Provinces and Oudh*, Census of India, 1891, Vol. XVI (Allahabad: North-Western Provinces and Oudh Press 1894), Part I, 258-259.

[42] Speech in Azimabad, May 26, 1873, *Lectures and Speeches*, p. 82.

[43] See above, pp. 26-33.

keepers, artisans, and laborers faded out almost entirely by the time the M.A.O. College got started, but in his first formal scheme in 1872 he was still talking about a program that would touch all classes (*jamʿāt*), including the lowest (*ʿavām un-nās*). Following up ideas expressed while in England, he wanted to "inaugurate an educational system for future generations." Different groups, he argued, had different needs. There would be specialized courses of study suitable to government service, law and medicine, commerce, land management, and scholarship in arts, science, or religion. All would get a religious education as needed to carry out the obligations of Islam. Sons of artisans and other poor people would study in affiliated maktabs up to the age of thirteen; they would learn practical literacy, arithmetic sufficient for the needs of daily life, and simple theology. If such popular education could become widespread, Sayyid Ahmad commented, "Hindustan would no longer remain what it is. It would become a part of Paradise."[44]

Sayyid Ahmad's rhetoric was as comprehensive about geography as it was about economic class. His use of the word "Hindustan" slips back and forth in meaning from the Hindi-Urdu region to India as a whole. Although his efforts were with a few exceptions limited to the North-Western Provinces, Oudh, Bihar, the Punjab, and the Urdu outpost of Hyderabad, he freely cited All-India statistics, including Bengali-speaking Muslims with whom he had no contact whatsoever. His statements assumed that Hindustanis would provide the leadership for all Indian Muslims.

The founders of Aligarh spoke in the name of all the Muslims of India, but offered a program designed to make contact with a considerably narrower group: the north Indian Muslims literate in Urdu who formed the reservoir of Muslim intelligentsia and government servants. Geographically, this meant a huge spread, though not so huge as all of India. Aligarh was also to transcend sectarian narrowness includ-

[44] *Report of the Select Committee*, pp. 53-70.

ing both Sunnis and Shīʿahs among its students. After 1873, partly in response to Hindu donations, all plans assumed that there would be Hindu students as well. But when concrete plans for the college were formulated, the idea of serving the full socio-economic spectrum fell by the wayside. There was never any thought of educating women. Aligarh was for the ashrāf, men of the respectable classes.

CURRICULUM

The kind of people most likely to take advantage of English education at Aligarh or elsewhere were the sons of government servants, legal practitioners, and teachers. Would-be engineers were trained at the government engineering college at Roorkee for the Public Works Department; would-be physicians went to the Medical College in Lahore to become "Native" Civil Surgeons. As Sayyid Ahmad himself pointed out, an English education usually led to a modest teaching job, or a clerkship, or a small legal practice.

At the outset of the new educational movement, Sayyid Ahmad had hoped to attract wider interest in English education by going beyond contemporary perceptions of occupational opportunity in north India. One approach was to appeal to some accessible nerve of self-respect, to inspire people in the name of Islam: by ignoring opportunities for advancement, Muslims were failing to live up to the heritage of their ancestors and even the commandments of God. They were discrediting Islam itself. More positively, Sayyid Ahmad wanted to stimulate genuine intellectual excitement over new modes of thought. Throughout the 1860s he had devoted himself to the popularization of European rationalism, empiricism, and dynamism. Islam, he now argued, was consistent with these intellectual attitudes and had declined by ignoring them. Political subordination was the surest indication of this decline. The initial rationale behind starting a Muslim educational movement was to cultivate intellectual change. Since British-sponsored education had failed to bring about a genuine transformation in world-view, private individuals would have to take education into their own hands. By creating new institutions outside the world of British administration, Sayyid Ahmad hoped to discover new fields of ambition, such as industrial and commercial entrepreneurship.

As Sayyid Ahmad conceived it in 1872, the curriculum would consist of general education from ages thirteen to eighteen, followed by specialized study, supposedly analogous to the tripos at Oxford and Cambridge. At the preparatory level there would be four subject areas—religion, literature, mathematics, and natural science. Natural science, a subject neglected by British public schools, would deal with elementary physics; mathematics, with algebra, geometry, and "higher" branches. Literature was defined as including language, composition, history, geography, logic, politics, and various topics in philosophy. The course in religion would cover the life and sayings of the Prophet, commentaries on the Qur'an, jurisprudence, and general principles.[45]

These subjects could be pursued in either English or Urdu. Students hoping for high government posts would study in English: "The time was fast approaching when high proficiency in English would be the only path to high rank and position in the world."[46] At the same time the English department could train people capable of transmitting modern learning to the wider Indian public. Aside from English, these students would have to learn Latin and either Arabic, Persian, or Urdu.

But in 1872 Sayyid Ahmad was still committed to vernacular education. Learning in a foreign language only imposed a greater obstacle. With Urdu one could teach the same course of studies to more students, and teach them better. Students in the vernacular track would be able to complete the equivalent of the B.A. in arts and sciences by the age of eighteen. For a second language they could choose English, Arabic, or Persian up to the level of the Calcutta University

[45] *Ibid.*, p. 58.

[46] *Ibid.*, p. 61.

entrance examination. Thus the early planning tended to underemphasize linguistic achievement.

Having finished the general course of study, a student would be ready to embark on a specialized program. If his second language had been Arabic, he might continue in advanced religious studies; Persian would be more appropriate for people going on in literature. There would also be a wide choice of scientific fields, including engineering, animal physiology, anatomy, zoology, botany, geology, mineralogy, and chemistry. A student who had done his preparatory studies in Urdu might decide at this point to spend the next three years concentrating on English. This could be followed by another three years preparing for examinations in law, government service, or some other profession.

Such was Sayyid Ahmad's educational dream in 1872. Nearly a year later Sayyid Mahmud, just back from England, presented an equally visionary scheme, this time for an independent "university" or "dār ul-'ulūm." Students would enter the preparatory level at age ten and pursue the general course of study for five years. They would all have to do advanced Persian and elementary English. Arabic was to be optional, and there was no provision for Urdu language. (In his first proposal of February 1872, Sayyid Mahmud had called for a wholly Urdu medium of instruction, with English taught as a foreign language.) Besides language there would be geography, Indian history, elementary mathematics, and, of course, religion—but no natural science. To move on to the college department students would have to pass a matriculation examination by the age of seventeen. The college would teach "subjects which are not exactly of any practical importance, but which improve the mind." The major aim was "to change the mode of thought of our students, and thus to produce men who may afterwards prove as so many instruments . . . for spreading enlightened notions amongst the people at large." The Lower Department of the college would prepare students for semiannual and annual examinations and one equivalent to the B.A. at the end of four years. Students would attend three hours of lecture a day, one in language and literature, one in mathematics and physics, and one in a third subject. They would have to study two languages out of a list including Arabic, English, Sanskrit, Latin, and Greek. The mathematics and physics course would duplicate the one at the University of London, including integral and differential calculus, statistics and dynamics, optics, acoustics, and astronomy. In the third hour students would read general history the first year; logic, rhetoric, and political economy the second; philosophy the third; and natural sciences (chemistry, biology, and geology) the fourth. At the college level theology was to be optional. Thus, unlike the scheme presented by his father, Sayyid Mahmud's prolonged general education through the B.A. level. It gave greater attention to language, less to science and religion, and it dismissed popular education entirely. There was considerably less flexibility about differing educational interests and needs. In its basic contours, Sayyid Mahmud's curriculum was much the same as that of Calcutta University, but at a more ambitious level of difficulty.[47]

The real departure in Mahmud's scheme was his plan for an Upper Department, which students could enter after completing their B.A. At this level students would specialize. One field would be language, and it would include Zend, Hebrew, Anglo-Saxon, and Pali, besides the more routine classical languages. Other areas would be moral science, natural philosophy (science and mathematics), and Islamic jurisprudence and theology. After a year or two a student would take an examination and write a dissertation; he would then be eligible to compete for one of thirty fellowships. These fellowships would offer a stipend of six hundred rupees a year for seven years. Devoted to the promotion of research, they would not carry any official responsibilities.[48] In proposing this scheme to promote the highest level of scholarship, Sayyid Mahmud was drawing upon currents of thought

[47] Sayyid Mahmud, "Scheme," SDAA, pp. 222-237.
[48] *Ibid.*, pp. 234-237.

that were at that time transforming Cambridge University. But the idea was also in the tradition of Islamic scholarship, where students were often supported by stipends and guided by a love of learning.

The report of Mirza Rahmatullah Beg's committee, presented in 1874, retained Sayyid Mahmud's curriculum, but gave a student a number of options. He might prepare for the Calcutta University exams, and he could choose Urdu or English as a medium of instruction. Furthermore, it would not be necessary for a student to pass in all subjects in order to continue at the college; he might continue in the subjects in which he had been successful.[49] In general, Rahmatullah's modifications had the effect of returning to the ideas of Sayyid Ahmad: the curriculum should be flexible enough to appeal to a broad variety of purposes. The point was to reach as many people as possible with whatever kind of education they might be willing to pursue.

RESIDENTIAL AND RELIGIOUS MILIEU

The proposed residential framework for the college, rather than the curriculum itself, was what represented a real departure from the existing system of English education in India. What Sayyid Ahmad advocated was the creation of a "total institution," where young men would be cut off from ordinary life and raised in highly controlled surroundings.[50] "Unless boys are kept at a distance from home . . . they will always remain ignorant, worthless, and exposed to all sorts of evils."[51] There were in Sayyid Ahmad's view two kinds of education, *taʿlīm* and *tarbiyat*: one prepared a person for an occupation, the other was designed to bring out innate qualities of character. Neither was necessary to the other, and the problem with indigenous Muslim education—as well as with the English educational system established in India—was

[49] *Ṭarīqah-i intiẓām.*
[50] See Goffman, *Asylums*, pp. 1-124.
[51] *Report of the Select Committee*, p. 60.

that it left "the inner spirit dead."[52] Not just book learning, but the moral influence of a planned social environment would be needed to raise up the new generation. As Sayyid Mahmud put it: the teachers and students of the college would "form a society of their own, whose notions and objects should be different from the present day society of Indian Musalmans."[53]

Sayyid Ahmad called for the building of boarding-house quadrangles, each a world unto itself with dining room, mosque, library and reading room, debating club, garden, and playground. To wait on the boys, clean rooms, and make beds there would be boarding-house servants, but no boarder would have a servant of his own. Children from rich and sharīf families would be educated in the same way as those from more ordinary backgrounds.[54] "Just as the students at Oxford and Cambridge have to visit the Church and attend the prayers regularly . . . the students will have to offer the congregational prayer five times a day." They would all eat, play, and study together at fixed times. Relatives and friends would not be allowed to visit without special permission. Name calling was against the rules, as was any punishment that might insult a student's dignity. British students wore black gowns: so would the Muslim students—along with red Turkish caps. It would be forbidden to wear laced, colored, tight, or thin garments, long hair over the ears, rings, or scents.[55]

In Sayyid Mahmud's scheme only students above the level of matriculation would have had to reside in the boarding house. The Rahmatullah plan exempted Hindu students. It followed Sayyid Ahmad's earlier statements but amended the wearing of uniforms to permit students to wear the customary dress of their homes, provided it was the dress of

[52] *Maqālāt*, VIII, 15-16.
[53] Sayyid Mahmud, "Scheme," p. 225.
[54] *Report of the Select Committee*, pp. 58-59.
[55] TA, 1 Rajab, 1289 H.; translated by Professor K. A. Nizami in *Sir Syed Speaks to You* (Aligarh: Sir Syed Hall, 1968), pp. 13, 15, 17.

the ashrāf. Students could make separate arrangements for their meals, but still had to eat them at the scheduled hour. Aside from the accommodations for poor students, everyone would have his own separate room for sleeping, studying, and washing.[56] These modifications had the effect of making the residential establishment less like a collective pressure cooker, but not much.

The rationale for a Muslim college was that a proper Islamic upbringing could only be assured under Muslim auspices. English education was only acceptable if it was accompanied by religious instruction and supervision of the day-to-day lives of the students. Although Sayyid Ahmad conceived of a far-reaching program touching on every aspect of learning and student life, the subject that occupied his most intense attention was religious thought and practice. Reformist articles in *Tahẕīb ul-Aḵẖlāq*, as well as his other extensive religious writings, went hand in hand with his efforts to start a Muslim college. The preface to *Essays on the Life of Muhammad* states that "the work was specially intended for the use of those Mohammedan youths who are pursuing their English studies."[57] In the meetings of the founding committee he repeatedly demonstrated a vehement irreverence toward the commonly held pieties of Islamic practice, belief, and scholarship. Calling for abandonment of the standard madrasah curriculum, he wanted emphasis put on comprehension of basic principles and the study of scriptural as opposed to scholastic texts. Islamic classics in philosophy, logic, and natural science he dismissed as out of date.[58]

Already the target of strong criticism for the "innovations" of his London trip—the improperly slaughtered chickens, the Turkish dress—Sayyid Ahmad continued to antagonize

[56] *Ṭarīqah-i intiẓām*, pp. 28-31, where there is a good deal of detail on forbidden dress and hair styles.
[57] Sayyid Ahmad, *Essays*, p. xii.
[58] *Report of the Select Committee*, pp. 55-56.

sharʿīah-minded Muslims with a whole series of theological and ritualistic reforms: it was all right to wear shoes for prayer in the mosque, to participate in Hindu and Christian celebrations, to eat at a European-style table, to think of angels and devils, heaven and hell as metaphorical.[59] What he was asserting in the end was his own right to skip over received tradition and make his own interpretation of the original scriptural sources of God's revelation to Muhammad. Such thoughts were by no means original with Sayyid Ahmad; the tradition of Shah Vali Ullah, in which he himself had been schooled, made room for interpretation, *ijtihād*, in the light of new circumstances. But such interpretation was to be made by a qualified member of the ʿulama, one steeped in the scholastic tradition. Opponents were quick to point out that Sayyid Ahmad was giving unwarranted scope to the meaning of ijtihad; and, especially in view of his limited theological education, it was outrageous for him to set himself up as one of the ʿulama.[60]

Criticism of Sayyid Ahmad's personal religious views threatened, in fact, to undermine his whole educational movement. Several members of the committee that first considered the proposal withheld approval pending reassurance concerning the religious textbooks to be selected for the college.[61] The fact that Sayyid Ahmad was on the textbook committee did not reassure them.[62] But aside from these internal disagreements, the M.A.O. College campaign became the target of well-publicized attacks on behalf of orthodox Islam. The two most vocal critics, Ali Bakhsh Khan and Sayyid Imdad Ali, were not opposed to English education but to the spread of religious reform. Themselves

59 Ḥālī, *Ḥayāt-i jāvīd* (pp. 517-599) and Baljon, *Reforms and Religious Ideas* (pp. 76-119) summarize the religious controversies raised by Sayyid Ahmad; for Sayyid Ahmad's defense of shoes in the mosque see TA, 1 Muḥarram, 1289 H.

60 Baljon, pp. 106-114; Sayyid Imdād ʿAlī, *Imdād ul-āfāq binjām ahl-i vifāq ba javāb parcah Tahẕīb ul-Akhlāq* (Kanpur, 1290 H.).

61 *Report of the Select Committee*, pp. 71-72.

62 "Rū'idād-i ijlās," May 12, 1872.

not ʿulama, they were, like Sayyid Ahmad, long-standing servants of the British government and active supporters of local educational efforts. The intensity of their opposition may even have had something to do with factional rivalry within the kacahri milieu. Deputy Collector Sayyid Imdad Ali, another "loyal" Muslim of 1857, had been friendly in 1862, when Sayyid Ahmad was launching his Bible commentary and earliest educational activities.[63] When Sayyid Ahmad was receiving the "C.S.I." in London—thus adding to his bad reputation because the initials sounded like *ʿisāʾī*, Christian—Imdad Ali was acquiring the same honor in India.[64] Ali Baksh, a subjudge like Sayyid Ahmad, also received official British recognition for his work on behalf of English education.[65]

Imdad Ali started publishing pamphlets and then a regular journal attacking *Tahẕīb ul-Akhlāq* and calling on Muslims to boycott Sayyid Ahmad's movement. Meanwhile, Ali Baksh travelled to Mecca to get *fatvās* condemning both Sayyid Ahmad's religious views and anyone who would aid such a heretic in starting a madrasah.[66] Sayyid Ahmad responded to these attacks with anger and irony: maybe he was a heretic, apostate, or atheist, but the college was for the glory of Islam and his opponents were therefore doing harm to the religion. In effect, they were "demolishing a mosque simply because an unclean and sinful man sat in it."[67]

[63] Sayyid Ahmad to Imdad Ali, July 3, July 16, and August 3, 1862, in Mushtāq Ḥusain, ed., *Makātīb-i Sar Sayyid Aḥmad Khān* (Lahore: Star Book Depot, n.d.), pp. 6-12.

[64] For biographical information on Imdad Ali see *Imdād ul-āfāq*, pp. 6-7; Sayyid Ahmad expresses pleasure that Imdad Ali got the C.S.I. title in a letter to Mahdi Ali, London, September 10, 1869 (*Maktūbāt*, p. 69); on the pun see Ḥalī, *Ḥayāt-i jāvīd*, p. 177. C.S.I. stands for "Companion of the Star of India."

[65] Āl-i Aḥmad Surūr, *Naē aur purānē cirāgh* (Lucknow: Idārah-i Farogh-i Urdū, 1963), pp. 115-140; Niẓāmī Badāyūnī, *Qāmūs* II, 94; see also RDPI/NWP, 1871-72, Part I, p. 97.

[66] Ḥālī, *Ḥayāt-i jāvīd*, pp. 526-529.

[67] The statement comes quite a bit later (AIG, July 12, 1887), but is typical of the general tone of apology that Sayyid Ahmad adopted from 1870 to the end of his life.

To reassure the public, Sayyid Ahmad made every effort to portray his co-workers as men of immovable orthodoxy. His views—which he reported at great length in published committee proceedings—were by his own account listened to "with abhorrence" by all the other members.[68] By 1873, however, some further reassurance was necessary in view of increasingly vocal opposition. Sayyid Mahmud stipulated in his formal scheme that "No controversial point of Theology should be included in the course, and strict regard should be paid to choosing books which contain doctrines received in general by the Musalmans of India."[69] This reassurance did not command immediate confidence. Ali Baksh suggested that Sayyid Ahmad might be guilty of a feint toward orthodoxy in order to obscure his ultimate intentions once the college got started. Pointing out Sayyid Ahmad's dominant role in the movement, he asked for some further guarantee that the college would not eventually become a vehicle for unacceptable religious ideas.[70] Sayyid Ahmad replied by agreeing to an entirely separate governing body to supervise religious instruction and, furthermore, suggesting that Ali Baksh should be in charge. "The whole arrangement for religious education is on your head."[71] Mushtaq Husain, a man of notable piety, followed up this invitation by arranging a meeting between the two antagonists, as a result of which Sayyid Ahmad pledged to withdraw himself from all religious matters and Ali Baksh pledged to donate eight hundred rupees.[72] The agreement fell apart, however, when other members of the Fund Committee refused to disqualify themselves on grounds of guilt by association with impiety.[73]

[68] *Report of the Select Committee*, p. 57.

[69] SDAA, p. 229.

[70] Ali Bakhsh Khan to Sayyid Ahmad, n.d. (1874), SDAA, pp. 251-260.

[71] Sayyid Ahmad to Ali Bakhsh, AIG, July 17, 1874 (SDAA, pp. 260-262, dates letter June 7, 1873, but it is probably 1874).

[72] TA, 1 Sha'bān, 1292 H.

[73] Mahdi Ali to Sayyid Ahmad, July 16, 1873 [1874?], SDAA, p. 263.

By then Sayyid Ahmad had abandoned the hope of using the college directly to spread his religious ideas. Instead he decided to be safe and noncontroversial.[74] He even pledged to have no personal contacts with the students.[75] There remained some difficulty, however, in finding an acceptable committee—or rather two committees, one Sunni and one Shīʿah. ʿUlama remained unsympathetic; nor was there sufficient unity among them to make consensus a simple matter.[76] An invitation to the founders of Deoband met with an emphatic refusal: they would not associate with a college that had room for Shīʿahs.[77] The distinguished *imām* of the Aligarh Mosque first accepted, but then withdrew—taking with him several big zamindar donors, including the Navab of Chatari. In the end a highly orthodox committee took over Sunni instruction, though few were ʿulama, The Shīʿah committee, on the other hand, included Ciragh Ali, a man at least as radical as Sayyid Ahmad. Sayyid Ahmad suggested to the committees that they assign Urdu and Persian books as well as Arabic to cover the language options students might take.[78] Otherwise he stepped aside.

GOVERNANCE AND FINANCIAL CONSTRAINTS

According to Sayyid Ahmad, education suitable to Muslim religious needs could not exist under British management; it was a "moral impossibility." Aside from specific allegations about anti-Islamic passages in the government textbooks, Sayyid Ahmad argued that the whole enterprise of public education was "a grave political error": foreign rulers were

[74] See Wilfred Cantwell Smith, "Ek Savāl," *ʿAlīgaṛh Megzīn*, Aligarh Number, Part I (1953-54), pp. 81-83.

[75] TA, 1 Muḥarram, 1292 H.

[76] Nazir Ahmad to Sayyid Ahmad, Azamgarh, July 20, 1874, *Urdū Adab*, No. 2 (1971), p. 46.

[77] TA, 1 Ramẓān, 1291 H.

[78] Sayyid Ahmad to members of the Fund Committee, n.d. [1875], *Maktūbāt*, pp. 207-211; *Report on the Progress of Education at the Muhammadan Anglo-Oriental College, Aligarh* (hereafter RMAOC), 1875, p. 2.

inherently unable to take on the burden of cultural policy. By 1872 the idea of a separate madrasah had transformed itself into a dream of an entirely autonomous educational system of far-flung preparatory schools affiliated to a central Muhammadan Anglo-Oriental College.[79] With a curriculum that offered wider options in subject matter and medium of instruction, and that moved more rapidly into advanced levels, this system would make no effort to mesh with the government-sponsored schools. The new madrasah at Deoband had started with much the same independence in 1867, but without any pretension to covering non-Islamic subjects.

When it came down to it, however, Sayyid Ahmad was not prepared to reject the government's role altogether. He suggested that government should pay fifty percent of the costs of local Muslim schools if Muslims chose not to participate in government ones.[80] While seeking to limit the sphere of government power, the founders of the college also wanted to achieve access to it. The sequence of schemes for the M.A.O. College came before both the North-Western Provinces authorities and the Government of India with letters soliciting both state and private funds—a request that was greeted with a mixed reaction from British officials.[81]

One thing that put the British off was Sayyid Mahmud's plan for a "university," able to set its own standards, issue its own degrees, and "perfectly free from any control of the Government beyond mere supervision." Like his father, Mahmud summoned up the Victorian ideology of private enterprise in education in order to carve out an interstice of self-rule within the British Raj. In Europe, he claimed—rather inaccurately, on the basis of his observations in England—that education was mostly in private hands: "With how much greater force does this argument hold good in the case of India where the Government is almost wholly . . .

79 *Report of the Select Committee*, pp. 57-71.
80 *Ibid*., p. 70.
81 GOI, Home Department, Education (A), June 1873, Nos. 69-73; October 1873, Nos. 15-17.

different from us in language, in religion and in mode of thought. . . . It is next to impossible for the British Government in India to understand fully our wants with respect to education." The university might hope for some financial patronage from the government, but should not depend on it. There would have to be a self-sustaining endowment sufficient to keep the institution "independent of any external aid." But such a financial base could not depend on sporadic public charity. Once set going, the university would be self-financed and also self-governed, free of both government and outside public control. In Mahmud's plan the governing body would be the Fellows, the advanced research scholars, as he believed to be the case at Cambridge.[82]

The demand for a separate governing body to supervise religious studies undercut Sayyid Mahmud's proposal for complete academic autonomy. The Rahmatullah scheme vested governing authority in the M.A.O. College Fund Committee on behalf of India's Muslims. To carry on its work, this body would create subcommittees made up for the most part of nonacademic members. Another significant revision was the decision to have a British headmaster, though under the control of the governing bodies.[83]

Despite brave words at the outset about independence from the British government, it was no easy thing to carry off. Deoband, after all, trained ʿulama; but most people who might go to an English-style college would be able to find employment only if they met government qualifications. A college that failed to meet these requirements, no matter how good it was, would be a dead-end street. In fact, it would be a college without students. As Sayyid Ahmad descended from his dream, it was the short-range, practical view that took over. One by one the features of independence—a curriculum different from Calcutta University's, a vernacular medium of instruction, independence of government con-

[82] SDAA, pp. 236-237.

[83] "*K̲h̲ūd hamārī quam kō sab ṭarah kā ik̲h̲tiyār hō.*" (Our quam itself should make all the decisions.) *Ṭarīqah-i intiẓām*, p. 33.

trol—fell by the wayside. By and large he had to surrender in the area of secular control as he did in the religious. When the British government told him that he had a choice between having an independent college or university and getting government financial assistance, he was not willing to risk his chances of creating a viable institution.[84]

But it was not easy to get much out of the British authorities. For some years Sayyid Ahmad had been a vocal antagonist of the North-Western Provinces' Department of Public Instruction. *Strictures on English Education* and the report of the Select Committee that reviewed the essay contest both brought down emphatic refutations, particularly from Mathews Kempson, the Director. Kempson, who considered Sayyid Ahmad's criticisms a personal attack, suggested that he was untrustworthy, inaccurate, unrepresentative of Muslim opinion, and harmful to the cause of education.[85] He had little inclination to be of assistance. It was government policy to retrench on educational expenditure by cutting down on government schools and colleges, and instead making grants to missionary and Indian-sponsored institutions. But the condition of a grant was that the institution accept the standard rules about admissions, fees, scholarships, enrollment, attendance, and staffing, that it conduct itself according to the government curriculum and participate in the standard examinations.[86] Sayyid Mahmud's proposal for an independent university was unacceptable: there were only four universities in India, they were under official British control, and their jurisdiction was territorial. There was no room for a rival "university."

Despite setbacks and feelings of suspicion held by some

[84] Alfred C. Lyall, Secretary, GOI, to C. A. Elliot, Secretary, NWP, June 24, 1873 (GOI, Home Department, Education [A], June 1973, No. 73); Sayyid Ahmad to C. A. Elliot, Benares, July 24, 1873 (GOI, Home Department, Education [A], October 1873, No. 15).

[85] Kempson to Elliot, August 28 and September 3, 1872 (GOI, Home Department, Education [A], September 1873, Nos. 48-49).

[86] Grant-in-Aid Rules, Government Order No. 187A, March 28, 1873, RDPI/NWP, 1872-1873, pp. 135-138.

British officials, Sayyid Ahmad managed to get valuable assistance from the British government, assistance for which he was appropriately grateful. The reason for this encouragement was that he had good friends in high places. Most important was his old superior as Moradabad collector, John Strachey. First as Financial Secretary of the Government of India and then as Lieutenant Governor of the North-Western Provinces, Strachey cleared a path for Sayyid Ahmad's efforts. In July 1872, when the earliest scheme was presented to the Viceregal establishment, Strachey said it "deserves . . . every encouragement the Government can give. It does infinite honor to Syud Ahmed Khan—a man whom I have long been proud to call my friend."[87] As a result of this recommendation, the central government pledged financial support, and the Viceroy, Lord Northbrook, even made a private donation of 10,000 rupees. Later Strachey cut through bureaucratic interference to put the new college in possession of the old Aligarh cantonment parade ground as site for the campus.[88] And despite obstruction from the Department of Public Instruction of the North-Western Provinces, the M.A.O. College was made a special case with regard to grant-in-aid rules.[89] In thus overcoming British official opposition, however, Aligarh moved more securely into the orbit of the British educational system. The result of this official encouragement was to extinguish Sayyid Ahmad's role

[87] Note by J. S. (John Strachey), July 25, 1872, attached to GOI, Home Department, Education (B), August 1872, Nos. 38-45 (NAI); see also Strachey, *India*, 2d ed. (London: Kegan, Paul, Trench, Trubner & Co., 1894), pp. 205-206; for further negotiations between the Aligarh founders and the government see GOI, Home Department, Education (B), October 1875, Nos. 44-45; also in the same proceedings, February 1876, Nos. 21, 24-25; the Despatch Book, Secretary of the Fund Committee, 1872-1877, summarizes letters from the Aligarh Magistrate to Sayyid Ahmad, October 14, 1874 and March 1, 1875 (AA).

[88] *Lectures and Speeches*, p. 419.

[89] RMAOC, 1877, p. 4; copy of letter from officiating secretary, NWP to Director of Public Instruction, NWP, June 18, 1875, enclosed in a letter from Sayyid Ahmad to C. Robertson, Secretary, NWP, May 14, 1878 (98A, AA); Sayyid Ahmad to Robertson, August 1, 1878 (99A, AA).

as political dissenter, and ultimately the aspiration of making Aligarh into a genuinely independent center of learning.

An important reason why Sayyid Ahmad gave in to the British government was that money was not forthcoming from the Muslim public. The original plan was to spend nothing until at least one million rupees were in hand; the goal was a million and a half.[90] Sayyid Ahmad had had experience with public subscriptions from his various causes in the 1860s, and he knew that great sums of money had been raised in Britain. But there was considerable public skepticism about whether such a vast sum could be collected through voluntary donations, and considerable distrust over the fate of the money should the project fail.[91] In the first year of fund raising the amount pledged was about 75,000 rupees, of which only one-third had been collected. The subscription lists for the first 62,000 as printed in *Tahẕīb ul-Akhlāq* contained about 250 donations, of which 16 accounted for over 25,000. The big donors included the Navab of Rampur (5,000), Salar Jang of Hyderabad (4,000), some other navabs, rajahs, and zamindars, as well as Sayyid Ahmad and Sami Ullah, who each gave donations of 1,000 rupees and were to give much more over the years to come. The smaller donations came from a variety of north Indian vakils, ra'īses, and government functionaries. Except for Salar Jang and the Navab of Dacca, the donations were from the area between Patiala and Patna [92] (Figure 2).

The amount of money was sadly inadequate for the ambitious schemes of the founders. Sayyid Ahmad's plan had called for a system of affiliated schools so that local donations could be used for local needs. On this score, however,

90 "Qavā'id-i Kāravā'ī, Kamiṭī Khāzan ul-baẕā't ul-tāsīs madrasat ul-'ulūm ul-Musalmānān," TA, 15 Rabī' us-Ṣanī, 1289 H.

91 Ali Bakhsh to Mahdi Ali, n.d., SDAA, p. 212.

92 TA, 1 Jamādī ul-Aval, 15 Jamādī us-Ṣānī, 1 Rajab, 15 Ramẓān, 1289 H.

Figure 2. "Naicarī Jōgī" (Naturist Yogi)—Sayyid Ahmad Khan as a Snake Charmer. The snakes are marked "candah" (subscriptions), and their scales represent rupees. Cartoon from the *Oudh Punch*, August 4, 1881

a disagreement developed over whether to start "branch schools" right away, or wait till the whole apparatus was ready to set in motion. Mushtaq Husain, noting the slow rate of fund collection, pointed out the dilemma: the preparatory schools would lead nowhere if the college was not there to receive the prepared students. And since the college was not designed to pick up students from government schools, it could not start independently either.[93]

Clearly, however, one million rupees were far off; by 1876 only one-fifth of the goal had been reached and, in fact, the total sum collected by 1898, the year of Sayyid Ahmad's death, was only a little over 600,000 rupees.[94] Donations from the general public came sporadically over the years, and were largely earmarked for building costs. The annual operating expenditures of the college, which rose from 25,000 rupees in 1881 to 73,000 rupees in 1898, relied on the government grant (20-25 percent), tuition and boarding house fees (20-25 percent), permanent endowments of land revenue income set aside by Hyderabad State and the estate of Salar Jang (about 15 percent, increased to 30 percent after 1891) and smaller endowments from Rampur, Patiala, Vizianagram, Mahmudabad, and a wealthy commercial figure in Bombay, Muhammad Ali Rogay. Such support was insecure, often withheld, and sometimes terminated. The college established a small capital endowment of about 110,000 rupees, invested in government promissory notes that yielded less than 2,000 rupees a year.[95] Quite aside from raising the

[93] Mushtaq Husain to Sayyid Ahmad, May 7, 1873, SDAA, pp. 247-250.

[94] Note by Auckland Colvin, officiating secretary, NWP, December 9, 1875, GOI, Home Department, Education (B), February 1876, Nos. 24-25 (NAI); table of funds collected, 1873-1898, Muhammad Amin Zuberi, *History of the M.A.O. College* (Urdu ms., no title page, no date, in possession of the All-Pakistan Historical Society, Karachi), I, 100-101. My thanks to Dr. S. Moinul Haq for permitting me to see this.

[95] RMAOC, 1881; "Report on the Financial State of the M.A.-O. College," August 31, 1880 (AIG, September 4, 1880); Allahabad University Calendar, 1889; Principal's Annual Report, 1898-1899, p. 31 (AA).

odor of usury in apparent defiance of the sharʿīah, the money received from this endowment was not sufficient to suggest the slightest hope of financial independence for the college.

Sayyid Ahmad would have waited a long time, then, to initiate his educational proposals were it not for the more practical action taken by his kinsman and co-worker, Sami Ullah Khan. A man of "concrete things" where Sayyid Ahmad was a man of "dreams," as Khvajah Yusuf put it,[96] Sami Ullah decided in 1873 to start a "branch school" in Aligarh, chosen site for the future college. Sayyid Ahmad opposed this move as premature, but Sami Ullah set up a separate fund and finally got the M.A.O. College Fund Committee to authorize his actions. His argument was that people would give money if they saw that the school was consistent with orthodox Islam. The point was to get Muslims started on English-style education in a religiously acceptable atmosphere. With the standard government curriculum and a British headmaster, the school started classes in June 1875. This was the M.A.O. College. There were to be no branches.[97]

PERSUASION AND REINTERPRETATION

In the course of promoting and expounding his proposals, Sayyid Ahmad was forced to whittle down his original hopes and fit them to the demands of potential patrons and clientele. But this process of planning and revising left a residue of ideological commitment that tells at least as much about what Aligarh meant to people as the everyday workings of the college. Aligarh became a symbol. In numerous articles, in public speeches at such widely dispersed places as Patna, Mirzapur, Gorakhpur, and Lahore, Sayyid Ahmad set down arguments that had not been heard before, but have been heard ever since.[98] His effort to persuade Muslims

96 Khvājah Muḥammad Yūṣuf, *Izālat ul-auhām* (Aligarh: Muhammadan Press, 1897), p. 17.

97 RMAOC, 1877, p. 9.

98 *Lectures and Speeches*, pp. 78-157.

of the advantages of an institution based on a foreign model required him to translate the significance of that institution into ideas that were meaningful to his audiences—and to himself. He was involved in a subtle process of finding continuities with the values and ideas of his own culture in terms of tenuously analogous concepts in a foreign one. The result was a change in the meaning of both.

First of all, Sayyid Ahmad redefined the meaning of "qaum." The word had been a loose one for any group defined by a concept of common ancestry—"tribe," "caste," "lineage," "family." Now it referred to the Muslims of British India, not just north India but places as far flung as eastern Bengal and even the town of Trichinopoly in Tamil Nad.[99] Sayyid Ahmad continually emphasized that he was acting not out of self-interest but for the sake of *qaumī bhalā'ī* and *qaumī hamdardī*, the qaum's welfare and sense of fellow feeling. The term replaced the concept of *ummah* or *ahl-i Islām*, the people who had submitted to God, and *maẕhab*, the category of a religious group, sect, or school. It referred now to "Indian Muslims," an ethnic group. The closest English equivalent to qaumi hamdardi would have been patriotism; later the word "communalism" was coined to represent the concept. There was a territorial dimension, but most inhabitants of the territory were not included. The word "Muslim" would now apply to voluntary associations, membership lists, annual reports—all in a style different from the sense of shared confession and history that had united Muslims in the past.

But this mode of conceptualizing group identity had roots in the past. Unlike "Hindu," a Persian word and outsider's construct, "Muslim," one who submits to God, had always expressed a profound and conscious sense of identity. And this identity always had a corporate and political dimension: one was accountable to God as an individual, but the jihad of an Islamic army, or the *ijmā'* (consensus) of the 'ulama

[99] Speech in Azimabad (Patna), May 26, 1873, *Lectures and Speeches*, pp. 84-86.

were collective means of making worldly power conform to the will of God. Sayyid Ahmad frequently pointed out that Islam transcended the distinction between *dīn* (religion) and *dunya* (world): the one must manifest itself in the other. To him the triumph of Islam on this earth became bound up with the economic and social position of an interest group under a colonial regime.

What Sayyid Ahmad emphasized was not conformity to the example of Muhammad, the *sunnah*, but the concepts *ʿizzat* (honor) and *daulat* (prosperity). Here he was influenced by the findings of Hunter and a Government of India enquiry into the condition of Muslims throughout India.[100] But he was also basing what he said on beliefs about the rightful attributes of ancestry (*nasl*) and social status. Thus his tears for the grass cutters of Tughluqabad. Appealing to his audiences as members of the ashrāf and descendants of the former rulers of India, he called upon them to act in conformity to their hereditary rank. Their ability to do so would manifest itself in wealth, power, and the deference of others. Indian Muslims would join the British as the rulers of India. Muslims had "fallen" because they had neglected the cultivation of the virtues associated with their position in society, especially the sense of social duty and the acquisition of knowledge. They claimed to be acting in conformity with received practice, *taqlīd*, but what they had received was itself a corruption. Now, since the world had changed, they must take drastic steps to recover what they had lost.

In Islam, knowledge (*ʿilm*) was the basis for all actions or decisions. Men of knowledge, the ʿulama, were the arbiters of conduct and belief. Knowledge was obtained by studying books with learned teachers, books that explained what God's revelation to Muhammad meant in people's lives. But ʿilm was also a kind of spiritual electricity, communicated by the touch of men who possessed it. Adjuncts of this spiritual knowledge were the whole range of classical Greek and

[100] *Ibid.*, pp. 78-80.

Arabic sciences from algebra to zoology, all of which enhanced man's understanding of God's order. It was in the context of such beliefs that Sayyid Ahmad spoke of the need to acquire knowledge, and if the knowledge he spoke of was derived most immediately from nineteenth-century Europe, it still had the same kind of power. And, once again, this power would be manifest in the prosperity and social position of those who held it. "Ignorance is the mother of poverty."[101]

To create a society in accordance with God's commandments Muslims established social institutions—mosques, maktabs, madrasahs, khanqahs. A Muslim must pray in the mosque side by side with other Muslims under the leadership of an imām. The same was true for the acquisition of knowledge: there must be a physical institution, involving communal effort and a set discipline. This was why the holding of a bi'smi'llāh ceremony for initiating a four-year-old boy to study was a public act. But according to Sayyid Ahmad, Indian Muslims had kept the ceremony and forgotten its purpose; they spent fortunes on the feast and nothing on the education to follow. Once again Sayyid Ahmad's madrasah was to be a return. And the insistence that every aspect of life be controlled, that dress and the hours of the day follow rules—all this was consistent with the Islamic belief that social conformity represented obedience to the example of Muhammad's original community of Muslims. The only difference was that Sayyid Ahmad fused this kind of social discipline with British public-school practices and Turkish caps.

Finally, it was consistent with Islamic values to join together in a united public enterprise. The collection of funds had its basis in *zakāt*, the giving of alms, which was one of the five pillars of the faith. The institution of *vaqf* existed for the endowment of educational institutions. In traveling about, making speeches, trying to inspire Muslims with a sense of their religious duties, Sayyid Ahmad was acting like thou-

[101] *Ibid.*, p. 84.

sands of Muslim leaders before him, such as his namesake from Bareilly who earlier in the century had gathered together funds, arms, and men for the sake of jihad. To the later Sayyid Ahmad, jihad meant organized social action on behalf of the ʿizzat of the Muslims, rather than the military imposition of an Islamic world order. The task for this age of Muslims, he argued, was the advancement of learning. The means, quite specifically, was the Muhammadan Anglo-Oriental College at Aligarh.

IV

Aligarh: A Planned Community

THE SITE

WHY Aligarh? Located eighty miles from Delhi, fifty miles from Agra, less than forty from Mathura and Brindaban, Aligarh was a place armies had been passing through for thousands of years—and, if they had any luck at all, leaving well behind. Aligarh was the most recent name for the eighteenth-century fortress four miles north of the old town of Koil, but under British rule the town and surrounding district came to be known by that name too. Koil's most striking feature was the Balai Qila, a large, steep mound in its center, the accumulation of a succession of settlements going back at least as far as the Buddhist Kushanas of the first century. Later came the Dor Rajputs, then Qutbuddin Aibak, the Turkish slave who conquered north India at the end of the twelfth century. A temple was torn down, a tall minar constructed from the old Hindu stones—to be demolished in turn by the British in 1862. Overshadowed by its famous neighbors, Aligarh made no political or architectural mark for six hundred years of Muslim rule. A semiautonomous Mughal official carved out a seat of power there in the early eighteenth century, rebuilt the mosque at the top of the mound out of the coarse local limestone called *kankar*; at sunset, seen from a distance through the gray-reddish dust of the town, that undistinguished building looked awesome, almost like one of the great mosques of Istanbul. Then descended in breathless succession a series of marauding and occupying regimes—the Jat kingdom, driven out by the

Afghans, replaced by the Mughals, taken over by the Marathas, given over to a sequence of French soldiers of fortune, and then conquered by the British in 1803.[1]

By the time the British took possession, Aligarh and its surrounding countryside had declined considerably. Politically unimportant but agriculturally quite prosperous in Mughal times, the area of cultivation had contracted drastically during the eighteenth century. British efforts to improve the situation, notably construction of the Ganges Canal in the 1840s, were of dubious value. Aligarh was located in a topographic depression between the Ganges and Jumna rivers, but not very near either of them. Canal irrigation only tended to saturate the poorly drained territory, leaving fly-infested pools and salt-laden soil. By the latter part of the century, however, drainage cuts helped restore agricultural production to the Mughal level. But meanwhile, the heavy forest of the area had been ravished as farmers sought new lands to take best advantage of British irrigation efforts and the expanded market for crops such as indigo and cotton. The long expanse of flatness was now broken only by an occasional sand ridge rising above the plane, a small cluster of neem or pipal trees at a village settlement, or the ruins of a zamindar's mud fort.

With the disappearance of the forest also went most of the wild animals; now wolves, leopards, nilgai, jackals, foxes, boars, or porcupines rarely came into human sight. But there were plenty of monkeys, and one result of the poor drainage was the creation of ponds where beautiful flocks of waterbirds would congregate during the cold, sometimes rainy months from October to March. Then the fields were filled

[1] Sources for the history and geography of the region are H. B. Nevill, *Aligarh: A Gazetteer* (Allahabad: Government Press, 1909); H. F. Hirt, "Aligarh, U.P.: A Geographic Study of Urban Growth" (Ph.D. dissertation, Syracuse University, 1955); see also Sayyid Ahmad, "The Minaret Situated at Koil," AIG, May 17, 1887. Most of all, I am indebted to Professor S. Bashiruddin, who frequently took me along on his daily walks at dawn, throughout the various seasons of the year.

for miles with golden wheat, scattered bits of pulses and sweet peas, barley and gram, and also a little tobacco. After the winter harvest came hot, dry months and dust storms that turned the land to khaki, the color of dust. Monsoon rains would break in July, making possible a second harvest of cash crops, indigo and cotton, as well as some American corn, sugar, rice, and hemp.

Indigo had been the big crop in the early nineteenth century, and Aligarh had drawn quite a number of permanently settled European planters. A speculative bust forced many of them out in the 1830s, but the local lawyers and money lenders who took over their lands carried indigo cultivation to further heights in the closing decades of the century. Cotton was even a bigger crop, and was tied in with adjunct town industries such as ginning and weaving, sometimes capitalized by British firms but often in the hands of local entrepreneurs such as the vakil Khvajah Muhammad Yusuf, one of the founders of the Aligarh College.[2]

The prosperity of cash-crop agriculture gave new prominence to the town, now economic center for a 2,000-square-mile hinterland, and headquarters for British judicial and revenue administration. By the 1870s, Aligarh had a population of 60,000. The inner town, Koil proper, was a set of concentric circles focused on the Balai Qila mound at the center. Most thickly settled within what used to be the first wall of the town, it was a helter-skelter bunching of winding, narrow lanes, fronted by earthen shop platforms at the foot of low, two-story buildings, all skirted by the open sewage that gathered at the foot of the Balai Qila. The area was thick with mosquitoes and flies. From here the town expanded, comprising in all twenty-seven muhallahs, the outer ones called sarais in memory of their function in Mughal times. These neighborhoods took their names from the jatis, lineages, occupational groups, or bazaar people who inhabited them. The Muslim groups, forty percent of the town,

[2] Nevill, *Aligarh*, p. 60.

consisted of weavers, fruitsellers, lockmakers—since mid-century an Aligarh specialty—butchers, and a few religious teachers, mostly from a group claiming both Afghan and Jewish descent, the Bani Israil. These were what the British called "the low Musalman rabble"; they had, for example, joined the "jihad" of 1857.[3] They were to have little to do with Sayyid Ahmad Khan. At the outer edge of the town was another class of Muslims, somewhat more well disposed, the lawyers and some rural landholders who had established interests in Koil.

North of the town, across the Grand Trunk Road that connected Aligarh with Delhi and Peshawar to the north and Allahabad and Calcutta to the east, was an entirely different area—the "station," Aligarh proper. From 1821 to 1869 the area half way between Koil and the old fort was a military cantonment with barracks for the soldiers, bungalows and gardens for the officers, a parade ground, and shops. Closer to the town were the "civil lines," which included a church, race track, theater, post office, and a large jail. There was also a post office workshop where postal equipment such as scales and mail bags were manufactured. This was, most important, the section where the kacahri, the courts and the collectorate, was located. Nearby were the houses of British civilian officials—collector, judge, policeman, engineer. And in similar houses—large bungalows with wide verandahs and thatched roofs—lived private British persons, in particular those involved in indigo. For all of these people there was an English club.

When Sayyid Ahmad Khan was transferred from Ghazipur in 1864 he had never before seen Aligarh.[4] That was the year the railway was opened up, connecting his native city of Delhi with the British capital at Calcutta. Aligarh was on the main line; Ghazipur, previously important in the

[3] *Ibid.*, p. 186.

[4] Sayyid Ahmad, "The Minaret."

Ganges river trade, was not. The railway shifted the economic center of gravity west, into the old Mughal heartland. In Aligarh Sayyid Ahmad found an enthusiasm for his educational efforts that he had not previously encountered. Here were well-to-do landholders, some of them newly created in return for backing the winner in 1857, who were ready to participate in his Scientific Society. Originally it was intended that the Society would find its permanent home in Allahabad, once its founder retired from his peripatetic career.[5] But within a year a permanent building was started just on the edge of the military parade ground, and the *Aligarh Institute Gazette* was coming out weekly on Sayyid Ahmad's private printing press. It was here that he succeeded in getting the government to establish a local education committee. Before leaving the place to take up his next assignment in Benares in 1867, Sayyid Ahmad had bought himself a bungalow near the new Institute building.[6] When he returned from England he only paid a pro forma visit to Delhi, and then went to Aligarh to spend a few weeks before taking up his Benares post.[7] The tragedy of Delhi, both personal and historical, had been decisive: "I left my relatives and beloved city"; the town of Aligarh was to be his home.[8] Or rather the civil station of Aligarh, for in Koil Sayyid Ahmad was always an outsider.

So Sayyid Ahmad must have been predisposed to making Aligarh the site of the central Muslim college. But to be consistent with open, deliberative procedures, this decision was to be reached by consensus. As with the essay contest, the question was opened to the public; Sayyid Ahmad placed

[5] See above, pp. 79-80.

[6] *Lectures and Speeches*, p. 405; interviews with Dr. and Mrs. Jamil Khwaja, who live in the house. This house was sold to Sami Ullah when Sayyid Mahmud bought a new bungalow further to the north and east of the kacahri. Sayyid Ahmad lived in this latter house as Honorary Secretary of the college.

[7] Sayyid Ahmad to Mahdi Ali, London, May 27, 1870, *Maktūbāt*, p. 115.

[8] AIG, July 12, 1887.

announcements in newspapers and sought opinions from a variety of sources.[9] What seemed important was that the place be centrally located so that it could draw the widest possible patronage. Sayyid Ahmad, remembering the distractions of his youth, also wanted to avoid such major old cities as Delhi. He preferred a small town—accessible but also isolated. Students should not have contact with the outside world, especially the world of pigeon keeping, kite flying, and courtesans. "The students should have as few temptations as possible, . . . their thoughts and notions, instead of wandering astray, should take a turn to calmness and serenity."[10]

There was, however, some support for Allahabad, the new provincial capital. Sayyid Ahmad had no personal connection with the place, but several members of the committee were vakils at the High Court. One drawback was that Allahabad already had, since 1870, a new central government college, a tough competitor. Agra was also mentioned, but it had the drawbacks of both Allahabad and Delhi—three colleges and numerous brothels. In Aligarh the competition was on a smaller scale; there was, for example, a new district high school. Admittedly, Aligarh was not a famous town, but the college would bring it fame—like Oxford and Cambridge.[11]

There was good reason for placing the college in the western part of Hindustan, an area strengthened and made more accessible to all parts of India by the new railway. Here there was hope of reaching up into Delhi and the Punjab as well as the North-Western Provinces and Oudh. The British government had plans to retrench the colleges in Delhi, Bareilly, and perhaps Agra; there was none in important northern towns like Moradabad, Saharanpur, Muzaffarnagar, and Meerut, all places with large Muslim populations and wealthy

[9] TA, 1 Jamādī ul-aval, 1289 H.; see SDAA, pp. 168-169, 178-179, 184-185.

[10] Proceedings, M.A.O. College Fund Committee, November 8, 1872 (AIG, November 29, 1872).

[11] *Ibid.*

Muslim zamindars. This area, the Rohilkhand, was connected through a branch line to the main railway in 1872; the junction was Aligarh.[12]

In 1872, Sami Ullah Khan left private law practice in Allahabad to take up Sayyid Ahmad's old post as subordinate judge at Aligarh. One of the clerks in his court was Mushtaq Husain, who came from Moradabad District. Among the permanent residents was the vakil Khvajah Yusuf, who was anxious to have the Muslim College in Aligarh. An active local version of the M.A.O. College Fund Committee also included members of two branches of the Shervani family, and there was "some hope (though a meagre one)" of drawing in other wealthy zamindars from the districts of Aligarh and Bulandshahr, such as the Navabs of Pahasu, Pindrawal, and Chatari.[13] A number of them had been participants in the Scientific Society.

Another attraction of Aligarh was the availability of revenue-free land. In 1869 the military camp was abolished because of the presence of malaria and the absence of adequate water.[14] Some villages that adjoined the camp had already been confiscated and demolished in retaliation for the 1857 Revolt.[15] A number of private English residents of the civil station were leaving and selling their houses.[16] Thus, with many usable buildings and open land, it was an excellent place to start a college—except for a little malaria. And according to the British Civil Surgeon, malaria was not in fact so serious a threat, far less so than in the Rohilkhand cities. "Allygurh is one of the healthiest Stations in the North Western Provinces." There was also some cholera, but it was not

[12] *Ibid.*

[13] *Ibid.*; SDAA, pp. 153, 178-179, 181-182, 184.

[14] Nevill, *Aligarh*, p. 205.

[15] Papers connected with suit filed against the college in 1876 over possession of the village of Bhomala, leveled by the British government in March 1858, in Sayyid Ahmad to District Collector, Aligarh, February 27, 1877 (23a A, AA).

[16] Advertisements in AIG, e.g., January 14, 1882.

as bad as elsewhere.[17] In the years to follow Aligarh was to have its share of floods, droughts, and epidemics, but few places were free of such disasters. Good, healthful climate was one of Aligarh's selling points.

For all these reasons Sayyid Ahmad formally recommended Aligarh as the site for the college; the Fund Committee ratified the choice in February 1873. When Sami Ullah Khan and his Aligarh committee decided to defy Sayyid Ahmad and open a school, they purchased three of the old cantonment bungalows. Later, with the help of John Strachey, the college was granted the seventy-four-acre parade ground on the condition that the Public Works Department approve all new buildings and that the government have the right to resume the land if it were misused. The committee also purchased about twenty more acres of adjoining land. The college property, then, was located just north and east of the Institute Building, at the outer edge of the civil station (Map 1). It was about a mile to the railway station and beyond that, to the south and east, was the town of Koil. Roads on both sides of the site joined beyond the college land, further to the north, leading past the ruined residence of an eighteenth-century French mercenary and then on to the old abandoned fort. The Muslim College was to be built on what had become wasteland, "a piece of land rich in brambles, ruled over by jackals and serpents."[18]

In 1872 the British principal of Roorkee College turned down an invitation to be architect for the college at Aligarh.[19] From then on the planning of buildings and the supervision of their construction was the special province of Sayyid Ahmad himself. The Public Works Division reviewed plans for most of the buildings—those constructed on the government land—and the college employed a full-time man to

[17] Memo of Dr. James R. Jackson, Officiating Civil Surgeon, Aligarh, October 18, 1872, SDAA, pp. 202, 203.

[18] [Sayyid Ahmad], "The Mahomedan Anglo-Oriental College Aligarh and its Supporters," AIG, December 15, 1885.

[19] Principal, Thomason College, Roorkee, to Sayyid Ahmad, August 23, 1872, SDAA, pp. 188-189.

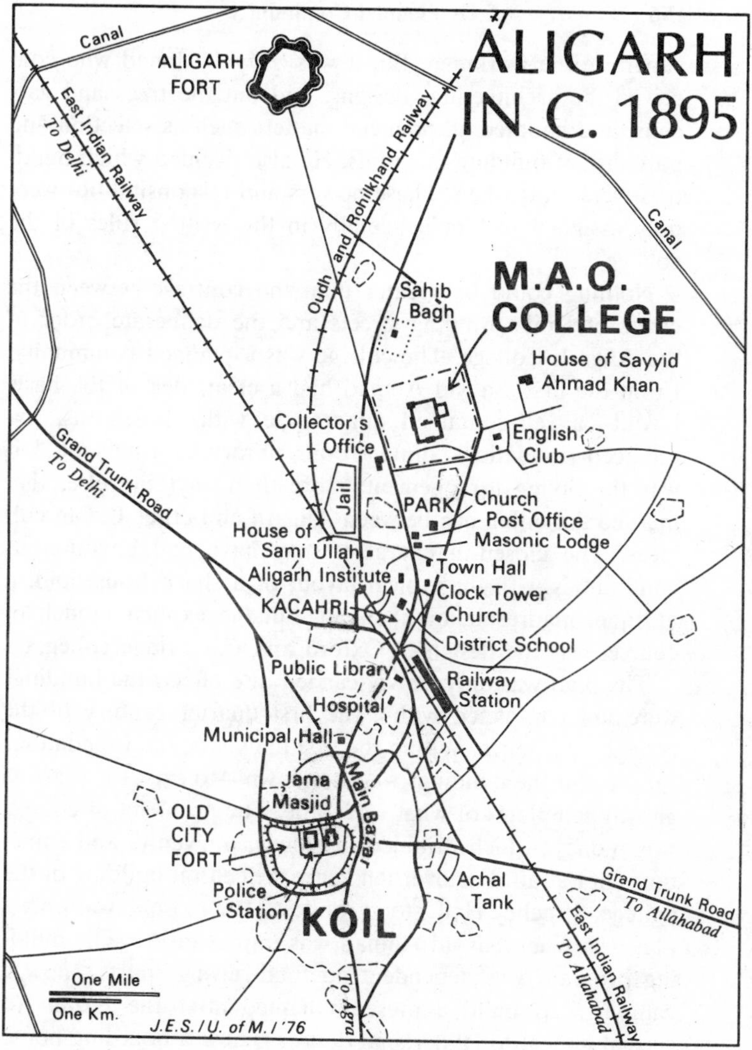
ALIGARH IN C. 1895
Canal
ALIGARH FORT
East Indian Railway
To Delhi
Oudh and Rohilkhand Railway
Canal
M.A.O. COLLEGE
Sahib Bagh
House of Sayyid Ahmad Khan
Collector's Office
English Club
Grand Trunk Road
To Delhi
Jail
PARK
Church
Post Office
Masonic Lodge
House of Sami Ullah
Town Hall
Aligarh Institute
Clock Tower
KACAHRI
Church
District School
Public Library
Railway Station
Hospital
Municipal Hall
Jama Masjid
Main Bazar
OLD CITY FORT
Achal Tank
Grand Trunk Road
To Allahabad
Police Station
KOIL
East Indian Railway
To Allahabad
To Agra
One Mile
One Km.
J.E.S./U. of M./'76

Map 1.

supervise the workmen. But it was Sayyid Ahmad who conceived the architectural designs, laid out the trees and gardens, and handled all financial matters such as selection and purchase of building materials. He also decided which buildings were built when. These powers and responsibilities were duly assigned to him personally in the written rules of the college.[20]

Nothing could be greater than the contrast between the chaos of Koil's winding streets and the deliberate order of the Aligarh College. The college was a planned community. From the first, Sayyid Ahmad had a clear idea of the basic layout—a self-contained quadrangle with classrooms, living accommodations, dining room, library, and mosque.[21] It was this living arrangement, more than anything else, that marked the difference between Aligarh and other Indian colleges. The closed-in character may have had unconscious continuities with the typical layout of a sharīf household, a mosque, madrasah, or khanqah, but the explicit model, of course, was the design of Oxford and Cambridge colleges.

The plan was only slowly carried into effect; the buildings were not completed within the first quarter century of the college's existence. Within the first ten years, the foundations for most of the buildings were set down—to exist for years as ghostly templates of what was to be. The problem, of course, was money, which dribbled in slowly, unevenly, and sometimes not at all. For over ten years the central building of the college, Strachey Hall, stood roofless. The mosque was only a platform when Sayyid Ahmad was buried in it.[22] The building program was dependent on fund-raising spurts—now a campaign to build a museum named after the Nizam (a special appeal to Hyderabad donors), now a boarding house

[20] AIG, August 4, 1877; W. Coldstream, "Sir Syed Ahmad (Some Reminiscences)," *Aligarh Monthly*, April 18, 1903; Sayyid Ahmad later stated that he had drawn up plans for the buildings while in London (*Lectures and Speeches*, p. 401); Sami Ullah to Sayyid Ahmad, March 6, 1875, *Urdū Adab*, No. 4 (1971), pp. 32-35.

[21] See above, p. 129.

[22] Photograph in the collection of Justice Mushtaq Husain, Lahore.

for Sayyids, or a classroom in honor of Queen Victoria's Jubilee. The major means of attracting donations was to offer people immortality in stone—for twenty-five rupees you could get your name carved on a railing of the outer wall, for five hundred it would be engraved on a marble plaque inside Strachey Hall. Above each student room would be the name of the donor, sometimes in English, usually in Urdu. Each fund drive would get publicity in the *Aligarh Institute Gazette*, which printed the names of the donors, but usually the effort would peter out, often leaving a partially built structure in its wake.

In the meantime the college had to resort to temporary measures—the old bungalows of the British cantonment continued to be used as classrooms and "boarding houses"; lines of kacca barracks—mud brick and low, slanting, tile roofs—and temporary walls to fill out the quadrangle enclosures. An effort was thus made to simulate the total concept before it was achieved, but the results were imperfect. The first building effort was to be a low stone wall to surround the college grounds and three fairly large entrance gates at different corners; ultimately two gates were built, and the wall covered only about a quarter of the college's perimeter. Originally there were to be two mosques—one Sunni and one Shīʿah; for most of Aligarh's first generation prayers were conducted on the ground under a tree.[23] The incomplete quadrangle had a tendency to leak students, who could slip out into the town without detection.[24]

Despite these shortcomings, the college designed by Sayyid Ahmad developed with a fine harmony of architectural style. The basic material was red brick and red sandstone, and the buildings had the strong straightforwardness that characterized their architect. The European element was most obvious in the simple gable-shaped roof of Strachey Hall, but the

[23] AIG, December 15, 1885.

[24] Boarding House Report, 1881, p. 7; Beck to Sayyid Ahmad, January 18, 1891 (AIG, January 20, 1891); Beck to Sayyid Ahmad, April 30, 1892 (AA).

pointed and cusped arches in the college buildings were Islamic, not Gothic. There were, in fact, few ornaments; the buildings were conceived in flat planes, like the earlier architecture of the Mughals. The most ambitious building was to be the mosque, designed out of a composite of Delhi prototypes, and decorated with old inscriptions from an abandoned tomb by the seventeenth-century calligrapher whose work appears on the Taj Mahal; white onion-shaped domes suggested on a small scale the Jumʿah Masjid of Delhi. But this building was not completed until World War I.[25] (Figure 3). The spirit of the place was simplicity, and in a day when colleges and railway stations were built to look like palaces, fortresses, or tombs, the Aligarh College did not pretend to be anything other than what it was.

Arriving, say, in the mid-1890s at the Aligarh Junction railway station, one was greeted by a crowd of thin, ragged *ekkah* drivers, heads wrapped in dirty turbans, all anxiously competing for passengers on their rickety, horse-drawn carts. To the west and south lay the town of Koil; the bridge over the railway tracks provided the best view of the big eighteenth-century mosque. On that side, but much closer to the railway station, was a new section of town, which included the district hospital and a new Hindi-oriented public library. But anyone going to the Aligarh College would head in the opposite direction along one of the two north-bound roads, the sides of a triangle with the college at its base. Taking the left-hand road, one would pass a series of public buildings on the west—first the District School and then the kacahri with its four separate court houses. On the eastern side of the road, just opposite the District Magistrate's Court, was a rather startling clock tower, elaborately decorated in the finest Indo-Victorian Gothic style. North of this lay park land, a town hall, Masonic Lodge, post office, and church. On the right side of the road, beyond the courts, the only major

[25] Sayyid Ahmad to Delhi Commissioner, April 15, 1886 (partly torn) (116A, AA); S. K. Bhatnagar, "The University Mosque—Its Forgotten Past," *Muslim University Gazette*, April 28, 1963.

Figure 3. Design for the College Mosque

building was the Aligarh Institute; further west, down a side road, lay Sayyid Ahmad's first Aligarh house, now the residence of Sami Ullah. The Scientific Society had ceased to function once Sayyid Ahmad turned his attention to the Muslim College, but the two-storied Institute building was still headquarters for the *Aligarh Institute Gazette*. In the 1880s it had been used for public meetings, political agitations, and British social gatherings. Now its main room was set up with benches for the M.A.O. College law class.[26] The room was much wider than it was long; from the small stage a speaker faced only a few long rows, and would have to pivot drastically right to left to keep in touch with his audience.

Continuing up the road, one reached on the right side an iron entrance gate to the college a mile from the railway station. Marked in English and Urdu with the name of the gate's donor (a pleader from Moradabad), and the name of the college, the simple brick columns on either side connected with the engraved railings of the outside wall.[27] Through the gate a road led north into the college grounds (Map 2). On the right was a garden thick with handsome trees and plants —several varieties of mangoes, oranges, flowers, and a well named for one of the Shervanis. On the left, beyond a small piece of garden, there extended to the west and north a large grassy field for cricket, which separated the public road from the college buildings. There was a spectator stand in the southwest corner of the field.

The college road bent east, away from the field running along the outside southern wall of the quadrangle. In the center of this line was a high, arched, partly marble entranceway

[26] Sayyid Ahmad to M. Harrison, District Collector, February 19, 1892 (35A, AA).

[27] The following description is based on [Ṯufail Aḥmad], *Muḥammadan Kālij Ḍairakṭaṛi* [Muhammadan College Directory] (Aligarh: Muhammadan Press [1895]), pp. 55-67; Sayyid Iftikhār ʻĀlam, *Muḥammadan Kālij Histaṛī* [*College History*] (Agra: Mufīd-i ʻĀm Press, 1901), pp. 227-251; Theodore Beck, "The College at Aligarh," *Cambridge Review*, V (1884), 178-179.

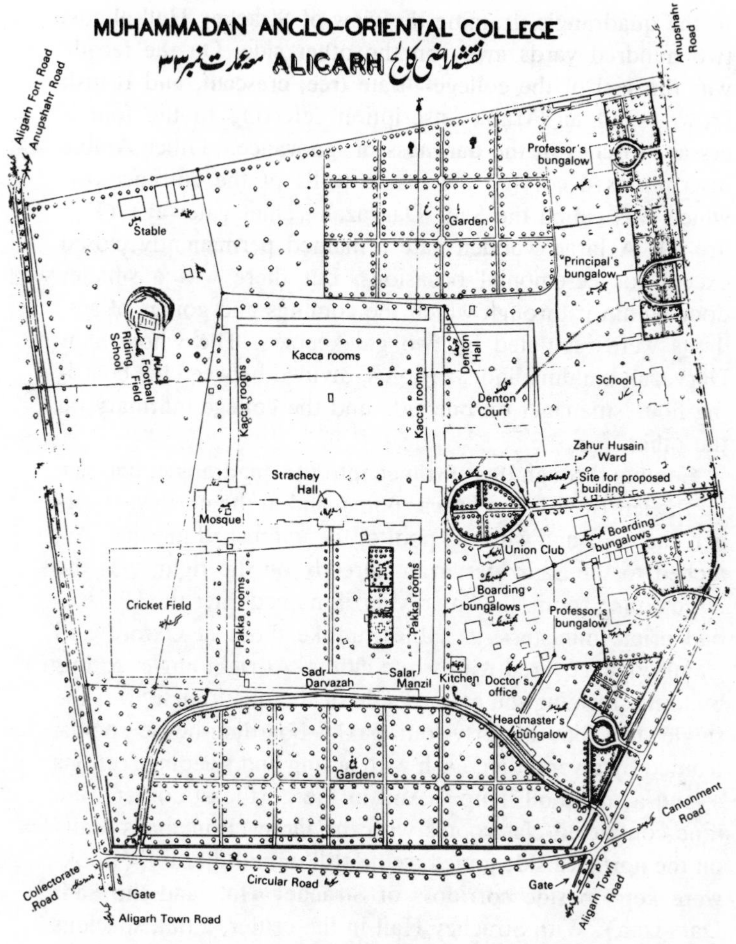
MUHAMMADAN ANGLO-ORIENTAL COLLEGE
ALIGARH
Aligarh Fort Road
Anupshahr Road
Anupshahr Road
Stable
Riding School
Football Field
Garden
Professor's bungalow
Principal's bungalow
Kacca rooms
Kacca rooms
Kacca rooms
Denton Hall
Denton Court
School
Zahur Husain Ward
Site for proposed building
Strachey Hall
Mosque
Union Club
Boarding bungalows
Boarding bungalows
Professor's bungalow
Cricket Field
Pakka rooms
Pakka rooms
Sadr Darvazah
Salar Manzil
Kitchen
Doctor's office
Headmaster's bungalow
Garden
Cantonment Road
Circular Road
Gate
Gate
Collectorate Road
Aligarh Town Road
Aligarh Town Road

Map 2.

to the quadrangle, framing the view of Strachey Hall almost two hundred yards away on the other side. On the facade was the seal of the college—date tree, crescent, and British crown—and an Arabic inscription referring to the founders as "torches in the darkness of ignorance." Other Arabic inscriptions decorated the inside walls of the entranceway, which was called the Sadr Darvazah (chief gateway) (Figure 4). A large wooden gate remained permanently closed except for ceremonial occasions, but there was a smaller door within it through which the comings and goings of students were regulated by two gatekeepers. The whole Sadr Darvazah building had six rooms, divided between the boarding-house manager on one side and the college infirmary on the other.

Coming through this entrance into the quadrangle, one saw on the left twenty-one kacca rooms, and in the northwest corner, the floor and washing pool of the unfinished mosque. Attached to the Sadr Darvazah, directly on the right, was the large dining room, the Salar Manzil, named after the Hyderabad prime minister—its tables, unlike those at Oxford and Cambridge, covered with white cloths. At right angles to this building, forming the eastern side of the quadrangle, was the single-story line of forty-four pakka boarding-house rooms, fronted by a verandah, each with sitting and sleeping sections —and a single oil lamp.[28] And in the northeast corner were nine completed classrooms with the large "Principal's Hall" on the northern side joined to the still unbuilt library. (Books were kept in side corridors of Strachey Hall and the Sadr Darvazah). With Strachey Hall in the center, a tall, spacious building, its assembly room some sixty by eighty feet (Figure 5), the northern side of the quadrangle was otherwise incomplete. On either side of this main building were gateways leading into the northern quadrangle, eighty kacca rooms on

[28] Sayyid Abbas Husain and Sayyid Asghar Husain to Collector, Muzaffarnagar, February 14, 1887 (AA). (These students were government wards and had to clear requests through the collector of their home district; they wanted an extra lamp.)

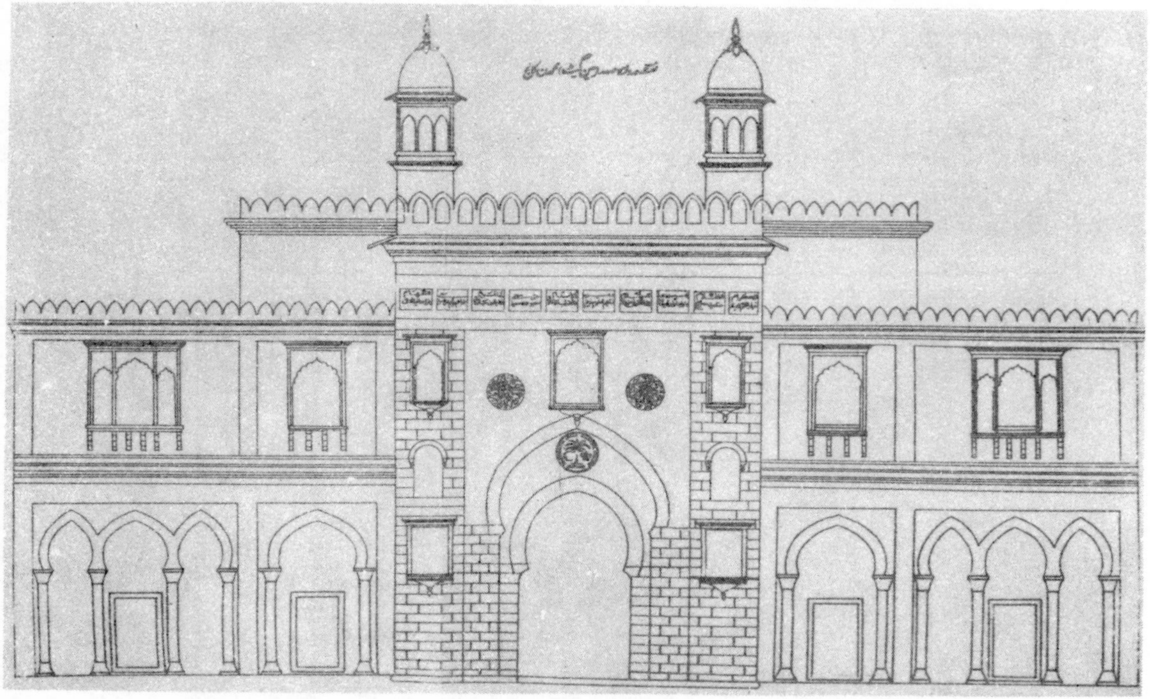

Figure 4. The Sadr Darvāzah (Chief Gateway)

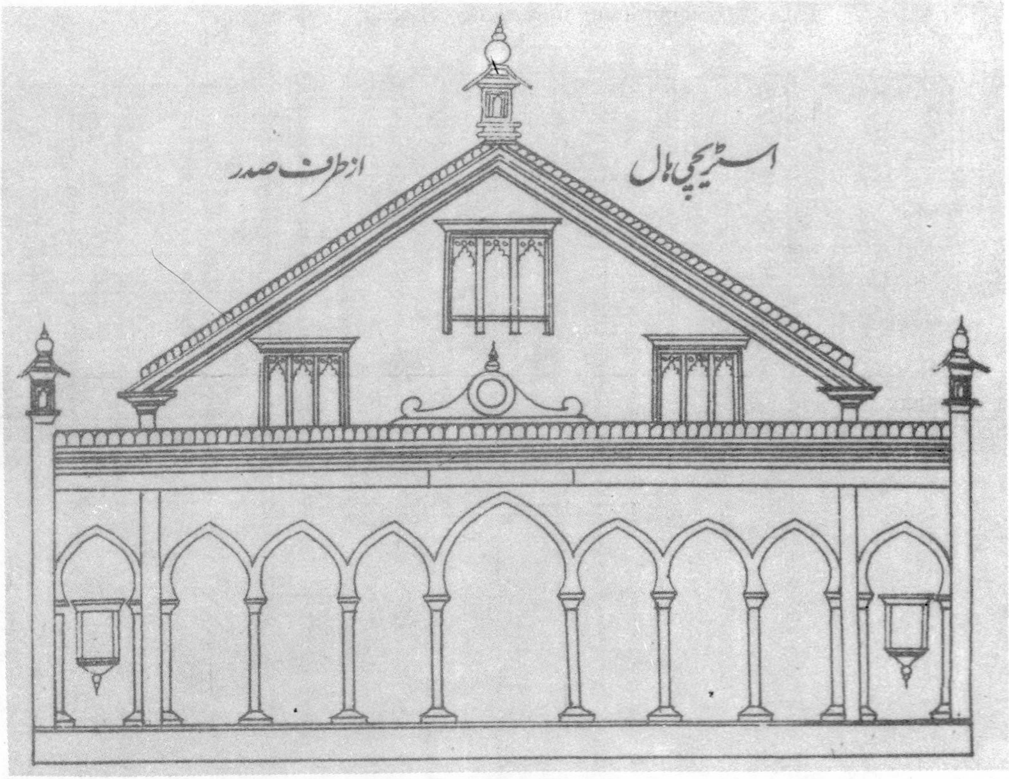
اسٹریچی ہال
از طرف صدر

all three sides. In both quadrangles the sizable grounds around which these buildings sat were fitted out with gardens —and latrines. Where a Cambridge college might be graced with a statue or fountain in the center of the quadrangle, Aligarh had an outhouse. The truth is, Aligarh was notable for its smell; the jails, someone said, were "sweeter." The latrines were poorly drained and overtaxed; but, on the other hand, students often used any convenient part of the college grounds.[29]

There were a number of other buildings outside and to the east of this quadrangle area. The original bungalows purchased by the college from former British residents were still very much in use. Six of them were boarding houses, some generally earmarked for Hindu students who ate out of a separate kitchen. There was also a large, old, dilapidated building used for school-level classes. Just east of the southern quadrangle was the Union Club, built in the early 1880s; it had a library, reading room, and main room for debates. North of this, two boarding-house courts were built in the mid-1890s for school students, one kacca and one, for the youngest boys, pakka. On the eastern edge of the college grounds, along the public road and amidst small gardens and orchards, were four thatch-roof bungalows for the European professors. Across the road was the Aligarh Club—exclusively for Europeans. To the south the second and more elaborate of the outer entrances led out to the eastern road, back to the railway station. Sayyid Ahmad's house, actually the property of his son Sayyid Mahmud, lay still further east.

Sayyid Ahmad managed the smallest details of building maintenance; he was the one the European professors notified when they wanted their houses whitewashed.[30] These houses were fitted out with servants' quarters, separate

[29] Theodore Morison, "Report of the Sub-committee to the Managing Committee on the Sanitary Arrangements of the M.A.-O. College," July 10, 1896 (332B, AA).

[30] W. C. Horst to Sayyid Ahmad, August 11, 1893 (AA).

kitchen buildings, and a *pankhā*, that long rectangular cloth fan pulled back and forth by a servant holding a rope outside the house. There were pankhas in the classrooms, too, but no servants' quarters; the college servants must have slept on the floor of the kitchen or verandah, or lived in the town. *Mālīs*, the groundskeepers, tended the gardens and pruned the trees to sell the branches privately in the town for firewood.[31] And when there was money in the building fund workmen came from the town to build. Water was supplied by wells and irrigation channels from the canal, but the sewage of the college had to be carried away in leather bags by "dirty water carriers" from Koil.[32] Food supplies, building materials, even some of the Indian teachers came from the town; and many students lived there too, attending the classes as "day scholars." At least one student kept a woman in the town until he was discovered and duly expelled.[33]

THE RECRUITMENT OF STUDENTS

The inhabitants of this planned settlement were to be students and teachers. According to the concept of education that the founders had adopted, students would have to come in a steady stream and pass through an articulated structure of academic levels: classes, examinations, and degrees. And their money, in the form of tuition fees, boarding house rents, and other charges had to come in a steady stream as well, in order to meet a significant portion of the expenses of the establishment. Most important if Aligarh was to fulfill its ambitions, the students had to stay on long enough to become full members of a community of shared values, divorced at least for the time being from the life of their families and the world at large.

[31] Theodore Beck to Sayyid Ahmad, December 31, 1896 (679B, AA).

[32] Sayyid Ahmad to Beck (as member of the Aligarh Municipal Board), May 13, 1896 (222A, AA).

[33] Sayyid Ahmad to the District Commissioner of Kheri, September 4, 1884 (374A, AA).

But attracting students to the new school was not easy; the founders were quite aware of the apathy, cultural resistance, and absence of incentive that stood in the way. Five years of publication and speech making before the college was even started had yielded only limited support and much significant opposition. A month before the opening, notices began to appear in the newspapers, but the managers of Aligarh realized that they could not rely on generalized publicity to gain students; personal connections among relatives and friends were more likely to produce results. The first student was the son of Sami Ullah Khan, Hamīd Ullah, eleven years old, who the year before had been introduced to audiences in the Punjab as an example of the kind of person the new institution would serve.[34] Some were relatives and friends of Sami Ullah and Sayyid Ahmad from Delhi; others were sons and nephews of old associates in the various kacahri headquarters of the North-Western Provinces. Inayat Rasul of Ciryakot delivered nine students, including seven from his own family, from the eastern end of the province.[35] In June 1875, the first month of classes, the average attendance was twenty-three; in December it was sixty-six, and about ninety students had entered their names in the register book during the year. Despite an early announcement of an admissions deadline, students came at scattered intervals throughout the year and were not turned away.[36]

Sami Ullah, whose well-publicized piety served as a counterweight to Sayyid Ahmad's unorthodoxy, was the chief recruiter in the early years; according to Masud Ali, there were few students who had not come as a result of his efforts. Such was the case with Masud Ali himself, whose uncle and guardian was persuaded to send the boy to Aligarh when Sami Ullah got the gentleman employment with the Raja of Pindrawal nearby.[37] Aziz Mirza's father, also an employee of

[34] Khwaja, *First Student of the M.A.O. College*, p. 4.
[35] RMAOC, 1875, pp. 6-9; interview with Muzzamil Abbasi.
[36] RMAOC, 1875, p. 2; AIG, April 30, 1875.
[37] Mas'ūd 'Alī, II, 130-131, 159-160.

a nearby magnate, the Navab of Pahasu, was bitterly opposed to his son going to Aligarh; but the boy went anyway at the urging of his sister's husband, an Aligarh vakil associated with Sami Ullah.[38]

At the outset, many students entered with only a maktab education similar to what their fathers had received. Masud Ali had supplemented this by starting the English alphabet with a retired munshi in Delhi; nevertheless, when he entered Aligarh at the age of fourteen he was put in the beginning-level elementary school class.[39] Hamīd Ullah had a more thorough preparation, had read through the Qur'an by the age of five and sat in the company of learned vakils and 'ulama. At the age of seven he started receiving private tuition not only in Arabic, Persian, and Urdu, but also in English. Zaka Ullah, mathematics professor at the new Muir College in Allahabad, started him on arithmetic; and Sayyid Mahmud, recently returned from England, spent a good deal of time with the boy in order to influence him with the spirit of English culture. When Sami Ullah moved from his private legal practice in Allahabad to his post as subordinate judge in Aligarh, he employed a retired government servant as tutor for his son and some other boys. Hamīd Ullah entered the M.A.O. College on its opening day at the age of eleven; within three years he was ready for the Calcutta University entrance examination, although still too young to satisfy the minimum age requirement.[40]

The new educational establishment had to start modestly as a precollege school with most of its students at the more elementary levels, but this was hardly adequate to support the ambitions of the founders and to build the reputation of Aligarh in the eyes of the public. Efforts were made to entice higher-level students from other English-style schools with promises of good preparation for the university examinations and the offer of scholarships, quite aside from the more in-

[38] Qamruddīn Aḥmad Badāyūnī, pp. 104-105.
[39] Mas'ūd 'Alī, II, 159.
[40] Khwaja, *First Student of the M.A.O. College*, pp. 1-8.

tangible benefits of the residential system and religious atmosphere. Announcing the opening of college-level classes in January 1878, an advertisement suggested that students might want to come from Bareilly, Moradabad, Saharanpur, Muzaffarnagar, or Delhi—all sizable towns with no colleges; in Delhi and Bareilly government college classes had just been terminated as part of an official policy of retrenchment. It was pointed out that the M.A.O. College had been able to send up four candidates for the Calcutta University entrance examination, and all four had passed.[41] The potential student clientele or their elders kept close watch on such information; a college that could pass a high percentage in the examinations was more likely to achieve respectable enrollment figures.

Sayyid Ahmad and Sami Ullah were reluctant to attract students with money—sharīf individuals would not be so motivated—but they realized the importance of producing some palpable statistics of educational success. It was with little enthusiasm that Sami Ullah took Sayyid Ahmad's advice and offered a ten-rupee monthly scholarship to a boy from the Shahjahanpur Government High School, where he had been in the second to the last class. Two students, from Delhi and Badaun, were drawn away with lesser scholarships.[42] Some years later Mir Vilayat Husain, the son of a poor family in Rewari, was attracted to Aligarh after doing his university entrance examinaiton; on the advice of a Hindu headmaster in his home town he answered an advertisement for an Aligarh scholarship.[43] Clearly such students had been willing to go to schools run under non-Muslim auspices. There is little reason to believe that students came to Aligarh who would otherwise have avoided English education on religious grounds.

Movement of students from school to school upset the con-

[41] AIG, January 1, 1878.

[42] Sami Ullah to Sayyid Ahmad, June 21, 1875, SDAA, pp. 271-273.

[43] Vilāyat Ḥusain, *Āp bītī*, p. 28.

tinuity of teaching and jeopardized the financial security of an educational establishment. Aligarh itself suffered from the comings and goings of such birds of passage. The government required transfer permission from the headmaster of the previous school, and this was often withheld pending the payment of all overdue fees, or merely to discourage such shifting. In 1878 the Aligarh management decided to admit students without collecting transfer documents, but some years later the Department of Public Instruction sternly informed Sayyid Ahmad that this practice would be grounds for suspending government aid.[44]

Aligarh was often criticized for attempting to raid and even absorb other schools and colleges. The most immediate competition was the government high school in the town of Aligarh itself; when the M.A.O. College was founded, there was some talk that the government establishment would now be superfluous. Sayyid Ahmad severely reprimanded Aligarh's English headmaster when he was caught making a private arrangement with his counterpart at the government school not to raid the town students.[45] Later on, Aligarh was accused of trying to replace Agra College, when the government decided to retrench its last university-level institution in the western part of the province.[46] Again in the 1890s, efforts to establish a Muslim College in Lahore had to overcome alleged opposition from Aligarh.[47] In all these cases, however, Sayyid Ahmad publicly disavowed any such intentions.

Although Aligarh was founded primarily for Muslims, it openly welcomed Hindu students both as day scholars from the town and as boarders in separate Hindu bungalows. In the first year the student body had been all Muslim, but thereafter there was always a significant number of Hindus. In addition to being consistent with Sayyid Ahmad's fre-

[44] AIG, March 9, 1878; cf. *ibid.*, July 25, 1885; E. White [DPI, NWP], "Inter-College Rules of 1889," (Printed Notice, 249B, AA).

[45] Sayyid Ahmad to Siddons, March 8, 1878 (29A, 30A, AA); AIG, February 23, 1878; RMAOC, 1879, p. 7.

[46] AIG, December 15, 1885; EC/NWP, pp. 325, 328, 411-416.

[47] AIG, March 5, 1895; cf. AIG, January 16, 1894.

quently proclaimed principles of fellow feeling between Muslims and Hindus, and expressive of gratitude for Hindu financial assistance to the college, the presence of Hindus added to the general enrollment and, in particular, the number of Aligarh students passing university examinations. In the early years a high proportion of the student body was Hindu; at the college level Hindus equaled or even outnumbered Muslims until 1889. Many Hindus came from outside Aligarh and lived on the college grounds. In the 1890s, however, there was a significant decline in the relative number of Hindu students, and very few of them were residential. By this time the college was usually full to capacity with Muslims, and there were more educational alternatives available in the region (see Table 2).

The intention of the college all along was to shift the balance of the student population in favor of Muslims living in the boarding house and preparing for university examinations. Until the 1890s the school-level enrollment overwhelmed the relatively small numbers in college classes, but eventually the gap began to close, particularly in the boarding house. The school attracted a large proportion of day scholars, both Hindu and Muslim, whereas day scholars in the college tended to be Hindus. By 1895 there were as many college as school students in the boarding house, and all but a handful were Muslim.[48] Until that time students at both levels and of all ages lived side by side; only in the 1890s were separate accommodations available for the younger boarders. Even within the same class there could be a considerable variation in ages: among twenty-five Aligarh high school students who passed the University of Allahabad entrance examination in 1889, the ages ranged from fourteen to twenty-one, with the median at seventeen.[49]

Aligarh's managers were quite aware that they could in-

[48] [Morison], *The Principal's Annual Report*, 1899-1900, p. 6; data on college versus school students in the boarding house was not usually reported on an annual basis.

[49] *Allahabad University Calendar*, 1890, pp. 248-249.

TABLE 2

Annual Enrollments, M.A.O. College, Aligarh, 1875-1900

Year	*Boarders*		*Day Scholars*		*College*		*School*		*Total student enrollment*[a]
	Muslim	*Hindu*	*Muslim*	*Hindu*	*Muslim*	*Hindu*	*Muslim*	*Hindu*	
1875	66[?]	—	—	—	—	—	66	—	66
1876	65	—	24	6	—	—	89	6	95
1877	64	—	49	12	—	—	113	12	125
1878	74	11	69	30	—	—	143	41	186
1879	[27][b]	—	58	30	8	7	77	23	116
1880	[91][c]	[9][c]	[?]	[?]	8	8	114	32	163
1881	150	22	36	65	11	15	175	42	244
1882	156	26	23	27	13	14	166	39	233
1883	156	26	36	27	13	14	179	39	246
1884	146	22	46	55	24	23	168	54	270
1885	142	18	45	53	19	20	168	51	260
1886	129	18	60	78	27	22	152	74	287
1887	105	13	54	74	19	22	140	64	237
1888	104	10	31	70	29	20	106	60	218
1889	142	9	54	53	42	23	154	39	259
1890	154	9	56	48	60	19	150	38	269
1891	182	12	56	58	76	26	162	44	310
1892	[206][d]	9	50	60	80	22	176	37	[316][d]
1893	228	3	72	55	[101][d]	20	199	38	359
1894	257	5	106	88	130	28	233	65	456
1895	322	8	135	101	168	37	289	27	566
1896	[333][e]		172[e]		168	30	249	58	505
1897[f]	[255]	[1]	[58]	[58]	[134]	[25]	[179]	[34]	372
1898	248	2	137	62	126	23	159	41	349
1899	311	2	63	53	157	17	217	38	429
1900	[352][f]	6	41	58	160	16	232	48	457

SOURCE: Iftikhār 'Ālam, *Muhammadan College History*, pp. 135-36 (except as noted in brackets). Day scholar figures have been calculated on the basis of the other data.

[a] Total includes Christians or Parsis not otherwise tabulated.

[b] Typographical error in Iftikhār 'Ālam corrected by reference to Theodore Morison, *The History of the M.A.-O. College, Aligarh* (Allahabad: The Pioneer Press, 1903), p. 60, and memorandum of Theodore Beck to Sayyid Ahmad, March 19, 1896 (AA). The low enrollments in 1879 were due to an epidemic.

[c] Iftikhār 'Ālam's figures are not consistent here; figures are supplied from [Sayyid Ahmad], *Rīporṭ sālānah kāravā'ī borḍing haus, Madrasat ul-'ulūm Musalmānān*, 1881 (Aligarh: Aligarh Institute Press, 1882), p. 6 (AA); these figures probably were taken at a different time of year from the school and college enrollments so they cannot be used to calculate the number of day scholars.

[d] Typographical error in Iftikhār 'Ālam corrected by reference to Beck's memorandum to Sayyid Ahmad, March 19, 1896 (AA).

[e] Hindu-Muslim breakdown not available.

[f] Missing data supplied by reference to [Theodore Morison], *Principal's Annual Report, 1899-1900* (n.p., n.d.), p. 6.

fluence the composition of the student body by manipulating the costs of studying and living in the college. Their ability to do so was limited, however, by Aligarh's financial needs and also by government rules that set down minimum fees and limited the granting of scholarships even in privately operated establishments. When the M.A.O. College opened, Sami Ullah instituted a sliding scale of fees according to the monthly salary of the student's father or guardian: students would pay one rupee a month for every hundred rupees that their fathers earned.[50] These terms assumed that fathers would generally be salary earners; it is not clear whether other financial resources were taken into consideration. In the first year, monthly fees ranged from four annas to five rupees, with a mean average of a little over two rupees, indicating a very well-off but not fabulously wealthy clientele.[51]

The charges for room and board that residential students had to pay were a separate matter, but here too a concession was made to varying levels of wealth. Aligarh rarely had sufficient accommodations to meet the demand, and this frustrated plans for creating a public school milieu or for drawing students from far-flung parts of India. In particular, it was difficult to provide rooms and food adequate for a wealthy clientele in the style to which they were accustomed. For the first two years students were put up in old bungalows or the homes of people such as Sami Ullah and the printer of the *Aligarh Institute Gazette*. Then for the next ten years, as the college quadrangle gradually materialized, students were divided among three classes of boarding-house accommodation, like the railways: a relatively larger number of kacca barracks (for second and third-class boarders) and a few pakka structures, set off by a line of nonresidential classroom buildings with Strachey Hall in the center. For most of the first dozen years of the college the three classes ate separately, with appropriately graduated charges. The basic costs for room and board in 1881 ranged from about

[50] Sami Ullah to Sayyid Ahmad, May 16, 1875, SDAA, p. 265.
[51] RMAOC, 1875, p. 3.

twenty-four rupees a month for the first class to eight and a half for the third class, with various gradations in between. That year among the Muslim boarders—Hindus had separate arrangements—there were forty-two in the first class, sixty-one in the second class, and fifty-two in the third.[52]

Despite the shortage of first-class accommodations, Aligarh made a particular effort to attract high-paying students. In 1885 third class was abolished, and two years later all students were eating together for the same relatively high price.[53] It was the special role of the college, Sayyid Ahmad maintained, to popularize English education among "the influential classes." In his first annual report he claimed that "gentlemen of family and position have sent their children from distant parts of the country to receive their education at this College, a fact which proves that the scheme of the Committee is esteemed by the people for the benefit of whose children the institution has been established."[54] And two years later he reported that it was not the increase of enrollment that was gratifying so much as the fact that it included "sons of respectable nobles and gentlemen of good family and position."[55] The next year, however, he had to confess that the wealthier Muslims of the districts near Aligarh "have hitherto preferred burning thirst to tasting the waters of the pure and sweet stream which is flowing at their doors."[56]

Many of the so-called aristocratic students of the college were, in fact, sent there by the British government. They were wards of the state, their upbringing as well as their property managed by district collectors and deputy commissioners. Sayyid Ahmad solicited the patronage of such students, often resorting to fairly prolonged negotiations with the various provincial governments and the viceregal

[52] [Sayyid Ahmad], *Rīporṭ sālānah kāravāʾī borḍing haus, Madrasat ul-ʿulūm Musalmānān* [hereafter BH Report], 1881 (Aligarh: Aligarh Institute Press, 1882), p. 6.

[53] AIG, December 14, 1886, and July 17, 1888.

[54] RMAOC, 1875, p. 4.

[55] *Ibid.*, 1877, p. 4.

[56] *Ibid.*, 1878, p. 4.

establishment. It was agreed in one case that a certain Oudh taluqdar might come to the college with an entourage of servants, including a groom for his horse and a grass cutter.[57] The young Navab of Mamdot wanted to hold on to his gun and two swords, as had been permitted him under special dispensation of the Arms Act.[58] But these were not typical cases: the Oudh Raja never came in the end, and the young Navab stayed only a few months while his private English tutor was on leave.

Most of the wards were of less substantial background. Sayyid Ahmad was distressed that two wards from Muzaffarnagar District had been placed in the second-class boarding house because of the very limited means of their estate. He wrote the Collector that the boys were ashamed to be living at a lower level than their peers, and suggested that other expenses could be lowered somewhat if the boys were permitted to shift to the first class.[59] Most wards stayed only briefly at Aligarh; they had little incentive to take a degree. There was one ward, however, who fulfilled Sayyid Ahmad's hopes as to wealth, status, and the success of his career at the college: Raja Rampal Singh, later a founder of the Hindu Mahasabha.[60] But in most cases wards were a great deal of trouble "because they belong to wealthy families and pay but little attention to their studies, and find the observance of strict discipline and conformity to the regulations of the Boarding House as somewhat unbearable. . . . Consequently, it takes much longer to make *men* of them."[61]

When fees were first announced in May 1875, a number of Urdu newspapers complained that they were too high, that as an Islamic madrasah Aligarh should not require stu-

[57] Deputy Commissioner of Gonda to Sayyid Ahmad, June 22, 1882 (82B, AA).

[58] Sayyid Ahmad to District Magistrate, Aligarh, October 2, 1878 (69A, AA).

[59] Sayyid Ahmad to District Collector, Muzaffarnagar, August 13, 1877 (56A, AA).

[60] RMAOC, 1883, p. 8; *ibid.*, 1885-1886, p. 6.

[61] *Ibid.*, 1883, p. 8.

dents to pay at all.[62] It was only after these complaints that the *Aligarh Institute Gazette* announced that twenty scholarships would be available, ranging from five to ten rupees a month.[63] As Sami Ullah pointed out in a letter to Sayyid Ahmad, five rupees were inadequate to cover expenses. He also remarked that the scholarship applications seemed to mistake the college for a workhouse.[64] The first year only nine students actually received scholarships, but the principle of a sliding scale of fees according to income was at least a partial concession to need.

Sayyid Ahmad was ready to concede that there were respectable Muslim families who were poor—or, as he put it, had been reduced to poverty. Boys from such families might be given vazīfah support in the form of money and exemption from fees. Mir Vilayat Husain got a free room in addition to a special gift from Mushtaq Husain.[65] The college did not want "openly to maintain students with a charity fund like common beggars"; instead poor students received aid in secret, and lived in the third-class boarding house along with paying students. In 1879 eleven students received free room, board, and tuition along with four or five rupees' stipend a month. To qualify, a student had to demonstrate his poverty; the college authorities attempted to investigate the accuracy of such claims by enquiring into the reputation of the family. Sayyid Ahmad frequently complained that families were willing to spend great sums of money on weddings and other domestic rituals, but were quick to claim poverty when it came to education. Vazīfah assistance was intended as a temporary boost; the poor students had to prove their worthiness in the annual examinations, at which time the vazīfah would be replaced by a scholarship "won by their industry and merit, with the object of keeping alive a spirit of independence in them and enabling them to appreciate the value of a living obtained by one's own labour and industry."[66]

[62] *Panjābī Akhbār*, May 22, 1875 (SVN, 1875, p. 23).
[63] June 11, 1875. [64] June 21, 1875, SDAA, pp. 271-272.
[65] Vilāyat Ḥusain, *Āp bītī*, pp. 30-31, 36-37.
[66] RMAOC, 1879, p. 8.

Scholarships, as opposed to vazīfahs, were not matters of secrecy. In addition to attracting more advanced students from other schools and colleges, they were a source of income for the college, donated by individuals or provided by the government to students who had done well on university examinations. Small scholarships were available for the best students in the school classes, but the bulk of scholarship funds was reserved for those studying at the university level. Until the mid-1880s all of the students in the college classes were on some scholarship, ranging from ten to sixteen rupees a month, depending on how far along they were toward a B.A. and how well they had done on previous examinations. Such scholarships were not based on need, but according to Sayyid Ahmad, all but one of the thirty-four Muslim students who had passed the First Arts or B.A. examinations up to 1887 would not have been able to do so without scholarship assistance.[67]

All scholarship holders were required to live in the boarding house. Although there were a few scholarships and prizes set aside for Hindu students, fund-raising appeals to the general public were often pitched in terms of providing assistance to poor Muslims. The search for scholarship donations was also an effort to enhance and expand the reputation of the college. In 1887 Sayyid Ahmad proposed that the residents of a locality might want to get together to raise funds for sending their own local boys to Aligarh.[68] That same year he made a successful appeal to the Punjab government for special scholarships in honor of the jubilee year of Queen Victoria's reign; the M.A.O. College was the one institution outside the Punjab at which such scholarships were tenable.[69]

When the college managers offered to supplement government scholarships with additional money to help pay boarding costs, however, they almost lost this special concession from the Punjab; once again Aligarh was accused of raid-

[67] Sayyid Ahmad to Director of Public Instruction, North-Western Provinces and Oudh, June 17, 1887, in AIG, July 5, 1887.

[68] AIG, June 25, 1887.

[69] W.R.M. Holroyd to Sayyid Ahmad, June 27, 1889 (144B, AA).

ing.[70] Indeed, that was the intention: Aligarh hoped in reaching out to the Punjab to establish itself on something more than a provincial basis. From the outset it had been the ambition of the founders to project the college as the educational center for all the Muslims of India. On several occasions—in 1873, 1884, and 1888—Sayyid Ahmad made speaking tours of the Punjab amidst much fanfare on behalf of the college.[71] In 1889, Aligarh's enthusiastic English principal, Theodore Beck, wrote to Sayyid Ahmad, "The Punjab is ready, with a little encouragement, to rush into our arms."[72]

The measures Beck proposed to achieve that happy consummation involved a revision in the structure of fees and scholarships. For one thing, he proposed to write off the school as a major focus of concern; Aligarh could never hope to monopolize the preuniversity education of Indian Muslims, and it would be sufficient to confine the school to the rich by abolishing reduced fees, scholarships, and vazīfahs at that level. "But our College cannot afford to . . . let any college in India approach it in the number of Mahomedans reading in the College Department. We require them all—rich & poor—in the College. In the school we require only the rich." Beck's proposal was to establish a system of reduced fees for food, along with the scholarships. Since 1887, all boarders had been eating together regardless of class; Beck now proposed to provide a cheaper breakfast for the students on reduced rates. In 1889 there were about twenty scholarship holders and thirty vazīfah holders in the college; Beck estimated that the reduction in food costs would enable the college to cut back on individual assistance and use the money saved to reach more students.[73] He also urged Sayyid Ahmad to push hard on the building program to make room for these additional numbers: "To be satisfied with our pres-

[70] J. Sime, Undersecretary to Government of Punjab, Home (Education) Department, to Sayyid Ahmad, June 12, 1891 and July 11, 1891 (B?, AA); Sayyid Ahmad to Sime, July 18, 1891 (250A, AA).

[71] *Lectures and Speeches*, pp. 111-139, 195-316, 377-397.

[72] Beck to Sayyid Ahmad, December 8, 1889 (238B, AA).

[73] *Ibid.*

ent limited number of students would be to abandon our position as the National College of the Mahomedans."[74]

The adoption of Beck's scheme was a well-tuned response to the rise in demand for college education. In 1889 there were already ninety-seven students in the college, and forty-six of them received no financial assistance; only nine of them, however, were paying first-class rates.[75] Probably the major reasons for the expansion of the college population were the availability of more students who had studied up to matriculation at other institutions, and the increasingly stringent educational requirements for government employment and the practice of law. The British authorities attempted to stem the flow to some extent by mandating higher fees at government and aided institutions, but this served to reduce the competitive disadvantages of Aligarh's own costs.[76] In the mid-1890s the official universities made a further attempt to moderate the demand by making examinations more difficult; by that time Aligarh was experiencing internal troubles of its own, which combined with these more general discouragements to inflict at least a temporary setback on the college's expansion.[77]

As an aided school Aligarh was required to keep a standard folio register book for periodic examination by the school inspector. The first ritual of initiation for an entering student

[74] AIG, January 20, 1891.

[75] Beck to Sayyid Ahmad, July 1, 1889 (147B, AA).

[76] For Sayyid Ahmad's attitude to government regulations on fees, see Sayyid Ahmad to Director of Public Instruction, North-Western Provinces and Oudh, August 8, 1884 (349A, AA); on a British official's feeling that too much encouragement of college education would only produce insatiable demands for government employment, see GNWP, General (C), Nos. 1-14, File 728 (U. P. Government Archives, Lucknow).

[77] See below, p. 314; for a good statement of the rationale behind harder examinations see W. J. Goodrich, "Educational Reform in the N. W.-P.," AIG, September 12 and 19, 1893; for Beck's critique of this policy see *Muhammadan Anglo-Oriental College Magazine* [hereafter MAOCM], June 1, 1896.

was to render up certain one- or two-word descriptions of his identity for the benefit of annual education reports. The register also helped to keep tabs on a young man's movements through the educational system. As one former student recalled the scene in later years, he was ten years old when his father brought him to Aligarh: weeping bitterly, he was taken to the English headmaster and given a chit to present to the teacher in charge of the register, a man with a large bunch of keys tied to the end of his handkerchief. The information the boy had to give was his name, his father's name, residence, father's occupation, caste, and age. But the overriding memory that stayed with him in later years was his fear of being hit with the keys.[78]

Unfortunately, the only old register book that has been preserved in the Aligarh Archives is blank, but various lists published from time to time in annual reports or alumni directories make it possible to gather some of the information that these registers provided. The missing information is on age, caste, and father's occupation, although there are enough scattered references in other sources to provide some preliminary impressions of the kinds of self-definitions that an entering student might offer. The first annual report of the college reprinted all the registration entries. Fifty of the eighty-eight students listed their fathers' occupations simply as "service," with no distinction of public or private; ten others specified the government post their fathers held. There were eleven zamindars, five pleaders, five traders, the relative of a navab, and a "manager." As for the "castes" of these Muslim students: twenty-eight were Sayyids, twenty-seven Shaikhs, twenty-two Pathans, seven Mughals, two Kambohs, one was a Khvajahzadah, and one an Alvi.[79] One of these Shaikhs later called himself a Sayyid, perhaps in accordance with the proverb: "Last year I was a weaver, this year I am a

[78] [Anon.], "My College Life: Twenty Years Ago," *Aligarh Monthly*, May 1904, p. 42.

[79] RMAOC, 1875, pp. 6-9; the totals given here ignore the fact that some were brothers.

Shaikh and next year if the price of wheat goes up I shall be a Sayyid."[80] Subsequently, the standard government form only asked the caste of Hindus, but at this time Muslims seem to have been ready enough to answer such a question if somebody took the trouble to ask.

In all, some 3,463 individuals registered at Aligarh from 1875 to 1900: 2,803 in the school section, 924 in the college, with an overlap of 264 in both.[81] For most of these people, however, the period at Aligarh was ephemeral. An 1895 directory of former students confined itself to those who had lived in the boarding house for at least a year and studied beyond the first three elementary classes; day scholars were only included if they took their B.A. from Aligarh, although a few others at the college level were added for whom the compiler happened to have some information. In all, 476 former students, about 22 percent of those registered up to 1895, were considered by these criteria to have had a substantial experience at Aligarh.[82]

The 476 students came from 154 different places; 43 percent of them came from places that in all sent fewer than 5 individuals (see Map 3). About two-thirds of the places, representing 54 percent of the students, were distinctly rural, old fortresses now torn down or small market centers. Some students listed their traditional vatan, even though their connection with it was tenuous. Masud Ali, for example, put down Fatehpur, near Lucknow, although most of his childhood had been spent in Delhi. Nine students listed their homes as Bilgram, although most of them grew up in Hyderabad. A rural address did not necessarily mean a landed income: although Aftab Ahmad Khan spent his early years in Kunjpura, where a senior lineage of relatives held all the

[80] Compare entries for Sajjad Husain in BH Report, 1875, p. 7 and *ibid.*, 1879, p. 6; the proverb appears with slightly different wording in Elliot, *Memoirs*, I, 185.

[81] Totals based on Ṭufail Aḥmad, *Muḥammadan Kālij Ḍairakṭaṛī* [Muhammadan College Directory], 2 vols. (Badaun: Nizami Press, 1914).

[82] *Ibid.* (1895 ed.), pp. 91-123.

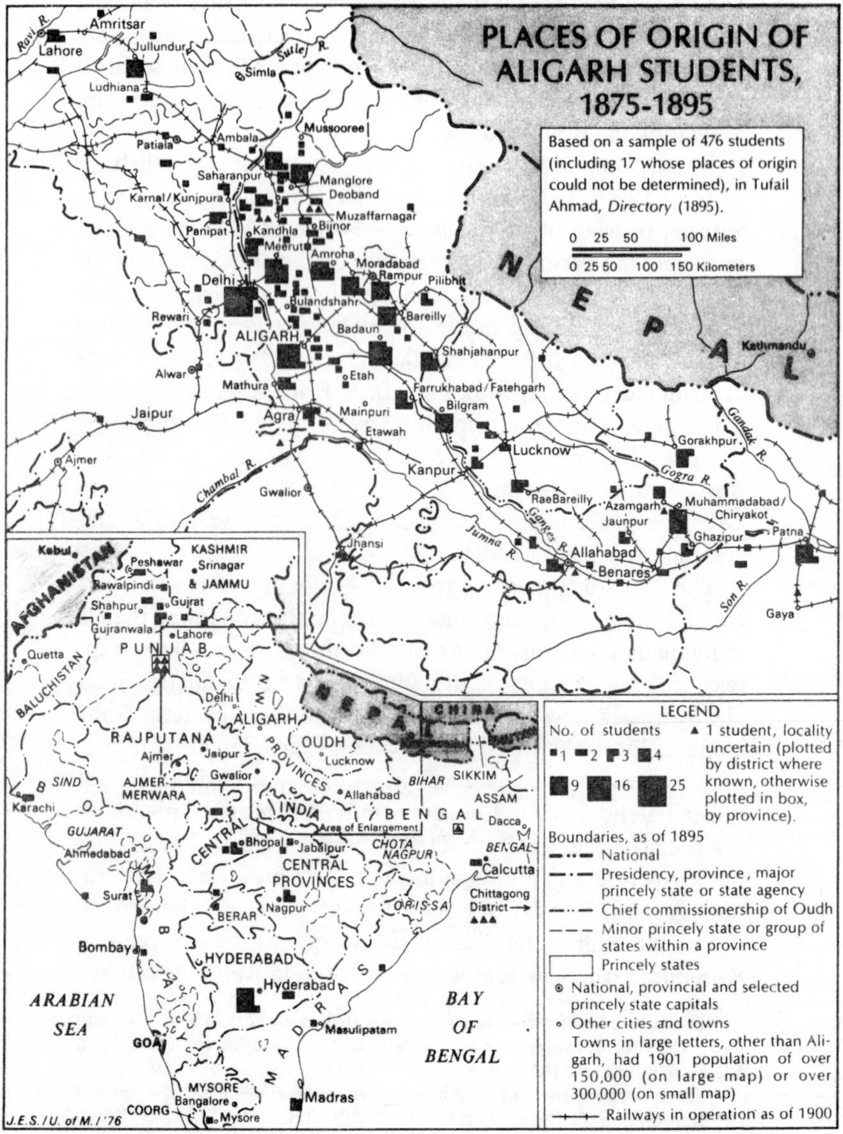
PLACES OF ORIGIN OF ALIGARH STUDENTS, 1875-1895
Based on a sample of 476 students (including 17 whose places of origin could not be determined), in Tufail Ahmad, Directory (1895).
0 25 50 100 Miles
0 25 50 100 150 Kilometers
LEGEND
No. of students
1 2 3 4
9 16 25
▲ 1 student, locality uncertain (plotted by district where known, otherwise plotted in box, by province).
Boundaries, as of 1895
National
Presidency, province, major princely state or state agency
Chief commissionership of Oudh
Minor princely state or group of states within a province
Princely states
National, provincial and selected princely state capitals
Other cities and towns
Towns in large letters, other than Aligarh, had 1901 population of over 150,000 (on large map) or over 300,000 (on small map)
Railways in operation as of 1900
NEPAL
Amritsar
Lahore
Jullundur
Ludhiana
Simla
Patiala
Ambala
Mussooree
Saharanpur
Manglore
Deoband
Karnal / Kunjpura
Muzaffarnagar
Panipat
Kandhla
Bijnor
Meerut
Amroha
Moradabad
Rampur
Pilibhit
Delhi
Bulandshahr
Bareilly
Rewari
ALIGARH
Badaun
Shahjahanpur
Alwar
Etah
Mathura
Farrukhabad / Fatehgarh
Jaipur
Agra
Mainpuri
Bilgram
Etawah
Lucknow
Gorakhpur
Ajmer
Kanpur
Chambal R.
Gwalior
RaeBareilly
Azamgarh
Muhammadabad / Chiryakot
Jaunpur
Ghazipur
Patna
Jhansi
Jumna R.
Ganges R.
Allahabad
Benares
Son R.
Gaya
Kathmandu
Gandak R.
Gogra R.
Sutlej R.
Ravi R.
Kabul
AFGHANISTAN
Peshawar
KASHMIR & JAMMU
Srinagar
Rawalpindi
Shahpur
Gujrat
Gujranwala
Lahore
PUNJAB
Quetta
BALUCHISTAN
Delhi
ALIGARH
RAJPUTANA
OUDH
Ajmer
Jaipur
Lucknow
Gwalior
PROVINCES
AJMER-MERWARA
SIND
Allahabad
BIHAR
SIKKIM
ASSAM
Karachi
INDIA
BENGAL
Area of Enlargement
Dacca
GUJARAT
CENTRAL
Bhopal
Jabalpur
CHOTA NAGPUR
BENGAL
Ahmedabad
CENTRAL PROVINCES
Calcutta
Surat
BERAR
Nagpur
ORISSA
Chittagong District
Bombay
HYDERABAD
Hyderabad
ARABIAN SEA
BAY OF BENGAL
Masulipatam
GOA
MADRAS
MYSORE
Bangalore
Madras
COORG
Mysore
J.E.S./U. of M./'76

Map 3.

land, his own immediate family income came from his father's official post in Gwalior.[83]

Perhaps the recent loss of landed property or the threat of such loss for those unfamiliar with the ways of British administration propelled some families to send sons to Aligarh to bolster or replace their sources of livelihood. It has been argued that insecurity among Muslim landholders was particularly rife in the region from which the largest proportion of Aligarh students came—the Rohilkhand and Ganges-Jumna Doab.[84] But this was also an area of thriving district towns, such as Meerut, Moradabad, Saharanpur, and Aligarh itself. Of the former students in the 1895 directory, 207 (43 percent) came from this region. The closing of the government colleges at Delhi and Bareilly in the 1870s left few alternatives there and in the area just west of the Jumna (Hariana and the eastern edge of Rajasthan), which accounted for another 65 (13 percent). The cultural center of this region was still Delhi, and it was Delhi that provided the largest single contingent of students, 27. Further to the south and east, the attraction of Aligarh fell off drastically, probably because the colleges in Agra, Allahabad, Lucknow, and Benares were sufficient to satisfy the demand. These major cities, all together, account for only 13 of those listed in the directory. In all, 23 came from Oudh (including the Bilgramis), and 10 from the Allahabad region. In contrast, there was a relatively large number of students, 30, from the eastern end of the North-Western Provinces, largely attributable to personal connections with particular individuals. For example, 9 students came from the town of Muhammadabad in Azamgarh district, the home of Maulvi Muhammad Karīm, a founder and manager of the college, who had served as Deputy Collector in Aligarh. For similar reasons, Aligarh was able to draw a small number of students from further east in

[83] See above, pp. 42-43.

[84] Francis Robinson, "Municipal Government and Muslim Separatism in the United Provinces, 1883 to 1916," *Locality, Province and Nation*, ed. John Gallagher, Gordon Johnson, and Anil Seal (Cambridge: Cambridge University Press, 1973), pp. 82-85.

Bihar, particularly the city of Patna, which sent 10. There were 14 students from such Central Indian towns as Jabalpur, Jhansi, and the princely state of Bhopal, for whom Aligarh was about as convenient as any of the other distant colleges. The well-cultivated relationship with Hyderabad far to the south, which provided such a sizable portion of the college's income, also managed to get 13 students to make the long trip north, in addition to the Bilgramis and some others whose fathers served the Nizam.

For all its geographical dispersion, there was a good deal tying together the territory from which the overwhelming majority of Aligarh students came. Although there was much linguistic variation, it could be subsumed under the broad category of "Hindustani": the mother tongue or familiar second language of the young men who came to Aligarh was basically the sharīf style of Urdu. Most came from places where Muslims were a minority in the general population, but were represented in fairly substantial numbers in the kacahri and other centers of relative privilege. Meeting at Aligarh, students might well think that the Muslim population was essentially homogeneous.

Recruiting students from beyond the great heartland of Hindustan was considerably more difficult. The most immediate concern was the Punjab, a region of cultural transition that had much in common with the territory to the east, and only gradually shaded off into a distinct configuration. Delhi and the nearby districts to the west and north were under the jurisdiction of the government of the Punjab, but were culturally very much of a piece with the Ganges-Jumna Doab to the east. Aligarh was easily accessible to this region, and the only obstacle was an occasional jurisdictional conflict between the provinces or the universities of Allahabad and Punjab with regard to matriculation requirements or educational qualifications for government service and the law.[85] Of the 75 students from the Punjab, 45 were in fact from this Hin-

[85] AIG, May 27, 1890.

dustani enclave. Further west and north, potential seekers of English education were drawn into the sphere of Lahore, linguistically distinct and increasingly Muslim. If one takes the present Indo-Pakistani border as a dividing line, then 17 students came from the eastern Punjab, where Muslims were a minority, and 18 from the western part, where they were a majority. Although Aligarh students sometimes made much of the Hindustani-Punjabi division, it is likely that sharīf culture in the two regions was very much the same. Urdu was a second language for Punjabis, but it was very much the first language for literate activity and, probably, polite conversation. As for other parts of India, the number of students attracted to Aligarh was negligible: the Pushtu region (still part of Punjab), 3; Sind, 2; Bombay and Kathiawar, 4; Mysore, 2; Madras, 4. Bengal, the largest region of Muslim population, sent 6 students in all, counting a Hindu whose father was a judge in Aligarh.

But if the number of students that passed through the M.A.O. College was extremely small and their representativeness of the Muslim population of the subcontinent was doubtful, it is important to bear in mind that the English-educated population in India as a whole was very small. In 1903 Theodore Morison, then principal of the Aligarh College, compiled a table to show the proportion of Aligarh alumni among all the Muslim graduates from the five universities of India. Between 1882 and 1902, Aligarh had sent up 220 Muslim graduates, or 18.5 percent of the 1,184 in all of India. Aligarh accounted for 53.6 percent of the Muslim graduates of Allahabad University; and after reaching its full stride in the 1890s, it almost equaled by itself the number of B.A.s from either Calcutta or Punjab University.[86] In statistical terms, Aligarh students made up a significant portion of the English-educated Muslim population of India; it remains to be seen whether this significance was something more than statistical.

[86] Morison, *The History of the M. A.-O. College*, p. 63.

THE TEACHERS

In the older forms of education for Indian Muslims, a student would seek out particular teachers of good reputation rather than make an impersonal choice of institution. And even in the English-style schools of India, the educational backgrounds and teaching skills of the faculty weighed heavily in the recruitment of students. To learn English well and get through examinations were the minimal educational goals of an English education, and popular opinion made coaching by teachers decisive in their achievement. It is for this reason that the recruitment of staff commanded as much attention as the recruitment of students. Still another consideration, more special to Aligarh than to other English-style establishments, was to find at least some teachers of good religious reputation with regard to both learning and piety.

A month before the beginning of classes, advertisements in the *Aligarh Institute Gazette* and other papers gave notice of teaching openings at Aligarh. Within two weeks another announcement appeared saying that so many applications had been received that unless a candidate had been notified, he should assume that he had been rejected.[87] In that first year there were seven teachers, three for English education, two for Arabic, and two for Persian. The third master for the English curriculum and the two Arabic professors, one Sunni and one Shiʿah, each earned 60 rupees a month; the Persian teachers earned 30 and 20. They were all Muslims. The second master was a Hindu and a B.A. He arrived three weeks after the start of classes and received a salary of 120 rupees. Five days later came the headmaster, an Englishman but not a B.A. His salary was more than all the others combined, 400 rupees.[88]

Although criticized by a hostile newspaper, the decision to hire an English headmaster and in the first year to pay him more than half the budgeted expenditure of the school does

[87] AIG, May 23, 1875.

[88] RMAOC, 1875, p. 14; K. Deighton to Sayyid Ahmad, May 31, 1875, SDAA, p. 268.

not seem to have been debated among the "managers" of the college.[89] It was of a piece with Sayyid Ahmad's conversion from vernacular to English medium of instruction: "If I had the means in my power, then I should like to have ABC taught to the boys through an English teacher who may not know a single word of Urdu."[90] If Indians were to get an English education, they would do best to get it from a native informant. There were few Indians available to play that role anyway, and hardly any of them were Muslim. A good English headmaster would probably be an important drawing card for potential students, not only for the intellectual authority of his cultural origins, but for the political authority that being English denoted in the eyes both of Indians and of the government itself. And to Sayyid Ahmad, the involvement of an Englishman in the enterprise was part of his long-cherished hope of establishing close personal relations with members of the ruling qaum.

Finding a suitable Englishman was the problem. There was a small floating world of English schoolmasters in the resident community; bringing someone from England was not really a possibility so early in the game. It was unlikely that anyone could be convinced to come out to such a new and uncertain post, even if the Aligarh committee could afford to pay transportation and guarantee some measure of security. In any case, an English master had to be paid on an English scale, to support a colonial life style and assure savings for the ultimate return home.

The pool of available Englishmen was such that they carried their reputations before them. When Sami Ullah heard that one had applied to Sayyid Ahmad, he sent off a warning to Benares that the man could not leave off liquor and was lazy in his teaching. Two other possibilities were the headmasters of the Delhi and Shahjahanpur government schools, but neither had applied yet, nor would they be available for

[89] TA, 1 Sha'bān, 1293 H.
[90] Sayyid Ahmad to Siddons, February 1, 1878 (15A, AA).

the start of classes.[91] Finally Kenneth Deighton, principal of the Agra College and a well-wisher of Sayyid Ahmad's scheme, made arrangements for H.G.I. Siddons to come from Shahjahanpur to Aligarh. "Mr. Siddons is far too good a man to lose," he wrote, "being both intellectually and socially much above the mark of Headmasters in Govt. Schools."[92]

In 1875 Siddons was about twenty-three years old. He was the posthumous child of a captain in the Bengal Army who had served with "Thugee" Sleeman both in military and civilian capacities.[93] His brother was also in India, as personal assistant to the commissioner for North Indian Salt Revenue.[94] The new headmaster had spent time at Worcester College, Oxford, before embarking on his career as Indian schoolmaster. At Aligarh he was headmaster of the school for two years and principal of the college for seven. His salary rose to 500 rupees, sometimes supplemented by private tuition. Although he found the Indian climate a severe strain, he spent nearly his entire adult life in the plains of Hindustan. He left his Aligarh position on grounds of health, but later tried unsuccessfully to retrieve his post, and finally had to settle for a variety of less lucrative jobs at the government colleges in Benares and Bareilly and at a special secondary school in Lucknow for Oudh taluqdars. He never could get beyond the subordinate levels of the government educational service because he had not passed the required examination in an Indian language.[95]

Muhammad Akbar, professor of Arabic and Sunni theology, was the brightest jewel in the staff. He was from a well-

[91] Sami Ullah to Sayyid Ahmad, May 16, 1875, SDAA, p. 264.

[92] Deighton to Sayyid Ahmad, May 31, 1875, *ibid.*, p. 268.

[93] Joseph Foster, *Alumni Orienses*, IV (Oxford: Oxford University Press, 1888), 1295; for his father, see *The Bengal and Agra Directory and Annual Register*, 1845 (Calcutta: Samuel Smith and Co., n.d.), pp. 133, 256, 300.

[94] AIG, April 17, 1883.

[95] Note by W.J.S., September 14, 1891, attached as "Keep With" to GOI, Home, Education (A), September, 1891, Nos. 45-46 (NAI); RDPI/NWP, 1892-1893, pp. 8, 67.

known ʿulama family in Kandhla, and this fact was intended to reassure people who were put off by Sayyid Ahmad's religious ideas. Muhammad Akbar's father, a long-time friend of Sayyid Ahmad, was a distinguished ʿalim, but had taught Arabic in government colleges, so the departure into this kind of role was not a complete novelty.[96] Like Sayyid Ahmad, the Kandhla family were disciples of the school of Shah Vali Ullah. Sayyid Ahmad considered Muhammad Akbar "a profound scholar of Arabic, very advanced in Arabic literature as well as science." He was also supposed to be a skillful teacher.[97] Besides his academic post, he was manager of the boarding house until his death in 1886, and was second only to Sayyid Ahmad in the practical administration of the college. He sent two sons as well as several nephews to Aligarh; virtually his whole income was devoted to their education.

The teachers at Aligarh during its first ten years were unambiguously the hired employees of the managing committee. Recruitment and salary negotiations were handled by Sami Ullah and Sayyid Ahmad, with some help from Deighton. The decision had to be approved by the committee, but the staff had no role in the matter, except that Muhammad Akbar was part of the management by virtue of his social position. During this earliest phase Indian teachers were generally hired from government schools, and Englishmen from the resident community. They could only be retained if their previous posts were of a fairly low-grade and temporary sort, because a full-fledged government appointment was generally conceded to be more desirable. "There is no doubt," Sayyid Ahmad admitted, "that if any of our European or native professors or masters could get government employment of this same salary as he gets here or even less, he would naturally prefer the government employment in the hopes of better future prospects."[98] A government post offered secur-

[96] AIG, June 4, 1875; on Muhammad Akbar's father see *Report of Select Committee*, p. 15.

[97] Sayyid Ahmad to Beck, March 8, 1884 (106A, AA).

[98] Sayyid Ahmad to A.A.I. Nesbitt, December 3, 1884 (471A, AA).

ity, a larger range of promotion possibilities, and a pension on retirement. Also, in government schools the members of the teaching staff controlled things, not a private management. As a result quite a few teachers on the Aligarh staff used it as a way-station as they prepared for examinations or waited for employment elsewhere.

The opening of college classes made it necessary to hire a mathematics professor, and to Sayyid Ahmad's regret there was not enough money to get a European. The new professor, Pandit Rama Shankar Misra, M.A., came to Aligarh after a brief stint as substitute mathematics professor in Benares. He was about twenty-three. In his brief stay he established a cricket club and publicly broke through the Hindu-Muslim barrier to attend a social gathering. Within a year, however, he was whisked away by an appointment as professor at Agra College. As a matter of fact, he left at a most inopportune time for the college, with examinations close at hand, but the Aligarh authorities did not consider it fair to hamper his "prospects" by attempting to force him to see the year through according to his contract. Misra's prospects turned out to be very good indeed: within a few years he had gone from the Agra post to School Inspector to Deputy Collector and member of the Statutory Civil Service.[99]

There followed a series of mathematics professors: a Bengali, a north Indian Kayasth, an Englishman, a recent graduate of the college, and then from 1888 to 1916 Babu Jadav Candra Chakravarti, M.A. Chakravarti seems to have answered an advertisement in a Calcutta newspaper at a time when Aligarh was famous for its anti-Bengali diatribes; in later years he was to comment "I have become a Muhammadan at heart, so far at least as the interests of the college are concerned."[100] He started at 200 rupees and in 1905, after

[99] *History of Services of Gazetted Officers, North-Western Provinces and Oudh*, July 1900 (Allahabad: Government of the North-Western Provinces and Oudh, 1900), pp. 194-195; AIG, February 16, 1878 and February 5, 1878.

[100] Chakravarti (to Mahdi Ali or Morison?), May 2, 1905 (File "Sālānah Ijlās-i Bajaṭ Mīṭing [Budget Meeting], 1906," AA); Morison,

seventeen years, was getting 300; but at the same time he had achieved widespread fame and a comfortable income as author of a series of popular textbooks used throughout India.

For the first three years of college classes, Siddons and the mathematics professor had to cover all subjects but the teaching of Arabic and Persian. Then in 1881 Aligarh hired Maulvi Amjad Ali, M.A., as professor of philosophy and logic at 200 rupees a month. One of the first north Indian Muslims to take a degree, Amjad Ali remained at Aligarh until 1887, when he took the post of professor of Arabic at Muir College, Allahabad.[101] Also in 1881, the college hired a Sanskrit professor for its Hindu students, Pandit Shiva Shankar Tripathi, who had studied not quite up to the matriculation level at Sanskrit College, Benares, and then taught Hindi at a missionary school in Allahabad. Shiva Shankar remained at Aligarh until 1897, when his post was abolished because of the decline in Hindu students; his salary was 35 rupees a month, a sign of the low priority put on languages and literatures other than English.[102]

Such was also the case in 1883, when the college hired Muhammad Shibli Numani as professor of Persian and assistant professor of Arabic at 40 rupees a month. When Muhammad Akbar died, Shibli took over in Arabic as well as continuing in Persian; his salary was raised to 70 rupees. The son of a wealthy vakil and landholder of Azamgarh, Shibli had come to Aligarh in the company of a younger brother who was enrolling as a student and later went on to Cambridge. In his fourteen years at the college, he rose to great fame as a scholar of Persian literature and Islamic history, and was probably the leading intellectual light of Aligarh's formative phase. He left Aligarh in 1897 to pursue other in-

---

History of the M.A.-O. College, p. 11; S. K. Bhatnagar, *History of the M.A.O. College Aligarh* (Bombay: Asia Publishing House for Sir Syed Hall, Aligarh Muslim University, 1969), p. 285; Sayyid Ahmad to Manager of *Bengalee*, November 23, 1888 (322A, AA).

101 AIG, March 15, 1887.

102 Sayyid Mahmud to Beck, May 27, 1898 (No. 199, AA).

terests, particularly as a founder of a new college for ʿulama at Lucknow; salary was probably not a consideration, but he was concerned about having time for his own research.[103]

Muhammad Akbar's role as religious exemplar was only partially filled by Shibli. Muhammad Akbar had only been professor of Sunni theology, and Maulvi Abbas Husain, his Shīʿah counterpart since 1876, remained. But aside from the teaching of theology and Arabic, part of Muhammad Akbar's role was to guarantee the religious atmosphere of the boarding house. He was the only member of the staff to have authority over the living arrangements of the students, although several of the managers, particularly Sami Ullah, Muhammad Karim, and Mushtaq Husain, were also closely involved in these matters. These arrangements were overturned at Muhammad Akbar's death, although for a brief period his younger brother, Muhammad Sulaiman, held the post of boarding-house manager without teaching responsibilities.[104] In 1893, the college hired as "dean" Maulvi Abdullah, the son-in-law of the famous founder of Deoband, Maulvi Muhammad Qasim. After receiving permission from his spiritual teacher in Mecca, Maulvi Abdullah accepted the post, which involved living in special quarters near the mosque, conducting prayers five times a day, delivering sermons on appropriate occasions, and counseling students who might waver in their faith. His salary was 80 rupees.[105]

In 1889 the college opened up a law class; for the first two years lectures were delivered without salary by Khvajah Yusuf and two Hindu members of the local bar. From 1891 to 1895 the professor of law was Sayyid Karamat Husain of Lucknow, a man who years later was to become a justice on the Allahabad High Court. Karamat Husain continued to practice law in Lucknow, residing in Aligarh for brief so-

[103] Shibli (to Mushtaq Husain), October 19, 1897 (N.M. 1966. 97/52 National Museum of Pakistan, Karachi).

[104] See below, p. 265.

[105] Sayyid Ahmad to Beck, October 28, 1893 (347A, AA); Sayyid Ahmad to Munshi Saʿīd Ahmad, June 5, 1893, *Maktūbāt*, pp. 617-622.

journs in order to deliver a course of lectures, for which he received the almost European salary of 300 rupees. Following his withdrawal from the faculty, his place was taken by Aftab Ahmad Khan, now an alumnus and only recently returned from England. Aftab Ahmad continued to practice law in Aligarh, and donated his salary to the college.[106]

As the focus of Aligarh's attention shifted from school to college-level classes, less effort was put into the recruitment of schoolmasters. At first the schoolmasters teaching at the higher levels were Hindu graduates of other colleges, and their salaries were relatively high, up to 135 rupees for the second master. Bakhtawar Lal, B.A., the third master from 1877 to 1886, was paid 80 rupees; for much of the time he was the only teacher in the school or college competent to prepare students for English-Persian translation questions on the university examinations. He left to take a clerical post in the Commissioner's Office, Ajmere.[107] From the mid-1880s, teaching positions in the school were offered as temporary employment for recent graduates of the college. The first to take such a post was Khvajah Sajjad Husain, son of the poet Altaf Husain Hali, who served as sixth master at 60 rupees a month before taking a more profitable post as assistant inspector of schools in the Punjab. Virtually the only Aligarh graduate to remain as a teacher for any extended time was Mir Vilayat Husain, who started as schoolmaster upon his graduation in 1883 and remained until a forced retirement in 1920, for all but the first four years serving as second master. Complaining of his salary of 150 rupees in 1905, after twenty-two years of service, 100 for his teaching and 50 as "proctor" of the boarding house, Mir Sahib compared his career to that of Sajjad Husain and others who went into government service: "I foolishly stuck to this place. . . . In Govt. schools where the highest pay of the Headmaster is Rs. 400, the Second Master generally gets Rs. 200 or 250, but here the Head-

[106] AIG, March 12, 1889; September 15, 1891; January 30, 1897.

[107] Sayyid Ahmad to Beck, March 8, 1884 (106A, AA); Bakhtawar Lal to Sayyid Ahmad, May 4, 1885 (File "1885-86," AA).

masters get Rs. 450 and sometimes Rs. 500, but the Second Master is never destined to rise beyond Rs. 100."[108]

The reason the headmasters got so much was that they were British. In 1880, with Siddons serving as principal of the college, A.A.I. Nesbitt, an M.A. in classics, was hired as headmaster of the school, held that post until 1883, then became professor of English in the college for two more years. Nesbitt played cricket, football, and tennis; he wrote on stationery embossed with a coat of arms. In 1885 he returned to England with hopes of establishing a small boarding school for boys with parents in India. Soon, however, he was back in India as successor to Siddons in the principalship of Bareilly College.[109] Nesbitt's successor as headmaster in 1883 was W. C. Horst, formerly a schoolmaster at Mussoorie in a school for British youth in India. Horst applied two years later for Nesbitt's post as English professor, on the latter's departure. Sayyid Ahmad replied, however, that the committee had decided that in the future it would confine professorships in the college to men who had studied at Oxford or Cambridge.[110] Horst did not qualify, but he remained as headmaster until 1896.

The recruitment of young professors from Oxford and Cambridge was consistent with the basic decisions that Sayyid Ahmad had made during his stay in England. Once again the mediating role was played by Sayyid Mahmud, who returned to Cambridge on a visit in 1883 with the intention of finding a successor to Siddons. The man selected, Theodore Beck, was presented to Sayyid Mahmud at Trinity College by John Strachey's son, Arthur.[111] Beck had grown up in London; his father, a Quaker and a Tory, had gone from an apprenticeship at the old Goldsmith's Hall to a partnership in an optical firm in Cornhill, and a seat on the

[108] Vilayat Husain to Morison, January 20, 1905 (Budget Meeting, 1906, AA).

[109] AIG, August 15, 1885; RDPI/NWP, 1892-1893, p. 8.

[110] Sayyid Ahmad to Horst, December 9, 1884.

[111] AIG, September 7, 1886; MAOCM, April, 1899; Sayyid Mahmud to Beck, November 25, 1898 (No. 438, AA).

Corporation Council.[112] The new principal had matriculated to Cambridge from University College, London, and fallen in with members of some prominent families, in particular the Stracheys and the Stephens. He achieved a good deal of prominence of his own as president of the Cambridge Union. Beck took his Tripos examinations in mathematics, and was also elected to the elite secret society called the "Apostles."[113] According to his later statements, he had not been aware that there were Muslims in India, but he very quickly accepted Sayyid Mahmud's instruction, and decided to devote his life to the Aligarh cause.[114] Beck was a man of extraordinary talents and extraordinary enthusiasms. He decided that he would prefer "living in India to living in Anglo-India," and defined that India as what he saw from Aligarh.[115] Wilfred Scawen Blunt, establishment gadfly of British imperialism, described Beck shortly after the young man had arrived in Aligarh as "a pretty little young man with pink cheeks and blue eyes, certainly not an average [Englishman]; and an average Englishman certainly could not succeed here. So Beck may succeed. He is probably clever."[116]

Beck was anxious to bring out his friends from Cambridge to share the experience with him, and as the college expanded, room was made for them. Two other Union presidents joined the Aligarh staff in 1885, Harold Cox and Walter Raleigh, the former as a relatively low-paid professor of mathematics, the latter in English and philosophy. Cox had gone to Tonbridge, and was thus the first real public-school

[112] Obituary for Joseph Beck, *North London Guardian*, April 24, 1891, reprinted in AIG, May 23, 1891.

[113] AIG, September 7, 1886; Venn, *Alumni*, Part II, I, 210 (all subsequent references in Venn are to Part II); Beck to Sayyid Ahmad, April 27, 1892 (?B, AA); C. W. Previté-Orton, *Index to Tripos List, 1748-1910* (Cambridge: Cambridge University Press, 1923), p. 19, DNB, 1901-1910, p. 439.

[114] AIG, January 8, 1889; see below, p. 218.

[115] Beck, *Essays on Indian Topics* (Allahabad: Pioneer Press, 1888), no page number [first page of preface].

[116] Wilfred Scawen Blunt, *India under Ripon: A Private Diary* (London: T. Fischer Unwin, 1909), p. 156.

man at Aligarh; his elder brother was mathematics professor at Muir College, Allahabad. Raleigh, son of a Congregationalist minister, had gone to the City of London School, Edinburgh Academy, and had done a B.A. at University College, London, before going up to Cambridge to study history. Raleigh was also a man with sisters: one of them married a son of John Strachey, the other married Theodore Beck. Cox and Raleigh stayed for only two years, returning to England to take up highly successful careers, Cox as a journalist—he eventually became editor of the *Edinburgh Review*—and Raleigh as a famous professor of English literature at Liverpool and then Oxford.[117] Although their stay at Aligarh was brief, the college was never the same afterwards.[118]

While Beck filled in for Cox in mathematics—generally he taught history—Raleigh recruited his own successors. For English literature he chose a man from Lincoln College, Oxford: Percy Wallace, who had the misfortune to have come out 11th out of 189 in the Home Civil Service examination in a year when there were only 3 vacancies. Described in a letter of recommendation as "an elegant scholar, well read and enthusiastic," Wallace came to Aligarh with the intention of spending twenty years, lasted three, and then seems to have died or disappeared into obscurity.[119] Far more important in the history of Aligarh was the man Raleigh got to replace him in philosophy, T. W. Arnold of Magdalene College, Cambridge. Arnold had done poorly in the classics Tripos, but this was attributed to his wide reading in other fields, including the study of Sanskrit. Son of a Devonport ironmonger, he had also attended the City of London School,

[117] Venn, *Alumni,* II, 160; *ibid.*, V, 235; Previté-Orton, *Tripos List*, pp. 64, 226; on the marriages of Raleigh's sisters, see Beck to Sayyid Ahmad, August 20, 1891 (304A, AA) and Venn, *Alumni*, VI, 61; D. Nichol Smith, "Sir Walter Raleigh," DNB, 1922-1930, pp. 701-704; Francis W. Hirst, "Harold Cox," DNB, 1931-1940, pp. 195-196.

[118] See below, Chapters V and VI.

[119] AIG, June 28, 1887; Foster, *Alumni*, p. 1489; letter to his mother, August 5, 1887, as communicated to me by Mr. Harlan Pearson from the original in the Duke University Library.

and even there had become interested in Sanskrit. More subdued than Beck, his enthusiasm was almost as great—marked, for example, by his occasional wearing of Indian dress. He also bound himself to the community by marrying Beck's niece. Although he left Aligarh in 1898 to take up an attractive post at Government College, Lahore, he remained intensely concerned with what he began under Sayyid Ahmad's auspices, and he ultimately achieved great distinction as a leading figure at the School of Oriental Studies at the University of London.[120]

Theodore Morison was a contemporary and friend of Beck, Cox, and Raleigh at Cambridge, though not quite so prominent. The son of a well-known Victorian writer, James Cotter Morison, and grandson of the inventor of Morison's Vegetable Pills, he had also grown up in London and had attended the Westminster School. After graduation from Cambridge in classics, he took a post as private tutor to the young maharaja of Chatarpur, on which occasion he visited his Cambridge friends at Aligarh in 1886. On his return to London, he became agent for an Aligarh-based political campaign against the Indian National Congress, so when he came in 1889 as professor of political economy and history he knew a good deal about the Aligarh ideology. He succeeded to the principalship of the college on Beck's death in 1899, and remained in that post until 1905, when he returned to England as a member of the India Council attached to the Secretary of State for India.[121]

Subsequent recruits from Oxford and Cambridge were a good deal less notable than Beck, Cox, Raleigh, Arnold, and Morison. One young Oxford man, the son of a colonel, was flushed out rather unceremoniously when he proved to be an ineffective teacher; he was able, however, to secure a post

[120] Venn, *Alumni*, I, 77; H.A.R. Gibb, "Sir Thomas Walker Arnold," DNB, 1922-1930, pp. 25-26.

[121] Sayyid Ahmad to Sayyid Mahmud, March 18, 1888 (73aA, AA); Venn, *Alumni*, IV, 466; J. C. Powell-Price, "Sir Theodore Morison," DNB, 1931-1940, p. 630.

at Bareilly College and ultimately succeeded Nesbitt, who had succeeded Siddons, as principal.[122] Llewelyn Tipping from Jesus College, Cambridge, had been born in India. He taught at Aligarh from 1895 to 1903, after which he joined the Indian Educational Service and spent the next sixteen years as professor, principal, and headmaster in a variety of institutions from Presidency College, Calcutta, to Islamia College, Peshawar.[123] Two other Cambridge men, Gerald Gardner Brown and J. R. Cornah, both of Pembroke College, came in 1899 and remained until 1908. Extremely unpopular among the students, they were considered to represent a new, unsympathetic attitude, in marked contrast to their enthusiastic forerunners. Both were virtually forced out of their posts as a result of a student strike and opposition from the trustees; they too found refuge in the Indian Educational Service.[124]

THE MANAGERS

Sayyid Ahmad was not only the founder of the Aligarh College; in the earliest phase of its existence he was very much the day-to-day administrator of its most detailed operations. For extended periods of time, Sami Ullah, Khvajah Yusuf, Mushtaq Husain, and Muhammad Karim were also on the scene, and a number of other men took a lively interest in the workings of the college. These unpaid directors of Aligarh's affairs were collectively known as the "managers"; as members of the all-Muslim M.A.O. College Fund Committee, their names were submitted annually to the Registrar of Joint Stock Companies in Allahabad. Most of them were fathers and uncles of Aligarh students. They were sturdy, independent-minded men of the older generation, not educated

[122] G. S. Carey to Sayyid Ahmad, December 9, 1895; GNWP, Education (B), July, 1895, No. 17, File 22 (U.P. Government Archives, Lucknow); RDPI/NWP, 1895-1896, p. 10.

[123] Venn, *Alumni*, VI, 196.

[124] *Ibid.*, I, 407; II, 138; Bhatnagar, *History of the M.A.O. College*, pp. 144, 203-205.

in English but well-versed in the arts of administration, the *kār o bār* of government offices and landed estates. They respected Sayyid Ahmad's energies and abilities, but were by no means deferential; they were prepared to overrule him and sometimes did so, as in the decision to initiate the school at Aligarh in 1875.

To have detailed influence on the college administration, it was necessary to live in Aligarh. The out-of-town managers —about seventy-five out of the eighty or so members of the Fund Committee—were conscientiously consulted on important issues, but only a few of them would actually travel to Aligarh to take a more detailed look at what was going on.[125] The business of running the institution remained primarily in Sayyid Ahmad's hands, although it was important to show the public that this "*kāfir*" was under the control of more orthodox Muslims.

Sayyid Ahmad moved to his new Aligarh home in July 1876, on retirement from his post in Benares. In the previous year, Sami Ullah had frequently corresponded with him about college business, such as the recruitment of students and teachers. For the first three years, until Sami Ullah was transferred out of Aligarh, there was a virtual duumvirate running the madrasah. Continuing the procedures of the prefoundation organization, a great deal of attention was devoted to establishing a committee structure and a code of rules and by-laws for the governance of the college.[126] Most of the managers were in government service or the legal profession, and there is an odor of legal formality in much of the college business. Sayyid Ahmad wrote letters pursuant to such and such clause in such and such section of the rules, with a full denotation of the official capacity in which he was speaking,

[125] List of 82 members of the M.A.O. College Fund Committee, Sayyid Ahmad to Joint Registrar of Stock Companies, February 14, 1884 (60A, AA).

[126] *Code of Rules for the Muhammadan Anglo-Oriental College at Aligarh* (Calcutta: n.p., 1883); "Meeting of the Members of the Select Committee appointed to revise the Code of rules of the M.A.-O. College, Aligarh, held on the 11th May 1884," English ms., AA.

even in correspondence with his son, Sayyid Mahmud. At one point he rather overwhelmed Siddons on a point of law—only to be taken aback when he realized that the relevant rules had not been translated into English.[127]

The Committee of the Directors of Instruction in Secular Learning made decisions on course of study and scholarship allocation. Deighton was president, and there were three other Englishmen on the twenty-two man body, including Siddons and John Eliot, then professor of natural science at Presidency College, Calcutta. The Sunni and Shīʿah Arabic professors were also members *ex officio*, but all the rest were representatives of the Fund Committee. They included Inayat Rasul Ciryakoti, Zaka Ullah, Sayyid Mahmud, Mahdi Ali, Ciragh Ali, Hali, and Sayyid Husain Bilgrami. At first Sami Ullah was secretary and Sayyid Ahmad vice president, but Sayyid Ahmad took over the post of secretary when he settled down in Aligarh.[128] The committee's business was generally carried on through the mails. An example was the case of a disagreement between Sayyid Ahmad and Siddons as to whether a student should lose his scholarship for poor academic achievement. A printed bilingual statement of the dispute, with extracts of the correspondence between the principal and secretary, was sent out to committee members. Siddons' more lenient position received support from most committee members.[129] The committees for religious instruction, one Sunni and one Shīʿah, operated in the same way, but since Sayyid Ahmad was not a member they were considerably less active.[130]

The most active committee was the Managing Committee, responsible as an executive body for the internal management of the college and boarding house. It had about twenty-five

[127] Sayyid Ahmad to Siddons, August 14, 1876 (55A, AA).

[128] Details of committee membership were published on the first pages of RMAOC and differ slightly from year to year.

[129] Printed letter from Sayyid Ahmad to members of Secular Studies Committee with extracts of correspondence between Sayyid Ahmad and Siddons, August, 1877 (128B, AA).

[130] See above, pp. 133-134.

members, most of them local zamindars and vakils, although it also included Zaka Ullah and Sayyid Mahmud as nonresident members. There were six Hindus, including Jaikishan Das, a Jat raja of the district, and some local vakils. There were no Englishmen. Usually only a handful of members attended the frequent meetings, and sometimes there were as many Hindus as Muslims. The verbatim proceedings appeared regularly in the *Aligarh Institute Gazette.* Generally matters such as finances, salaries and fees, expansion of the staff, rules of admission, and alterations in the boarding-house arrangements would be presented to the meeting by Sayyid Ahmad, and after discussion the members would pass an appropriate resolution. The procedure was that of a formal deliberative body, presided over by a "president" and recorded by a "secretary." From the Scientific Society on, most of the members had had experience with such matters of public decision making.

Through most of this first period the president of the Managing Committee was Muhammad Karim. Sami Ullah was secretary for two years until his transfer to Moradabad, and he was responsible for major administrative matters, such as boarding-house supervision and the appointment of teachers. Sayyid Ahmad, who at first held the honorific post of vice president, moved into Sami Ullah's office in June 1877, with Sami Ullah becoming Life Honorary Secretary. But Sami Ullah's boarding-house responsibilities were assigned to Muhammad Karim, probably on the grounds that Sayyid Ahmad's religious views made him the wrong man to oversee ritual and moral behavior. When Mushtaq Husain temporarily lost his post in Hyderabad in 1879, he came to Aligarh as a member of the Managing Committee, and actually resided in the boarding house for two years, sharing its supervision with Muhammad Akbar.[131] From 1878 to 1882, Sayyid Ahmad had to spend a few months each year in Calcutta as a member of the viceroy's legislative council; his college responsi-

[131] BH Report, 1879, p. 9; Ikrāmullāh Khān, *Viqār-i Ḥayāt*, pp. 387-389.

bilities were taken up by Khvajah Yusuf and, after his reassignment to Aligarh from 1881 to 1886, by Sami Ullah.[132]

A Fund Committee member and active supporter of the college in Patna visited Aligarh in 1880. In an article for the *Aligarh Institute Gazette* he took great pains to show that Sayyid Ahmad had nothing to do with the students. According to this account, Sayyid Ahmad would sit in his house during the day, working on correspondence with the government, fund-raising operations, and building construction. It might be added that he also corresponded with the principal of the college, the letters being translated back and forth between English and Urdu by a personal assistant. In the evenings he would come over to the college grounds to talk with the construction workers and check on what they had done. He would leave without running into any of the boys, so there was no danger that they would be contaminated by his religious ideas.[133] Sayyid Ahmad made the same point on several occasions: he only asked permission, infidel that he was, humbly to serve the qaum by doing some of the more laborious tasks.

In fact, Sayyid Ahmad's influence on the whole milieu of the college was pervasive. It is true that his technical views on theology and ritual were not propagated among the students, but otherwise he touched decisively all aspects of Aligarh's life. If students saw him as an awesomely distant figure, this was probably no more the case than at many educational institutions: a student does not often see the chief administrator, just as a seaman rarely sees the captain of a ship. Such men as Sami Ullah and Mushtaq Husain were more in evidence as far as ordinary personal relations went, but on public occasions as well as in the basic form and substance of Aligarh's institutional life, Sayyid Ahmad was the

132 AIG, December 17, 1878; January 10, 1882; Sami Ullah was absent for part of 1884 in order to accompany Lord Northbrook to Egypt (*History of Services*, N.W.P., 1887, p. 118).

133 Sayyid Riẓā Ḥusain, "Kāfiyat-i Madrasat ul-ʻulūm," AIG, May 15, 1880.

presiding genius. This was conceded by all observers at the time, sympathetic and otherwise. From the beginning there were expressions of anxiety about Aligarh's viability after the old man's death.[134]

It was Sayyid Ahmad who received and dispersed money, kept the daily accounts, drew up budgets and reports, supervised all publications and public relations, corresponded with parents, government officials, and financial benefactors, oversaw the teaching, discipline, and general life of the college, designed the buildings and supervised their construction, hired teachers, granted them leaves of absence, nominated scholarship holders, arranged the administration of examinations, and scheduled vacations. To hold such powers it was necessary to wear more than one fez: he was secretary of the Fund Committee; he was in charge of various Aligarh satellites, such as the *Institute Gazette* and the many committees set up to champion educational, political, and social causes under the Aligarh aegis, as well as the moribund Scientific Society and the intermittent journal, *Tahẕīb ul-A<u>kh</u>lāq*. With the advent of the young men from Cambridge, and particularly after 1887, Sayyid Ahmad began to divest himself of some of these powers, although his activity and attention to detail remained prodigious until his death in 1898. The authority of the other managers, however, fell by the wayside, and for a time Aligarh lost much of its connection with the older generation.

134 Note by D. B. attached to GOI, Home, Education (B), February, 1876, no. 45 (NAI); for statements about Sayyid Ahmad's indispensability see EC/NWP, pp. 211, 242, 319.

V

The Life of the Mind

EXCEPT for theology, the curriculum at Aligarh College was set by external authorities. Aligarh students had to study the same books for the same examinations as students from other colleges. The layout of the educational system—graded progression through classes, definition of subject areas—was dictated by uniform government rules. There was some slight room for maneuver among overlapping authorities (the universities of Calcutta, Punjab, and Allahabad, for example), and it was possible for the college authorities to exercise some influence, formal or informal, on academic policy. Aligarh was represented on some governing bodies; Aligarh teachers sometimes set the examinations. There were also decisions to be made as the educational system gradually provided optional courses of study, such as the bifurcation of science and humanities. After 1892 Aligarh authorities were free to decide *not* to prepare students in science. They could choose to ignore the Anglo-Vernacular Middle School Examination or the terminal School Final Examination, which after 1894 was offered as an alternative to matriculation. They also could take a few of the positive options, such as preparing students for law examinations after 1890. But within any subject, the topics covered and even the books assigned were uniform, and the public—prospective students and contributors, for example—knew from the published examination results which colleges could deliver the goods. A college's claim to distinction rested on its style and quality of teaching. Like ghazal poets, Aligarh professors and masters had to work within a restricted genre.

THE BURDEN OF ENGLISH

The Oriental Department might have been an independent educational effort, but it tended to hover uncertainly around the government model. Sayyid Ahmad still had not given up his long-established belief in vernacular education when the college was founded, although he now conceded that higher professional and governmental posts would require English education. At the outset of the Oriental Department in 1876, he made suggestions about Urdu textbooks in science and mathematics, and stated that if the government would not institute adequate Urdu examinations the college could hold its own.[1] But the course would follow the lines of the Calcutta University curriculum, except that Arabic or Persian would be the language of literature, logic, and philosophy; Urdu, of history, geography, science, and mathematics; and English would be the second language. Several of the original Aligarh students, sons of ʿulama families from Ciryakot and Kandhla, switched over to the Oriental program; in all 20 out of the college's 95 students enrolled in its first year. The following year the number was 36 out of 125, split evenly between the Arabic and Persian branches.[2]

But 1877 was the peak year in Oriental Department enrollment. Already in 1874 the North-Western Provinces authorities had responded to the vernacular education movement by establishing through the government college at Allahabad a vernacular examination, supposedly equivalent to the standard of Calcutta matriculation. But when Aligarh students, prepared only in Arabic or Persian literature, presented themselves for this examination in 1877, only one passed. Sayyid Ahmad, rather disappointed, commented that there was no reason to have the department if students did not use it to learn "modern" subjects. Still, he expressed

[1] TA, 1 Shaʿbān, 1293 H.; see also GNWP, General (A), May 1875, Nos. 6-8.

[2] "History of the Muhammadan Anglo-Oriental College, Aligarh" (1882), p. 2 (printed brochure, AA); AIG, December 27, 1884.

hope that the experiment would work out.[3] But as he took up residence in Aligarh and watched the effort in action, he became increasingly disillusioned. So were many of the students; they either switched to the English Department or, more often, dropped out.[4] Among those who stayed, some in the Arabic branch performed "brilliantly" under the teaching of Maulvi Abbas Husain, the Shīʿah theology professor whom Sayyid Ahmad considered "a great scholar in Arabic."[5] On the other hand, "the existence of [the] Persian branch is no better than its non-existence." English Department students were doing better with Persian as their second language.[6] Soon the program was reduced to a handful of Shīʿah students in Arabic. In 1885 it was finally abolished altogether.[7]

In 1882 Sayyid Ahmad explained his disillusionment with higher-level vernacular education in testimony before W. W. Hunter's Education Commission. "I confess I am the person who had first entertained the idea," he stated; but he now believed that the language of ruling power must become the language of scholarship. Although he conceded that some of the exact sciences might require only a very rudimentary English, since they consisted so much of universal symbols and technical terms, what now concerned him more were what he called the "uncertain sciences," such as history, logic, philosophy, political economy, and jurisprudence. Here, not only were there difficulties over technical vocabulary, or keeping up with the literature. The major obstacle was the style of expression communicated in ordinary Urdu prose. In Urdu, according to Sayyid Ahmad, it was virtually impossible to write without exaggeration, to separate metaphor from concrete reality. "As long as our community does not, by means of English education, become familiar with the exactness of thought and unlearn the looseness of ex-

[3] RMAOC, 1877, p. 6. [4] *Ibid.*, 1878, p. 5.

[5] *Ibid.*, 1879, p. 4; Sayyid Ahmad to Beck, March 8, 1884 (106A, AA).

[6] RMAOC, 1880, p. 5. [7] *Ibid.*, 1884-1885, p. 1.

pression, our language cannot be the means of high mental and moral training."[8]

The major goal of education, then, was the mastery of English. Whatever concepts were taught in subjects such as history, philosophy, logic, or natural science, what was primarily being taught was English: not only its vocabulary and grammar, but genres and styles of exposition and expression as they had developed in the historical tradition of English literature. English was no neutral tool; it was to be an intentional instrument of acculturation to Victorian values and ideas. Yes, Sayyid Ahmad said it: the aim of the college was "to form a class of persons, Muhammedan in religion, Indian in blood and colour, but English in tastes, in opinions, and in intellect."[9]

But what, in fact, was communicated to the students? In the earlier years, when Aligarh still had ambitions of teaching at a higher standard than other colleges, it offered examinations of its own to determine who deserved scholarships, and also as practice for the ones given by Calcutta University. These internal examinations reveal what teachers at Aligarh expected their students to know—and presumably what they taught. Parallel evidence for a later period, after 1890, is available from those Allahabad University examinations set by members of the Aligarh faculty. Although there was limited difference in the curriculum between the two periods, there was a significant shift in how it was presented and in the style of expression that students learned.

The required course in logic did not differ significantly from the equally Aristotelian system taught in the old madrasahs. But students really learned how to string ideas together by close, sentence-by-sentence study of works of

[8] Sayyid Ahmad's testimony to EC, in AIG, Supplement, August 5, 1882.

[9] "History of the Muhammadan Anglo-Oriental College" (1882); the statement alludes to a famous passage in Macaulay's Minute on Education, 1835 (de Bary, *Sources*, II, 49).

English literature and contemporary British philosophers and historians. Except on the elementary school level, there were few textbooks especially prepared for Indian students; when textbooks were used, they were written for British and American audiences. But most of the books studied were, in the contemporary view, the best British culture had to offer. This included Shakespeare, Milton, Johnson, Burke, Wordsworth, Macaulay, and Mill, as well as contemporary writers then considered the leading scholars in their fields.[10] Thus Indian students were included in the audience of British culture.

This can even be seen in a passage to be translated from English into Persian on a B.A. level examination given in 1883. "Among the many phenomenal outgrowths of our century," the passage began, "is the strange creed of the so-called spiritualists . . . a possible last refuge of compromise [between industrial progress and] the tottering ruins of religion." Genuine religion was ignored, the passage continued; as a Brooklyn preacher has argued, if Jesus appeared in today's world he would be arrested as a public nuisance. This passage, selected by Amjad Ali for a Persian examination, was not intended as a vehicle of indoctrination; nor was it considered inappropriate or inaccessible. Students would be able to identify with "our century," with the bemused detachment of such words as "phenomenal," "strange," "so-called"—the criticism of one European point of view by another. The idea of possible tension between industrialization and religion would be familiar, and students would not be confused or offended by the boldness of expression in a phrase like "the tottering ruins of religion." They might agree with the sentiment expressed in the passage or not, but they would be able to respond to its style of argument. What is more, they were expected to translate it into Persian.[11]

[10] See Ellen E. McDonald, "English Education and Social Reform in Late Nineteenth Century Bombay: A Case Study in the Transmission of a Cultural Ideal," *Journal of Asian Studies*, XXV (1966), 453-470; the authors mentioned are taken from the examinations discussed below.

[11] B.A. Test Examination No. XIV, 1883 (AA).

Many examination questions seem to call for a genuinely critical interpretation of the texts, leaving wide scope for original thought; argument, one might think, was a large part of a student's education. "Briefly criticize Wordsworth as a poet, a philosopher and a politician. . . . What was the 'leading idea' in Coriolanus and did it represent Shakespeare's political views? . . . How did the poetry of Dryden and Pope differ from Elizabethan poetry?" History questions often called for evaluations and comparisons, usually of famous people such as James I and Charles I, Walpole and the younger Pitt. Or the questions could be scholarly, such as an evaluation of the different kinds of evidence for dating Shakespeare's plays.[12]

In philosophy, strongly emphasized in the curriculum, students were drawn into the major controversies of British thought, in particular the opposition between Intuitionist and Utilitarian views of epistemology and ethics. In Britain during the nineteenth century, this classic battle between the belief in innate mental faculties and environmentally conditioned ways of thought was held to possess immediate political implications. Moral philosophy was necessary to the training of political leaders. Could society reorganize its institutions by rational calculation? Could individuals maintain independence of mind and action despite the pervasive pressure of a particular social environment? At its widest poles, the controversy represented the full tensions of a newly industrial society, one viewing man as an interchangeable cog in the great machine, the other emphasizing often intangible feelings of virtue and faith.[13] Indian students were to be included in this pressing philosophical dispute:

> It is objected to the doctrine of utility that it is impossible to trace an action to all its consequences. Answer this objection.

[12] *Ibid.*, No. I; "English Prose," Annual Examination, First Year Class, 1883; "History of England," B.A. Test Examination No. XII, 1883; "Shakespeare," Annual Examination, Third Year Class, 1883 (AA).

[13] See Rothblatt, *Revolution of the Dons*, pp. 98-147.

> What according to Hamilton is the relationship between the proof of the existence of God and human freedom? Accepting his position, how do you account for the fact that many necessitarians have believed in God?
>
> What is Truth? Is there any absolute test of truth? What are the tests available to us? Answer these questions fully and critically.[14]

What did such questions mean to the students of Aligarh? The course of study made little concession to the fact that they were not bound up in the mainstream of British concerns. Or maybe they were. Half the history questions dealt with the history of England; only a quarter with India, and most of those with the British in India:

> Sketch the administration of Lord Amherst. Characterize the state of Indian finance at this time.
>
> Trace the progress of education in India during the present century. Mention any measures relating to the press during the same period.[15]

Such questions seem to represent the full extent of efforts to draw connections between British ideas and Indian concerns.

There is no evidence to indicate what students did with such questions before the arrival of the young professors from Cambridge, but few of them did satisfactorily in the eyes of the examiners. On Aligarh's own examinations a passing grade was usually 33 percent; sometimes it was 25 percent. A mark over 50 percent was a rare thing. In the college-level examinations of 1883, 16 out of 35 students passed.[16] Such results were typical not only for Aligarh but for all colleges. Aligarh's results in the university examinations were not distinguished, but they were not notably dif-

[14] "Psychology," Annual Examination, Third Year Class, 1883 (AA).

[15] "History of India," B.A. Test Examination, No. X, 1883 (AA).

[16] RMAOC, 1883, Appendices I, III.

ferent from the university as a whole.[17] Again, in the period before Beck, 69 out of 99 passed the entrance examination, 34 out of 58 passed the First Arts, and 7 out of 14 passed the B.A.[18] Even among those who passed, only the bravest went on to try the next level.

It is likely that students learned their subjects pretty much by rote, relying on the painstaking lectures of their professors and, sometimes, booklets that summarized the texts and anticipated likely examination questions.[19] It is unlikely that students under Siddons' principalship became involved, either as students or in later life, in the genuine intellectual issues presented in the course of study. It was hard enough to learn English.

In 1881 the *Aligarh Institute Gazette* published some short student essays in order to show the public what the students were learning. The subject was "College Life," in particular the advantages of going to a residential school. Laboriously written over a period of three hours, the essays are devoid of concrete detail, wit, or straightforward feeling. Ahmad Husain Khan, then just at the start of his college years after six years in the school, won a prize of fifteen rupees for his celebration of "hard, untiring labour" and the need to "command the attention to fix itself on the hard, dry lesson and master it." Students must not be distracted, he argued, by "sensual pleasures [such as] drinking, eating, operatic performances, shows, games, jokes, gay companies &c." The motive for such self-denial—all that time saved by not going to the opera, for example—was the hope "for future greatness" and "becoming a famous man."[20]

[17] Comparative examination results were regularly reported in AIG.

[18] Bhatnagar, *A History of the M.A.O. College*, p. 75, but corrected on 1878 Entrance Examination (RMAOC, 1878, p. 5).

[19] Bazaar notes are listed in the quarterly statements of registered publications, *North-Western Provinces and Oudh Gazette* (e.g., March 13, 1886; August 31, 1889; March 18, 1893; September 21, 1895); for an attempt of the Director of Public Instruction to ban the use of such publications see AIG, March 11, 1890.

[20] AIG, February 12, 1881.

Ahmad Husain Khan did not want to be a clerk like his father,[21] and contrary to the accusations of Sayyid Ahmad and others, the official British educational system was not designed to make him one. It was not an education to inspire meek submission. At least the curriculum was not designed for that purpose. It was a curriculum conceived as training for leadership. Men who lead other men, it was assumed, must understand the moral foundations of individual action and social institutions. They must also have the verbal skills to articulate goals and persuade others. They can develop such understanding and skill by the close study of language as it has been used by great men of the past. And a necessary condition of such learning is self-discipline and the ability to overcome difficulty.

But something was wrong. Students were not being inspired; they were giving up. What they learned was the ability to accept drudgery. They found no excitement in their schooling, no vigor of intellectual involvement. The British schoolmasters hired in India to transmit this high civilization—Siddons, Nesbitt, and Horst—did not reveal any great vigor of intellectual involvement, either. They were apparently diligent teachers, but they have left no trace of independent thought or personal commitment to ideas. Siddons could occasionally urge the students to be "good boys."[22] Horst managed to publish *A Key to Nesfield's Senior Reader, Part III*.[23] Their contribution to Indian intellectual history was not overwhelming.

THE APOSTLES

Sayyid Ahmad had long denounced any system of education that left "the inner spirit dead." His major complaint against English education in India was that it failed to inspire

[21] For Ahmad Husain Khan's father, see note by Pānipatī, *Maktūbāt*, p. 15.

[22] AIG, March 6, 1880.

[23] *North-Western Provinces and Oudh Gazette*, March 18, 1893.

creativity. The initial designs for Muslim education represented a bold departure toward a different kind of intellectual community; but in the early years, it was by no means obvious that the college at Aligarh was headed in any such direction. A change came in 1883, however; Sayyid Ahmad managed to recruit two young men who were able in the years ahead to breathe genuine life and vigor into the Aligarh College. One of them was Maulana Muhammad Shibli Numani of Azamgarh, then about twenty-six. The other was Theodore Beck of London and Cambridge University, aged twenty-three. Shibli came alone and developed a special enclave that both opposed and complemented the dominant theme. That dominant theme was the work of Beck and a chain of Cambridge recruits—Harold Cox, Walter Raleigh, T. W. Arnold, and Theodore Morison. These men carried to Aligarh a particular subculture of British intellectual life, one that suited the aspirations and priorities that Sayyid Ahmad considered appropriate to his educational efforts.

"The students are alive," Alfred North Whitehead once wrote, ". . . [and] the teachers also should be alive with living thoughts."[24] Whitehead was a classmate of Beck's at Trinity College and a fellow member of the Apostles. Raleigh was also an Apostle. Membership in this society was hard to come by, and could not be sought. Its procedures and even its existence were supposed to be secret. There were only about ten undergraduate members at any one time, only a few openings every year. Selection was made with great care, but without regard to social status, wealth, learning, moral worth, or even intelligence. The requisite quality was "an apostolic spirit." The philosopher Henry Sidgwick described this as "the spirit of the pursuit of truth with absolute devotion and unreserve by a group of intimate friends, who were perfectly frank with each other and indulged in any manner of humor, sarcasm and playful banter, and yet each respects the other and when he discourses tries to learn from him and

[24] *The Aims of Education* (New York: Mentor Books, 1949), p. xi.

see what he sees."[25] The Society delighted in the widest divergence of opinion, in aggressive, even brutal disputation. That was what brought ideas to life.

Even when the Apostles gave themselves over to comedy, it was underpinned with those earnest Capitalized Abstractions of Victorian culture. Once Walter Raleigh read a paper "Is Sense of Humour or Personal Integrity More Potent for Pleasure to its Owner?" The argument, humorously made, was for humor, but the issue was the seminal moral concern of Victorian thought, represented in the conflicting tradition of Apostle philosophers, Sidgwick, M'taggart, Russell, and Moore. Raleigh's essay was a parody of utilitarianism, an argument for higher qualities of mind. Humor was Olympian, above the mundane—like poetry. Aesthetic feelings were truer than "facts."[26]

Such detachment, argued in terms of Platonic perfection by his Apostolic contemporary G. Lowes Dickenson, was one major current in the Society. But another was an intense desire to communicate this higher enlightenment to the world of human institutions. One of the original formulators of the Apostle ethos, F. D. Maurice, the passionate advocate of "Christian Socialism," constructed an alternative to intuitionist and utilitarian ethics by turning from philosophical inquiry to religiously inspired sociology. Morality was based neither on innate faculties nor calculation of the general good, but on the extension of family love to wider social circles—the community, the nation, and ultimately to all mankind. The social bond of shared values was consummated in public worship, but the whole structure would crumble if men ceased to believe in it. The movement in British thought from collectively based values to a morality posited on the individual threatened the basis of human existence. That basis was to be found in the loyalty and intimacy of human relationships.[27]

[25] A. S. and E. S[idgwick], *Henry Sidgwick* (London: Macmillan, 1906), p. 34.

[26] Walter Raleigh, *Laughter From a Cloud* (London: Constable & Co., 1923).

[27] Rothblatt, *Revolution of the Dons*, pp. 143-151.

Whatever their philosophical positions, Apostles shared Maurice's belief in social intimacy and the power of ideas. For a later generation, more famous as "the Bloomsbury group," such values drifted into aestheticism and flamboyant homosexuality.[28] But Victorian Apostles followed Maurice in his earnest dedication to a social mission. Thus Henry Sidgwick, successor to Maurice as Professor of Moral Philosophy, returned to utilitarianism by looking to common understandings of moral concepts and their practical implications for social action.[29] Apostles tended to move from their clandestine gatherings into active lives as public men. As politicians, writers, and educators, they sought influence over the working institutions of society.

J. R. Seeley, Professor of History at Cambridge, was not an Apostle—though Sidgwick felt he should have been—but his thinking was very much part of the intellectual atmosphere of Cambridge in the late nineteenth century. Like Maurice, he built his theory of society and history on the primacy of kinship ties. He argued that political institutions were extensions of family feelings. This concept was also familiar in the writings of an early Victorian Apostle, Henry Maine, but Maine considered such feelings an evolutionary artifact, not a necessary condition of the social order. In Seeley's view, civilization had achieved its highest moments when men had been capable of transferring such feelings from the particular to the universal, as with the Roman Empire and then, more perfectly, the Christian Church. And such universality was the historical mission of the British Empire.[30]

The work of education was a vitally important area of social action. So thought Seeley and Sidgwick, who in the decade that intervened between Sayyid Ahmad's trip to Eng-

[28] Michael Holroyd, *Lytton Strachey* (Harmondsworth: Penguin Books, Ltd., 1971); Holroyd, *Lytton Strachey and the Bloomsbury Group* (Harmondsworth: Penguin Books, Ltd., 1971).

[29] Henry Sidgwick, *The Methods of Ethics*, reprint ed. (Chicago: University of Chicago Press, 1962), pp. 1-14.

[30] Rothblatt, *Revolution of the Dons*, pp. 155-180.

land and Theodore Beck's admission to Trinity College, had transformed Cambridge and formulated a new understanding of the role of higher education in modern society. Democracy and industrialization did require a new kind of education, but it was not to be a simple surrender to vocational training. What was needed was a generation of intellectuals capable of rigorous scholarship and research, but also sensitive to the totality of human needs. Such men would be the leaders of the new society. To achieve these ends courses of studies were revised to emphasize general ideas over detail, and the role of the professor and don was redefined to include real personal involvement in intellectual dialogue with the students. The residential character of the Cambridge colleges was crucial to the emotional as well as the intellectual purposes of the university: the extension of family feelings to universal concerns.[31]

For many Apostles the first venture into public life had been the Cambridge Union; the Union was one place where the Society spotted prospective members. Beck, Cox, and Raleigh were all presidents of the Union during their undergraduate years. Here, too, the business was disputation, but in the form of parliamentary debate. The issues were almost always matters of political concern and social policy. The audience was not select, the discussion was formal, and the highest virtue was oratorical skill, not truth or sincerity. At the Union one played to win. When the Apostles met secretly on Saturday evenings a member read a paper, but he was always free to change his mind. The meeting ended with a vote, but it was based on the major issue raised in the course of discussion rather than the argument of the initial paper. In the Union, with far more people and no wine, there was a set "resolution" argued initially and in conclusion by two speakers, pro and con. The vote decided which speaker had been more convincing. Such was the difference between private inquiry and public persuasion.[32]

In the Union debates Beck was a Tory "Radical" and

[31] *Ibid*., pp. 167-179, 260-273.

[32] For Union debates see *Cambridge Review*, I-VI (1879-1885).

Cox, a socialist. They frequently found themselves in opposition to their well-connected Apostolic friends, sons of John Strachey and Fitzjames Stephen. Cox was in favor of nationalizing landed property, forcing landlords to work, and offering them only "charitable consideration."[33] Beck spoke eloquently on behalf of abolishing the House of Lords, Home Rule for Ireland, women's rights, "pure democracy," the right of revolution, and the creation of a classless society. Cambridge should be open to the working class, and students should have power in governing the university.[34] He denounced British rule in India for not "fulfilling our duty, training the nation and leaving it, when strong enough, to itself."[35] Supporting Morison's motion that "John Bull is a revolting National ideal," Beck declared, "The Englishman abroad [is] a most objectionable character. . . . In India," he went on, "we have sent out young Englishmen to domineer over and insult our subject races."[36]

Apostles were not bound to consistency; it was sufficient to be sincere. In later life Harold Cox was to be an outspoken opponent of socialism, an upholder of classical economic liberalism.[37] Walter Raleigh, the aesthete, denigrated his own able literary scholarship and was killed in 1923 after trying to be an aviator in Iraq.[38] As for Beck, he was very soon speaking with envy of the colonial administrators he met on the way out to India—"men of action, not of literature."[39]

"THE CAMBRIDGE OF INDIA"

"You will, I think, be interested in hearing about the new Cambridge founded by the Indian Muhammadans," Beck

[33] *Cambridge Review*, V (1884), 312-313.

[34] *Ibid.*, IV (1882-1883), 64, 188-190, 312, 397, 428; II (1880-1881), 129, 257.

[35] *Ibid.*, IV (1883), 205.

[36] *Ibid.*, IV (1883), 268.

[37] Hirst, "Cox," DNB.

[38] Smith, "Raleigh," DNB; see also Holroyd, *Lytton Strachey*, p. 110.

[39] Theodore Beck, "A Journey to Aligarh," *Cambridge Review*, V (1884), 147.

wrote Raleigh soon after arriving in Aligarh at the end of 1883.[40] From the start of the Aligarh College, Sayyid Ahmad and Sayyid Mahmud had projected on to it the image of Cambridge. Over their own clothes, college students wore gowns modeled after the one Mahmud had worn at Christ's College.[41] In 1880, when Mahmud opened a reading room in the boarding house, again hallowed by the Cambridge example, Sayyid Nabi Ullah, soon to be a Cambridge student himself, called him "the first civilized Musalman gentleman." The ideal of liberal education, as Nabi Ullah put it, was bound up with "fellow feeling" and "national sympathy"—an ideal common to Sayyid Ahmad and the Cambridge dons. Another student said Aligarh would become "the Cambridge of India," and recalled the idea of its eventual apotheosis as a university.[42]

When Sayyid Mahmud traveled to Cambridge in 1883 to recruit a principal, he knew very well the kind of man he wanted, and Arthur Strachey was able to find him such a man. As Strachey put it years later, "Mr. Beck's sympathetic enthusiasm enabled him to identify himself with Sir Syed Ahmed's ideals." Theodore Morison was to describe him as a man of "ardent enthusiasm . . . romantic and generous," who was prepared to devote his life to restoring "a people who once thronged the palaces and commanded the armies of the great Moghul."[43]

But if Beck had the right temperament, he also needed some ideological orientation. Accompanied on the long trip out to India by Sayyid Mahmud and subjected to endless political conversation, he was soon an ardent convert to the Aligarh party line. He summed it up for Raleigh shortly after his arrival:

> The Muhammadans were, you know, for two centuries the rulers of Upper India. . . . The British empire involved

[40] *Ibid.*, p. 146.
[41] Beck, "The College at Aligarh," *Cambridge Review*, V (1884), 178.
[42] AIG, November 13, 1880.
[43] MAOCM, December 1, 1899, pp. 7-8.

> new conditions of individual success. The most downtrodden of the Hindoos, the Bengalis, eagerly embraced the opportunities offered them of English education, while the proud Muhammadans held sulkily aloof. . . . Under these circumstances what was wanted was a college which would give an English education, and at the same time teach the Muhammadan religion. . . . Accordingly our founder, Syed Ahmed Khan, set to work to mould the opinion of his countrymen.

The word "our" kept cropping up as Beck communicated his enthusiasm for Sayyid Ahmad and the Aligarh College. A "Radical" no more, he spoke with awe of Sayyid Ahmad's "illustrious descent" and was appropriately impressed by "the Rajas, Nawabs, etc., I have met."[44]

In this frame of mind, he set out on his appointed task to bring the breath of Cambridge to Aligarh. Soon after taking over from Siddons, he wrote an article in the *Institute Gazette* holding out the prospect of affiliation to Cambridge.[45] At the opening of the Siddons Union Club, he emphasized his experience with the Cambridge prototype and promised to hang a picture of it in the room.[46] At his instigation the Cambridge Union even passed, with one dissent, a vote of good will.[47] A reception for the cricket team was likened to "Bump suppers" for Cambridge rowing teams, and there were also to be occasional meals fitted out with a "Fellows' Table."[48]

The most important of these Cambridge-like institutions was the Union Club. Sayyid Ahmad had included a debating society in his earliest "dream" of the Muslim College, and in 1880 there had been an abortive attempt to start a "Union Club" with required attendance and written essays on topics assigned by Sayyid Ahmad and other adult authorities.[49] The idea was revived by Sami Ullah shortly after Beck's arrival

[44] "The College at Aligarh," p. 210.
[45] AIG, May 24, 1884. [46] *Ibid.*, September 20, 1884.
[47] *Ibid.*, December 20, 1884.
[48] *Ibid.*, November 25, 1884; March 20, 1886.
[49] *Ibid.*, September 28, 1880.

as a way of honoring Siddons. This time money was raised to renovate one of the old bungalows east of the quadrangle, and student membership was voluntary—for a fee (one rupee entrance and eight annas a month). The club was fitted out with a reading room containing 350 books, some daily newspapers, and magazines such as the *Times Weekly, Nineteenth Century*, and *Cassels Family Magazine*.[50] The Principal would be permanent president and Sayyid Ahmad, treasurer, but the students would elect a vice president and secretary.

Inaugurating the Union in August 1884, Beck laid out ideological boundaries for the students with a neat synthesis of the ideas of J. L. Seeley and the "school of native political thought" led by Sayyid Ahmad. In contrast to the bitter antagonisms of "Anglo-Indian" settlers and Bengali nationalists, the basic theme at Aligarh was warm personal relations between Englishmen and Indians. Each culture had much to learn from the other, and Beck expressed his own excitement at discovering the wonders of Mughal architecture. One of the major purposes of the Union would be discussion of what things India might want to borrow from Europe and what things it should hold on to: for "remember, gentlemen, that you have a civilization of your own." Politics would be an important topic, but it would have to be considered "in a spirit of investigation and in the light of history." Some subjects, however, would not be open for debate—British rule in India, for example. Unlike the Cambridge prototype, Beck warned, he would have veto power over any discussion, and would not permit the Union to become a forum for Bengali-style "sedition." He offered as an alternative approach to politics the ideas of Seeley about universal empire. The goal was the unity of man. This was the purpose of the British empire today, just as it had been of Akbar in former times.[51]

Beck's speech accurately reflected ideas often expressed by

[50] *Ibid.*, September 11, 1883; August 6, 1884; Aziz Mirza to Sayyid Ahmad, May 9, 1886, AA.

[51] AIG, September 20, 1884.

Sayyid Ahmad, but it contrasted significantly with Sayyid Ahmad's own words on the same occasion. The difference was above all in tone: Beck's bright optimism versus the heavy irony and pathos of Sayyid Ahmad. Once again the old man set out to shock his audience with insults. As in his London letters, he turned to animal imagery: Indians were like monkeys, as some Englishman had remarked; they imitated "men." On the other hand, if Darwin was right even Indians could evolve some day to the human level. The means would be an amalgamation of cross and crescent, a concept he represented graphically with a picture of a crescent lying on its back, a cross mounted above it. "Why should we not try and be equal to European nations?"[52]

Following Sayyid Ahmad's speech, Beck's statement of admiration for Indian civilization was especially gratifying and appealing. So were Beck's enthusiastic, open manners: "When I saw Mr. Beck for the first time mixing cordially and sincerely with my countrymen," said Khvajah Yusuf in the concluding speech, "my surprise though very agreeable was very great."[53] It was Beck's special mission to inspire the students of Aligarh with self-respect—a sense of superiority with regard to the humdrum of textbooks and examinations, a belief in one's own ability, within limits, to form and express opinions. And for many students the Union was just such a liberating experience. But it might also commit them to ways of thinking with far greater effectiveness than rote preparation of assigned textbooks.

The Club met Wednesday evenings. As few as ten, as many as fifty students might seat themselves on benches underneath the large chandelier. A six-man executive committee would sit facing them at the head of the room. Beck, now permanently a Union president, would enter, accompanied by the two student officers; with all due ceremony they would take their chairs just in front of the committee. Four days earlier the resolution had been posted outside the

[52] *Ibid.* [53] *Ibid.*

Club building, along with the names of speakers pro and con. The pro speaker rose first, and the debate would proceed—in English—amidst heckling and parliamentary cries such as "no" and "question," until finally a vote was called.[54] In 1887 a student strike temporarily undermined the Union's popularity, but in its first three years the *Aligarh Institute Gazette* published the proceedings of twenty-seven debates. The topics could be divided almost evenly under four headings—private belief, social relations, future occupation, and politics.[55]

Debate on religious principles was not permitted, except when those principles came under non-Muslim auspices. On one occasion two visiting Christian missionaries defended belief in ghosts as part of religious faith. Most Hindu and Muslim students disagreed, although Sayyid Ahmad recounted how he had once seen a ghost in a London theatre—Hamlet's father.[56] Another time a Brahmin student held forth on the virtues of vegetarianism. His only support came from another Hindu student and Harold Cox, who was a practicing vegetarian. Muslim students argued that meat eating was part of the natural order and a sign of strength. Sajjad Husain, Hali's son, said simply that he happened to like "a good dish of roast mutton or Indian kabobs." And Walter Raleigh, characteristically, maintained that the expulsion from the Garden of Eden was a direct result of vegetarianism: mankind would still be there if Adam and Eve had "confined themselves to roast beef."[57]

This sort of wit became part of the Aligarh style, but there could also be serious discussion on moral and philosophical questions like the relative virtue of truthfulness. Ahmad Husain Khan, the student who had suffered so in his "hard, dry" studies, could now rise to the occasion with "a learned dis-

[54] *Ibid.*, October 6, 1885.

[55] *Ibid.*, November 22, 1884 to March 31, 1888; it is possible there were other debates, since there are gaps in the Azad Library holdings of the AIG.

[56] *Ibid.*, January 19, 1886.

[57] *Ibid.*, December 22, 1885.

cussion on the nature of conscience and the moral faculty." Aziz Mirza replied with an appeal to "general happiness." Another student quoted the Qur'an in support of truthfulness, while Ahmad Husain Khan concluded the debate by speaking of death on the battlefield for the sake of truth and glory in the afterlife. In the vote truthfulness lost, 31-20.[58]

Like truthfulness, human equality was generally a losing cause. When Sajjad Husain introduced a cautiously worded resolution in favor of female education in the home, it went down to defeat by a close vote; but even those who favored it held out for the continuance of pardah. The majority view was expressed by Shibli's younger brother, Mahdi Hasan: "all that [is] needed for a woman is to lead a virtuous life."[59] In another debate Mustafa Khan argued that there should be no division between high and low, that all men are brothers. In support, Sajjad Husain startled the audience by claiming that he could even prefer a good Camar to an evil Sayyid. Against this the learned Ahmad Husain Khan quoted Plato, Shakespeare, and Alexander Bain about the superiority of certain lineages; and Aziz Mirza offered the analogy of animal pedigrees.[60] On still another occasion the issue was whether certain occupations were contemptible. The students were closely divided, with many words of praise for the honest artisan, but also much in support of social exclusiveness. "Would you like to eat with a shoemaker or a sweeper?" asked Sami Ullah's son, Majid Ullah. "No, I hope never."[61]

"It is utterly wrong to say that . . . different races of mankind are naturally brave or naturally timid." This resolution, moved by Sajjad Husain, alluded to British theories and policies concerning "cowardly" Bengalis and allegedly "martial races" like the north Indian Muslims.[62] Sajjad Husain opposed this notion, arguing that bravery was a matter of education and circumstances. The other side was led by the learned

[58] *Ibid.*, August 22, 1885.
[59] *Ibid.*, November 22, 1884.
[60] *Ibid.*, December 6, 1884.
[61] *Ibid.*, February 14, 1885.
[62] Nirad C. Chaudhuri, "The 'Martial Races' of India," *Modern Review*, LXVIII (1931), 41-51, 295-307.

Ahmad Husain Khan, "who exhibited an intimate acquaintance with his 'Bain' which boded well for his approaching examination." (Bain argued that there were innate physical and mental differences among men which made them respond differently to environmental stimuli.)[63] The discussion came down to whether a Bengali raised in Kabul would turn out like an Afghan; thirteen against nine felt he would not.[64]

The military self-image of Muslims was a common area of disagreement; many did not identify with it. Usually the staunchest advocates of the idea were students claiming Afghan descent.[65] Despite his learning, Ahmad Husain Khan glorified the military life as superior to the intellectual. Aftab Ahmad Khan argued that generals were more important than statesmen. One non-Afghan agreed: the life of a civil servant was boring. "I prefer a military life, though I am not a Pathan, or a Jat, or a Rajput, or a Maharatta. I am only a poor Sheikh. It is from reading tales that I have come to prefer the military life, which does not agree with my constitution."[66] Sajjad Husain and Aziz Mirza were the steady defenders of intellectual superiority. On different occasions the gathering supported opposite positions—often by decisive margins.

The opposition of pen and sword was bound up with the content of student ambitions. What was this English education leading them to? Overwhelmingly the students agreed with Sajjad Husain when he argued that they should not aim for government employment. The only thing said in its favor was that there was often no alternative. Most speakers maintained that one obtained a government post at the cost of narrow examination preparation, rather than true learning. Raleigh argued that it was menial to be a government "servant." It was better to be a cook, a builder, or a philosopher who "possess their souls in calm." Beck took a different position: "man's faculties [are] better called out in conducting an

[63] Alexander Bain, *Mental and Moral Science*, 3d ed. (London: Longmans & Co., 1872).

[64] AIG, April 14, 1885.

[65] *Ibid.*, October 10, 1885; October 23, 1886; November 30, 1886.

[66] *Ibid.*, October 23, 1886.

industrial enterprise than when engaged in clerk's work."[67] In another debate Mustafa Khan condemned students who chose the legal profession; it was better to be a doctor. In a close vote a majority of students disagreed.[68]

Finally, the Union members addressed themselves to the question of power in Indian society, where they fit into the political structure of the country. Freedom of the press received overwhelming support, but students were evenly divided on whether the British government should take responsibility for the educational system.[69] Some students expressed opposition to the Burmese and Afghan wars, but more declared a good deal of enthusiasm for them.[70] Few people attended debates on representative government and the Indian National Congress, which took place after a student strike. Beck used the occasions to argue that representative institutions would harm Muslim interests, and most students agreed. The Congress was condemned nine to one, with a Hindu as the sole dissenter.[71]

All these Union debates—or most of them—revealed that Aligarh students were not all cut out of the same cloth. There was genuine diversity of opinion. The most active of the Union students held fairly consistent points of view through the different debates. Often they put their studies to work in support of their arguments. Mahdi Hasan pointed out the main purpose of the Club: to give a student "confidence in his opinions." It was possible to have political influence within the British raj, but "we lose our rights because we do not know how to ask for them." The Union, he said, bound students together in "friendship" and enabled them to work out opinions in public and learn how to present them persuasively. A good speaker could look forward to "loud cheers and applause."[72]

Whatever their disagreements, Aligarh students were beginning to develop a style of their own. The Calcutta Uni-

[67] *Ibid.*, December 5, 1885. [68] *Ibid.*, March 14, 1885.
[69] *Ibid.*, March 9, 1886; September 3, 1887; December 3, 1887.
[70] *Ibid.*, March 31, 1885; March 31, 1888.
[71] *Ibid.*, January 24, 1888. [72] *Ibid.*, December 9, 1884.

versity course of study purported to encourage independent thought, but preparation for examinations tended to inspire students with a tight, dull, irrelevant approach to intellectual problems. With the coming of Beck and his friends Aligarh students were constantly exposed to combative conversation and speech making. Controversy was no longer confined to textbooks and examinations, it was now a means of social competition within a residential student community. A student could score points by skillful use of literary allusion, philosophical principles, and humor. There were several rewards: the immediate gratification of an audience's reaction, the annual "Cambridge Speaking Prize," and, most of all, election as officeholder in the Union. To be vice president or secretary was "a coveted distinction" and a matter of intense competition among student factions.[73]

Verbal competition was a familiar feature of Urdu culture. Many students could recall the witty, learned conversation of fathers, uncles, and their friends in the mardanah of their homes.[74] The home of Sayyid Ahmad was even then a center for theological disputation, although that subject was out of bounds for the college.[75] The munāzarah, or formal disputation, the mushā'irah, or poetic symposium, were occasions for men to exhibit their skill with words. Often the idea expressed was considerably less important than the manner in which it was expressed. "This is an open challenge to subtle-minded friends," wrote Ghalib, but he was hardly committed to every theological and mystical proposition that entered his poetry.[76] Above all, facility with language was a way of calling attention to the speaker.

By recruiting a series of Cambridge Union presidents, the managers of Aligarh College found a way of pouring new content into old forms of social intercourse. Once again, they

[73] *Ibid.*, October 6, 1885. [74] See above, pp. 55-56.

[75] Khvājah Muḥammad Yūṣuf, *Izālat ul-auhām*, p. 3; see theological correspondence between Sayyid Ahmad and Mahdi Ali, Maktūbāt, pp. 131-183.

[76] "Ṣalā'ē 'ām hai yārān-i nuktahdān kē liyē."

selected a particularly congenial feature of British culture. These young men from Cambridge possessed unusual eloquence, a power with words that often, as with their Urdu counterparts, inspired one with admiration for their fluency quite apart from what they were saying. Literary skill had been Muhammad's one miracle; Muslims knew how to appreciate it.

EXAMINATIONS AND THE UNIVERSITY

In April 1885, Ahmad Husain Khan and two fellow students, both Hindus, took the train to Allahabad to participate with forty-six other students in the Calcutta University B.A. examination for the North-Western Provinces. In the previous three years seven Aligarh students had achieved this rare and coveted set of initials. To get them one had to sit for a grueling series of three-hour papers lasting over a period of ten days. The examinations demanded mastery of the texts, critical understanding of their major ideas, and clear expression in English. A student could not be sure what was coming the next day. In philosophy Ahmad Husain Khan was all set to be tested first on his old favorite, Alexander Bain's *Mental and Moral Science*; instead he got Mansel and Jardine. In English he had not been expecting such emphasis on Macaulay at the expense of Burke. Nevertheless, all three Aligarh students were able to get through.[77] Ahmad Husain Khan, captain of the cricket team and son of the construction munshi, received a twenty-rupee-a-month scholarship to stay on at Aligarh—at the urging of Beck and against the advice of Sami Ullah—to serve as librarian, translate for the *Aligarh Institute Gazette*, play cricket, and prepare for his M.A.[78]

The first year of Beck's tenure had produced satisfactory

[77] Ahmad Husain Khan (to Beck?), five letters, from Allahabad, two undated, others April 15, 16, 17 of 1885 (AA).

[78] Beck to Sayyid Ahmad, n.d. [September, 1885?] (AA); Ahmad Husain Khan died two years later (AIG, September 13, 1887).

results: three out of three on the B.A., ten out of thirteen on the F.A. True, only half the students taking the entrance examination had passed, but the school was not Beck's department.[79] The arrival of Cox to teach mathematics and political economy and Raleigh to teach English and philosophy made Aligarh an exhilarating place. The message communicated to the students was that personal style was superior to the plodding work of examination preparation; nothing could be more slavish than to study hard in the hope of securing some government post. A talented, cultivated gentleman would naturally find his appropriate station in life. It was best to hold the university curriculum at an ironic distance. Raleigh tried to inspire a proper feeling of irreverence toward the poems of Tennyson and the essays of Helps—both old Apostles—and described his teaching method as "the jack-in-the-box system." It was based on "suddenness of intrusion upon surrounding phenomena. . . . I devise a new sort of manner of conducting my class every morning, pop examinations round corners, make them discuss with each other (limited this), change classes and repeat."[80] He was clearly enjoying himself.

But the young Apostles could not help chafing at the ever-present university, "the Calcutta Mill," as Raleigh called it.[81] Even at Cambridge Beck had attacked the Tripos examinations as contrary to "original research and individual culture."[82] At Aligarh he wrote Sayyid Ahmad that it was "inefficient" to judge a college by examination results while ignoring "the other influences of College life which go towards making students men & gentlemen."[83] Raleigh complained that the Calcutta authorities not only prescribed what subjects to study but what books to read, "even in

[79] AIG, May 9 and 19, 1885.

[80] Raleigh to his sister Kate Raleigh, November 9, 1885, in *The Letters of Sir Walter Raleigh*, ed. Lady Raleigh (New York: Macmillan, 1926), I, 41.

[81] Raleigh to W. R. Sorley, November 16, 1885, *ibid.*, I, 42.

[82] *Cambridge Review*, II (1880), 49.

[83] Beck to Sayyid Ahmad, February 4, 1886 (59B, AA).

mathematics." Teaching procedure was "to pig through the books at so many pages a day." Students spent five hours a day in class: "they slept, and were able under examination to pass by recalling their dreams."[84]

During the hot months of 1886 Beck, Cox, and Raleigh went off on a long, utterly joyful excursion through Kashmir. Traveling by horse and boat, stopping at mud huts and old serais, they were thrilled by the beauty of that beautiful land, and also by their own adventurousness.[85] One morning, while they were eating breakfast at a small Kashmiri shop, they received a letter from Sayyid Ahmad. He was glad to hear that they were having a pleasant journey, he would order cricket equipment from London, work was in progress on the gateway and Strachey Hall—and six out of eight students had failed the B.A. examination.[86] All the other colleges had done exceptionally well; Aligarh's results were "utterly disastrous."[87] Raleigh wrote back, "We are very much depressed at the result of the examination; . . . we did not think we should fall so far below mediocrity. If good examinational results are all important there is more than one way to effect them."[88] Dreams, it would seem, were not good enough.

Sayyid Ahmad was afraid that as a result of the poor examination results students would transfer to Agra College and the enrollment would fall. It did; there were fifty fewer students the following year.[89] Beck tried to reassure him: ". . . I hope rumours as to bad teaching will not spread more than our last bad result warrants. I am myself convinced," he wrote in November, "that never since I joined the College have the College classes been working so well. . . . I do not think there is the least ground for anxiety as to

[84] Raleigh to Sorley, November 16, 1885, *Letters*, I, 45.

[85] Raleigh to Sayyid Ahmad, Mansibal Lake, Kashmir, June 9, 1886 (AIG, June 22, 1886).

[86] Sayyid Ahmad to Beck, May 8 [1886] (AA).

[87] AIG, May 11, 1886.

[88] Raleigh to Sayyid Ahmad, June 9, 1886 (AIG, June 22, 1886).

[89] Above, Table 2, p. 172.

our next results."[90] Once again Beck was overly optimistic. In February all those high hopes and good feelings came crashing down: the students walked out en masse in a dispute with Sayyid Ahmad over boarding-house discipline.[91] Eventually most of the strikers straggled back and made formal apologies in time for the university examinations. They did fairly well; seven out of ten passed the B.A., four of them Hindus. Aziz Mirza, secretary of the Union and leader of the strike, even got honors in English and History. But meanwhile the other colleges once again did much better, nearby Agra passing fifteen out of sixteen.[92] The next year Aligarh's enrollment fell again by another nineteen students.[93] Raleigh and Cox tired of their Indian adventure and returned to England to take up distinguished literary careers.

Beck, however, remained, finding new impetus in the campaign against the Indian National Congress and the establishment of Allahabad University. Opposition to the Congress represented a marvelous way of dramatizing the Aligarh cause and asserting Aligarh's leadership of the Muslims of India. The new university for Hindustan, breaking off from Bengal-oriented Calcutta, held out the prospect of reformulating higher education in the direction of the Cambridge prototype. At least Aligarh would now have a voice, since Beck, Sayyid Ahmad, and Sayyid Mahmud were Fellows and members of the Syndicate. In an educational system run on different principles, the students of Aligarh might look better in comparison to their rivals.

When Sayyid Ahmad's old idea for a regional university at Allahabad was revived in the mid-1880s, he was emphatically unsympathetic. Borrowing from the Punjab University experiment, the proposal called for a strong emphasis on "Oriental" learning. But Sayyid Ahmad, who was then presiding over the demise of Aligarh's own Oriental Department, damned the whole idea as an attempt to keep Indians

[90] Beck to Sayyid Ahmad, November 22, 1886 (AA).
[91] See below, pp. 266-269. [92] AIG, May 28, 1887.
[93] Above, Table 2, p. 172.

down. The British were afraid educated Indians would make trouble for them. They had no intention of turning government offices or commercial enterprises over to "Oriental" procedures; there was no prospect that "the discoveries of art and science, medical and engineering work, would be thrown into an Oriental form." A person with that kind of education "would not be of any use in the world." Furthermore, such learning always had a religious tinge, and was therefore inappropriate for the British government.[94]

Sayyid Ahmad argued that it was better to be affiliated with the best university, Calcutta, than with an inferior new one.[95] But the following year, 1886, he was able to look on the proposal for Allahabad University in a new light. The idea of imitating Punjab had been abandoned, and he could now look forward to seeing "the education of our Province directly in our hands."[96] By this time he was convinced that the way to obtain the highest quality of education, the education of the British ruling class, was to imbibe the spirit of Cambridge—as embodied by Theodore Beck. From this would come the new generation of Muslim leadership.

Allahabad University started off in 1887 with a carbon copy of the Calcutta University curriculum, but Beck immediately set about to alter it. His efforts won support from Sayyid Ahmad as well as some of the British professors associated with other colleges. The basic idea of Beck's proposal was to encourage greater specialization by reducing the number and diversity of courses. Thus the Intermediate Examination would call for compulsory English and only two other subjects chosen from among four options: classical

94 Quoted in Naik, *Selections from the Educational Records,* II, 367-374.

95 *Ibid.*

96 AIG, October 12, 1886; see also Sayyid Ahmad to Auckland Colvin, Lieutenant Governor, NWP, January 21, 1888, communicating a resolution passed by the Muhammadan Educational Conference in Lucknow, December 29, in support of the Allahabad University "provided that it prove an instrument for spreading English higher education among Mahomedans" (43A, AA).

language, mathematics, history, and physical science. The old curriculum had demanded preparation in five subjects. Beck's proposal was enacted as a bifurcation of studies: an A course with language and history (and philosophy at the B.A. level), a B course with science and mathematics.[97] Beck said he was skeptical about teaching science, at least at Aligarh, because to do so properly required full laboratory facilities. He himself had studied more science than was required for his B.A. degree in mathematics, and considered it "useless" to teach "homeopathic doses of science" out of textbooks.[98] He proposed that no provision be made for science at the entrance examination level.[99] He also proposed that the university encourage "original research" by offering a gold medal for a postgraduate dissertation.[100]

Although Sayyid Ahmad tried to make some room for science at Aligarh—a short-lived class in the school to prepare students for Roorkee Engineering College—the basic thrust of Beck's proposal received his enthusiastic support. Returning to arguments he had made back in 1869 in his pamphlet *Strictures on English Education*, he declared "that the system adopted by the older Indian Universities, however useful it may have been to provide government with subordinate officers and officials for the purposes of administration, has failed to produce men who can in any sense be regarded as belonging to a rank higher than . . . mediocrity. . . . Not one man of genius has arisen." He went on to argue that the intellectual potential of Hindus and Muslims was equal to that of Europeans; this was proven by the historical achievements of their two great civilizations. It was unfair to

[97] Papers relating to proposed amendments in the Faculty of Arts (?B, 263B [1887], AA); Bhargava, *History of Secondary Education*, pp. 64-65.

[98] "Principal's views on special committees' report for Entrance Examination," addressed to P. K. Ray, Registrar, Calcutta University, August 12, 1887 (269A, AA).

[99] Amendment to regulations in Arts (Beck's handwriting) (263B [1887], AA).

[100] Amendment proposed by Beck and M. J. White, Canning College (?B [1887], AA).

blame Indian students for failing to love learning for its own sake; their motivations were bound up with the kind of education they got, an education that prepared them only for government employment or the legal profession. "The decision rests, *not* with the original intention of the young student who enters a university but his determination after he has undergone the course." Initial motivations were no different in Europe—"I cannot easily believe that human nature is radically different in various parts of the globe"—but there universities stimulated students with the excitement of ideas. Indian university education, on the other hand, blocked off many occupational choices "because it leaves them the supposed knowers of many subjects and the masters of none."[101]

The Aligarh proposal made considerable headway. No gold medal dissertations were forthcoming, but in 1894 a separate B.Sc. course with physics and chemistry further specialized the curriculum. In 1896 the university made provision for a student to concentrate two-thirds of his time on one subject for the B.A. examination and allowed the professor to select his own textbooks. Philosophy was made optional.[102] "The essential principle," wrote Beck, "is that . . . intellectual discipline rather than the acquisition of a miscellaneous mass of general information is the true aim of education."[103] Critics charged that Allahabad University had become an affiliate of Aligarh, that Beck wanted the course of study watered down for the benefit of Aligarh's inferior students.[104] It is true that Beck's major aim in revising the curriculum was to make Aligarh look better, attract students, and gain national prominence.[105] On the other hand, he

[101] Ms. English translation of Urdu original in Sayyid Ahmad's handwriting (263B [1887], AA).

[102] [Beck], "The Allahabad University," MAOCM, April 1, 1896, and December 1, 1896.

[103] Principal's Report, 1895-1896.

[104] *Hindi Pradīp* (Allahabad), March, as quoted in *Native News Reports, North-Western Provinces and Oudh*, 1891, p. 359.

[105] Beck to Sayyid Ahmad, October 28, 1896 (521B, AA).

feared the domination of Muir College, Allahabad, the largest and best endowed, which supplied most of the examiners and threatened to monopolize the more advanced levels of education.[106] To ward off this challenge he proposed that colleges specialize in their areas of strength. Muir had two science professors; Aligarh would be strong in English, history, mathematics, and Arabic.[107] The logical conclusion of these efforts was the old proposal, revived once again at Sayyid Ahmad's death in 1898, to create an independent teaching and residential Muslim university.[108]

Meanwhile Aligarh students had to live with the standards set by Allahabad University, and these were not always comfortable. As Indians increasingly perceived English education as a means of social mobility under colonial rule, there was a deliberate effort by some British authorities to stem the rising tide of enrollment by failing all but the best students. In the name of excellence they raised the standards of the examinations and curriculum still further beyond the standards of teaching that were possible with a small government investment.[109] It became harder to cram for examinations. In English, for example, students now had to answer a large proportion of questions—forty percent on the entrance examination—based on unseen passages. The textbooks were changed almost every year.[110] On the other hand, the examiners were also different every year, so the level of difficulty varied greatly. For the university as a whole the percentage of passing students on the entrance examination was once as low as 31; it was never higher than 55. For the Intermediate it was even worse, varying from 27 to 48 percent. The B.A. was better—48 to 71 percent—but few reached that stage.[111]

[106] *Idem,* December 8, 1889 (238B, AA).

[107] Principal's Report, 1895-1896.

[108] *Ibid.*, 1898-1899 (in MAOCM and AIG [combined], July 15, 1899); Beck, "The Mahomedan University," MAOCM, March 1899.

[109] RDPI/NWP, 1892-1893, p. 17; 1893-1894, p. 13; 1894-1895, pp. 21-22.

[110] *Ibid.*, 1894-1895, p. 17.

[111] *Ibid.*; also Bhatnagar, *History of the M.A.O. College*, p. 135.

Beck was one Englishman who protested against the high failure rate of the university; he considered it a tremendous waste of human effort, a deliberate discouragement to education. By defining education solely in terms of examination success, the university was making it impossible for students to give adequate attention to other educational concerns.[112] He complained, for example, that the other affiliated colleges were not interested in sports.[113] Addressing the students of Aligarh, he told them to consider passing examinations "a disagreeable necessity."[114] Since the government and the public at large evaluated a college by examination statistics, "it is not only to your personal interest but it is a patriotic duty for you to accumulate in your heads a large supply of information of a kind available for reproduction in the examination hall."[115]

Since Aligarh did not choose to provide instruction for the science track, the supply of information it provided covered much the same ground as the old Calcutta curriculum. For example, Beck himself as an examiner in history asked students to summarize the plot of the Ramayana, give the dates of the first six Mughal emperors, and tick off the provisions of the Magna Charta and the 1832 Reform Bill.[116] In the classroom, however, Beck was apparently a lively lecturer, often swept away in the drama of historical narrative. One old student used to recall with admiration as well as amusement Beck's excitement at telling of Babur's conquest of India: all the fallen Hindu warriors were dispatched directly to hell.[117] The reading in history generally consisted of one self-confident author for any topic, but some of these rose above factual narrative to far-reaching interpretive essays about the rise and fall of civilizations. In Bryce, Seeley, Bagehot, and Guizot students came in contact with some

112 MAOCM, June 1, 1896.

113 *Ibid.*, April 1899.

114 *Ibid.*, December 1, 1894.

115 AIG, July 9, 1889.

116 *Allahabad University Calendar*, 1893-1894, pp. 239-240, 262-263.

117 Interview with Dr. Abid Ahmad Ali, Lahore, September 1969, recollecting what he was told by his father, Sayyid Ahmad Ali.

major contemporary European thought about the moral basis of political community and the "progress" from particularist to universalist loyalties.[118] Authors on Indian history such as Strachey and Hunter tended to emphasize the decadence of India at the time of Britain's providential conquest, and Lane-Poole's handsome book about Muslim Spain ended with the same message about how great civilizations decay.[119] The history course now also included the study of political economy—the theory of rent, the law of supply and demand, and other doctrines of classical liberalism.[120] It was as if the British wanted to teach Indians the secrets of their success.

Though history now put less emphasis on didactic biography and more on the analysis of institutions, some of the loss was made up in English and philosophy. Biographical studies of people such as Locke and Milton now accompanied readings in the original literature. Sometimes popular readings on current science were also included in the English course. There was new attention paid to translation, composition, and oral command of English, even at the college level. But the greater part of the course continued to be a sampling of the major English authors since the time of Shakespeare. Examination questions dealt with comprehension and memory of the texts, but they also called for aesthetic and moral evaluation.[121]

In philosophy the focus continued to be on ethical conduct and its psychological basis, and here students were again confronted with both sides of contemporary philosophical controversy. For a brief period there was also an optional unit on "natural theology." Such readings may have

[118] *Allahabad University Calendar*, 1898-1899, pp. 181-182.

[119] *Ibid.*, 1891-1892, p. 92; 1893-1894, p. 127; 1897-1898, p. 184; Strachey, *India*; Strachey, *Hastings and the Rohilla War* (Oxford: Clarendon Press, 1892); W. W. Hunter, *The Indian Empire* (London: Trübner & Co., 1882); Stanley Lane-Poole, *The Moors of Spain* (London: T. Fisher Unwin, 1885).

[120] *Allahabad University Calendar*, 1893-1894, p. 135.

[121] See annual examination texts in the *Allahabad University Calendar*.

been treading on dangerous ground—the problem of evil, the possibility of miracles—but there is no evidence that students were either upset or engaged by these issues.[122] Most students found philosophy tiresome and difficult, though Zafar Ali Khan was inspired to write an imaginative story about meeting the devil after hearing Arnold lecture on Locke's theory of idea association.[123] There was general relief when philosophy was made optional in 1896.[124]

Although Beck and Sayyid Ahmad had advocated deeper and more advanced study in particular disciplines, Aligarh itself failed to develop in this direction. The college could offer M.A. instruction in English, history, philosophy, mathematics, Arabic, and Persian, but there were few takers. Ziauddin Ahmad, who eventually received doctoral degrees both in India and Europe, was J. C. Chakravarty's only advanced student in mathematics. No one took advantage of Morison in political economy or Arnold in philosophy. The ten students besides Ziauddin who did Master's degrees were in Arabic, Persian, and English.[125] The LL.B., which became a postgraduate degree in 1896, was awarded to twenty-four Aligarh students of the first generation. The law examinations were virtually unique in their practical relevance to Indian concerns and their demand for problem solving. Test questions, sometimes set by Sayyid Mahmud, called for legal opinions on hypothetical cases.[126] It was possible for students to take up law for the sake of intellectual pleasure as well as occupational ambition.

For most Aligarh students, then, their hard labors with the Allahabad curriculum did not turn them in the direction of scholarship or original thought. Nor did it win them distinguished results on the university examinations. Aligarh

122 *Ibid.*, 1895-1896, pp. 390-391.

123 MAOCM, contained in AIG, May 8, 1894.

124 RDPI/NWP, 1897-1898, p. 17.

125 The Muhammadan Anglo-Oriental College, Aligarh, *Calendar*, 1911-1912 (Allahabad: The Indian Press, 1911), p. 118.

126 *Allahabad University Calendar*, 1891-1892, pp. 555-562; see MAOCM, June 1, 1896.

shared the high failure rate of the university as a whole, and sometimes did much worse than the average.[127] The main point was to give some of them, at least, tools of expression and philosophical and historical concepts considered necessary for political leadership. A disciplined political community, led by men capable of rising above selfish concerns and of persuading others about the proper focus of loyalty and duty—this was the message of the classsroom. But in the Aligarh view the classroom could only contribute a small part of the students' moral and emotional education. The real work of inspiring students belonged to the planned social milieu of the college—sports, clubs, prayers, meals, friendships.

Beck now argued that his old preference for "men of action" over "men of literature" in fact conformed with the immediate needs of Indian society. He thus took up one side of Sayyid Ahmad's original motivations for founding the college: intellectual reformulation of Islamic thought finally lost out to finding a place for a small circle of Muslims within the new political structure. For Beck the business of the college was to

> work more at developing strength of character, a sense of public duty, and patriotism, than at cultivating the imagination, the emotions or the faculty of pure speculation. . . . We must reluctantly abandon the cultivation in the majority of our students of the poetic, artistic, or philosophic temperament, and devote our attention to turning out men who in appearance are neatly dressed and clean, of robust constitution and well-trained muscles, energetic, honest truthful, public spirited, courageous and modest in manner, loyal to the British Government and friendly to individual Englishmen, self-reliant and independent, endowed with common sense, with well-trained intellects, and in some cases scholarly tastes.[128]

[127] Bhatnagar, *History of the M.A.O. College*, p. 135; see annual examination results in RDPI/NWP.

[128] Principal's Report, 1895-1896.

Since Aligarh students were gentlemen, university examinations, even failure, could now become a fit subject for humor. Although Beck complained of the "intellectual stagnancy" and "dullness" of India, he assured his students that "Renaissance" did not mean obtaining diplomas; "B.A." just stood for "big ass."[129] On failing his B.A., Sayyid Zainuddin, football captain, wrote a witty third-person essay entitled "Sentiments of a Student Plucked at the University Examination." Shaukat Ali, cricket captain, thought the article was so fine that he led a delegation to Zainuddin the next year to beg him to fail again so that he could write another such article.[130] But Zainuddin passed and went on to an M.A. and then a Deputy Collectorship on Sayyid Ahmad's recommendation.[131] Shaukat Ali passed too, and wrote "How I Passed My B.A.," in which he described his carefree life in the college—until he realized he had six months and twenty-eight books to go before the crucial test. "There is a class of students . . . who have unusual brains, bright intellects and good memories, but withal this, are extremely careless and lazy. . . . They always have a silly contempt for regular industrious students, whom they term '*smugs* or *book worms.*' "[132] Shaukat Ali was proud to belong to this easygoing group; he was also one of Beck's favorite students.[133]

INTELLECTUAL CROSS-CURRENTS

Despite Sayyid Ahmad's unsympathetic words about "Oriental" scholarship, this was the one area where Aligarh developed some scholarly distinction. Disillusioned with undergraduate concentration in Persian and Arabic literature, Sayyid Ahmad nevertheless remained personally absorbed in the study of Islamic theology and history. At Aligarh he continued to write and publish; his *K͟huṭbāt-i Aḥmadiyyah*, the

[129] AIG, September 6, 1892. [130] *Ibid.*, June 6, 1893.

[131] Sayyid Ahmad to Sayyid Zainuddin, January 23, 1896 (47A, AA); telegram from Sayyid Zainuddin to Sayyid Ahmad, February 17, 1896 (95B, AA).

[132] MAOCM, September 1894. [133] See below, pp. 284-286.

final Urdu version of *Essays on the Life of Muhammad*, was followed by his commentary on the Qur'an and a revival of *Tahẕīb ul-Akhlāq* in the 1890s. He was an avid collector of manuscript and modern editions of Arabic texts published in Europe and the Middle East. Much of his interest was an antiquarian fascination, but throughout, his primary motive was to reformulate the ideas and practices of Muslims so that they might become full participants in the power and prosperity of the British empire.

The fact that Sayyid Ahmad's religious ideas were not admissible in the Aligarh curriculum may explain why he was so unenthusiastic about putting strong emphasis on an uncongenial version of the subject. Required classes in "what was euphemistically called 'Theology' "—as Muhammad Ali put it—were not a serious enterprise.[134] They met once a week and required little reading; students sometimes skipped the examinations.[135] Overwhelmingly, students chose easy Persian over difficult Arabic as their second language, despite efforts to encourage them to learn the language of the faith.[136] The Sunni professors, Muhammad Akbar and his successors, were learned ʿulama from Kandhla or Deoband, men of the Vali Ullah tradition like Sayyid Ahmad himself, but they did not do original research or writing. After 1889 the supervisory committees seem to have fallen into disuse, and readings were set by Shibli and other members of the staff. The theology course may have been almost unique in India in including some Vali Ullah in the readings—but only a few pages.[137]

When Shibli arrived at Aligarh in 1883 to take up a post in Persian and to assist in Arabic, he could not be counted as

[134] Mohamed Ali, *My Life: A Fragment*, p. 21.

[135] Sayyid Ahmad to Siddons, May 11, 1883 (116A, AA); Beck to Sayyid Ahmad, July 6, 1886 (205B, AA).

[136] BH Report, 1881, p. 20; statistics on second-language electives are included in annual reports submitted to the Inspector of Schools, Meerut Division, e.g., April 14, 1885 (149A, AA).

[137] Sayyid Ahmad to Beck, December 11, 1894 (415A, AA); MAOCM, May 15, 1899.

a member of the ʿulama. Like many other educated Muslims, he knew Arabic and Persian; he could even write poetry in those languages as well as in Urdu. It was as a man of literature that he was taken on to the Aligarh faculty. He had studied briefly at Deoband and Lahore Oriental College, but most of his education came from individual teachers sought out in a variety of north Indian towns. He had also made a pass at the legal profession, the occupation of his father and younger brothers, at least to the extent of passing the vakil examination.[138] But probably the most important influence on his life previous to Aligarh was his teacher Maulana Muhammad Faruq of Ciryakot, younger brother of Sayyid Ahmad's old teacher and collaborator, Inayat Rasul. Ciryakot was a center for a uniquely rationalist and ecclectic school of ʿulama. Their studies included Muʿtazilī theology, the early Arabic development of Hellenistic science and philosophy, as well as non-Islamic languages such as Sanskrit and Hebrew. Inayat Rasul had participated in the founding of Aligarh and helped recruit some of its first students. Maulana Faruq, however, was unsympathetic to Aligarh; he believed in the continuing validity of *kalām*, Islamic scholasticism. One of his early writings, a poetic reply to Hali's *Musaddas*, denied that the alleged failure of Islamic intellectual life was responsible for the decline of worldly power among the Muslims.[139]

Shibli carried on this defense of the Islamic heritage, but at Aligarh he turned to the writing of history to achieve this purpose. History, though often neglected by Indian Muslims, was an accepted branch of Islamic learning. There were many chronicles of Muslim dynasties in India, but few scholars had turned their attention to such great Arab historians

[138] Nadvī, *Ḥayāt-i Shiblī*, pp. 71-116.

[139] Shaikh Muḥammad Ikrām, "Maulānā Muḥammad Fārūq Ciryākōṭī aur un kā naẓrīyah-i ʿulūm aur taʿlīm," *Al-Maʿārif* [Lahore], 1969, pp. 3-13; Raḥmān ʿAli, pp. 457-464. Hali's long poem, "The Ebb and Flow of Islam," was a popular statement of ideas associated with the Aligarh movement.

as al-Tabari and Ibn Khaldun. Shibli followed Sayyid Ahmad's example in concentrating on the early history of Islam and pre-Islamic Arabia. Like Sayyid Ahmad, he enthusiastically gathered all possible sources and information, such as geographical data and the etymology of words, in order to explain institutions in their historical context. Shibli was, furthermore, indebted to the genre and style of Urdu prose that Sayyid Ahmad had helped create. Perhaps the turning point of his life came when he saw Sayyid Ahmad's library, full of European editions of Arabic texts and other examples of recent Orientalist scholarship. Sayyid Ahmad encouraged him to use these books, and soon after his arrival in Aligarh he took up residence in the compound of Sayyid Ahmad's house.[140]

Shibli's earliest writings took up themes that Sayyid Ahmad had himself attempted: a study of the old system of Muslim education, and an essay to prove that Muslims were not responsible for destroying the Alexandria Library. Like Sayyid Ahmad's, these early writings were cast as responses to European criticism. Similarly, he wrote essays to show that pardah and the jizyah poll tax on non-Muslims were of pre-Islamic origin, justifiable in historical context, but not part and parcel of the religion. He wrote of the underlying tolerance of Islamic rule toward non-Muslims primarily in terms of Middle Eastern Christian and Jews, but the relevance to British rulers and Hindu "brothers" was not lost. The ideal of government was to be found in the history of Muslim political authority. The major works of his Aligarh years were biographical studies of the caliphs Umar and al-Māmūn, both influenced by the biographical works of Hali as well as the Arabic translation of Carlyle's *Heroes and Hero Worship*. These biographical works were didactic efforts to portray exemplary human beings at the height of early Islamic civilization. Beyond this biographical concern, however, was an attempt to find the roots of Islamic social institutions at the point closest to God's revelation to Mu-

[140] Nadvī, *Ḥayāt-i Shiblī*, p. 126.

hammad. Like Sayyid Ahmad, Shibli looked outside of India and past a thousand years of history for his golden age.[141]

In this historical work, Shibli was aided by T. W. Arnold, who came to Aligarh as philosophy professor in 1888. Arnold was a man of shy, scholarly temperament. At Aligarh he shifted his interest from Sanskrit to Arabic, and studied under Shibli. The two men developed a close working partnership—Arnold helped Shibli locate European sources, taught him some French, and acquainted him with the conventions of European scholarship. Shibli was Arnold's major guide to Arabic literature. This was the British-Muslim friendship of Sayyid Ahmad's dreams, and he helped both of them obtain books and manuscripts for their research. He also made sure they were known to the scholarly world and that their writings got published.[142]

Arnold's two major works of scholarship during his ten years at Aligarh were *The Preaching of Islam* and the publication of an extract from an Arabic manuscript on Muʿtazilī theology. *The Preaching of Islam*, which came out piece by piece in Urdu translation before being published in English, presented evidence that Islam had spread more as a result of missionary effort than military conquest. The chapter on India went so far as to argue that most Indian Muslims were descended from converts—not a welcome idea in some contexts, though it defended Islam from some familiar European accusations. (Shibli himself made no attempt to disguise his Hindu ancestry.)[143] The book was based mostly on sources in European languages, though he did draw on a few Arabic books and manuscripts. In his preface Arnold apologized for the preliminary nature of his research and expressed appreciation to Sayyid Ahmad and Shibli for their assistance.[144]

141 "Pardah aur Islām," *Maqālāt-i Shiblī* (Azamgarh: Maʿārif, 1954), I, 103-120; Habibullah, "Historical Writing in Urdu," pp. 486-488; Aziz Ahmad, *Islamic Modernism*, pp. 77-86.

142 Nadvī, *Ḥayāt-i Shiblī*, pp. 139-144.

143 *Ibid.*, pp. 58-60.

144 Reprint ed. (Lahore: Sh. Muhammad Ashraf, 1961).

But for all this close cooperation of scholarly effort, there was an element in Shibli's underlying assumptions that separated him not only from Arnold but from Sayyid Ahmad as well. Shibli did not attack *taqlīd*, following received belief and practice, and he accepted the principle that such matters should be decided by the consensus of the ʿulama. Unlike Sayyid Ahmad, he tended to be more conventional in evaluating the validity of *hadīs̱*, the sayings of Muhammad, as historical sources. Shibli himself was gradually recognized as an ʿālim in the 1890s; through Sayyid Ahmad's efforts, the British government conferred on him the title Shāms ul-ʿulamā, and he was an original participant in the new national association of Sunni religious authorities, the Nadvaʿt ul-ʿulamā, which was formed in 1894. At the first gathering of this organization he argued that it was not sufficient for Muslims to mobilize themselves in terms of loyalty to the qaum, Sayyid Ahmad's recurrent theme. Muslims would achieve real unity and political power only when they acted in the name of the religion of Islam. The ultimate goal was a society organized in accordance with the revelation of God to Muhammad, a society in which political power belonged to the only people qualified to interpret this revelation, the ʿulama.[145] With this speech Shibli rejected the foundation of Sayyid Ahmad's movement.

It was Shibli's role at Aligarh to give content to the ethnic loyalty Sayyid Ahmad and Beck sought to inspire in the students. "Our communical consciousness," wrote Muhammad Ali, "was . . . far more secular than religious, and although we considered Islam to be the final message for mankind and the only true faith, and could strenuously and even intelligently enough argue about the superiority of its chief tenets, we were shamefully ignorant of the details of its teaching and of its world-wide and centuries-old history." According to Muhammad Ali, Shibli was the one exception, the one person who made the symbols of Islam a living real-

[145] " ʿUlamā-i Farāiẓ," Kẖuṭbāt-i Shiblī (Azamgarh: Maʿārif, 1965), pp. 28-46.

ity for the students.[146] Although Sayyid Ahmad and Beck did not agree with the ultimate implications of Shibli's thought, they realized the emotional value of his contribution to the Aligarh culture.

Both Shibli and Arnold were active in creating extracurricular centers for intellectual and literary activity. Neither of them had the opportunity to teach in class the subject of their scholarly research. Islamic history received little attention in the Allahabad university curriculum. Shibli taught a related subject, Arabic and Persian literature, but Arnold had to devote himself to European philosophy. On occasion he was also assigned two hours a day teaching English in the school classes.[147]

In 1891 Arnold called for efforts "to foster an intellectual life" at Aligarh. Although the original idea of having resident fellows was beyond the resources of the college, it might still be possible to invite outside lecturers: Nazir Ahmad might lecture on Arabic literature; Hali, on Persian literature; Inayat Rasul, on Hebrew; Ismail Khan Shervani, on Turkish; Zaka Ullah, on natural science and mathematics; Shibli, on the intellectual history of Islam. "The minds of our students would thus occasionally be taken out of the narrow groove of their university curriculum, and these lectures might also contribute in some degree to arresting the (unfortunately) increasing decay of sympathy between the English educated Mahomedans and the representatives of the old learning."[148]

In 1889 Arnold had established a competition for the best poem in Urdu and encouraged the Akhvān us-Ṣafā, a society in which students submitted and discussed essays in Urdu. Before this time Urdu literature had received no recognition at Aligarh. Although there had been some provision for teaching Hindi (to Hindu students), Urdu was never part of the

[146] Mohamed Ali, *My Life*, pp. 22-25.

[147] Beck to Sayyid Ahmad, n.d. (1890-1891), AA.

[148] Arnold, "Comments on Principal's Report," 1891 (AA); proposal to invite outside lecturers, signed by Arnold, Morison, and Sayyid Ahmad, July 9, 1891 (AA).

curriculum. Students learned it before coming to Aligarh, often as a byproduct of Persian. Arnold now attempted to bring Urdu to the forefront. In poetry he encouraged the students to follow the style of Hali, the so-called "natural poetry," which avoided complex metaphysical imagery and erotic themes in favor of descriptions of nature and salutary moral instruction. The student who embodied this style was Khushi Muhammad "Nazr."[149] Among the many other student poets there were some who looked to more traditional models. The verse of Zafar Ali Khan, passionate or humorous, was a self-conscious display of difficult Persian and Arabic diction in the style of Shibli. Zulfiqar Ali "Gauhar" and his more famous younger brother, Muhammad Ali "Jauhar," both considered themselves followers of Dagh Dehlvi. The most famous Aligarh poet, Hasrat Mohani, arrived just after the departure of Shibli and Arnold.[150]

The A<u>kh</u>van us-Ṣafā (Brothers of Purity), named after the classical Baghdadi literary circle, was dedicated to high morality, brotherly feelings among members, and the development of literary tastes. It was the closest Aligarh got to the Apostles, though it made no claim to secrecy. Although it sometimes drifted into English, the society was committed to the belief that Indian Muslims should develop Urdu as the medium of intellectual expression. One of the recurrent themes in the society's meetings was the shortcomings of English education. Shibli, an active participant, continually emphasized the religious ideals of Islam, a subject rarely if ever raised in the Siddons Union. Probably the quintessential member of the society was its founder, Ghulam us-Saqlain, a relative of Hali, who carried on Sajjad Husain's tradition

[149] See review by Abdul Haq, MAOCM (contained in AIG, August 1, 1893).

[150] <u>Gh</u>ulām Ḥusain <u>Z</u>ūlfiqār, *Ẓafar 'Alī <u>Kh</u>ān* (Lahore: Maktubah-i <u>Kh</u>ayābān-i Adab, 1967), pp. 60-63; *Dīvān-i Jauhar*, ed. Nūrur Raḥmān (Lahore: Shaikh Ghulam Ali and Sons, 1962); Sayyid Viqār 'Azīm, "Ḥasrat," *'Alīgaṛh Megzīn*, Aligarh Number, Part II (1954-1955), pp. 85-106.

of moral earnestness, often at the cost of ridicule by his fellow students.[151]

In 1891 Shibli and Arnold also joined forces on a new student journal in English and in Urdu, the *Muhammadan Anglo-Oriental College Magazine*. First published as part of the *Aligarh Institute Gazette*, it became a separate enterprise in 1894. The journal was the vehicle for the Akhvān us-Ṣafā essays by Shibli, Ghulam us-Saqlain, Abdul Haq, and Zafar Ali Khan—all notable figures in modern Urdu writing. There were also articles by other students and alumni, poems, summaries of Union debates, and reports on college activities.

In 1892, Shibli and Arnold sailed off together from Bombay, parting company in Egypt. Both of them were to use their vacations and leaves to carry on their research. One result of Shibli's trip in the Middle East, besides the acquisition of a well-publicized decoration from Sultan Abdul Hamīd, was a society he formed on his return in 1893 as an adjunct to the Union. The purpose of the Lajnat ul-adab was to give students an opportunity to speak Arabic; the society also subscribed to Arabic newspapers.[152]

Both Shibli and Arnold considered themselves spokesmen for an opposing current of thought at Aligarh. Probably only a very select group of students fell into their orbit; few could live up to such heavy intellectual demands. Arnold argued that English education would be a hollow thing without "a high national ideal"; Muslims must have confidence in "the grandeur of Islam both of the past and present."[153] Years later he called his role at the college one of "protest": "All good in advancing civilization can be absorbed without

[151] Morison, quoted in memo by R. Burn, January 4, 1911, in *Correspondence in Connection with Muhammadan Affairs from 1912-14*, Meston Papers, IOL, p. 77; Khvājah Ghulām us-Saiyidain, "Ek Mard-i Darvaish- Khvājah Ghulām us-Ṣaqlain," *'Alīgaṛh Megzīn*, Aligarh Number, Supplement, p. 8; 'Abd ul-Ḥaq, *Cand Ham 'Aṣr*, p. 109.

[152] AIG, May 7, 1893; Ṭufail Aḥmad, *Muhammadan College Directory* (1895 ed.), pp. 34-35.

[153] Speech to Akhvān us-Ṣafā, MAOCM (in AIG, June 6, 1893).

adopting foreign follies."[154] Shibli had a low opinion of English-educated Muslims, bitterly taking them to task for their apathy toward the achievements of the past. Once, after discoursing on the greatness of the Urdu poet, Anīs, he challenged his students to come up with anybody of equal stature: "Have you, gentlemen, produced anything worth keeping[?]"[155] After leaving Aligarh and establishing a rival "university" or *dār ul-ʿulūm* at Lucknow, the Nadvaʿt ul-ʿulamā, he was to speak disparagingly of Aligarh and its claim to lead the Muslims of India, but his son was an Aligarh student, and Shibli himself remained active in Aligarh affairs.

While Shibli and Arnold remained at Aligarh, their presence was greatly appreciated. When they threatened to leave, great efforts were made to convince them to stay. Shibli was offered an annual half-year leave for his research.[156] Arnold went off to Government College, Lahore (where he was a major intellectual influence on Muhammad Iqbal), but Aligarh authorities went so far as to persuade the government of the North-Western Provinces and Oudh to request the transfer of his services back to Aligarh.[157] The effort was unsuccessful, and a few years later, in 1904, Arnold returned to England to take up—first at the India Office Library and then at the London School of Oriental Studies—a distinguished career as historian of Islam. No doubt he benefitted much from Aligarh, but Aligarh gave him no intellectual disciples.

THE NEW LIGHT

Arnold and Shibli served to confer some measure of legitimacy on Aligarh's claim to be a Muslim college as well

154 "The New Light," ms. lecture notes, n.d., Arnold Papers, Box II, School of Oriental and African Studies, University of London.

155 AIG, January 3, 1893; see also comment on Amīr ʿAli in "Pardah aur Islām," pp. 103-104.

156 Shibli [to Mushtaq Husain], October 19, 1897 (N.M. 1966.97/52), National Museum of Pakistan, Karachi.

157 Officiating Chief Secretary, Government of the Punjab to Secretary, GOI, July 23, 1900, including numerous telegrams from Aligarh trustees calling on the government to lend Arnold's services to the college (Arnold Papers, Box VIII).

as a college for Muslims. The same conflict that troubled the Akhvān us-Ṣafā, the conflict between the older and younger generations, Islamic and English cultural styles, tended to discredit Aligarh among the wider public of Indian Muslims. The first book by an Aligarh student, written in 1890, was a response to this conflict. Mustafa Khan wrote *An Apology for the "New Light"* because he felt that it was time for the new generation of English-educated students to speak on their own behalf instead of relying on Sayyid Ahmad and Theodore Beck. Aligarh students, he claimed, felt "isolated" from the Indian Muslim public. Yet, writing in English, Mustafa Khan was more assertive than apologetic about the manners and beliefs of his Aligarh contemporaries. Urdu poetry was "stale," pardah was "unfavorable to honest love," the old etiquette was dishonest and "effeminate," the Muslim conquerors of India had been "mere warriors." On the other hand, Mustafa Khan takes on a different tone when he speaks of the sons of the "New Light." They "want to walk erect, though in doing so they unfortunately now and then stumble." They "are sufficiently miserable without being jeered at." He denies that their attitudes are due to English education, "a tribute to which I do not think it is entitled," but he concedes the importance of exposure to the European model of civilization. The important thing for the new generation is to resist blind following of either the old Indian Muslim culture or the culture of the Europeans. In adopting fez and Turkish coat, for example, they would have an efficient, simple form of dress without losing their "national identity." "Mahomedans are scattered all over India; but still, to all intents and purposes, they are a nation having identical interests." Having learned the virtues of "sympathy" and "common sense," it was the task of the "New Light" to unite among themselves as leaders of the Indian Muslim people—even though they are "few" and "unpopular." To win such a role they must be "cautious." For example, even though they were convinced by John Stuart Mill about the ultimate goal of female equality, they would be unwise to force the issue.[158] The sons of Aligarh would have to be good politicians.

Reviewing Mustafa Khan's book in the *Aligarh Institute Gazette*, Ghulam us-Saqlain praised it for an English prose style worthy of John Morley, but complained of the "extravagant admiration by the writer of European manners and dress." Ghulam conceded that "the New Light"—"a phrase of meaningless expressiveness"—had learned to reject superstitious saint worship and the prejudice against educating women. But who had taught them that lesson? It had been the previous generation, unschooled in English, Sayyid Ahmad Khan, the great "Conservative Genius," reaching for enlightenment into the heritage of Islam. English-educated Muslims had done nothing and were inadequate for the tasks ahead. They lacked "a fierce and pure earnestness without which no movement can go on for a moment."[159]

If other students found Ghulam us-Saqlain's earnestness "quaint," as Morison later recalled, they nevertheless shared that yearning for energetic purpose that his words expressed. Again and again they were told that they were to be the leaders, the hope of the Muslims of India. Yet on all sides lay choices to be made, options that had never confronted their fathers. What language should they speak or write? How should they dress—as their fathers did, like Englishmen, like Turks? Their British teachers told them that British civilization was superior—and that they should not imitate it. All these issues kept returning in the Union debates of the 1890s, in the magazine articles and papers read to student societies. Sajjad Haidar, Ghulam us-Saqlain's successor as student intellectual in residence, moved back and forth between admiration for all that was British and assertions that contact with British culture had done them more harm than good.[160] Ultimately, he found the answer in the

[158] Mustapha Khan, *An Apology for the "New Light"* (Allahabad: Pioneer Press, 1891).
[159] AIG, June 9, 1891.
[160] MAOCM, November 15, 1899.

thought and writings of young Ottoman intellectuals, which he translated into Urdu; but that was after his student days.

Anxiety about their role and their cultural options was a continuing concern for this first generation, but it was often mediated through the playful competition of student debates and other extracurricular activities. It was, after all, the favorite literary pose of an Urdu poet to face sorrow and rejection, defeating it with the secret victory of eloquence. Anxiety was the occasion for brilliance. There is no doubt that Mustafa Khan, Ghulam us-Saqlain, and Sajjad Haidar enjoyed their ability to express themselves so skillfully in English as well as in Urdu. And this ability was their best claim to leadership. "When the nightingales heard my lamentations," says Ghalib, "they became poets too."

Aligarh communicated to its students something more than the body of information and skills set down in the university curriculum; it communicated a special style of intellectual energy and emotional involvement. The knowledge, even if it were imperfectly learned, was useful in gaining access to networks of communication within the British imperial system. The verbal skills that students acquired not only in their studies but in such extracurricular activities as the Union were especially suitable for public life in a world of deliberative political procedures. But as everyone at Aligarh insisted, the transmission of information and skills was subordinate to the college's role in forging a social bond that reached into the inner feelings of the new generation. Ideas and the way they were communicated by such people as Sayyid Ahmad, Beck, Raleigh, Arnold, and Shibli made significant contributions to this emotional education. These ideas were most effectively transmitted in a spirit of playfulness, not work. The wit and carelessness of the Cambridge Apostles replaced the grim, intense labor of examination preparation as the dominant theme of the college. Ideas became a matter of pleasurable competition, as they had always been in the verbal joustings of sharīf society. The intellectual and religious counterculture led by Shibli fell easily into the same mode of competition and student clubs. Even classes and examinations could be approached in this light spirit; like Union debates, they were part of the game and it would be unsportsmanlike to take them too seriously.

What was most important was the social milieu. As fellow players, the students of Aligarh, all living together and cut off from the ordinary world of family and adult society, established bonds of solidarity with each other that were more profound and enduring than a piece of information or a technique of disputation. Mughal ideology about personal loyalty, Sayyid Ahmad's plea for close social relations as the basis of political institutions, the developed thought of Cambridge dons like Maurice and Seeley about human society as the extension and transformation of kinship ties—all these came together, not only as intellectual formulations, but in the emotional lives of Aligarh's first generation. And the major educational strategy for communicating this message was to get the students to play games, intellectual and otherwise.

VI

"Brothers of the *Akhārā*"[1]

ONE night in March 1886, two Englishmen, Cox and Raleigh, were sitting on the verandah of their bungalow drinking tea. The moon was full, the air heavy with the scent of roses. Raleigh was holding forth in his witty way on the romantic power of the Indian atmosphere—were it not for the utter lack of "human material"—when suddenly they noticed the sound of voices and clapping coming from the Hindu students' bungalow nearby. They rose to follow the noise. A small gathering of Hindu and Muslim students were having a party; they welcomed the two professors, seated them on chairs, then continued with a speech about Hindu-Muslim brotherliness and a magic lantern show.

As the gathering broke up—it was already eleven o'clock —one of the students, a member of the cricket team, asked the young professors if they would like to play kabaddi. The invitation was irresistible; they all went along to the boarding house quadrangle, rounded up some twenty students from their rooms, divided into two teams on opposite sides of a line of scrimmage. A member of one team ran across the line, calling out "kabaddi, kabaddi, kabaddi . . ." all in one breath while trying to tag as many of his opponents as possible. If he was good, he could tag out several players and escape back to his side of the line before running out of breath and being tackled in enemy territory. The Englishmen,

[1] Shaukat Ali in *Old Boy* (March-April 1913), as quoted in ['Azizuddīn Aḥmad], *Rīpōrṭ-i Kamiṭī-i taḥqīqāt muṯ'aliq ba Aulḍ Boiz Āsōsīaishan, Madrasat ul-'ulūm, 'Alīgaṛh* (Aligarh: Institute Press, 1917), p. 21; see below, pp. 327-334.

dressed only in white trousers and shirtsleeves, threw themselves into the game, shouting and running about with the students.

Then there was a sudden hush and everyone froze. Maulvi Muhammad Akbar, professor of Arabic and Sunni theology, majestic in his flowing robes, appeared in the moonlight. With deliberate authority he began to reprimand the students for their unseemly behavior. Sheepishly Cox and Raleigh came forward out of the shadows to claim responsiblity and apologize. Now the maulvi was startled, made his own apologies, and bade the game go on. It was embarrassing on all sides. Raleigh wrote a formal apology the next day. He also revised some of his notions about his students as "human material." "It must be a handful to keep them in order," he wrote his sister, "they are all so fearfully independent and some of them with a genuine recklessness I admire."[2]

THE PLAYING FIELDS OF ALIGARH

Kabaddi was not a regular activity at Aligarh; neither was kite flying, wrestling, or Indian clubs.[3] But from the start the design for the college made room for play—of authorized games at authorized times. At first such activities were optional and informal; there is some mention of cricket and lawn tennis, but not much.[4] Early in 1878, Rama Shankar Misra, professor of mathematics, presided over the establishment of a cricket club, limited to twenty-two dues-paying members; they had to pay three rupees in advance and wear a uniform of "blue flannel coat, shirt, knickerbockers and cap." Although they played occasionally with the English "rulers" of the station, the club was not overwhelmingly successful. In 1881 the college tried to make sports compulsory and required all boarders to pay the cricket fee, but two years later Siddons wrote Sayyid Ahmad that the club was in danger of expiring because of the difficulty collecting the

[2] To Jessie Raleigh, March 20, 1886, Raleigh, *Letters*, I, 58-60.

[3] See above, pp. 54-55.

[4] RMAOC, 1877, pp. 7-8.

money.[5] The only other physical activity in these early years was the annual "Athletic Sports Meeting," in which students competed in such activities as the hundred yard dash, shotput, broad jump and, finally, a mass tug-of-war. For comic relief the day featured a three-legged race, blindfold race, and a separate race for the watercarriers. The incentive was great: cash prizes distributed by a woman, the District Collector's wife.[6]

With the arrival of Theodore Beck, sports, particularly cricket, became much more important at the college. Although Beck himself was a complete "duffer" at the game, he made it a major part of his educational program.[7] During his first year as principal he led the cricket team on a well-publicized tour of the Punjab; spectators could see what Aligarh was all about whenever a match stopped for prayers.[8] Commenting on official criticism of Aligarh's poor examination results, Beck argued that the college had too many other concerns to concentrate on one, narrow aspect of education. He pointed out Aligarh's distinction in "fostering a spirit for manly games and manly sentiments." In all the North-Western Provinces and Punjab, Aligarh could boast of having the best team in the "noble and manly game of cricket."[9] This demonstrated, he said, that the college was "suitable for the landed gentry" and not merely for "the intellectual training [of people] who look on education purely in its commercial aspect."[10] Beck repeatedly emphasized that cricket could serve to establish bonds between Aligarh and significant

[5] BH Report, 1879, p. 7; 1881, pp. 21-22; Siddons to Sayyid Ahmad, November 4, 1883 (302B/83, AA); for an anonymous student recollection of the absence of any serious commitment to sports at Aligarh before Beck, see "My College Life: Twenty Years Ago," *Aligarh Monthly*, May 1904, p. 43.

[6] AIG, March 4, 1882.

[7] Shaukat Ali, "The Late Mr. Beck and His Pupils," *Aligarh Monthly*, December 1905, p. 7; for Beck's own confession, see AIG, March 30, 1886.

[8] AIG, November 15, 1884. [9] AIG, March 19, 1887.

[10] "M.A.O. College Students' Race," ms. in Beck's handwriting (1886-1887), AA; probably the draft of an article for AIG.

groups outside. Traveling to other cities, playing host to visiting teams, even British teams, from far away, put Aligarh students in an exclusive network. What is more, Aligarh usually won: "the reputation of the College depends to a very large extent on the success of our cricket and foot-ball elevens."[11]

Football (that is, soccer) and a few other sports came in 1888 with the arrival of Theodore Morison and the assignment of the boarding-house supervision to the British staff. An active athlete, Morison was himself the star of the football team and an avid sponsor of parallel bars and rope climbing.[12] In 1893 he started a riding school in which the wealthier students received instruction from a retired jamadar of the Bengal cavalry. Horseback riding was a necessary skill for any of the higher civilian or military posts; it was also, of course, the mark of a gentleman.[13] Another physical activity introduced about the same time was compulsory drill; disciplined marching maneuvers became part of an Aligarh education. According to Beck, such physical education enabled a man to face his country's enemies in time of war.[14]

Other north Indian colleges lagged far behind Aligarh in sports. When Allahabad University established an annual intercollege competition in the provincial capital in the 1890s, Aligarh almost invariably captured first and second prizes in each event.[15] This athletic success did not always earn praise. The principals of some colleges considered the tournament a

[11] AIG, February 28, 1893; an example of Aligarh's fame in sports is that it is mentioned in Rudyard Kipling, *Kim* (New York: Modern Library, n.d.), p. 197.

[12] Principal's Report, 1891, p. 6; MAOCM, December 1894, pp. 157-158; Beck to Sayyid Ahmad, November 22 and November 23, 1889, AA; Iftikhār 'Ālam, *Muhammadan College History*, p. 188.

[13] AIG, April 6, 1894; Iftikhār 'Ālam, *Muhammadan College History*, pp. 189-192; see also Sayyid Ahmad to Navab Viqar ul-Umara, Prime Minister of Hyderabad, n.d. [1893] (377A, AA).

[14] AIG, August 15, 1893; Ṭufail Aḥmad, *Muhammadan College Directory*, pp. 51-52.

[15] MAOCM, February 1, 1896, pp. 57-60; RDPI/NWP, 1895-1896, pp. 16-17; Shaukat Ali, "The Late Mr. Beck," *Aligarh Monthly* (December 1905), p. 9.

waste of time and money.[16] Muslim critics such as Khvajah Yusuf charged that Aligarh was winning games at the expense of providing a good education. Some of the top players, he claimed, were poor students, elderly hangers-on in the high school, who could never get through the entrance examination.[17] Even Aligarh's English headmaster, W. C. Horst, agreed; he had no sympathy with the efforts of Beck and Morison to make sports such a crucial part of the school. In response to such complaints, Sayyid Ahmad felt called upon to remind Beck that studies came first.[18] And despite all sorts of rules, many students did not participate in sports.[19]

But for a significant group of students, the Aligarh experience was very much bound up with games, and this was an important part of the face that the college presented to the general public. Before Beck, it had been sufficient to justify physical exercise as a matter of health; later came talk of being gentlemen, social intercourse with Englishmen, even military preparedness. Sports were charged with symbolism. And the Aligarh sport par excellence was cricket. Why? What could possibly be the attraction of cricket? Certainly not exercise. Certainly not military preparedness. Hardly what Shaukat Ali claimed for it, "the unity of thought and action."[20] It may be worthwhile to speculate on the attractions of this peculiarly English game, and to wonder what it did for the Indians who played or watched.

Like kabaddi, cricket was a team game, in which one player at a time faced the entire opposition. The image of combat, bravery, heroism was clear enough in kabaddi, and similar overtones were not absent from cricket. One difference not intrinsic to the games themselves was the permanence of the teams. No one had ever heard of an organized

16 MAOCM, April 1899, pp. 60, 87-88.

17 Khvājah Muḥammad Yūṣuf, *Izālat ul-auhām*, pp. 43-44.

18 Sayyid Ahmad to Beck, July 10, 1895 (239A, AA).

19 MAOCM, August 1, 1896, pp. 335-337; MAOCM/AIG (combined), April 1, 1900, English section, p. 1; Riza Ali, *Essays on Moslem Questions*, p. 80.

20 AIG, July 5, 1892.

kabaddi team electing a captain, meeting opposition squads, compiling records, wearing uniforms. Kabaddi had always been a simple, spontaneous game between improvised teams. It was not taken so seriously.

Cricket, of course, could be played in the same way, and no doubt was. But the emphasis put on the team's role in defending the college's reputation could not be taken so lightly. Membership on the college eleven represented a real commitment; it meant traveling together during vacations as virtual missionaries of the Aligarh cause. There is reason to believe that this commitment created a special solidarity among many of the players.[21] It also brought them into a network of relationships with similar but opposing teams, relationships that often would not have been possible were it not for cricket. As with any game, these matches took place within defined limits of time and space, according to rules freely accepted for the sake of a special kind of enjoyment not available in the "real" world of everyday activities.[22] In a match with a British regiment team, it became temporarily irrelevant that they were in India as an army of occupation. The only relevant mark of status was athletic skill. Obviously, this was a major motivation for playing cricket: it was the game of India's rulers, and there was something to be said for playing them at their own game—especially if you could win.

But there were also formal features to cricket that set it apart from other games. Cricket differed from Indian games like kabaddi in the elaborateness of its rules and the differentiation of roles among the players at any particular time. The "bowler" had to heave a ball of a particular size in a proscribed fashion from a designated spot on the field toward a formation of stakes that were set in a position and at a distance determined by the regulations. A "batsman" on the other team stood in front of the stakes with a peculiarly

[21] See below, pp. 292-297.

[22] J. Huizinga, *Homo Ludens* (Boston: Beacon Press, 1950), pp. 7-11.

shaped piece of wood with which he attempted to prevent the ball from hitting the stakes and knocking off the cross-bar set on top of them, called the "wicket." If he failed, he was "out" and another member of his team, according to a preestablished order, took over the same responsibility.

At another set of stakes on the opposite side of the bowler was a second batsman. An "over" consisted of six balls bowled at one of the wickets before turning to the other. A successful batsman not only "defended" the wicket but was able to hit the ball so that it would not be caught in the air by the opposing players, who were stationed at named positions on the playing field. If he hit it far enough he would then have an opportunity to exchange positions with his teammate at the other wicket before an opposing player on the field could get to the ball and use it to knock off the wicket. Every time he made such an exchange of positions he scored a "run," and the winning team was the one that compiled the most runs during a determined period of play. Each of the eleven players would have the opportunity to bat, after which the opposing team had its "innings."[23]

Cricket matches were a matter of record; each player's performance was recorded in detail according to an esoteric system, and was available for future reference as part of the evaluation of his worth among other players and of the worth of his team. For most of the game any single player watched and waited his turn. Where football, for example, required something like perpetual alertness and continual movement, a game of cricket unfolded with slow, well-considered deliberateness. But when a person's turn came to handle the bat, he became the object of total concentration. Like a poet reciting a ghazal, he offered up his skill for public appreciation. There was only a very limited area for maneuver: a pitch, the movement of the bat, each was a couplet in the appropriate meter.

[23] George H. Selkirk, *Guide to the Cricket Ground* (London: Macmillan, 1867). Needless to say, my knowledge of cricket is untainted by experience. I have, however, benefitted from conversations with a number of cricket enthusiasts in India.

The ball comes in, an obstacle, an object of dread; the batsman hits it and it becomes an extension of himself, an expression of his power. Each movement has a purpose, but the ball always threatens to diverge from human control, to take on a life of its own. Between batsman and bowler the ball is an item of exchange, a weapon, and a prize. It is the "catalyst of movement," the object of a man's effort to control the amorphousness of experience.[24] "See what a drop of rain must undergo before it becomes a pearl."[25]

Legalism and poetry, team play and solitary confrontation, such was the symbolism of cricket. Within the context of accepted rules, assigned responsibilities, group cooperation toward collective ends, the burden of the moment was always on a lone individual. Conversely, to excel as an individual was also to serve the purposes of the team, the college, and the Muslims of India. This sense of civic membership was where Aligarh cricket differed from the competitions of the akhara or the mushāʿirah. Victory or defeat belonged to the group. Cricket, then, symbolized the personal achievement of a trustworthy official, the ability to take active initiative within the confines of a highly restricted and regulated role for the sake of the larger whole.[26] It was this combination of independence and responsibility that Beck referred to as "manly."

At the same time, it is important to remember that cricket was, after all, a game. One could lose, and there would still be an opportunity to win some other time—or the other way around. No victory or loss was permanent. On the field it was ultimately safe to let out aggressiveness or to be its victim. And, as one psychoanalytic interpretation of the game suggests, such contests were held within the reassuring, nurturing

[24] Marcel Bouet, *Signification du Sport*, 4th ed. (Paris: Editions Universitaires, 1968), pp. 106-113, 133-134.

[25] There is no evidence that Ghalib was thinking about cricket.

[26] Letter of a District Collector, N.W.P. and Oudh, to a former cricket captain, MAOCM, June 1, 1896, pp. 243-244; see also Mabel Jane Reany, *The Psychology of the Organized Group Game*, Monograph Supplement IV, *British Journal of Psychology* (Cambridge: University Press, 1916), p. 34.

grounds of a familiar green field, the field of the college or one like it. Dressed in white clothes, moving slowly through the sleepy, sunny game, the players almost appeared like cattle on some idyllic pasture. The whole complex of college buildings and grounds, one may imagine, resonated in the emotions of the students like some great symbol of maternity.[27] Nurtured from this same mother, they could even begin to think of themselves as brothers.

A CRISIS OF AUTHORITY

A teacher should be a father to his students. So wrote one of the young British professors, probably Beck, in the summer of 1886. In government schools "a master is a member not of a school but of a Department and . . . his duty to his pupils is supposed to be finished when he has taught them their lessons." But Aligarh would be guided by the "graceful sentiments" of " 'the East,' in other words Islam," not by the standards of an impersonal bureaucracy. In the old days a student was bound to his teacher by feelings of loving deference, performing menial tasks in a spirit of profound devotion. Even the great Shah Ismail carried the shoes of his spiritual guide, Sayyid Ahmad Barelvi, and walked humbly behind his palanquin.[28]

That was heady stuff for a young Englishman fresh out of Cambridge: to be a murshid, a spiritual guide. The Roman tradition of a teacher standing "in loco parentis," which Beck cited some years later, did not offer quite the same perquisites.[29] It was a founding principle of the college that the boarding-house quadrangle would replace the homes of the pupils, allegedly backward and degenerate, but there was no expectation that British teachers would take over as substitute par-

[27] Adrian Stokes, "Psycho-Analytic Reflections on the Development of Ball Games, Particularly Cricket," *The International Journal of Psycho-Analysis*, XXXVII (1956), 185-192.

[28] "Teacher and Pupil," AIG, August 10, 1886.

[29] Beck to Deputy Secretary to the GOI, Foreign Department, December 9, 1896 (631B/96, AA).

ents. That role was clearly staked out for the Managers. One stipulation Beck agreed to in coming to Aligarh was that "the Principal would not be called on to interfere in the finances of the College or the domestic arrangements of the students."[30] Maulvi Muhammad Akbar was in charge of the boarding house. For some time, between 1879 and 1882, Mushtaq Husain lived there, too, keeping an eye on his own son and the other students as well. Khvajah Yusuf, Muhammad Karim, and especially Sami Ullah made a special point of looking after the boarding house. The presence of these pious gentlemen on the scene was a matter of frequent comment in Aligarh publications, an explicit reassurance that they were, in fact, behaving as fathers to the students. If the college quadrangle was a symbol of nurturing motherhood, it was also, as Sayyid Ahmad said, "like a woman with four husbands."[31]

But Sayyid Ahmad himself was to have no personal contact with the students, lest they be contaminated with his heretical ideas. One came into personal contact with the founder only under special circumstances: "A good thrashing from the old Syed's stick," wrote one old student reminiscing about the early 1880s, was said to be "very efficacious in improving one's prospects in life. It brought Barristerships, Deputy Collector-ships and various other emoluments."[32]

British professors had no such prerogative; their job was to teach. When Siddons inflicted corporal punishment on a student, he was severely reprimanded for disobeying the college rules, rules "based on the circumstances of the people which an English gentleman is not expected to be aware." To some extent this was a concession to public opinion: the rule

[30] Proceedings, Managing Committee, M.A.O. College, Number 29 (August 28, 1883), in AIG, September 1, 1883.

[31] Quoted in Raleigh to his mother, February 22, 1887, *Letters*, I, 102.

[32] "My College Life: Twenty Years Ago," *Aligarh Monthly* (May 1904), p. 45; also incident recounted by Masud Ali to a meeting of the Aligarh Old Boys' Club, Hyderabad, as recollected by Justice Sharfuddin Ahmad (interview, Hyderabad, July 1969); Ḥabībullāh Khān, *Ḥayāt-i Aftāb*, p. 13.

would have to stand "until the college becomes more popular and fully established." But more than that, such punishment was "contrary to the very principles on which the college is founded."[33] One thing was clear: parents of Aligarh students were not going to permit teachers, including British ones, to beat their children.

Beating was something you did to servants.[34] Of course, not everyone approved: Sayyid Ahmad carried around a childhood memory of being thrown out of the house by his mother for slapping a servant.[35] There was always some protest when one of the sahibs kicked a servant to death for falling asleep at the pankha. Still in general, "one's servants are often very provoking," as Beck put it in 1886, when the government disciplined the District Collector of Saharanpur for hitting one.[36]

If servants in general were a problem, the most difficult to deal with must have been the servants in the Aligarh College boarding house, subject as they were to divided authority and unconventional responsibilities. Student complaints against them were numerous: they were disobedient, they lounged around on the boarding-house verandah as if they owned it, they usurped the status of the students by forming their own athletic teams and playing kabaddi on the college grounds. Worst of all, they reported to the college authorities when a student broke a rule.[37] It was therefore necessary to remind

33 [Sayyid Ahmad or Sami Ullah] to Siddons, August 14, 1876 (54-55A, AA); note formal rules on corporal punishment, AIG, February 2, 1877, allowing punishment with strap or switch in the boarding house; but the point is that the English staff had nothing to do with the boarding house. Cf. 1889 code, SDAA, p. 369.

34 Aziz Mirza, quoted in Badāyūnī, *Maḥfil-i 'Azīz*, pp. 130-131; Aziz Mirza says that in ordinary home life one might occasionally strike a servant—or a younger brother—notwithstanding adult prohibitions against such acts.

35 See above, p. 40.

36 Beck to Sayyid Ahmad, Murree, May 3, 1886 (AIG, May 15, 1886; reprinted in SDAA, pp. 305-306). For public controversy on British assaults on pankha coolies and other servants see SVN/NWP, 1897, pp. 25-26; also S. Gopal, *British Policy*, pp. 261-265.

37 Badāyūnī, *Maḥfil-i 'Azīz*, pp. 121-122.

them of their menial position from time to time by giving them a good thrashing. "The servants are very cheeky," said Raleigh sympathetically, "and it is the habit to slipper them for offences."[38]

But in the new social world of a residential college it was not always clear who were the servants and who were the masters. The idea of students waiting on their teachers in devoted servitude may have been appealing to Beck, but the truth remained that the teachers at Aligarh College were hired employees subject to the authority of the Managing Committee. British members of the staff were a special problem by virtue of their membership in the ruling qaum, on the one hand, and their extreme youth, on the other. In all the correspondence between them and Sayyid Ahmad, it was clear that it was Sayyid Ahmad who gave the orders. The relationship of teacher to student, however, remained ill-defined. Beck heard when he arrived that a student had beaten one of the professors, apparently a Hindu, in class with a shoe; when Siddons expelled the student, Sami Ullah had him reinstated.[39] Whatever the truth of this story, the authority of the teaching staff remained an open question, a question which did not often arise, however, when the teachers confined themselves to their classroom duties.

But now Beck was talking about becoming a father to the students. As a matter of fact, Maulvi Muhammad Akbar already combined the roles of manager, teacher, and father. He was boarding-house manager, professor of Arabic and Sunni philosophy, actual father and uncle to several of the students, and a member of the Managing Committee. As a respected member of the ʿulama, he could command the kind of deference that Englishmen wistfully hoped for. "I pine to know Urdu," said Raleigh, "to talk to this fine yellow

[38] Raleigh to his mother, February 22, 1887, *Letters*, I, 102-103.

[39] Beck to Sayyid Ahmad, March 19, 1896 (AA, the draft of a pamphlet, apparently published). Khvājah Muḥammad Yūṣuf's reply, *Izālat ul-auhām*, attempts to deal with Beck's statements point for point, but says nothing in refutation of this item.

robed professor."[40] Then the maulvi died in July 1886—despite illness he had insisted on observing the Ramzan fast during that hot and humid season.[41] A brother, Maulvi Muhammad Sulaiman, became the new boarding-house manager, but he was not a man of the same awesome presence. Students took the occasion to petition Sayyid Ahmad regarding the quality of food and other living accommodations. First-class boarders received permission to establish their own housekeeping committees to supervise food, servants, and sanitation.[42] But the new manager, who did not like sharing responsibilities with the students, soon found himself locked into a nasty dispute. According to later testimony by Beck, one student even threatened to beat the maulvi—like a servant. To make matters worse, Sayyid Ahmad was in Allahabad as a member of the Public Service Commission and Sami Ullah was posted as District Judge in Rae Bareilly. At this point Beck intervened to expel the student, though the rules gave him no such power. When Sami Ullah visited Aligarh in December, he had the young man readmitted.[43]

In the face of this rebuff Maulvi Sulaiman then reported to Sayyid Ahmad that the students were beating the servants and causing them to run away. From the students' point of view the maulvi's action was an effort to undermine their own precarious authority over the servants. And when Sayyid Ahmad issued a decree that the punishment for servant-beating was expulsion from the boarding house, they felt he was taking sides with the servants against them. It was a declaration that the college was not, in fact, a home at all; it was a place you belonged to conditionally, by accepting rules that denied to students their accustomed authority over servants. A student, after all, was "sharīf"; a servant was *kamīn*,

[40] Raleigh to his mother, October 4, 1885, *Letters*, I, 30.

[41] *Idem*, July 17, 1886, *ibid*., I, 90.

[42] "Darkhvāst farsṭ klās bōrḍarz kī," Aftab Ahmad, Inayat Ullah, Mustafa Khan et al., to Sayyid Aḥmad, August 25, 1886; and October 12, 1886; also, n.d., AA. See also Vilāyat Ḥusain, *Āp bītī*, p. 57.

[43] Beck to Sayyid Ahmad, March 19, 1896, AA; cf. Khvājah Yūṣuf, *Izālat ul-auhām*, p. 37.

a menial. If a servant could have a student expelled by informing the college authorities about some such incident, it meant that the hierarchy was reversed, that servants were superior to students.[44]

The issue came to a head early in February 1887, when a second-year college student disobeyed the new rule. Sayyid Husain, an "old Mahomedan bigot with a protruding chin and firm set mouth who wears spectacles and a dilapidated fez," had already inspired Raleigh's special comment over a year earlier for his way of interrupting classes with difficult questions: "he is an attractive character in many ways, and once fought a man for affronting his religion."[45] Humorless and pugnacious, he was not one of the more popular students; they called him "Bāngrū," meaning something like hillbilly. Still, he was one of them; he could count on their solidarity. One evening, having instructed a servant to leave the supper in his room in the kacca boarding house, he returned to find the dishes empty. He was told that the food had been eaten by a cat. Sayyid Husain accused the servant of eating the meal, struck him, and was duly reported to Sayyid Ahmad. The next morning came word from the Honorary Secretary's bungalow: Sayyid Husain would have to be out of the boarding house by evening.[46]

Word of Sayyid Ahmad's decision passed among the students. They began to gather in front of Room No. 1 of the kacca boarding house, the room of Aziz Mirza, secretary of the Siddons Union Club. An appeal was drawn up requesting Sayyid Ahmad to rescind his order lest the servants become all-powerful in the boarding house. Soon came Sayyid Ahmad's reply: anyone who was unwilling to obey the rules of the boarding house should go. The students took him at his word; they prepared to leave.

They did not, however, neglect their mid-day prayers.

[44] Badāyūnī, *Maḥfil-i 'Azīz*, pp. 123-124; see Sayyid Ahmad to Mushtaq Husain, February 16, 1887, *Maktūbāt*, p. 259.

[45] Raleigh to W. R. Sorley, November 16, 1885, *Letters*, I, 44.

[46] Vilāyat Ḥusain, *Āp bītī*, pp. 58-59.

But just as they were finishing, Sayyid Ahmad drove up in his coach. The old man got down and furiously waved his walking stick at Aziz Mirza and the other student leaders, calling them bastards and sons of pigs, shouting at them to clear out. It took two members of the Managing Committee to restrain him and take him away in the coach.[47] Then the staff members came on the scene, urging the students to make their peace with Sayyid Ahmad and accept his authority. Raleigh came rushing back from the English Club to join Beck in talking to the students. Anyone who left the boarding house would forfeit the right to take university examinations.[48] Aziz Mirza, a candidate for the B.A., had been an Aligarh student for twelve years. A first-rate student, there was no question that he would pass. But, he told the professors, he could not allow personal considerations to interfere. The students acted as a group, and he was their leader. Since Sayyid Ahmad had refused to act as a loving father, the students had to depend on each other. So sixty-six of them gathered up their belongings and went off to a sarai in the town; only thirty remained. The protest would be a "silent *hartāl*," an effort to establish the moral authority of the group's demands by enduring hardship and refusing to cooperate in an unfair system.[49]

When Mir Vilayat Husain, a recent graduate, now a schoolmaster, went to the sarai he found the students more adamant than ever: they would return only if Beck and Maulvi Sulaiman were dismissed. They also demanded the dismissal of Munshi Said Khan, father of the recently de-

[47] *Ibid.*, p. 60; for contemporary newspaper accounts see *Naiyar-i A'ẓam* (Moradabad), February 21, 1887 (SVN [Punjab, NWP, etc.], 1887, p. 141); *Najmul Akhbār* (Etawah), February 24 (*ibid.*, pp. 141-142); *Suhail-i Hind* (Benares), February 24 (*ibid.*, p. 157); *Najmul Akhbār*, March 4 (*ibid.*, pp. 158-159); *Āzād* (Lucknow), March 4; *Ṭūṭi'yā-i Hind* (Meerut), March 8 (*ibid.*, p. 159); *Saḥīfah-i Qudsī* (Delhi), March 10; *'Ālam-i Taṣvīr* (Kanpur), March 11, *Koḥ-i Nūr* (Lahore), March 10 (*ibid.*, pp. 173-174).

[48] Vilāyat Ḥusain, *Āp bītī*, p. 60.

[49] Badāyūnī, *Maḥfil-i 'Azīz*, pp. 127-128, 130-131.

ceased Ahmad Husain Khan, Beck's favorite—and Aziz Mirza's rival for student leadership. They claimed the munshi spied on the students and reported their misdemeanors. Mir Sahib also discovered that the students had one more father to call upon: they had wired Sami Ullah to come to their aid.[50]

When Sami Ullah arrived at the railway station a few days later, the students were there to greet him, in Raleigh's words, "as a *Deus ex machina.*" Urging the students to moderate their demands, he promised that they would all be pardoned. Then he went off to see Sayyid Ahmad. The old man was beginning to lose his nerve.[51] Newspaper accounts had appeared supporting the students, charging the Honorary Secretary with senility, warning the British professors that relations between students and servants were none of their business.[52] Most of the managers apparently felt the same. Only one group remained adamant against the students: the young Apostles from Cambridge. They held out for punishment of the "ring-leaders" and a formal apology from every student who had left the college.[53] Sayyid Ahmad would have to choose between them and the managers. "It has taken me ten years to create this college," he told them, "and you would destroy it in a day."[54] The Englishman argued that the college could not survive without due respect for authority, nor could public confidence and government support survive the resignation of the British staff. Reluctantly Sayyid Ahmad agreed. Sami Ullah told the students that they had lost, then returned to Rae Bareilly.[55] One by one most of the protesters trooped back, apologizing separately to Horst, Beck, and Sayyid Ahmad.[56] From a distance Aziz Mirza and Sayyid Husain repented their part in

[50] Vilāyat Ḥusain, *Āp bītī*, p. 61.
[51] Raleigh to his mother, February 22, 1887, *Letters*, I, 103.
[52] SVN as cited above.
[53] Raleigh to his mother, February 22, 1887, *Letters*, I, 103.
[54] Morison, *History of the M.A.-O. College*, pp. 6-7.
[55] Raleigh to his mother, February 22, 1887, *Letters*, I, 103.
[56] Iftikhār 'Ālam, *Muhammadan College History*, pp. 107-112.

the strike and reaffirmed their allegiance to Aligarh.[57] The college now had a new regime.

"It is an occasion of joy to us that we have routed the Committee," wrote Raleigh to his mother. "We are going to step into the incapable Committee's place. . . . We can none of us stay here unless College Discipline or Penal Law, in and out of class, is put entirely in our hands. The pettifoggers on the Committee love to show their power, but it is a characteristic of the English race in India that you can't have their service without giving them a share in dominion."[58] It was astute of Raleigh to sound the imperial theme: Aligarh was not just a college, it was part of the colonial situation, subject to circumstances of power beyond the college boundaries. That power was ultimately in British hands. Even within the college society, moreover, the strike had revealed a new cultural response to changing institutional configurations. The students may have been acting upon feelings for family and home, but it made all the difference in the world that those feelings had to be played out in a new institutional setting. The hartal, for example, may have been a familiar technique of protest, but now solidarity among the protesters was not based on birth-defined relationships. What united them was that they were all students at Aligarh and, as Sayyid Ahmad had made plain, all free to go. As with cricket, their participation was voluntary—so long as they accepted the rules.

Over the next two and a half years the British professors translated their victory into a formal set of governing regulations for the college. The first issue was job security for the Englishmen. The relevant rules were drawn up a month after the student strike; in their final form two years later all matters of recruitment, leave, salary, and tenure of

[57] *Ibid.*; Sayyid Husain to Sayyid Ahmad, July 1, 1886; Sayyid Ahmad to Sayyid Husain, July 3, 1886, AA; In'ām Ilāhī, " 'Azīz Mīrzā," *'Alīgaṛh Megzīn*, Aligarh Number (1954-1955), Part 2, pp. 29-30; see also AIG, July 31, 1888.

[58] Raleigh to his mother, February 22, 1887, *Letters*, I, 104-105.

position had to be mediated by Sayyid Mahmud—a man the Cambridge Apostles considered to be virtually one of their own. The rules provided that the principal, two professors, and the headmaster must all be Europeans and graduates of European universities. These provisions became the core of a lengthy code of "Laws and Regulations" covering all aspects of college governance. Known as the "Trustee Bill," it was drawn up in 1888 by another Cambridge Apostle, Arthur Strachey, at that time a barrister in Allahabad. Written into these rules was a clear provision that Sayyid Mahmud would be his father's successor as Honorary Secretary, a post that now conferred greater discretionary powers. Even though the old Managing Committee under Sami Ullah would still have general jurisdiction over the residential arrangements, the principal now received "full power to maintain discipline in the Boarding-House." The original draft of the bill also gave the British government special powers of intervention—powers that, as it turned out, the government was unwilling to take on, at least for the time being. The new body of lifetime Trustees, replacing the College Fund Committee, retained ultimate authority, but had little direct power in running the college.[59]

Before the strike Sayyid Ahmad had foreseen a divided successorship between Sami Ullah and Sayyid Mahmud.[60] Now this had become unthinkable. Feelings were bitter, and the fact of kinship only aggravated the matter. In 1888 Sayyid Mahmud married a bride originally promised to Sami Ullah's son; she came from the same family that had given

[59] "Draft of the Rules and Regulations for Appointment of the Trustees of the Mohommedan Anglo-Oriental College and for the Manner of Their Working, May 1899," SDAA, pp. 313-406; for revisions due to the unwillingness of the GNWP to undertake certain responsibilities, see AIG, September 10, 1889; see also Sayyid Ahmad to Members, College Fund Committee (Printed), May 20, 1889, AA.

[60] Alṭāf Ḥusain Ḥālī, "Khayālāt darbārah-i musavaddah-i qānūn-i ṭrasṭiyān-i madrasat ul-'ulūm 'Alīgaṛh" (*Samūr Gazette*, August 8, 1889), in Shaikh Isma'īl Pānīpatī, ed., *Kulliyāt-i Nasr-i Ḥālī*, I (Lahore: Majlis-i Taraqqī-i Adab, 1967), 429.

Sayyid Ahmad and Sami Ullah their wives and mothers.[61] Sayyid Ahmad used to refer to the younger man as his "little brother"; now, like some brothers, relations between the two reached a state of open hostility. In the midst of this tangle of family and college quarrels Khvajah Yusuf, a loyal supporter of Sami Ullah, called upon Sayyid Ahmad to step down as Honorary Secretary; like an old father on his prayer rug, he might now look on as his successors carried on the work.[62] But under the new rules it was Sami Ullah who was retired from the field. He responded with a bitter pamphlet charging that Sayyid Ahmad was making the college into his personal property, that Sayyid Mahmud was inadequately pious, that the boarding house was being turned over to Christian management, and that excessive power was to be surrendered to the British government. He reminded the public that Aligarh College existed in order to transmit English education through reliable Muslim auspices.[63]

Sayyid Ahmad replied by defending the need for British professors of the highest qualifications. Aligarh could never match the salary or job security of government colleges, but at least it could assure British recruits of sympathy and support. In the case of Beck, the college had a man who took the Muslim cause to heart and could be trusted to respect and maintain religious discipline. Committed to his longstanding belief in personal friendship between Muslim and Englishman, Sayyid Ahmad denounced Sami Ullah for attempting to treat the British staff as a batch of overpaid servants.[64] To others such a characterization seemed reasonable enough; Khvajah Yusuf called Beck the *mālī* of Sami Ullah's garden.[65]

[61] Vilāyat Ḥusain, *Āp bītī*, p. 67; cf. Ḥāli, "Khayālāt," p. 416.

[62] AIG, July 12, 1887.

[63] Quoted in Ḥālī, "Khayālāt," pp. 401-402; for contemporary newspaper comment see SVN (Punjab, NWP, etc.), 1889, pp. 444, 461, 545, 582-583, 641-643, 657-660, 673-674, 803; AIG, September 24, 1889.

[64] *Lectures and Speeches*, p. 430-432.

[65] Khvājah Yūṣuf, *Izālat ul-auhām*, p. 47.

Widely publicized, the battle between Sayyid Ahmad and Sami Ullah created enduring personal animosity. Sayyid Ahmad was not quite joking when he suggested a trip to Paris for a duel.[66] He was certainly serious when he threatened to disassociate himself from the college if the new rules failed to pass.[67] Some mediators, such as Mushtaq Husain, tried to dampen the dispute by postponing the issue of succession till after the old man died.[68] But at Sayyid Ahmad's insistence the Trustee Bill was finally steamrolled through the old Fund Committee in December 1889. Sami Ullah and his friends turned their attention to establishing a Muslim boarding house at Muir Central College, Allahabad—where they had to accept even more European intervention.[69] Meanwhile, Aligarh College had to carry on without its orthodox credentials and without a number of important contributors. Almost all the old backers from Aligarh town and vicinity marched off with Sami Ullah. The British government, however, made up the financial loss.[70]

The year 1889 was also the year that Mustafa Khan published *An Apology for the "New Light,"* dealing with the divorce between the generation of his peers and the world of their fathers.[71] Over the next decades that older world was increasingly excluded and even discredited at Aligarh. Sayyid Ahmad was the one member of the older generation who continued to play an active role in the college, but in the general life of the students the distant presence of this old man was only a vague accompaniment to the overwhelming dominance of the young faculty and older students. From

[66] Ḥālī, *Ḥayāt-i jāvīd*, p. 287.

[67] Sayyid Ahmad to Mushtaq Husain, August 7, 1889, *Maktūbāt*, p. 262.

[68] Ikrāmullāh Khān, *Viqār-i Ḥayāt*, pp. 392-397.

[69] GNWP, General, Education (B), February 1893, No. 391 (U.P. Archives, Lucknow); Ismail [Khan Shervani], "Muhammadan Boarding House, Muir College Allahabad," AIG, February 27, 1897.

[70] GOI, Home Education (B), September 1889, No. 13 (NAI); *Rū'idād No. 1: Ijlās-i Ṭrasṭiyān*, August 12, 1890 (Agra: Mufīd-i 'Ām Press, 1892).

[71] Above, p. 249.

time to time his carriage would come on to the college grounds: he might watch some cricket, check out construction operations, make a speech. He intervened when a student food monitor attempted to reorganize the system of food purchases from the town bazaar.[72] Twice he came into conflict with Beck. In 1894, prompted by Shibli, he revived the idea of uniforms—dark blue Turkish coat embroidered with the college insignia, red fez, English boots—and ordered the cloth from Kanpur.[73] But due to opposition from the press—the costume was expensive and un-Islamic—and from Beck, who may have preferred the romantic variety of student dress, the uniform was never compulsory in Sayyid Ahmad's lifetime.[74] The Honorary Secretary also attempted to replace Union elections with appointed officers and to control the subjects for debate, but Beck managed to convince him that such attentions were unnecessary.[75]

FACTORY AND FAMILY

Student unity was born out of resistance to authority, but the continuing encouragement of such solidarity went hand in hand with the tightening of supervisory control on the part of the teaching staff. This special combination of regulation and emotion was the foundation of a conscious strategy of moral education. For Sayyid Ahmad and Beck, the constant and explicit aim of the college was to raise up a disciplined cohort of public leaders for the Muslims of India. The lesson to be learned was the ability to act in close and sustained cooperation within the narrow restrictions of the

[72] Sayyid Ahmad to Morison, May 17, 1891 (123A, AA).

[73] AIG, July 2, 1892; Cawnpore Woolen Mills Co., Ltd. to Sayyid Ahmad, November 13, 1894 (?B, AA); *Lectures and Speeches*, pp. 527-528.

[74] *Naiyar-i A'ẓam*, September 5, 1894, and other newspaper comments in SVN (Punjab, NWP, etc.), 1894, p. 389; Muḥammad Amīn Zuberī, *Tazkirah-i Sir Sayyid* (Lahore: Publishers United, 1964), pp. 76-83.

[75] Sayyid Ahmad to Beck, January 25, 1893, and July 30, 1893 (AA).

British imperial system. The life in the boarding house was a model of the kind of political participation that might someday be available to the new generation. Raleigh had described the strike as "the rise of the English Democratic Spirit" among the students. True, the right they were defending, the right to thrash servants, was not among the more familiar precepts of the European liberal tradition. But the students had gathered together in an organized protest under an elected leader, so the crisis called for the familiar British strategy of reform. "By showing a decent regard for their feelings," said Raleigh, "it is easy to get unlimited authority."[76]

Beck and his colleagues now had the power to achieve that uniformity of social life that Sayyid Ahmad had dreamed of in his earliest plans for the college: students shut within the college compound, living together, eating together, following the same schedule of classes and activities, even wearing a standard college uniform. No one had ever challenged the desirability of Sayyid Ahmad's "dream," but it was far from fulfillment during the paternalistic days of Muhammad Akbar and Sami Ullah. Walling in the student population had to await the progress of building operations, but by the late 1880s there was at least a temporary enclosure on all sides. Almost all the Muslim boarders now lived in one of the two contiguous quadrangles, the kacca and the pakka. In 1887, just before the strike, first and second class students had started eating together in the same dining room.[77] Student life still fell short of perfect regimentation: the dining room was a scene of uncontrolled noise and chaos, and half the students ate in their own rooms—a practice that contributed mightily to student-servant tension.[78] Student attitudes were not in harmony with the new arrangement.

Having established the sure enforcement of rules and regu-

[76] Raleigh to his mother, February 22, 1887, *Letters*, I, 104.
[77] Above, p. 174.
[78] Beck to Sayyid Ahmad, December 8, 1889 (238B, AA).

lations, Beck proceeded to place day-to-day jurisdiction in the hands of recent graduates, who were now teachers in the school. They took up residence in the boarding house, each in charge of one side of a quadrangle. Under their supervision students had to study at fixed hours, sometimes in the classrooms, sometimes separately in their own rooms. The evening meal, now a required group activity for all Muslim boarders, was served under the watchful eye of the headmaster or Mir Vilayat Husain. School-level students had "their day mapped out for them in such a way as to leave them but little discretion; they are awakened before sunrise for morning prayers and until they go to bed at night they have hardly an hour which has not some particular work or pastime allotted to it."[79] Ten chowkidars stood guard to prevent unauthorized exits and entrances.[80]

The creation of student housekeeping committees in 1886 had been a source of friction with Maulvi Sulaiman, the manager, but in the new scheme of things such student responsibility received special encouragement. Squeezed out of his supervisory role, Maulvi Sulaiman resigned in 1891 and was not replaced. There continued to be a maulvi in the boarding house to lead prayers and perform religious duties, but he had no role in running the establishment.[81] The old nurturing role of the boarding-house manager was transformed as it passed into the hands of a carefully graded official structure —student monitors for prayers, house discipline, food arrangements, drill; the newly graduated schoolmasters as "sub-proctors"; Vilayat Husain as "proctor"; Morison, "the Provost," in overall command.[82] To the outrage of Sami Ullah and his friends, the Englishmen now had authority over the

[79] Morison, Principal's Annual Report, 1900-1901 (in MAOCM/AIG [combined], June-July 1901, p. 43).

[80] Sayyid Ahmad to Beck, May 11, 1894 (109A, AA).

[81] Sayyid Ahmad to Munshi Sa'īd Ahmad, January 5, 1893, *Maktūbāt*, p. 618.

[82] Beck, Principal's Annual Report, 1895-1896, p. 6; see also Shaikh Abdullah [librarian] to Sayyid Ahmad, October 14, 1896 (486B, AA).

smallest details of student life: Beck concerned himself with menus and dinnerware, Morison made periodic inspections of the student rooms.[83]

Under the new regime Islam itself came within the jurisdiction of the British professors; they enforced attendance at prayers with a determination unmatched by their pious Muslim predecessors.[84] Boys in the school were given little opportunity to miss prayers, but if any managed to slip away they were punished with "impositions." A prayer monitor kept an attendance register for the college students, who had to pay a fine for undue absence; they were reported to average three of the five prayers a day.[85] Visitors often commented on the impressive sight of students lined up in rows, prostrating their bodies in unison. Beck also instituted daily readings of the Qur'an, followed by a half-hour of translation and explanation by Shibli.[86] At Morison's urging, the college hired as "Dean" a maulvi from Deoband, Abdullah Ansari, who took over religious supervision of the Sunni students and replaced Shibli, with much less popularity, as expounder of the Qur'an. Parallel arrangements were made for Shī'ahs.[87] Muslim holidays such as Īd were celebrated in the college by feasting, speeches, and illuminations; students were expected to stay in the college rather than go home or into the town to join the community at large.[88]

[83] Beck to Sayyid Ahmad, November 19, 1889 (AA); AIG, January 31, 1891; Principal's Annual Report, 1895-1896, p. 61.

[84] Beck to Sayyid Ahmad, March 19, 1896; cf. Bilgrami, p. 86.

[85] MAOCM, June 15, 1899; Principal's Annual Report, 1895-1896, p. 7.

[86] AIG, June 19, 1894; Beck to Sayyid Ahmad, March 19, 1896 (AA).

[87] Sayyid Ahmad to Beck, October 28, 1893 (347A, AA; MAOCM/AIG, April 1901, p. 9); Shibli requested that Maulvi Abdullah relieve him of this obligation (Sayyid Ahmad to Shibli, January 20 and January 22, 1895, *Makātīb-i Sir Sayyid*, pp. 238-240); see also Mohamed Ali, *My Life*, pp. 23-25.

[88] In 1901 the college closed for Īd and students either went home or went to the prayers outside the town of Aligarh. "The practice of celebrating Eid in the college mosque as in the days of Sir Syed seems to have been abandoned." (MAOCM/AIG, April 15, 1900, English section, p. 8).

Although the classes in theology continued to receive minimal encouragement, Aligarh's English professors appreciated the value of Islam in promoting solidarity among the students and improving the reputation of the college among the outside public.

Cut off from the cultural milieu of their fathers' generation, Aligarh students now came in contact with an adult world as mediated by their teachers, especially the British ones. The memorable professors of the 1890s were, of course, Beck, Morison, and Arnold, but they never shared the warm camaraderie that Beck had known with Raleigh and Cox. Morison, efficient, self-confident, athletic, had none of the personal warmth that so attracted students to Beck and Arnold. Arnold, scholarly and awkward, avoided any administrative role and confined himself to a small circle of serious young men. But all three were committed to channeling the moral lives of Aligarh students in the direction of fellow feeling toward each other and public leadership over the Muslims of India. They exhorted the students, bluntly criticized the culture and morality of their parents' generation, organized them into voluntary associations stretching beyond their college years, and allocated among them their occupational careers. These three Cambridge men managed to communicate to the students in more than words what the "reality" out there was all about—not the reality of sharīf culture, but the reality of British dominance. It was to perform this task that Sayyid Ahmad had staked so much on retaining them.

From time to time the students would assemble in Strachey Hall to receive moral guidance in the form of an oration by Beck, Morison, or Arnold. There was, for example, the motley gathering of new college students at the start of each year—rough Punjabis, delicate young men from Oudh, their mouths full of pān, as well as the previously initiated matriculates from Aligarh's school classes. Such, at least, were the stereotypes recalled by Shaukat Ali in later years. They would hear Beck hold forth with all his skillful eloquence on the virtues of soap and water, well-washed clothes, even how to perform a restrained but graceful gesture of *salām*—at a forty-five degree angle from the perpendicular.[89] "After a year's stay in the College," wrote Shaukat Ali, "it was difficult to recognize 'who was who,' as all that heterogeneous material had been shaped in the 'Aligarh mould' "[90] (see Figure 6). Or in Beck's words: "A college or School may be compared to a factory which works up raw material into the finished products of civilization. . . . Its energies must be mainly devoted to producing one type only of many possible forms of excellence. For only by making this type predominant among its students can it exert the influence necessary to stamp its characteristics on fresh comers." The recognized virtues at Aligarh were defined as "practical energy," "strength of character," and "a sense of public duty." They were not intellectual or aesthetic.[91]

But if the image was sometimes industrial, Beck also made it his special concern to tell the students what it meant to be a "gentleman": the importance of a fixed schedule of work and play—"In Cambridge no one works in the afternoon"—the moral value of games and college societies, how to maintain a proper detachment from the vulgar necessity of examinations. He generally would close his speech with some catalog of relevant virtues: to be "courageous, independent, straightforward, truthful and honest; to be ashamed to do a mean trick; to be too proud to lie; to acquire such a feeling of self-respect as to make it impossible for you ever to take a bribe."[92] But the honesty that Aligarh endorsed referred more to matters of fact than matters of feeling. When a student at the Riding School showed that he was afraid of letting the horse go faster than a walk, Morison called him down before the whole student body: "No Aligarh boy ought

[89] Shaukat Ali, "The Late Mr. Beck and His Pupils," *Aligarh Monthly* (December 1905), p. 8.

[90] *Ibid.*

[91] Principal's Annual Report, 1895-1896, AA.

[92] MAOCM, December 1, 1894, pp. 156-157.

Figure 6. Theodore Beck and Student Leaders, 1898-1899. Seated on chairs, Beck is third from left, Sajjad Haidar is second from right, and between them is Llewlyn Tipping

[ever] to disgrace the College by letting it be seen that he is afraid"—on pain of ridicule.[93]

The implication of such remarks—and it was not always left to implication—was that dirt, dissipation, dishonesty, and cowardice were characteristics of the previous generation of Indian Muslims. Students were lectured on "the appalling evils of Oriental society," "the ignorant and bigotted mullas," "the intellectual poverty of this country," "the natural indolence of the East."[94] "The creation of this College," Morison told them, "is about the one noteworthy thing that the Musalmans of India have done for some time."[95] Such remarks were a familiar part of Sayyid Ahmad's own special rhetoric, but it made a difference that they were now uttered by British professors to the students of a tightly enclosed residential establishment.

The authority for such comments and exhortations received further reinforcement from the reality of British power beyond the college walls. These were not just individual opinions; they were part of a code of conduct for public life in British India. Viceroys and Lieutenant Governors on great ceremonial visits to the college would vouchsafe similar advice: to the extent that students lived up to the Aligarh code, they would be allowed to participate in the benefits of British rule. "To have been an Aligarh man," Auckland Colvin, Lieutenant Governor, told them in a much quoted remark, "is, I have over and over again found, a passport to the respect and confidence of both Englishmen and Indians. They carry with them the stamp of their training." They were suitable material for responsible public office.[96] Conversely, as Morison put it, students who did not live up to the Aligarh image in terms of their conduct in the

[93] MAOCM, August 1894, p. 47.

[94] Principal's Annual Report, 1898-1899, AA; speech by Beck at Prize Distribution (AIG, September 6, 1892).

[95] MAOCM, August 1894, p. 45.

[96] *Addresses and Speeches Relating to the Mahomedan Anglo-Oriental College, in Aligarh*, ed. Mohsin-ul-Mulk (Aligarh: Institute Press, 1898), p. 176.

boarding house and extracurricular activities, could not expect those valuable recommendations the British professors were in a position to provide.[97]

In the early days of the college, the relationship between Sami Ullah and the students had been built on parental love; he cared for them when they were sick and refused to disown them when they were disobedient. Maulvi Muhammad Akbar had been notable for his spirit of loving kindness. In the absence of women, such men provided almost motherly care; Sayyid Ahmad was the distant Muslim father figure.[98] But the victory for authority perpetrated by the British professors was a victory for written rules and conditions; it represented the fall of the parent-child paradigm of college social life. Both Sayyid Ahmad and Sami Ullah had failed as parents; the one had disowned them, the other had proven ineffectual. Now, in their unsuccessful strike, the students suddenly discovered a self-conscious solidarity of action in which the older generation had no part.

After 1887, the student body was older and a larger proportion was in college classes. In the new regime, authority rested with a group of men who were only slightly older than many of the students. Almost all the school masters were young former students of the college. The British professors, all in their twenties, played on student teams and participated in student societies. They had even been known to play kabaddi on moonlit nights. Their occasional pose as father figures was unconvincing: "I cannot pretend to regard in a parental light students who by their activities and their sentiments themselves discard the relationship," said Beck shortly after the student strike.[99]

The dominant paradigm of social relationships after 1887

[97] MAOCM, August 1894, p. 45.

[98] Vilāyat Ḥusain, *Āp bītī*, p. 29; see Z̲akā' Ullāh, *Samī' Ullāh K̲h̲ān*, pp. 64-65.

[99] AIG, April 12, 1887.

was one of solidarity among a society of peers; the kinship metaphor was that all students were brothers. Sayyid Ahmad ratified the change in a humorous act: in 1892 he enrolled as a student in the youngest school class in order to join the Brotherhood, a new society confined to students and former students.[100] Two years later he elaborated on the metaphor in an address to the students: they had come from many different places, were studying different subjects, but they were all together in "the lap of a wise mother"; they were all her children. The mother was the boarding house. In the all-male society of the college, the college itself would embody the missing female role. Now the students were bound together as brothers in love, friendship, fellow-feeling.[101]

Aligarh, Sayyid Ahmad told the students, was to be a distinct stage in their lives, a turning point into a new moral consciousness. "Every period of your life is a period of passing into a new life": the total dependency of infancy, followed by the ability to move around and feed oneself, then a time of learning language and religious principles, and some years later facing the "dangerous enemies" of youthful temptation. The students of Aligarh were fortunate enough to have found refuge in the abstract motherhood of the college; once again they had discovered a "new life." That new life was their solidarity as Aligarh students, a condition that partook of the unity of the Islamic ummah, even the unity of God. And from this student brotherhood they would someday forge together the Muslims of India into a fully mobilized political community. "The boarding house exists as a single whole [*ek kul*] in order to make the qaum really a quam."[102]

In accordance with this metaphor, the British professors did not limit themselves to enforcing boarding-house discipline or delivering formal pronouncements to ceremonial

[100] *Ibid.*, July 5, 1892.

[101] Lecture, December 7, 1894, *Lectures and Speeches*, pp. 525-526.

[102] *Ibid.*, p. 526. Deferring to C. M. Naim, I take *kul* to be the Persian "whole," not the Sanskritic "family"—though I would like to think that there is a play on words going on here.

assemblages; they sought to reach the students with a more personal touch. Although Beck referred to himself as a "professional educator," he defined his role in terms of the most diffuse responsibilities and relationships with regard to the students.[103] The opposition between emotional attachment and organizational formalism presented itself as a transition in the lives of the students from the family mode of social relationships to the bureaucratic and professional impersonality of their later careers. And the contrast between the metaphor of factory-like efficiency and the continual appeals to gentlemanly detachment replicated the seminal Victorian tension between utilitarianism and intuitionism more directly than the study of philosophical arguments. The shared belief of Sayyid Ahmad and the Cambridge Apostles in the primacy of human relationships even within the structure of a complex society found expression in the social milieu of Aligarh in a way that could never be communicated in the classroom.[104]

Of all the British professors, it was Theodore Beck who made the most complete personal commitment to Aligarh and its students. Determined to devote his entire life to the college, he even offered the allegiance of his family back in England. In 1891 he brought out his parents and a sister, Jesse Beck, and they were all introduced to the student body in a formal assembly marked with the exchange of gifts and addresses.[105] Miss Beck, who stayed on after the parents had departed, became the first woman to reside on the college property. "We were all terribly excited," recalled Shaukat Ali ten years later, referring to the first time they were invited for a social evening in the presence of "an 'English lady.'" "What a pleasure it was to have refined educated ladies to talk to. . . . Miss Beck . . . took each one in hand and in her charming sympathetic [way] put him

[103] Beck, "Work and Games," MAOCM (August 1, 1896), p. 331.
[104] Above, pp. 214-216.
[105] AIG, December 4, 1888; February 16, 1889.

at his ease."[106] The following year Beck went a step further and became the first English professor to bring a wife to Aligarh—Raleigh's sister—having first solicited Sayyid Ahmad's "blessing" and Sayyid Mahmud's brotherly approval.[107] Arnold and Morison soon followed the example, and all these women participated actively in the social life of the college. Like sons in a great joint household, the British professors had brought their wives to Sayyid Ahmad's college. The family bond reached back to England, especially in the case of the Becks, who provided warm and generous hospitality to Aligarh alumni studying at British universities.[108]

The Englishmen had their particular favorites among the students. Some were especially studious, but the attraction of others lay in their glamorous social background. A government ward sent down by the Foreign Department from Baluchistan spent three years of early adolescence at Aligarh and, in Beck's words, "won a unique place in my affections." He even accompanied the principal to the hills during vacations. Then suddenly the British government ordered him back home to occupy a chieftainship denied to his "rebel" father. Instead, he ran off to join his father, and died soon afterwards in battle. He was fifteen years old. Beck's deep personal grief must have been mixed with an unspoken sense of gratification at the young man's brave loyalty and dramatic death.[109]

Shaukat Ali has written the most vivid description of Beck's personal relations with a student. He recalls first seeing Beck in his home town of Rampur, when the Aligarh football team came to play a match. There was a special tent for the team, and when Shaukat looked in he was amazed to

106 Shaukat Ali, "The Late Mr. Beck and His Pupils," MAOCM, June-July 1901, p. 27.

107 Beck to Sayyid Ahmad (from London), August 20, 1891; Beck to Sayyid Mahmud, August 20, 1891 (304A, AA).

108 Aftab Ahmad Khan, *Diary*, 1892-1893 (AA).

109 Beck to Deputy Secretary to the Government of India, Foreign Department, December 9, 1896 (631B, AA).

see two Englishmen, Beck and Morison, sitting on a charpoy "laughing and chatting away" with the students. No Englishman had ever, in his experience, behaved with such easy familiarity toward Indians. Sometime later Shaukat visited his elder brother, Zulfiqar Ali, at Aligarh, and once again encountered Beck, this time eating with the students in the dining room. What is more, Beck himself noticed the young visitor. "Zulfiqar," he said, "your brother is a magnificent looking boy." As Shaukat remembered, "His words went right to my heart and I loved him from that moment."[110] Beck easily persuaded him to join the college at Aligarh, thus recruiting a star batsman for the cricket team.

Beck's recipe for eastablishing close personal bonds with this bright, boisterous student included what he used to call "friendly wiggings" or "a bit of plain talking." When Shaukat forgot about an invitation to tea with the principal and his wife, Beck berated him for a full half hour as a "disgrace to the College," "never to be treated as a gentleman," the kind of person who deserved to be "kicked out of one's house." In later memory such attention was obviously gratifying, but at the time Shaukat was deeply embarrassed and for a while did his best to avoid meeting the principal. Beck himself broke the ice some days later by inviting the guilty student for a walk up the road toward the old Aligarh Fort. Beck started off by joking, "forced" the young man to smoke a cigarette, and then lectured him gently about the importance of personal discipline. He himself was temperamentally lazy, Beck confessed. Even his best friend Arthur Strachey had the same problem. But they had learned that there was no alternative to energy and self-control. It was the only protection against starvation. As a matter of fact, Beck and Strachey came from notably warm, close families—but the ethic of the time was that a man must succeed on his own. And that was the principal's heart-to-heart advice to Shaukat Ali.

[110] Shaukat Ali, "The Late Mr. Beck" [1901], p. 22.

For Shaukat Ali what militated against this stern and lonely view of life was that Beck obviously cared for the students with a warmth that transcended any calculated educational strategy. Traveling with some students to Allahabad for the university athletic tournament, the principal was "quite as boyish and excited as any of his pupils. At such times, he could not keep himself from our company and would pay us four or five visits during each day at most unexpected hours."[111] For all the discipline and exhortation it was difficult for a student to resist Beck's affectionate enthusiasm. Such care and concern went a long way toward making an externally imposed code of conduct into genuine personal commitment.

BROTHERHOOD AND THE WRESTLING PIT

"Really I do not know so intimately any of my family members as I do of my Boarding fellows," said Aftab Ahmad Khan after completing eleven years as an Aligarh student.[112] Already married, the father of a three-year-old son, Aftab nevertheless found his fullest sense of belonging among the students of the college. He might visit his family in Kunjpura or his father in Gwalior, but Aligarh was his home base and remained so throughout his life. Profoundly serious and self-consciously pious, he was not generally popular; although he won the "Cambridge Speaking Prize" for his debating skills, he was never a Union Club officer. He was not a person to drop in casually upon a fellow student in the boarding house, and if one came by his room while he was studying he would be told unceremoniously to get out. Yet for a special group of earnest young men, Aftab was clearly the leader. Even in his early days as a school student he surrounded himself with a group of friends known as the "Aftab Party," a group that marked its separateness by not playing games with the other students.[113] One person who did not

[111] *Ibid.*, [1905], pp. 6-15. [112] AIG, April 21, 1891.

[113] Inayat Ullah, quoted in Ḥabībullāh K͟hān, *Ḥayāt-i Aftāb*, pp. 11-12.

participate in Aftab's circle was a slightly older student toward whom he was notably deferential, his older brother Sultan Ahmad Khan. Sultan did not make enemies.[114]

In 1886 Aftab Ahmad Khan was one of the students who petitioned Sayyid Ahmad for the creation of student housekeeping committees in the boarding house, but that year he also passed his entrance examination and took the opportunity to interrupt his education to get married. He does not appear to have participated in the student strike; in fact, he and his fellow petitioners had made a point of disassociating themselves from Aziz Mirza and the Union Club leadership.[115] Over the next five years Aftab remained at Aligarh without taking any examinations, was frequently absent, but retained his role as student leader. In 1891, he and his brother went off to Cambridge, but Aftab remained in close contact with the Aligarh scene. When he returned from Cambridge in 1894, he went back to Aligarh almost immediately after the most perfunctory visit to his family. Soon he settled there permanently, as a barrister in the Aligarh District Court and a Trustee of the college.[116]

In 1891, while still a student, Aftab Ahmad Khan wrote up a formal proposal in Urdu for the establishment of a new student organization, the Anjuman al-Farẓ, or Duty Society. The cricket team and the Union Club had been established at the behest of the college authorities; the Duty, as it was called, was entirely a matter of student initiative. Its purpose was to collect funds to enable poor students to come to Aligarh and to promote the reputation of the college among Indian Muslims in general. Aftab shared his idea cautiously with a select group of friends, then approached T. W. Arnold with the request that he be the one officeholder in the society, the *Amīn* or Keeper. The membership was to consist of "servants," who would unanimously elect any additional members after they had served a trial period in the Lajnat al-Akhvān, society of brothers.[117] The numbers were small, the

[114] AIG, April 21, 1891.
[115] "Darkhvāst Farsṭ Klās Bōrḍarz kī."
[116] Ḥabībullāh Khān, pp. 39, 45. [117] *Ibid.*, pp. 19-29.

servants well tested. They had to be persons of high moral character—as exhibited by their conduct in the boarding house—and energetically committed to the Duty's activities. By 1895 there had been thirty-six servants and twenty-four persons still in the status of associate. Beck, Morison, and Horst were in the latter category.[118] Five years later the cumulative number of servants had just barely doubled to seventy-four.[119] The Duty was a select group.

Aftab had listened well to the exhortations of Sayyid Ahmad and the British professors; the Duty represented exactly the kind of disciplined cohort of dedicated leaders that Aligarh was designed to create. Back in 1888 Sayyid Ahmad made one of his less successful attempts at establishing an organizational adjunct to the Aligarh movement by calling for the enlistment of "National Volunteers"—the term borrowed from the local militia groups that only Europeans were permitted to join. A member was supposed to go about with a purse around his neck begging money for scholarships for poor Muslim students.[120] The proposal, typical of Sayyid Ahmad's ironic style, was a response to the criticism that only the rich could go to Aligarh: people were quick to attack Aligarh, but only some dramatic act, a respectable man taking up the pose of faqir, could shame them into helping the college. It was left to Aftab Ahmad Khan to take the proposal seriously; only when the Duty was a going operation did Sayyid Ahmad become aware of its existence.[121] By acting with pious humility, by exemplifying the highest standards of personal morality, the servants of the Duty hoped to refute the notion that Aligarh and the generation of the New Light were inimical to Islam. They would prove the worth of Aligarh by begging from door to door, in town after town, during their vacation, and by setting up tea stalls

118 Ṭufail Aḥmad, *Directory* (1895 ed.), pp. 40-44.

119 "Sālānah Rapōrṭ Anjuman al-farẓ, Madrasat ul-'ulūm 'Alīgaṛh, 1900-1901," MAOCM/AIG [combined], October-December 1901, Urdu section, pp. 1-2.

120 AIG, February 7, 1888.

121 Ḥabībullāh Khān, *Ḥayāt-i Aftāb*, pp. 19-29.

at the annual Aligarh *Numā'ish* (a local fair) and at the Muhammadan Educational Conference—preparing the tea and washing the dishes themselves. And all this would be an intrinsic part of their own education, an education of the heart, as Aftab put it, not just of the mind. The Society aggressively excluded the college authorities, with the exception of Arnold; money was collected and spent according to its own rules and goals. Sayyid Ahmad had to apply formally to borrow from the fund—by 1895 the Duty had collected about 5,000 rupees—and could only use it as specified by rigorous conditions.[122]

At the same time that he was establishing the Duty, Aftab Ahmad Khan presented Beck with a formal scheme for the moral improvement of students in the boarding house. The proposal for careful supervision, Qur'an reading, periodic moral lectures by the British professors—all this was just what Beck and his colleagues wanted to hear, and were in fact instituting at the time. Aftab also proposed separating the students into three age grades with the dividing lines at twelve and seventeen, an idea that achieved partial realization in the creation of the Zahur Husain Ward for younger children in 1895.[123] Later, in 1897, as a Trustee of the college Aftab proposed a special "English House," where younger students would be placed in the care of an English governess; four years later this too came to pass.[124]

With so many public-spirited ideas for the realization of Aligarh's goals, Aftab Ahmad Khan stood forth as the Aligarh student par excellence, the hope of the future generation. When Aftab and Sultan were leaving for England, a special dinner was held in their honor attended by British government officials, many of the Trustees, even a few representatives of Sami Ullah's faction, and all of the boarders. There were speeches, nonalcoholic toasts, a full demonstra-

[122] Sayyid Ahmad to Mazhar ul-Haq, June 18, 1892 (176A, AA); Ṯufail Aḥmad, *Directory* (1895 ed.), p. 40.

[123] Ḥabībullāh Khān, *Ḥayāt-i Aftāb*, pp. 29-31.

[124] *Ibid.*, pp. 47-48.

tion that Aftab in particular, as founder of the Duty, represented what Aligarh was all about: the raising up of "vigorous public spirited men . . . the bone and sinew of a nation."[125]

The Duty was only one of a number of student societies that blossomed in the early 1890s. The intellectual counterculture gathered under the aegis of Arnold and Shibli also expressed itself in the vocabulary of brotherliness, but the brothers tended to be a different group of young men.[126] Ghulam us-Saqlain, founder of the Akhvān us-Ṣafā (Brothers of Purity), was not a member of Aftab's inner circle; he was a man of earnest piety and moral intensity, but he was much more of an intellectual, more given to advancing subtle arguments and to the display of wide reading. He too had won the "Cambridge Speaking Prize," but not an office in the Union. According to Morison, Ghulam us-Saqlain was given to "intellectual isolation."[127] Sayyid Ahmad called him "very virtuous," and commented that he read far beyond what the curriculum demanded of him.[128] In the Aligarh milieu such attributes were not altogether commendable: "As a student," said Morison many years later, "he was chaffed for his zeal and quaint ideas."[129] As with Aftab, his energetic participation in the Union debates did not win him any student offices; his leadership was confined to a more select group than the general student body. A composer of apothegms, poems, and numerous essays, he maintained his relation to the college after his graduation by frequent visits,

[125] AIG, May 5, 1891. When he returned three and a half years later, another dinner was held in his honor and he was hailed as "a typical Aligarh student . . . the very ideal of what an educated Musalman in India ought to be." (MAOCM, December 1894, p. 166.)

[126] Above, pp. 246-247.

[127] Morison, *History of the M.A.-O. College*, p. 12.

[128] English draft of Sayyid Ahmad's letter of recommendation for Ghulam us-Saqlain, July 27, 1893 (AA). See also an article by his son Khvājah Ghulām us-Saiyidain, "Ek Mard-i Darvaish," *'Alīgaṛh Megzīn*, Aligarh No. Supplement (1954-1955), pp. 1-40.

[129] Quoted in memorandum by R. Burn, January 4, 1911, in *Correspondence in Connection with Muhammadan Affairs from 1912-14* (printed), Meston Papers, No. 6, p. 102 (IOL).

continued participation in the Union and the A<u>kh</u>vān us-Ṣafā, and articles in the college magazine.[130]

In 1892, Mustafa Khan wrote to his friend Aftab Ahmad Khan, then at Cambridge, reporting that yet another student organization had been established, this one called the Brotherhood. "I am thinking of writing Mr. Beck," wrote Aftab in his diary, "asking him to make this newly created Brotherhood as one of the branches of the Duty."[131] The Brotherhood had been inaugurated with an eloquent speech by Morison, later inscribed in Urdu translation beside the entranceway of Strachey Hall, and distributed as a bilingual pamphlet to the general public. Student speakers on that occasion included Sayyid Vazir Hasan and Shaukat Ali, neither of them members of the Duty or the A<u>kh</u>vān us-Ṣafā. Only the student poet Khushi Muhammad "Nazr" managed to bridge all three organizations.[132]

The purpose of the Brotherhood was to bind Aligarh students, past and present, into an ongoing commitment to the college ideology and its propagation among the Muslims of India. Less exclusive than the other societies, it was open to all students, but only to students: Khushi Muhammad's "real" brother was refused admission as an Aligarh "brother" because he had never gone to the college.[133] As members of the Brotherhood, former students were expected to donate one percent of their incomes to the college and to form local societies of ex-Aligarh students wherever they might be located. Aside from promoting the college, the Brotherhood was to provide a network for ferreting out job opportunities suitable to an Aligarh man. And an annual dinner at Aligarh was supposed to bind past and present students together in sibling affection. After the departure of its initial student founders, however, the club depended on Morison's intermittent attention, and never succeeded in attracting

130 Above, pp. 250-251.
131 Entry for August 17, 1892 (AA).
132 MAOCM, printed as supplement to AIG, July 5, 1892.
133 *Ibid.*, September 6, 1892; December 6, 1892.

a significant number of alumni.[134] The idea was revived in 1899 with the founding of the Old Boys Association.[135]

The establishment of rival student societies seems to have been a response to the dominance, with Beck's enthusiastic sponsorship, of cricket and the Union Club. The prestige conferred on these two extracurricular activities made leadership in them a highly coveted distinction. Beck chose the captain of the cricket team in consultation with the previous captain, and tenure in the post lasted until the young man left Aligarh.[136] Vice presidency, secretaryship, and membership on the select committee of the Union, on the other hand, were all achieved through hotly contested elections. For three or four days before the election, day and night, Aligarh surrendered itself to intense campaigning on behalf of two opposing slates; when the results were announced, the losing candidates were given a mock funeral procession through the college grounds.[137]

In the early 1890s the Big Man on Campus was surely Shaukat Ali, captain of the cricket team and secretary of the Union. In cricket he was long remembered as "a good slogging player," one who hit the ball hard and far.[138] In the Union he was always a reliable source of humor, especially at "Penny Readings," where he did his "Bengali babu" and "Chinaman" imitations. In 1894, his last year at the college, he won the Cambridge Speaking Prize. As an initiator of the Brotherhood, he fulfilled his duty of service to the college. As a student he was capable of a safe second division without joining the "smugs" and "book worms" of the Duty and Aḵẖvān us-Ṣafā. He ignored college rules and schedules, living a boisterous, happy life, "joining in a rollicking noisy 'chorus' or loafing about from room to room . . . clothes

---

[134] AIG, March 6, 1894; MAOCM, May 1, 1896; Iftiḵẖār 'Ālam, *Muhammadan College History*, pp. 168-170.

[135] Below, p. 332.

[136] Shaukat Ali, "The Late Mr. Beck" [1905], p. 11.

[137] Shaiḵẖ Muḥammad 'Abdullāh, *Mushāhadāt o ta'aṣṣurāt* (Aligarh: Female Education Association, 1969), pp. 13-14.

[138] Morison, *History of the M.A.-O. College*, p. 14.

scattered over a dozen rooms and no regular hours kept." For months on end, or so went the boast, he never had occasion to enter his own room in the boarding house.[139] A new student would be taken to meet the great Shaukat Ali, and one of them recalled thirty-six years later as the happiest moment in his life that time when he was taken by the hand and swept away with great waves of personal warmth and laughing hilarity, ushered from room to room, dubbed with a nickname—"Pasha"—and then led off to the cricket field for a game he had never played because of studiousness and ill-health. From then on he was Shaukat Ali's man.[140]

When Shaukat Ali was appointed captain of the cricket team, the *Aligarh Institute Gazette* commented with some anxiety: "Our Eleven is not famous so much for their good play, as for their gentlemanly manners, and we hope the present Captain, who is a popular, young and energetic player, will keep up the former prestige of the College in the Cricket field."[141] Under Shaukat Ali, the team played to win. Shaikh Abdullah, a stalwart of the Duty, recalled years later that no one in his class went out for cricket: that was the preserve of "Shaukat Ali's party."[142]

Aftab Ahmad Khan, Ghulam us-Saqlain, and Shaukat Ali exemplify three types of student leadership at Aligarh and reflect conflicting signals from the college authorities about which virtues characterized "the Aligarh mould"—social service, intellectual enterprise, or the light-hearted comradeship of self-confident men. Every student generation gave witness to such conflicts. Far from being a united phalanx, Aligarh student society seems to have harbored within itself a number of highly competitive subcultures and cliques.

[139] Shaukat Ali, "The Late Mr. Beck" [1901], p. 23.

[140] Sīlānī [pseud.], "Yād-i Ayyām," *Old Boy*, I, No. 4 (January 1928), 32-37 (Salar Jang Library, Hyderabad, India); Sajjad Haidar has also left a vivid description of Shaukat Ali's "darbār," quoted in Allah Bakhsh Yusufi, *Life of Maulana Mohamed Ali Jauhar* (Karachi: Mohamed Ali Educational Society, 1970), pp. 38-39.

[141] July 5, 1892.

[142] Shai<u>kh</u> 'Abdullāh, *Mushāhadāt*, pp. 10-11.

Precise information on these student groups is not available, but it is possible to establish their existence and something of their characteristics.

The earliest appearance of open divisiveness among students coincided with the arrival of Theodore Beck as principal in 1883. Beck's bewildering sponsorship of the very virtues most foreign to his own character, athletic ability and gentlemanly leisureliness, as well as the tremendous emphasis that he placed on cricket and the Union Club, helped set the terms of competition in the intense social world of the Aligarh boarding house. The first round of this kind of competition took place when a student named Abdur Rauf attempted to organize a clique against Khvajah Sajjad Husain, vice-president of the Union from 1884 to 1886.[143] Soon afterwards there was a bitter battle between Ahmad Husain Khan, the cricket captain, and Aziz Mirza, the Union secretary.[144] Beck, who allegedly favored Ahmad Husain Khan, attempted to discourage the rivalry by preaching a "sermon," complete with quotations from both Qur'an and Bible. As he put it, "there is abroad in the College a spirit of backbiting, slander, of stirring up ill-feeling. . . . If you are to accomplish the work for which this college was founded, you must be friends, there must be no dissension. In unity is strength."[145]

Such principles were at the heart of the Aligarh ethos, but each little coterie of boarding-house friendships wanted unity established under its own leadership. And one reason that rivalries were often so intense was the emphasis placed on extracurricular success. In addition to prestige within student society, the mutual gratifications of friendship and enmity, and the desire to contribute to the great Aligarh cause, one motivation for seeking student leadership was that it might launch a young man on a successful career after leaving the college. Theodore Morison explicitly stated that in recommending students for government posts he would consider

143 Aftab Ahmad Khan, *Diary*, October 13, 1893 (AA).
144 Badāyūnī, *Maḥfil-i 'Azīz*, p. 115.
145 AIG, November 24, 1885.

their extracurricular achievements, not their scholastic standing.[146]

In the early 1890s the lines of student competition seem to have been fairly well defined. Following Shaukat Ali's victory as Union secreatry in 1893, a group of students, including Ghulam us-Saqlain and Khushi Muhammad, organized a breakaway debating club. News of this inspired Sayyid Ahmad to make one of his rare interventions into student affairs, scolding Beck for his failure to maintain tight supervision over student societies. If Union Club members could not select their officers by unanimous agreement, then Beck should step in and appoint them.[147] Both Khushi Muhammad and Ghulam us-Saqlain hastened to declare their own innocence to Sayyid Ahmad and to put the blame on Shaukat Ali and his friends. The annual Union elections, said Khushi Muhammad, were the cause of the trouble: there were always two parties and every year one of them swept all the offices by last-minute recruitment of school-level students as Union members. "Last year the two parties were ready to fight with cudgels and clubs." The winning party consisted of a rowdy bunch of students called the "chorus wallas" because they went around singing "obscene choruses" and making a "noisy stir." For his part, Khushi Muhammad had dedicated himself to "promoting mutual friendship" and "removing frictions"; for example, he once broke up a fight by holding up a copy of the Qur'an. He and his friends believed in "good behaviour" and "the observance of praiseworthy morals."[148]

According to Khushi Muḥammad, one of the major grievances was an anti-Punjabi attitude on the part of the Union leadership. He charged that Shaukat Ali "openly insulted & reviled the Punjabis" in the Union, and the club had stopped subscribing to newspapers from the Punjab. In response,

146 MAOCM/AIG [combined], June 1, 1900, pp. 2-3.

147 Sayyid Ahmad to Beck, January 27, 1893 (AA).

148 Petition from Khushi Muhammad to Sayyid Ahmad, July 30, 1893; letter from Khushi Muhammad to Sayyid Ahmad, n.d.; Sayyid Ahmad to Beck, July 30, 1893 (248?, AA); see also Yusufi, *Mohamed Ali Jauhar*, p.38.

Ghulam us-Saqlain initiated a separate debating club, and Khushi Muhammad was elected chairman. There were twenty to twenty-five members, mostly from the Punjab.[149] Then the following year, Shaukat's successor as secretary of the Union was a leading member of this circle of earnest intellectuals, Zafar Ali Khan, a Punjabi.

There had been a significant rise in the number of students from the Punjab in the early 1890s, but it is not clear how important the regional rivalry was.[150] It probably was not linguistic, since Ghulam us-Saqlain, who was from Panipat, was included among the Punjabis. Khushi Muhammad and Ghulam us-Saqlain may have had most of their friends from the Punjab, but insofar as one can identify Shaukat Ali's closest friends, some were also from the Punjab—and, of course, were cricket players.[151] The differences seem to have been temperamental, not regional; the two were by no means congruent. In general, student cliques do not seem to have been based on identities established at birth—religious sect, region, or lineage. It seems likely that students found their friends as fellow students in the classroom, boarding house, and playing fields, and that friendship was a matter of accidental juxtaposition as well as shared talents and inclinations.[152]

In 1894, there was a considerable dispute over whether the "tone" of the boarding house was declining. Morison, officiating principal while Beck was in England, raised the issue in one of those periodic exhortations to moral perfection.[153] Habibullah Khan, a recent graduate and close

149 Letter from Khushi Muhammad to Sayyid Ahmad (248?, AA).

150 See above, p. 178.

151 Examples are "Sīlānī" and Shaukat Ali's successor, Muhammad Abdullah, who died on a visit from his home in Jullundhur to Shaukat Ali's home in Rampur, and inspired his friend to write a heartfelt eulogy ("The Late Mr. Beck" [1905], pp. 13-14). Abdul Haq (from Hapur) and Ziauddin Ahmad (from Meerut) were leading non-Punjabis in the Akhvān us-Ṣafā group.

152 Note friendships discussed in Habībullāh Khān, *Ḥayāt-i Aftāb*, p. 25; Badāyūnī, *Maḥfil-i ʻAzīz*, pp. 107-112; Mas'ūd ʻAli, II, 160-162; Riẓā ʻAlī, *Aʻmāl nāmah*, pp. 80-81.

153 MAOCM, August 1894.

friend of Aftab Ahmad, took up the theme in a series of articles in the college magazine, bemoaning the falling standard of decorum and seriousness on the part of the present student generation. Muhammad Abdullah, Shaukat Ali's friend and successor as cricket captain, responded with a hard-hitting attack on Habibullah Khan and a strong defense of his own contemporaries.[154]

The dispute reflected differences among the English professors. In a letter to Sayyid Ahmad, Beck took issue with Morison's contention that dress, manners, and morals had deteriorated; indeed, they had improved and were now "more manly & honest."[155] And although Beck would probably have agreed with Morison's criteria for student distinction—"their social influence in the Boarding-House, their conversation and the part they play in the Clubs; a smug is one of the last people who . . . would bring credit to the College"[156]—even this latter group of hard-working students had their refuge in Arnold.[157] Endemic student conflict was built into the institutional culture that Aligarh's Cambridge contingent had worked so hard to create.

If competition set students against each other, the college also inspired powerful friendships among students, friendships that often lasted throughout life. Vilayat Husain, a Shīʿah and Barha Sayyid, and Habibullah Khan, a Sunni and Pathan, had a legendary friendship that they symbolized in later years by naming their houses after each other.[158] Ziaullah and Muhammad Abdullah, cricket players of the 1890s, were buried side by side.[159] Sayyid Riza Ali, Sajjad Haidar, Sirdar Muhammad Hayat Khan, and Haidar Hasan all lived in the kacca barracks, eschewed sports in favor of intellectual interests, and called themselves "the four dervishes."[160] Such friendships may have led to marriage ar-

[154] *Ibid.*, September 1, 1894 [*sic*].
[155] London, September 17, 1894 (AA).
[156] MAOCM, August 1894. [157] Above, pp. 245-247.
[158] The houses, both in Aligarh, are Habib Manzil and Vilayat Manzil; see Vilāyat Ḥusain, *Āp bītī*, pp. 180-181.
[159] Shaukat Ali, "The Late Mr. Beck" [1905], pp. 13-14.
[160] Riẓā ʿAlī, *Aʿmāl nāmah*, pp. 80-81.

rangements between far-flung families and further ratified the kinship bonds among students.

On the other hand, there seems to have been some anxiety among college authorities and certain students that the close, intense, all-male living conditions of the boarding house might encourage homosexuality. In the early 1880s some students were expelled for what seems to have been homosexual conduct.[161] Beck later claimed that putting the boarding house under his control ended a rather notorious state of affairs.[162] This statement was vigorously denounced by Khvajah Muhammad Yusuf as slander against the early students of the college.[163] In fact, the original rules of the boarding house that only "real" brothers or close relatives could share a room, and that no student could be in another's room at night fell by the wayside under Beck's regime.[164] Instead students received exhortations. Several times the Akhvān us-Ṣafā were reminded about the "purity" in their names: a warning that "the sin of immorality" was "bestial and degrading."[165] In the absence of evidence from some Aligarh version of Lytton Strachey, however, there is no reason to believe that overt homosexuality was particularly widespread; brotherly love had other ways of expressing itself.

Powerful friendships and equally powerful feuds constituted the informal core of the Aligarh experience. Student cliques had a great deal to do with the actual social education of the young men who went to the college. What many students learned was how to organize themselves for group cooperation—and for factional competition. The formal superstructure of the boarding house provided the context for such competiton; the results were often at cross purposes with

161 Sayyid Ahmad to Siddons, June 13 (or 3?), 1881 (121A); Muhammad Akbar to Muhammad Ghaus, n.d. (1885) (AA).

162 Memorandum from Beck to Sayyid Ahmad, March 19, 1896, p. 14 (AA).

163 Khvājah Yūṣuf, *Izālat ul-auhām*, p. 40.

164 *Code of Rules for the Muhammadan Anglo-Oriental College, Aligarh* (Aligarh, 1880), p. 27 (AA); BH Report, 1880, p. 3.

165 Speech by Gerald Gardner Brown to the Akhvān us-Ṣafā, MAOCM/AIG, December 1, 1900, English section, p. 7.

the goal of unity that Beck and Sayyid Ahmad so forcefully espoused. Aligarh students became political people, strategists, organizers, but beneath the rhetoric they were never the united brotherhood that they wanted to be; loyalty to friends and jealousy of enemies was always getting in the way. And the official ideology of the Aligarh movement could barely compete with such personal concerns, despite Beck's reiteration of the Victorian credo: "It is much better to talk about things than to talk about people."[166]

People at Aligarh were encouraged to feel all the complicated, diffuse emotions of family members toward each other. But personal relations were not determined by specific roles. At home social bonds were embedded in carefully graded rules of etiquette according to such things as age and kinship position. At Aligarh, on the other hand, students shared a relatively equal status except as their personalities and talents brought them to varying degrees of prominence. In sharīf culture, too, the transition between the sheltered world of women and children to the life of an adult male was mediated by the idea of brotherliness, but the brotherliness fostered in the Aligarh College compound was on a larger scale, more deliberate, and less subject to a predetermined hierarchy. Aligarh students belonged to a society of several hundred youths, isolated and close together, with only a dozen or so adults to represent the outside world. For many of them this very social milieu became the object of powerful nostalgia for the rest of their lives. They were prepared for the world of professions, bureaucracies, and voluntary associations by their experience of the *akhārā*, the wrestling pit of the Aligarh College; it helped them to translate the ideology of family to the public institutions of a complex society.

[166] AIG, November 24, 1885.

VII

The College and the *Qaum*

IN December 1893, when the Muhammadan Educational Conference gathered for its eighth annual meeting, Strachey Hall was still incomplete, covered only by a temporary roof. In the past the Conference had ventured to Lucknow, Allahabad, Delhi, and Lahore, but this was the fourth time that the meetings were being held at the M.A.O. College. There were 672 people on the membership rolls that year. They were drawn from a great scattering of cities, towns, and qasbahs in upper India, including a large contingent from the Punjab; there were also a few subscribers from far-off places—Hyderabad, Bombay, Madras, and even Rangoon. In occupational background they represented a broad range of government officials, legal practitioners, teachers, property owners, as well as a few merchants and doctors, both western and Yunani. Some held substantial positions in society, with titles like Navab and Khan Bahadur; many were of modest background—court clerks, school teachers, legal agents.[1] Of this membership, some 305 actually made the trip to Aligarh; 118 nonmembers came as visitors; and, vacation notwithstanding, there were 231 Aligarh students, there to stand as exemplars of the new generation. An elite corps of forty students, dubbed the "National Police" and organized into military ranks, served as guides and watchmen around the clock for the three days of the conference. One of the special features associated with holding the meet-

[1] The list of members is contained in *Muḥammaḍan Aijūkaishanal Kānfrans kā āṭhvān sālānah jalsah* [Muhammadan Educational Conference, hereafter MEC, 8th meeting], 1893 (Agra: Mufīd-i ʻĀm, 1894), pp. 8-56.

ings at Aligarh was that those in attendance got to live like Aligarh students, sleeping in the boarding house, eating in the dining room, attending a Union Club debate, and generally following the well-regulated schedule of collegiate life.[2]

It was an impressive conference. Shibli composed and recited a long Urdu poem for the occasion; an Aligarh student, Daud Bhai, offered one in Arabic. Nazir Ahmad gave one of his popular religious lectures, and the president, Mahdi Ali (Navab Mushin ul-Mulk), delivered endless speeches in his famed oratorical style. There were resolutions encouraging Muslim religious education in government-sponsored schools, scholarships for the study of Arabic, and the creation of local committees to promote English learning. For two full sessions Sayyid Mahmud delivered an elaborate lecture on the history of higher English education in India, with lengthy quotations from British public documents and an analysis of the 1881 and 1891 censuses, all aimed at showing the desperate backwardness of Muslims as opposed to Hindus in acquiring university degrees.[3] He was followed by an equally learned and statistics-laden analysis of Muslim education in the Punjab, offered by a young barrister from Lahore, Muhammad Shah Din, who emphasized the need for improving elementary education among the peasant population. Both lectures document the relevance of British official statistics in defining the self-image of Indian Muslims as an aggregate population in contrast to the aggregate population of Hindus.[4] For Theodore Beck, such statistics were not enough; he urged the Conference to make its own census of "respectable" Muslim families and the extent to which they were educating their sons. Beck's census operation, proposed initially in 1892, represented the first substantial

[2] *Ibid.*, pp. 2-7.

[3] *Ibid.*, p. 141; the lectures were continued the following year and revised for publication as Syed Mahmood, *A History of English Education in India* (Aligarh: M.A.-O. College, 1895).

[4] "The Education of Musalmans in the Punjab," reprinted in Bashir Ahmad, *Justice Shah Din* (Lahore: by the author, 1962), pp. 197-262.

effort of the Conference to go beyond speech-making and to reach out to the general public. The face-to-face encounter could be as significant as the information obtained.[5]

A large audience crowded into the hall for the final session of the conference; over two hundred people—students—had to stand. In regular parliamentary fashion the Honorary Secretary, Sir Sayyid Ahmad Khan, moved that he be permitted to hold the *bi'smi'llāh* ceremony of his four-year-old grandson as part of the conference proceedings. The child was on the platform, seated in the lap of his "dādā" (paternal grandfather), Raja Jaikishan Das, symbol of brotherly relations between Hindus and Muslims; the "uncles" were Mahdi Ali and T. W. Arnold, the latter serving as representative of the British "qaum." The child's name, Sayyid Ross Masud, incorporated the surname of Sayyid Mahmud's closest English friend. The maulvi sahib who taught the first words of the Qur'an was a member of the Kandhla family, linked over the generations with Sayyid Ahmad's family and previously represented at Aligarh by the late Maulvi Muhammad Akbar. Before the ceremony could take place, Sayyid Ahmad made a characteristic speech in which he denounced the customs of Indian Muslims: Masud was his only grandson, but instead of spending large sums on lavish feasting and entertainment he preferred to divert that money to public purposes, to a genuinely educational cause, and asked all gift givers to do the same in order to complete Strachey Hall. Then the old man put five hundred rupees on the table and said to his grandson, "Miyan, what should be done with this money?" "Give it to the college," came the reply.[6]

ALIGARH AND INDIAN NATIONAL POLITICS

The Muhammadan Educational Conference represented a kind of short course in the Aligarh ethos. In a political sense it was an effort to stake out Aligarh's claim to leadership of an All-India Muslim constituency. From a more immedi-

[5] MEC, 1893, pp. 151-157. [6] *Ibid.*, pp. 168-175.

ately practical point of view, the conference was one more in a series of efforts to widen the financial and recruitment base of the college. It was Sayyid Ahmad's contention that the best political strategy for *all* Muslims *all* over India was to pour every last bit of public energy and economic capital into the college at Aligarh, to build up one great center for a unified network of Muslim institutions. Not everyone agreed. Many who shared Sayyid Ahmad's general belief in the need for fundamental intellectual and moral reformation did not feel the necessity of working under his shadow. In the Punjab, for example, the Anjuman Ḥimāyat-i Islām, which was basically sympathetic to the aims of the Aligarh movement, nevertheless wanted to establish its own school and college rather than depend on Aligarh for the education of Punjabi Muslims.[7] Moreover, there were quite a few supporters of Aligarh as central headquarters for the Muslims of India who still considered themselves staunch defenders of religious orthodoxy and the ways of the past. This meant that Sayyid Ahmad's religious ideas had hardly more scope in the Muhammadan Educational Conference than they had at the M.A.O. College; like the college, the conference could only achieve legitimacy as a Muslim organization by paying due respect to the received pieties.[8]

Such conferences had become fairly widespread in the public life of modern India. Once a year subscribing members of an organization would gather together from far-flung locations; they would elect a president, hear him give a long oration, spend three days in formal British-style deliberations, making speeches and passing resolutions, all to be printed up along with the membership list for general circulation. Apart from these meetings, the organizations had little in the way of sustained activity; usually there were no headquarters or permanent staff. In order to attract an All-India interest, the conferences were itinerant, held each year in a

[7] AIG, February 6, 1892.

[8] Edward D. Churchill, Jr., "The Muhammadan Education Conference and the Aligarh Movement," paper read at the Association for Asian Studies meetings, New York City, March 1972.

different city with success or failure in the hands of a local reception committee. For this reason there was some difficulty in maintaining continuity of membership. The Muhammadan Educational Conference had the advantage of a home base, Aligarh, but it suffered from an inability to attract much interest in the more distant centers of Muslim population, such as the Bengal and Bombay presidencies.

At the same time as the 1893 meetings in Aligarh, the Kayasth Association was holding a much larger meeting just fifty miles away, at Mathura; some three thousand were in attendance.[9] The following February a new organization of Sunni ʿulama, the Nadvaʿt ul-ʿulamā, gathered for its first annual conference in Kanpur. Although cheered on by Mahdi Ali and Sayyid Mahmud, and though it engaged the active participation of Aligarh's own Shibli Numani, this association stood for a reassertion of ʿulama leadership in the face of changing organizational styles. It was, in fact, a direct challenge to the leadership of Sayyid Ahmad's "New Light."[10]

But the major competition for public attention at the time of the Aligarh meetings was the ninth Indian National Congress, held that year at Lahore, very close to Aligarh's own catchment. President of the Congress that year was Dadabhai Naoroji, whose recent victory as Liberal party member of Parliament in England had constituted a significant coup for the political movement that he had helped initiate. Congress stood for the establishment of representative institutions in India, widening access to the higher levels of the bureaucracy by allowing Indians to take the Civil Service examination in India itself, and a series of economic policy demands aimed at fostering Indian business enterprise. Most of all, Congress nationalists aspired to the creation of an All-India political identity, a sense of citizenship within the territorial domain of "India" as defined initially by the colonial government. Although the Congress sought to develop participation and ultimately control by the indigenous population, the goals of

[9] AIG, January 5, 1894. [10] Above, p. 244.

natonalism were conceived within the context of membership in the British empire. India would be another Canada, equally subject to British institutions and the British queen. And it was in this direction that the British Parliament had indeed moved the previous year in the Indian Councils Act of 1892, one more in a series of hesitant concessions toward the goal of representative government. Dadabhai's triumphal progress from Bombay to Lahore marked a renewed tide of hope for the cause.[11]

When the Indian National Congress was started in 1885, Sayyid Ahmad had remained conspicuously aloof. Surendranath Banerjea, founder of the National Conference (which merged with the Congress the following year), had written him that "no assembly of national delegates would be complete without your presence."[12] If that were the case, the Congress would have to remain incomplete. Though the founders warmly solicited his support, Sayyid Ahmad made no statement, and the *Aligarh Institute Gazette* gave no coverage.

Congress leaders had good reason to be disappointed, for by this time Sayyid Ahmad was probably the most prominent public man in northern India, and he had apparently supported aims like those of the founders of Congress. He had served as nominated member on the Viceroy's Legislative Council, where he had supported local self-government and the right of Indian judges to try European defendants.[13] As far back as 1858, he had called for Indian representation on government councils. In the 1860s he had used the British Indian Association and the *Aligarh Institute Gazette* to deliver some harsh criticisms of government policies, even at the cost of incurring considerable enmity within certain official British circles.[14] The cause of having Indians enter the

[11] K. Iswara Dutt, *Congress Cyclopaedia* (New Delhi: by the author [1967]), pp. 80-84.

[12] December 5, 1885 (recently typed copy in AA).

[13] AIG, January 20, 1883; March 17, 1883.

[14] Ḥālī, *Ḥayāt-i jāvīd*, pp. 152-157.

covenanted Civil Service was dear to his heart: he had written in defense of Banerjea's own claims in 1870,[15] and in 1877 he revived the British Indian Association at Aligarh to join with Banerjea in a campaign to restore the age of entrance from nineteen to twenty-one. Banerjea had attended a meeting at Aligarh at the time,[16] and in 1884 he returned to start a branch of a new political organization, the National Fund, with Sayyid Ahmad as president. In coordination with the National Fund, Aligarh College had just initiated a Civil Service Fund and a Civil Service Preparation Class. In his speech at the National Fund meeting, Sayyid Ahmad had emphatically supported the creation of a new organization for voicing general political grievances.[17] He was no revolutionary, of course, but neither were the founders of the Congress; they all spoke in terms of loyalty to the British Raj. When Surendranath Banerjea wrote Sayyid Ahmad six months later, he had good reason to expect a favorable reply.

The next year, 1886, Sayyid Ahmad started a Congress of his own, the Muhammadan Educational Congress—the name was changed in 1890—to be held at the same time as its Indian National counterpart. Although there were no explicit references, the gesture was widely taken as an act of opposition. During the next year Allan Octavian Hume, the retired civil servant who was now the most energetic sponsor of the Indian National Congress movement, wrote Sayyid Ahmad as "my dear old friend" and urged him to offer his support.[18] But meanwhile the new political movement had stirred up a good deal of controversy. Two Calcutta Muslim leaders, Abdul Latif and Amir Ali, had refused to join on the grounds that the establishment of elected representative bodies would not be in the interests of the Muslim population. Amir Ali's National Muhammadan Association had initially participated in Banerjea's National Conference; since 1877 it had pre-

15 AIG, April 8, 1870.
16 *Ibid.*, Supplement, June 26, 1877.
17 *Ibid.*, May 17, 1884.
18 March 3, 1887 (recently typed copy in AA).

sented itself as a base for Muslim political activity without paying any deference to Aligarh. Now Amir Ali was the first to test the waters of Muslim opposition to the Congress.[19] In Bombay, on the other hand, Congress had an outstanding Muslim supporter in Badruddin Tyabji, close friend and associate of Aligarh's major backer in that city, Muhammad Ali Rogay.[20] It seems that Sayyid Ahmad's first inclination was to keep silent, but when Tyabji was chosen as president of the third Indian National Congress, it became clear that such silence could be maintained only at the cost of forfeiting his claim to leadership of the Muslims of India.

Sayyid Ahmad chose the occasion of Tyabji's presidency to come out publicly against the Congress. Once again, in December 1887, the two organizations met simultaneously, the Indian National Congress in Madras, the Muhammadan Educational Congress in Lucknow. To maintain the non-political character of his own organization, Sayyid Ahmad chose to make his speech at a separate public meeting. In it he bluntly denounced the Congress as an attempt by frail-bodied Bengalis to take over India. Democracy and bureaucratic recruitment by merit were impossible in a land that lacked a homogeneous political community, he said; such a system would only lead to temporary domination by inferior breeds of men. The proper representatives of Indian opinion in the councils of government should be men appointed on the basis of "social position" as determined by ancestry, not ability.

> Would our aristocracy like that a man of low caste or insignificant origin, though he be a B.A. or M.A., and have the requisite ability, should be in a position of authority above them and have power in making the laws that affect their lives and property? Never! Nobody would like it.

[19] Rafiq Zakaria, *The Rise of Muslims in Indian Politics*, 2d ed. (Bombay: Somaiya Publications, 1971), p. 51.

[20] Husain B. Tyabji, *Badruddin Tyabji* (Bombay: Thacker & Co. [1952]), pp. 175-205.

(Cheers) . . . Think for a moment what would be the result if all appointments were given by competitive examination. Over all races, not only over Mahomedans but over Rajas of high position and the brave Rajputs who have not forgotten the swords of their ancestors, would be placed as ruler a Bengali who at sight of a table knife would crawl under his chair. (Uproarious cheers and laughter) . . . [I]f you accept that the country should groan under the yoke of Bengali rule and its people lick the Bengali shoes, then, in the name of God! jump into the train, sit down, and be off to Madras, be off to Madras! (Loud cheers and laughter.)

The result of the Congress proposals would be anarchy and violence, and only British rule could maintain peace between the warring segments of the population.[21]

Although Sayyid Ahmad spoke in one breath of a martial alliance of Rajputs and Muslims, he also foresaw the consolidation of Hindu votes in any electoral system against the Muslim minority. In 1882, at the time of Hunter's Education Commission, he had seen the revival of a campaign to establish Hindi as the official language of the north Indian provinces at the expense of Urdu.[22] That same year Dayananda Sarasvati, founder of the Arya Samaj, had initiated his movement for the outlawing of cow slaughter.[23] It was becoming clear that whatever deference may have been paid to Muslim sensibilities, whatever subordination may have been accepted for Hindu ones during the period when Muslims ruled much of India, such circumstances no longer applied under British rule. Aside from the fact that the British were neither Muslim nor Hindu, the institutions that they established encouraged non-Muslims to believe that they had as much right to

[21] *Sir Syed Ahmed on the Present State of Indian Politics* (Allahabad: Pioneer Press, 1888), reprinted in Shan Mohammad, ed., *Writings and Speeches of Sir Syed Ahmad Khan* (Bombay: Nachiketa Publications, 1972), pp. 204, 209.

[22] EC/NWP.

[23] Har Bilas Sarda, *Life of Dayanand Saraswati* (Ajmere: P. Bhagwan Swarup, 1946), pp. 278-279.

petition government as anybody else; in fact, more so because they were a majority—at least as an aggregate statistic. But many Muslims believed that they deserved both power and deference: by virtue of their ancestry, according to Sayyid Ahmad; by virtue of their acceptance of God's revelation, according to the pious. And, perhaps even more than the loss of worldly success, real or imagined, nothing could cause greater anxiety to sharīf Muslims of north India than the withdrawal of deference.[24]

Sayyid Ahmad's speech at Lucknow was followed up by a vigorous political campaign under the inspired direction of Theodore Beck. An anti-Congress organization came into being, the United Indian Patriotic Association, which claimed a monopoly on loyalty to British rule and purported to represent the politically significant sections of the population, not just the English-educated "babus" of the presidency towns. At first the organization included some prominent north Indian Hindus—Oudh taluqdars, the Raja of Benares, even Sayyid Ahmad's old antagonist Shiva Prasad—but it soon bifurcated, with the more energetic section devoted to the mobilization of local Muslim associations. All over India meetings were held to voice Muslim support for Sayyid Ahmad's stand.[25] In some Muslim circles Sayyid Ahmad's opposition may have have been a kiss of life for the Congress, but on the whole the anti-Congress campaign tapped a new vein of public sympathy for Aligarh. Sayyid Ahmad's arguments may have sounded closer to indigenous political assumptions than bold Congress talk of nationalism and representative government. Even supporters of the Congress, like Tyabji, had to speak in the vocabulary of qaums, but it was difficult for them to set forth a persuasive theory of social pluralism in terms of the British institutional model. If the aim of Sayyid Ahmad's opposition was to bring Aligarh to

[24] Cf. de Tocqueville in *L'Ancien Régime et la révolution*, Book II, Chapter 1, discussed in Hannah Arendt, *The Origins of Totalitarianism*, 3d ed. (New York: Harcourt, Brace & World, 1966), p. 4.

[25] Zakaria, *Rise of Muslims*, pp. 66, 73, 372-373; M. S. Jain, *The Aligarh Movement* (Agra: Sri Mehra & Co., 1965), pp. 124-125.

the center of the political stage, it was a consumate success. In 1889 Aligarh students gathered nearly thirty thousand Muslim signatures for an anti-Congress petition to Parliament; the college had never received so much attention.[26]

At the time and long afterwards, Theodore Beck was accused of playing Iago to Sayyid Ahmad's Othello. Sixty years later Sayyid Tufail Ahmad, an Aligarh student of the late 1880s, charged that Beck, like a British Resident in some princely state, had taken advantage of Sayyid Ahmad's senility to force Aligarh into the forefront of British efforts to undermine the nationalist movement.[27] Mir Vilayat Husain recalled, also much later, that upon his arrival in India Beck was greatly alarmed at Sayyid Ahmad's support for Surendranath Benerjea and set about to change the old man's mind.[28] This testimony notwithstading, Beck was a man more influenced than influencing: under intense indoctrination from Sayyid Mahmud on the voyage out, and anxious to give himself heart and soul to the Aligarh cause, Beck had abandoned his undergraduate sympathy for Indian nationalism and accepted the views of his Indian mentor.[29]

There was, however, gratification in winning the approbation of certain eminent Englishmen. Within a week of the Lucknow speech Sayyid Ahmad had become Sir Sayyid, a double honorific that went well with the Anglo-Oriental label he was so fond of using. He received fan mail from Fitzjames Stephen, and responded by showing that he was well acquainted with the latter's arguments against democracy in general and the possibility of national consolidation for India in particular.[30] Auckland Colvin, Lieutenant Governor of the North-Western Provinces and Oudh, and probably the leading official critic of the Congress, was a long-standing associate of Sayyid Ahmad; he had been cotranslator of

[26] Zakaria, *Rise of Muslims*, pp. 378-380.

[27] Sayyid Ṭufail Aḥmad Manglōrī, *Musalmānōn kā raushan mustaqbil* (Delhi: 'Alīmī, 1945), pp. 275-282.

[28] Vilāyat Ḥusain, *Āp bītī*, pp. 48-50.

[29] Above, pp. 217-218.

[30] Sayyid Ahmad to Stephen, February 17, 1888 (262B, AA).

Causes of the Indian Revolt in 1873. Mahdi Ali's official mentor, on the other hand, had been Allan Octavian Hume: caught in a conflict of personal loyalties, the Hyderabad official wavered for a considerable length of time before coming down on the side of opposition to the Congress.[31]

The ideological basis of Sayyid Ahmad's opposition to Indian nationalism had been clearly articulated well before either Beck or the Congress had appeared on the scene. Drawing from his Mughal roots, he had always conceived of India as a combination of unequal and mutually antagonistic ancestral groups brought to peace only by their relationship to an overarching power. When he supported the Local Self-Government Act for the Central Provinces, he told the viceregal council in January 1833 that he was not in favor of introducing elective government to India, "where caste distinctions flourish, where there is no fusion of the various races, where religious distinctions are still violent, where education in its modern sense has not made an equal or proportionate progress among the population. . . . The larger community would totally override the smaller community."[32] What he favored was representation by appointment, communication between government and the governed within the authoritarian framework of British rule.

For Sayyid Ahmad, being Muslim was defined in terms of membership in a qaum, a people of common descent, not the ummah of common belief. He did not base his appeal on Islamic revelation and its implications for the political order; high status for Muslims was their right by virtue of ancestral heritage as descendants of a ruling race. He realized that, in fact, not all Muslims were descended from the same progenitor, but kinship served as a living metaphor for forging Muslim solidarity in the midst of India's non-Muslim majority; Muslims were conceived of as an ethnic community. What Sayyid Ahmad could not accept for India was a notion of society based on individual citizenship within a nation-state and a government subject to the decisions of majority

[31] AIG, September 8, 1888. [32] *Ibid.*, January 20, 1883.

rule. If the elective principle were to come to India, Sayyid Ahmad and his supporters insisted that Muslims be guaranteed separate constituencies and a proportion of representation considerably in excess of what the Muslim population would warrant. Low-caste Hindus should be excluded entirely; then Muslims would be entitled to fifty percent of the seats on the major legislative councils.[33] The very censuses that were used to show Muslim backwardness in education and government employment also demonstrated Muslim vulnerability in the face of a universal electorate. Since the divisions of Indian society were based on identities established at birth, Sayyid Ahmad argued, there was little scope for a political system based on persuasion.

Although he could never accept the idea that India was or might become a united polity, Sayyid Ahmad was ready enough to organize people to make political demands and to carve out enclaves of autonomous action within the system of British rule. His campaign against Congress "agitation" was as much an agitation as anything the Congress could come up with, and shares with Congress some of the credit or blame for the development of India's political style. But Sayyid Ahmad had other things on his mind; the United Indian Patriotic Association lasted only two years and was followed by a long silence. Finally, in December 1893, just following Ross Masud's bi'smi'llah, a small group gathered at Sayyid Ahmad's house to start a Muhammadan Anglo-Oriental Defence Association. The new Indian Councils Act called for some political preparation. And the previous year had been one of unprecedented Hindu-Muslim rioting over the issue of cow slaughter, a grim reminder that religious sensibilities had political implications. The new organization, largely Beck's doing, kept its activities at a dignified minimum and never reached far beyond Sayyid Ahmad's domes-

[33] Beck and Sayyid Mahmud, "Musalmānōn kī ṭaraf sē laijislaiṭiv kaunsal aur myūnisipaliṭiyōn vag͟hairah mēn̲ intik͟hāb," MAOCM, December 1, 1896.

tic circle; like its predecessor, it was dead after two years.[34] As Sayyid Ahmad had maintained all along, the major commitment of energy belonged to the college at Aligarh.

Hindsight has rendered Sayyid Ahmad's opposition to the Congress the crucial event of Aligarh's early history. Seen from the perspective of the college, this political activity was sporadic and of limited importance. If one takes Sayyid Ahmad at his word and grants that he was primarily concerned with the educational institution he had founded, opposition to the Congress, like the Muhammadan Educational Conference, stands out as an attempt to enhance the college's prestige in moments of internal crisis. Thus the initial spurt of political activity coincides with the student strike, poor examination results, and the Trustee Bill controversy. In the face of declining enrollments and the withdrawal of support from a number of major patrons, the college relied more and more on backing by the British government. Sayyid Ahmad had no hesitation in soliciting such backing by claiming for Aligarh a peculiar role as outpost of "loyalty" to the Raj.[35]

The mid-1890s was a time of renewed internal crisis for the college and renewed public activity in the outside world. In 1892, Sayyid Mahmud, hope of the future, for whose sake the Trustee Bill battle had been fought, was forced off the Allahabad High Court under rather scandalous circumstances. A brilliant legal thinker, he had achieved the highest position available to an Indian—only two others had gone that far—but was continually harassed by his British col-

[34] Zakaria, *Rise of Muslims*, p. 84.

[35] Sayyid Ahmad to E. White, Director of Public Instruction, NWP, n.d. [1888] (301A, AA); examples of the government response were an increase in the monthly grant by 100 rupees (White to Sayyid Ahmad, February 22, 1888 [45B, AA]); a 15,000 rupee "advance" for the building of Strachey Hall (GOI, Home, Education [B], September 1889, No. 13 [NAI]); and the inclusion of Aligarh in the Punjab Jubilee scholarship program (above, p. 177); see also Morison, *History of the M.A.-O. College*, p. 10.

leagues and shunted off to specialized cases in civil law. He started drinking heavily and acting strangely on the bench.[36] His father attempted to bring him back to Aligarh, but he was not a man to live under his father's shadow. Instead he went off to Lucknow to take up private practice, leaving his wife and son with the old man. For the next six years his occasional appearances on the Aligarh scene would result in bitter factional entanglements and profound public embarrassment.

Then in 1895, Sayyid Ahmad discovered that his English-language clerk, Shiam Behari Lal, had managed over the years to embezzle some 115,000 rupees from the college funds.[37] In the aftermath of that scandal, Beck was able to add the role of Bursar to his administrative domain. Sami Ullah and Khvajah Yusuf now had an excuse to pounce on Sayyid Ahmad's mismanagement and Beck's usurpation.[38] Enrollment fell, the very existence of the college was in doubt. When Sayyid Mahmud returned to Aligarh in an attempt to get control of the college finances, a bitter quarrel developed between father and son. Sayyid Ahmad was ordered out of the house, and for several days he actually became a resident of the boarding house. Family emotions had been extrapolated on to public institutions with a vengeance. In March 1898, the incident was repeated, Sayyid Ahmad now moving to the house of his friend Ismail Khan Shervani. There, on March 27, he died, a bitter, utterly disappointed man.[39]

In 1895, the enrollment of the college and school at Aligarh had been 595; at the time of Sayyid Ahmad's death it had fallen to 323. By the following July it plummeted to 189.[40] Financial grants stopped; faculty, including Shibli and

[36] GOI, Home, Judicial (A), February 1893, Nos. 1-29 (NAI).

[37] *The Report of the M.A.-O. College Embezzlement by the Life Honorary Secretary of the M.A.-O. College Trustees*, January 1, 1896 (Allahabad: Pioneer Press, 1896).

[38] Khvājah Yūṣuf, *Izālat ul-auhām*; Beck memorandum to Sayyid Ahmad, March 19, 1896 (AA).

[39] Shaikh ʿAbdullāh, *Mushāhadāt*, pp. 71-72, 99-105.

[40] Principal's Annual Report, 1898-1899, MAOCM/AIG, July 15, 1899.

Arnold, left. There followed an unseemly struggle for power between Beck, Mahmud, Mahdi Ali, and, once again, Sami Ullah. Mahmud went on drunken escapades in the college boarding house, calling out the police to arrest a member of the staff for hitting students, and writing strange, long-winded legal briefs for every trivial piece of business. With his encouragement there was almost a repetition of the 1887 student strike.[41] Meanwhile, Sami Ullah intrigued with the Navab of Rampur: the Navab would bail out the college from its desperate financial position if Sami Ullah could be Honorary Secretary. As a counter move Beck joined forces with Aftab Ahmad Khan, now a Trustee, to put forward Mahdi Ali. Coming to their assistance, James La Touche, Chief Secretary of the North-Western Provinces and Oudh, and Anthony MacDonnell, Lieutenant Governor, publicly condemned Sami Ullah and visited Aligarh with an offer of more government money if the college management could restore order and provide the government with new supervisory powers. MacDonnell also promised substantial financial assistance from the Navab of Rampur, now forced to disassociate himself from Sami Ullah.[42] On January 31, 1899, the Trustees ratified the government demands, electing Mahdi Ali as Honorary Secretary in the place of Sayyid Mahmud, and guaranteeing Beck tenure for life. Students gathered to see the founder's son tearfully embracing his "uncle" Mahdi Ali on the steps of Strachey Hall, after which he left the college for

[41] Beck to Mahmud, n.d. [July 1899] in file marked "Copies of correspondence enclosed in a letter to Beck c/o Mr. [Thomas] Raleigh [Walter Raleigh's cousin] . . . Simla" (AA); printed Urdu letter from Sayyid Mahmud to Muhsin ul-Mulk, n.d. [1899] in binding marked Board of Trustees, 1899 (AA). See also newspaper comment, e.g., *Al-Bashīr* (Etawah), August 28, 1899 (SVN, NWP, etc., 1899), p. 476; *Riāz ul-Akhbar* (Gorrackpur), November 20, 1899 (*ibid.*, p. 651).

[42] Sami Ullah Khan, "Memorandum" (printed and containing extensive documentation in binding marked "Board of Trustees" [AA]); Ḥakīm Ajmal Khān, *Javāb-i maimōranḍam* (n.p.: published by the author, 1899 [Azad Library]); Ḥabībullāh Khān, *Ḥayāt-i Aftāb*, pp. 48-49.

good.[43] He died at a cousin's house in Sitapur in 1903. His son, Sayyid Ross Masud, whose public bi'smi'llah had touched the high point of Aligarh's symbolic drama, remained at the college under the guardianship of Theodore Morison.[44]

Following Sayyid Ahmad's death in 1898, Beck summoned up all his organizational and rhetorical powers to save the ship by leading a large-scale campaign to revive the old dream of an independent university for the Muslims of India. Aftab Ahmad Khan, Shaukat Ali, and their friends joined in this campaign, called the "Sir Syed Memorial Fund"; and even though it did not raise much in the way of money, it succeeded in preserving Aligarh as a living symbol for the ideal of Muslim consolidation. The 1898 meeting of the Muhammadan Educational Conference at Lahore was an unprecedented success. From Bombay came a letter of support from Badruddin Tyabji, along with 2000 rupees pledged to the university movement. Amir Ali also sent in his backing from Calcutta. The following year the Conference moved out of north India for the first time and gathered in Calcutta, with Amir Ali as president. The Muslim university movement developed into an effort to create an autonomous Muslim educational system on an All-India basis, centered at Aligarh. Ultimately, it represented a challenge to British control over the educational access to political power.[45]

For the time being, however, the goals were more modest. Enrollment at the college began to recover. According to Beck, this was due "to one cause only, viz. the efforts to collect money for the Memorial Fund, whereby knowledge of the aims and nature of the . . . College have [*sic*] been vastly extended." Everyone now realized that "the future prospects of the Indian Musalmans are bound up in [Aligarh's] prog-

[43] Riẓā 'Alī, *A'māl nāmah*, pp. 76-77.
[44] 'Abdul Ḥaq, *Cand Ham 'Aṣr*, p. 188.
[45] Gail Minault and David Lelyveld, "The Campaign for a Muslim University, 1898-1920," *Modern Asian Studies*, VIII (1974), 145-154.

ress."[46] This, surely, was an exaggeration, but at least Beck and the young alumni had managed to tide Aligarh over. Exhausted by the effort, Beck followed his leader to the grave on September 2, 1899; he was forty years old. His death was commemorated with a Beck Memorial Fund for the college.[47]

If opposition to the Congress and other attempts to mobilize public opinion by means of voluntary political association can be construed as a mere sideline in the general effort to promote the interests of the M.A.O. College, it nevertheless remains true that the college itself was a profoundly political enterprise. From the outset, the rationale for Aligarh's existence was bound up with an analysis of the relationship between being Muslim and the nature of political power in British India. According to Sayyid Ahmad, Muslims were a former ruling class now fallen on evil days. To recover their rightful position they had to cultivate new areas of knowledge and skill; they also had to develop a new level of consolidation as a qaum. Being Muslim could not be an assumed fact of religious and social identity; it required active participation in a whole range of new institutional activities spread over a vast geographical territory. That territory was not defined as dar ul-Islam, the realm of Muslim rule, but rather was congruent with the domain of the British government of India.

Sayyid Ahmad may have made light of the B.A.s and M.A.s of Bengal, but his idea for Aligarh was to raise a new

[46] Principal's Annual Report, 1898-1899, MAOCM/AIG, July 15, 1899.

[47] MAOCM, October 1, 1899; Thomas Raleigh, *Annals of the Church of Scotland* (London: Oxford University Press, 1921), pp. xxx-xxv; Miles Irving, ed., *A List of Inscriptions on Christian Tombs or Monuments in the Punjab, North West Frontier Province, Kashmir and Afghanistan,* II, Part I (Lahore: Government Printing Press, 1910), 51.

generation of Muslims who would have the knowledge, skills, and values necessary to qualify them for public leadership. Other colleges in the British Indian educational system gave the wrong kind of education to the wrong kind of people, but Aligarh would be no ordinary college. Its students would not be content with a watered-down curriculum in preparation for subordinate government posts. Nor would they be content with mere individual success. Their obligation was to all the Muslims of India, whether these many millions knew it or not. English education at Aligarh was a political strategy to enable Muslims to achieve, eventually, their rightful position of power, even within the British empire. "Pathans, Syeds, Hashimi and Koreishi whose blood smells of Abraham, will appear in glittering uniforms. . . . But we must wait for that time."[48]

Such rhetoric required a large dose of wishful thinking. An outside observer might have had some justification in doubting the unique character of the college. Curriculum, examinations, occupational horizons, these were not significantly different from any other English college in India. What was important from the point of view of the participants, however, was the ideological meaning poured into this standard institutional mold. As far as knowledge of the ideas, procedures, and structures of British rule went, Aligarh students had no overwhelming advantage over other English-educated Indians. What made at least some of them special was the ethos of solidarity that they learned by direct indoctrination, extracurricular activities and, most of all, the informal social milieu of the college.

Of direct indoctrination there was plenty. In numerous addresses to the students, Beck, Morison, and Sayyid Ahmad would reiterate the basic theme: that Indian Muslims, the former rulers of the country, had declined, and that the only hope for their regeneration was to mobilize them under the aegis of Aligarh. Selfless service to the qaum, not individual

[48] Lucknow Speech, 1887, in Shan Mohammad, *Writings and Speeches*, p. 215.

achievement, was to be the major aspiration of a rightly guided student, and student solidarity was a necessary condition for carrying out the mission of the college.

It was an axiom of the Aligarh party line that only in the context of British-Muslim friendship and complete "loyalty" to British rule could Muslims hope to improve their position in Indian society. According to the written rules of the Union Club, "no matter shall be discussed which raises the question of the permanence or stability of the British Rule, nor any subject which involves the necessity of the speakers . . . taking up a disloyal or seditious attitude toward the British Government in its internal policy or external relations. . . ."[49] Pro-Congress newspapers were barred from the Union reading room.[50] Anti-Congress exhortations, on the other hand, were a proper ingredient of moral education at the college; they were part and parcel of what Beck called "patriotism," without which no society could prosper.[51]

Opposition to the Congress does not seem to have been entirely convincing to the students. While studying in England, Aftab Ahmad Khan, that model of an Aligarh student, went off to have a talk with Hume and came back wondering what was wrong with the Congress after all.[52] For Riza Ali and his friends, the banned Congress newspapers had all the attraction of forbidden fruit.[53] The issue of support for the Congress was probably not all that important to the students, but one may also doubt their heartfelt allegiance to the British. The lesson they carried away was the idea of Muslim solidarity. In one Union debate students voted overwhelmingly that the Muslims would rise again.[54] As for the British, Aligarh students expressed the hope that they would embrace Islam.[55]

In 1889, Theodore Beck led a group of Aligarh students

[49] MAOCM, December 1894.
[50] Riẓā ʿAlī, *Aʿmāl nāmah*, pp. 73-75.
[51] AIG, August 15, 1893.
[52] Diary, May 8, 1892; November 27, 1893 (AA).
[53] Riẓā ʿAlī, *Aʿmāl nāmah*, pp. 73-75.
[54] MAOCM, December 1, 1899. [55] AIG, August 19, 1890.

to Delhi to sit at the gates of the Jumʿah Masjid on Friday noon and gather signatures for an anti-Congress petition to Parliament.[56] Such practices were not continued—the Lieutenant Governor of the Punjab declared that student agitation against the Congress was just as improper as student agitation in its favor[57]—but organized activities by students outside the college grounds on behalf of the Aligarh cause became a major extracurricular activity. The Duty, the Brotherhood, the National Police, the campaign for the Sir Sayyid Memorial Fund were all efforts to reach out to the qaum with student and alumni cadres. These activities supplemented the political education students received in the college as cricket players, speakers in the Union, and as members of competing student cliques. Learning how to organize themselves for cooperation and for competition, they acquired a variety of techniques to enable them to play significant roles in the outside world.

CAREERS IN LATER LIFE

Sending students into the outside world was the business of Aligarh College. Plans broached by Sayyid Mahmud in 1873 and T. W. Arnold in 1889 for creating a community of scholars were ignored and sometimes explicitly rejected.[58] A major impetus for founding the college was the changing criteria for government employment and professional occupations, and this surely had much to do with the college's success in recruiting students. It is true that Sayyid Ahmad and the young men of Cambridge who taught at Aligarh might sometimes denigrate the standard route of English education in India—the route to law and government service, as opposed to entrepreneurship or voluntary public service to the qaum—but they were not prepared to scrap the university curriculum and degrees required for admission to that well-trodden path. Forays in some other direction—a

[56] Vilāyat Ḥusain, *Āp bītī*, p. 70. [57] AIG, October 24, 1893.
[58] Above, pp. 127, 245.

preparation class for the engineering school at Roorkee, horsemanship, and "drill" to enhance martial aspirations associated with being Muslim—all came to nothing. On the contrary, government employment was an explicit inducement for students to live according to the college ethos and win the approval of their teachers; it was also part of the rationale for the Brotherhood's effort to extend student solidarity beyond the college years.

The routes to an occupational career for former students of the college ranged from personal patronage in the princely states to popular political agitation in the context of newly developing institutions of representative government. But a majority of former Aligarh students for whom there is information became employees of the British government, and the next largest category were lawyers practicing before British courts. As in the princely states, there was scope in the British government for personal patronage: one was qualified by nomination for admission to certain examinations, provided one had the requisite educational credentials. District collectors and, in some cases, college principals did the nominating. And there were some posts recruited by simple appointment. Formal bureaucratic rules probably constricted the influence of personal connections much more than in the princely states, but there was great continuity from the kacahri milieu of the previous generation despite the alteration in educational qualifications and relative elaboration of government structures. The question is, was it different to be a tahsildar, sarishtadar, or vakil after being a student at Aligarh and in a world of changing political institutions and ideologies?

If there was a difference, it was probably not so much in the administrative role as in the other aspects of people's lives. British regulations forbade membership by government servants in explicitly political organizations, and it was more difficult than in Sayyid Ahmad's day to lead an independent public life while holding a government job. Posts like High Court Judge and Deputy Collector were extremely tempting, and Sayyid Ahmad had done his share of launching favored students, such as his nephew Sayyid Muhammad Ali, on prestigious careers; but it was only by resignation or retirement that they had an opportunity to be of much service to the Aligarh cause. Akbar Allahabadi's comment on the later careers of Aligarh's graduates was that all the brave talk about future leaders yielded very little of importance:

What words of mine can tell the deeds of men like these,
our nation's pride?
They got their B.A., took employment, drew their pensions,
and then died.[59]

In 1914 Tufail Ahmad published a two-volume Urdu *Directory* of former school and college students of Aligarh. The project was an old one; nineteen years earlier he had compiled a similar, though much less thorough version. The 1895 directory limited itself to individuals who had been students for a substantial period of time. The 1914 version attempted to include all former students, even those who had been registered for a single day. From the old registration books, Tufail Ahmad managed to gather 5,924 names, of whom 1,070 were current students as of 1911. But the effort to track down information on residence, occupation, and activities for former students yielded disappointing results. Confining the analysis to students who entered college-level classes between 1877 and 1900, one discovers 924 names, but information on later careers for only 592. Sixty-four students had already died, but there is career information on fifteen of these that can be added to the cases of 577 living alumni of the college. Since most of the people for whom there is no information were students for extremely short periods of time, the 592 cases are probably adequate for a preliminary analysis of the occupational distribution of the alumni as of 1911 (see Table 3).

[59] Translation in Ralph Russell and Khurshidul Islam, "The Satirical Verse of Akbar Ilāhābādī," *Modern Asian Studies*, VIII (1974), 29.

TABLE 3

Occupations of 592 Former College Students at Aligarh (1877-1900) as of 1911

	British government	*Princely state*	*Private*	*Total*	
(1.0) Medicine	5	1	1		7
(2.0) Engineering	9	1	—		10
(3.0) Law					
(3.1) Judge	21	10	—	31	
(3.2) Government Pleader	3	—	—	3	
(3.3) Barrister	[5]	[2]	20	[27]	
(3.4) Vakil	—	—	86	86	
(3.5) Mukhtar	—	—	4	4	
Total Law	[29]	[12]	110	[151]	144
(4.0) Teaching					
(4.1) School	21	5	12	38	
(4.2) College	5	—	2	7	
(4.3) Private tutor	—	—	3	3	
Total Teaching	26	5	17		48
(5.0) Miscellaneous Government Service					
(5.1) Deputy Collector, etc.	31	1	—	32	
(5.2) Tahsildar, etc.	58	3	—	61	
(5.3) Police	30	1	—	31	
(5.4) Member of Council, Ministry, Secretary, etc.	—	8	—	8	
(5.5) Secretary of Municipal Board	15	—	—	15	
(5.6) Sub-Inspectors, Agents, Superintendents (Salt, Opium, Excise, etc.)	38	5	—	43	
(5.7) Sub-Inspectors, etc., Education Department	8	1	—	9	
(5.8) Sub-Registrar	10	—	—	10	
(5.9) Clerical	69	24	—	93	
(5.10) Other	11	4	—	15	
Total Miscellaneous Government Service	270	47	—		317

TABLE 3 (Continued)

	British government	*Princely state*	*Private*	*Total*
(6.0) Miscellaneous Private Employment				
(6.1) Business				
(6.1.1) Trade	—	—	*5*	*5*
(6.1.2) Industry	—	—	*1*	*1*
(6.2) Editors	—	—	*5*	*5*
(6.3) Private Service	—	—	*5*	*5*
(6.4) M.A.O. College				
(6.4.1) Administrative	—	—	*4*	*4*
(6.4.2) Teacher, School	—	—	[*4*]	[*4*]
(6.4.3) Professor, College	—	—	[*2*]	[*2*]
(6.5) Muslim League	—	—	*1*	*1*
(6.6) Students	—	—	*5*	*5*
(6.7) Zamindars	—	—	*25*	*25*
(6.8) Vatan-Unspecified Employment	—	—	*14*	*14*
(6.9) Political Pensioner	—	—	*1*	*1*
Total Miscellaneous Private Employment			[72]	[72] ~ 66
TOTAL	334	64	194	592

SOURCE: Ṭufail Aḥmad, *Directory* (1914 ed.), Vol. I. Table does not include 332 students for whom there is no information. Italics indicate subcategories. Brackets indicate double counting, not to be included in general totals, such as barristers, who have been counted as judges. "Etc." indicates similar posts with different titles, e.g., Extra-Assistant Commissioner (Punjab) is similar to Deputy Collector (United Provinces).

Two-thirds of the former students for whom there is information were government employees, 334 for the British and 64 for princely states. Government employment, however, embraced a multitude of occupational activities and a good many differences as to recruitment, status, tenure, and renumeration. Among those with professional qualifications, 6 of the 7 doctors and all 10 engineers were government servants; of the 144 lawyers, 34 were either judges or government leaders; and 31 of the 48 teachers worked in government schools. A large number achieved high posts in land revenue administration, ranging from naib-tahsildar to Deputy Collector; except in princely states, the highest posts were the preserve of British members of the Indian Civil Service. Only two Aligarh alumni held posts comparable to the I. C. S.; one was a judge of the Allahabad High Court, and the other a member of the Statutory Civil Service, a Joint Magistrate. Various forms of "Deputy," "Sub-" and "Assistant" append the titles of the more successful alumni in the police, post office, school, court of wards, excise, opium, salt, forest, and canal administrations. Below these were numerous subregistrars, office supervisors, translators, and assorted varieties of clerks. With the possible exception of one lieutenant surgeon in the army, Aligarh education failed to deliver much in the way of "glittering uniforms."

"Service," whether for government or private employers (such as the M.A.O. College or, in one case, the Muslim League), was the occupational fate of the overwhelming majority of former students. The major exception was private legal practice, which included 20 barristers (qualified in England), 84 vakils or pleaders, and 4 mukhtars. Although an unspecified number among the other occupational categories probably derived income from landed property, only 25 are listed as zamindars, that is, as persons actively engaged in agricultural management; another 14 are simply stated to be residing in their vatans. There are 15 people in business, generally wholesale or retail merchandizing; one of them actually went to England to study commerce. Only one was involved in some industrial enterprise, an employee in a Bombay textile factory. Five former students were editors and proprietors of newspapers or magazines, including Zafar Ali Khan, editor of *Zamindar* in Urdu, and Muhammad Ali, editor of the English-language *Comrade*, papers that achieved unprecedented levels of circulation as well as British official hostility. A third editor was Hasrat Mohani, and all three were to suffer long periods of incarceration in the course of their dramatic anticolonial struggles.

Very few people in "service," generally those in lower categories, lived in their place of origin; only 35 are so listed. Among the lawyers, one-quarter of the barristers, half the vakils, and all the mukhtars continued in their home towns. Those described as zamindars do not seem to have been purchasers of far-flung properties; they are listed as residing in their vatan. About half the businessmen and one of the editors were still at home. A full geographical analysis of residential distribution among former Aligarh students would probably show the same kind of dispersion through north India, with occasional outcroppings in Hyderabad and the presidency cities, as was characteristic of their places of origin.[60] Except for zamindars, one might expect a shift from villages and qasbahs to towns and cities, but it is important to remember that such moves were temporary. Service people were frequently shifted around; probably most of them retained their vatan ties.

Statistical analysis of alumni careers is important in the cultural history of Aligarh because Aligarh people took the trouble to compile this kind of data and often thought of social and cultural matters in statistical terms. The foregoing analysis of the 1914 directory, however, neglects those who went only to the school and, more important, fails to trace possible shifts in occupation in the course of an individual's total life. It also neglects the family context, which in many cases probably determined the choice of occupation.[61] But the greatest shortcoming of a tabular rendering of occupations is that it cannot show the dynamic interaction among Aligarh's alumni, and how their experiences and self-definitions as a cohort were refracted through the other institutions and social groups with which they came in contact. An account tracking the later lives of the first generation would necessarily require a detailed examination of numerous aspects of twentieth-century Indian history. A large part of

[60] Above, pp. 181-185. [61] Above, pp. 91, 100-101.

that history, political narrative and analysis, has already been the subject of extensive scholarly research.[62] It remains here, by way of epilogue, to suggest in a preliminary fashion what might be learned by searching out the continuities of student experience at Aligarh.

THE OLD BOYS

> When Indra, king of the giants, finished his work and passed on, his successor [Mahdi Ali] poured new life into the *sabhā*. He toured the heavens and beat the sabha's drum in the four corners of the world. But the response was so open-hearted and generous that it sometimes got tiresome.

So began Shaukat Ali's account, written in 1913, of how Aligarh's first generation carried on the task of public leadership in the fourteen years that followed the death of Sayyid Ahmad Khan.[63] In those years Aligarh had attracted a new measure of political attention, reaching out beyond Hindustan into most of the major centers of the subcontinent. First came the campaign to turn the college into a Muslim university, started as an effort to shore up Aligarh's failing fortunes in the wake of embezzlement, trustee disputes, falling enrollments, and the death of its early leaders. The Indian Education Commission of 1902 vetoed the idea of denominational universities, but eight years later the movement reappeared with an unprecedented level of popular enthusiasm and financial success. By that time the goal, clearly articulated in publications and meetings throughout India, was an autonomous university, affiliating far-flung

[62] Robinson, *Separatism*, pp. 358-418, offers biographical notes on some Aligarh alumni (including a few who are not noted as such and some other individuals who, incorrectly, are) and attempts to align them in political categories. Further work along these lines will be necessary.

[63] Shaukat Ali in *Old Boy*, March-April 1913, quoted in ʿAzīzuddīn Aḥmad, *Rīporṭ-i kamiṭī*, pp. 19-23; slightly paraphrased and condensed here in translation.

schools and colleges and responsible to popular constituencies within the Muslim community: little less than a separate educational system that would sift out Muslim loyalties from among all the overlapping geographical and cultural identities of South Asian society. Other Aligarh subsidiaries moved in the same direction. The Muslim Educational Conference now met in far-flung corners of India, and established regional offshoots. And at Dacca in 1906 the Conference gave birth to a new, avowedly political, association, the Muslim League, dedicated to mobilizing Muslims into a united, permanent party interest in national politics. Responding to the introduction of electoral institutions and the extension of bureaucratic criteria for official recruitment, the demands of the Muslim League for separate Muslim electorates, reserved seats, and more than proportional representation immediately acquired crucial importance in the political debates of modern India. And after 1912, events beyond India, particularly British-Ottoman opposition in the pre-World War alliance system of Europe, served to forge an alliance between Aligarh alumni and 'ulama, all by way of prelude to the great postwar agitation on behalf of the Ottoman Sultan in his role as Caliph for the whole Muslim world.

In the development of early twentieth-century Indian politics, Aligarh projected itself as central headquarters for the mobilization of a united Muslim response to changing idioms and institutions for the distribution of power at local, provincial, and national levels. By no means an accomplished fact, the image of that unity covered over a multitude of factional divisions and, no doubt, a great expanse of apathy toward Aligarh among many Indian Muslims. But Aligarh's claims were sufficient to generate a whole complex of political styles and policy formulations that became increasingly important in the years ahead. As Aligarh attained new heights of practical and symbolic prominence, it became an arena for competition among potential leaders, and a great deal of political history can be told in terms of these face-to-face battles within the confines of the Aligarh establishment.

What is striking in these developments is their continuity with the experience of student life in the era of Sayyid Ahmad and Beck. In the isolated and intense environment of Aligarh College, young men developed powerful feelings of friendship and rivalry as members of student cliques. They learned how to organize themselves for group cooperation or factional competition on the basis of personal attachment rather than fixed relationships determined by birth. They also confronted the reality of British power, as Beck and his colleagues increasingly took control over every aspect of college administration. Along with direct indoctrination of political skills and ideas, the unanticipated overtones of group interaction in the college made Aligarh students particularly sensitive to the relationship between personal loyalties and the acquisition of power and prestige.

Shaukat Ali's account summoned up, more as parody than epic allusion, the popular Urdu masque of mid-nineteenth century Oudh, Amanat's *Indra Sabhā*: Sayyid Ahmad was Indra, the sabha represented the Muslim community of India, the akhara or wrestling arena was Aligarh College. Before Aligarh's old students could come into their inheritance, the fable continued, they had to extirpate British faculty domination.

> In the excitement some foreign demons, disguised as giants, managed to infiltrate the sabha and take possession of the akhara, which they turned into a cess pool. The demons cast a spell on the real giants, paralysed their activities and maligned their reputations.

As Honorary Secretary, Mahdi Ali surrendered to Theodore Morison the last vestiges of power in the college and confined himself to public oratory well beyond the college grounds. Even that role was severely undercut when Mahdi Ali attempted to lead a pro-Urdu resistance to the establishment of Hindi as an official language in the courts: Anthony MacDonnell, Lieutenant Governor of what was now the United Provinces, broadly hinted that such political activity would put the government grant to the college in jeopardy. The old Hyderabad politician got the point.[64] Morison, on the other hand, carried on Beck's role as spokesman for approved Aligarh causes, actively working on the Muslim university campaign and presiding in 1904 over the Muslim Educational Conference.

Alumni of the college led the effort to wrest control over Aligarh from British hands. Aftab Ahmad Khan and his friends, many of them residing in Aligarh for that very purpose, gained power in college bodies and affiliated organizations, and used the press to attack the British staff and the weak older generation of Trustees who were content to remain on the sidelines. When Morison proposed the establishment of a postgraduate program in Arabic studies, he set off a hue and cry from among the old students; the scheme, they argued, was an attempt to turn Aligarh into a madrasah at the cost of its commitment to English learning. Aftab encouraged Morison's resignation in 1904, and over the next five years reestablished Trustee power with respect to admissions and discipline. In 1909, skillfully engineering a great public outcry, he warded off an attempt at direct government intervention on behalf of the British staff, and brought about the resignation of Morison's successor.[65]

"Aftab & Co." were not the only alumni to claim successorship in the cause of Sayyid Ahmad and to do battle with the British professorial usurpers. There was also Shaukat Ali and his younger brother, Muhammad Ali:

> Then arose the Red Giant and his brother, the Little Red Giant, to break the spell and rip off the imposters' masks.

On graduation Shaukat Ali, as the leading student of his day, received the reward of becoming subdeputy opium agent, a post generally held by British officials. Though posted in far-

[64] Zakaria, *Rise of Muslims*, pp. 303-309; Bhatnagar, *History of the M.A.-O. College*, pp. 141, 177-178; Robinson, *Separatism*, p. 137.

[65] Ḥabībullāh Khān, *Ḥayāt-i Aftāb*, pp. 54-61.

off towns, he maintained his special hail-fellow-well-met brand of involvement in Aligarh affairs, often to the discomfort of his earnest associates. Muhammad Ali had gone from Aligarh to Oxford, taken his degree and returned to India, "though not as a member of the much coveted Indian Civil Service, thanks to an English spring and a young man's more or less foolish fancy."[66] After a brief stint in the Rampur education department, he tried unsuccessfully to join the faculty at Aligarh. Finally he took a post in far-off Baroda, but attempted to keep his hand in Aligarh affairs by frequent visits, occasional articles, and active participation at the Muslim Educational Conference, the Muslim League, and the Old Boys' Association. A writer and orator of exceptional power in both Urdu and English, in 1904 he started issuing a series of speeches, articles, and pamphlets about what was wrong with Aligarh and what direction the movement should take. In 1907 he supported—some said fomented—a major student strike that resulted in the resignation of Mahdi Ali as Honorary Secretary and his replacement with his tough-minded old Hyderabad rival, Mushtaq Husain, a man more in harmony with the aspirations of the younger generation.[67]

There was little ideological difference between Aftab Ahmad and the Ali brothers, but there was a long-standing personal opposition between them, with roots back to their student days.

> The demons managed to create a disagreement in the ranks of the giants, particularly between the Red Giant and the White Giant. Both had been raised in the akhara and were devoted to it; but the Red Giant had a light-hearted disposition and was open to persuasion, while the White Giant was somber-minded and held on to his views with great tenacity.

66 Mohamed Ali, *My Life*, p. 30.

67 *Report of the Committee of Enquiry at Aligarh* (Allahabad: Pioneer Press, 1907), pp. 6, 24; Bhatnagar, *History of the M.A.-O. College*, pp. 202-210. For a detailed "exposé" of Muhammad Ali as an opportunist see Robinson, *Separatism*, pp. 178-189.

The initial conflict between these alumni concerned office-holding rules in the Old Boys Association—or what Shaukat Ali calls in his fable, the Sons of Giantland Society. The year before Sayyid Ahmad's death, Shaikh Abdullah, an ally of Aftab Ahmad Khan, sent around a letter regretting the demise of the Brotherhood and calling for an annual Old Boys' Dinner on the model of Eton and other English public schools. In the new spurt of energy that came with the Sir Syed Memorial Fund Committee, this proposal bore fruit: in July 1898, there was a dinner with thirty-five alumni in attendance. It was decided to ask every alumnus to give one month's salary to the Memorial Fund by the end of the year, to hold annual dinners, and to make Morison secretary-treasurer. Old students should get together on a local basis as well: "When an Aligarh student is transferred some place it is his duty to contact other students without regard to status and invite him to his house." There should also be periodic local meetings.[68] The following October, the annual dinner was formally transmuted into the Old Boys' Association with Bahadur Ali, yet another of Aftab's friends, as secretary. Forty alumni attended the 1899 meeting, many of them subscribing a month's wage to the new Beck Memorial Fund. All of them, in Shaukat Ali's words, "looked back with longing to their bright and happy undergraduate years."[69]

Membership in the Old Boys' Association was small, even relative to the general body of old students, who were either less taken with large social concerns, less convinced of Aligarh's special role, less happy in their memories, less energetic—or simply had other interests. It was the aim of the active nucleus to pull these others in, and the aim was pursued with greatest vigor by the Ali brothers, who remained at the fringes of Aftab's charmed circle.

In 1904, when Aftab Ahmad Khan himself became secretary, the organization had only fifty-six members. This was the time of Morison's Arabic studies project and Muhammad

[68] ʻAzīzddīn Aḥmad, *Rīporṭ-i kamiṭī*, pp. 12-15.
[69] MAOCM, November 1, 1899.

Ali's first articles and speeches. The previous year, the association had received the right to send three representatives to the seventy-man Board of Trustees, which otherwise consisted of a lifetime, self-electing membership. One of these representatives was Shaukat Ali, now joint secretary of the Old Boys. Growth of the association began to accelerate; soon over two hundred alumni were sending in the one percent assessment on their incomes required as dues. At its annual meeting in February 1905, the association took on the responsibility of providing three hundred rupees per month for the salary of the college's new science professor—science had become an alternative to Arabic.[70] The meeting coincided with the resignation and departure of Morison, an event welcomed by Aftab Ahmad Khan as an opportunity to reassert Muslim control over the college.[71]

Soon after, in April, Aftab had to go to Hyderabad on some legal work, and in the absence of any rules he appointed Mir Vilayat Husain, second master of the school, to officiate as secretary of the Old Boys. When Aftab's stay in the south was prolonged, Shaukat Ali, as joint secretary, wrote Mir Sahib demanding the post be turned over to him. He received no satisfaction, so he wrote Aftab directly. Aftab wrote back that he could have the post only if he resided in Aligarh. At the time Shaukat was posted in Bahraich, and he considered this reply typical of Aftab's effort to confine control of the society to his own entrenched clique.[72]

The Red Giant had many more supporters than the White Giant, but they were located in the sabha at large, not in the akhara.

Aftab Ahmad Khan returned to Aligarh in November, and resumed his post as secretary. The following month, the Muslim Educational Conference was held at the college for the first time since Sayyid Ahmad's death. For the occasion

[70] ʿAzīzuddīn Aḥmad, *Rīporṭ-i kamiṭī*, p. 16.
[71] Vilāyat Ḥusain, *Āp bītī*, pp. 149-150.
[72] ʿAzīzuddīn Aḥmad, *Rīporṭ-i kamiṭī*, p. 16-17.

Shaikh Abdullah, head of a new committee on female education, organized an evening exhibition of arts and crafts of Muslim ladies. Though Shaukat Ali was no opponent of women's education—at an earlier Conference he had spoken out on the need for educated wives for the new generation of educated men[73]—he resented the credit going to Aftab's circle. As the crowd was walking out of Strachey Hall after a meeting full of praise for Shaikh Abdullah, Shaukat Ali came up from behind, thumped his rival on the shoulder and said he deserved a beating for getting all that praise without having done anything. So saying, Shaukat Ali thumped the Shaikh again. An act of high spirits, it was also a shocking breech of gentlemanly conduct. That night the Trustees met and called for Shaukut's resignation. The next day the Old Boys' Association met in the Lytton Library and, despite Muhammad Ali's pleas on his brother's behalf, decided to put off the annual dinner, and issued an ultimatum to Shaukat Ali either to resign from the Board of Trustees or be expelled from the association. They also demanded that he apologize to Shaikh Abdullah. Shaukat, admitting what he had done had been rash, was forced to comply, but he resented Aftab Ahmad all the more for taking the lead in this public humiliation.[74]

> The Red Giant wanted to apologise, but no one would listen. As brothers of the akhara they could have embraced, but instead the Red Giant was ignominiously expelled from the special council of akhara.

A little over a year later Muhammad Ali underwent a similar humilitation, when a Committee of Enquiry on the student strike condemned him for encouraging unrest.

> He and his brother now realized that the only way to break the spell of the foreign demons was to organize a separate majlis [organization] for the protection of the akhara.

[73] MAOCM, January 15, 1900.
[74] Shaikh ʻAbdullāh, *Mushāhadāt*, pp. 186-188.

The Ali brothers and ten of their friends sent out a letter to the alumni calling for the establishment of an Old Boys' Reform League. The aim of the League was to break the power of Aftab's "clique wallas," put the Old Boys' Association in trustworthy hands, and then increase the power of the Old Boys in the Board of Trustees. Nonresidents would be allowed to hold the office of Old Boy Secretary, and members of the college teaching staff would be barred on the grounds that they were subject to the influence of the British staff. The League would meet two days before the annual meeting of the regular Association to formulate its program; all members would then vote in a bloc no matter what their personal views. And "since the college belongs to the public we might have to resort to agitation through the newspapers." It was also necessary to recruit more alumni for both the Association and the League.[75]

That same year, 1907, Muhammad Ali proposed in a series of articles for the *Times of India* (Bombay) that life membership on the Aligarh Board of Trustees be abolished in favor of a system of representation, with the Old Boys' Association electing thirty-five out of the seventy-five members. Another thirty would be elected by the old trustees, and the rest would be sent from the Muslim Educational Conference, the Muslim League, and Muslim organizations in the Punjab, Calcutta, Bombay, and Madras.[76] This effort to establish voting constituencies stood in significant juxtaposition to the Old Boys' Reform League. The Ali brothers were now playing politics in earnest. For the present their efforts were confined to Aligarh; the momentum was to carry them much further.

Aftab Ahmad's "clique wallas" and the Ali brothers' "league wallas" did not always have the akhara to themselves. The Board of Trustees was still dominated by members of the older generation under the leadership of Mushtaq Husain, and there were many members of both generations

[75] 'Azīzuddīn Aḥmad, *Rīporṭ-i kamiṭī*, pp. 26-36.

[76] The *Times of India*, May 13, July 6, July 26, 1909. (Thanks to Gail Minault for her notes on these articles.)

who supported the policies of the British government and the authority of the British faculty with regard to Aligarh affairs. Among the rising generation there were individuals and groups that had their own goals and ambitions. In 1909 Aftab Ahmad Khan defeated Ghulam us-Saqlain in an election from a Muslim constituency to the new provincial Legislative Council. The next year Ghulam us-Saqlain attempted to get elected to Aligarh's Board of Trustees; when he failed, he issued a scathing attack on Aftab Ahmad Khan's administration of the building funds of the college, which forced Aftab's temporary resignation from his college posts.[77] In 1914, as the Ali brothers began to test the edges of radical anti-British agitation, one hundred government officials who were former students of the college wrote a public letter to Shaukat Ali to tell him that his actions were "prejudicial not only to our personal interests, but also to the interests of our college."[78] This followed the line of cautious "loyalty" pursued by Dr. Ziauddin Ahmad, professor of mathematics, and for many years the most powerful member of the Aligarh faculty.[79] Even within radical alumni circles, anti-British and pro-Khilafat, there was an abiding rivalry between the Ali brothers and Zafar Ali Khan, who as a student had been one of the young intellectuals associated with Shibli and Arnold.[80]

The rise of overt factionalism among the Old Boys coincided with the institution of some major changes on the In-

[77] Ḥabībullah Khān, *Ḥayāt-i Aftāb*, pp. 197-198; Bhatnagar, *History of the M.A.-O. College*, pp. 255-256.

[78] English letter circulated by Muhammad Badrul Hasan and Qasim Beg Cagtai with the names of one hundred signers, printed as appendix in ʿAzīzuddīn Aḥmad, *Rīporṭ-i kamiṭī*, pp. 135-141.

[79] Muḥammad Amīn Zuberī, *Ẕiyā-i Ḥayāt* (Karachi: Maṭbūʿah Dīn Muḥammadīn, n.d.), pp. 49-63.

[80] Interview with Professor Hamid Ahmad Khan, half-brother of Zafar Ali Khan, Lahore 1969. See also Afzal Iqbal, *The Life and Times of Mohamed Ali* (Lahore: Institute of Islamic Culture, 1974), pp. 345, 349, 364.

dian political scene. In the summer of 1906, John Morley, the new Liberal Secretary of State for India, announced a number of concessions to the long-standing demands of the Indian National Congress for an increase in the representative element in the Indian government. This was one of those landmark decisions, like Ripon's Local Councils Act of 1882 and the Indian Councils Act of 1892, that raised the ante in political competition by adding to the power of elected representatives and increasing patronage posts in government service. This decision, following on the great *svādeshī* agitation in Bengal, gave new life to the stale Congress politics of the nineteenth century. For the first time, northern India began to become interested in All-India politics. In this new political climate, many of the central issues were construed in terms of Hindu-Muslim divisions: the contest between Hindi and Urdu, the partition of Bengal, the legality of cow slaughter. Now the fear that Sayyid Ahmad had enunciated in the 1880s was recalled: that a non-Muslim majority would use its power under democratic institutions to the detriment of Muslim interests and sensitivities. The low level of political activity that Sayyid Ahmad had fostered would no longer suffice to win the prizes or withstand the dangers of an expanding arena of political competition.

The Simla Deputation of October 1906 was an act of the Aligarh elders—Mahdi Ali, Mushtaq Husain, and Sayyid Husain Bilgrami—under the titular leadership of the young Agha Khan. Aligarh alumni had only background roles, though it was Aftab who pushed Mahdi Ali into taking the first step toward organizing the deputation, and Aligarh was central headquarters for the effort.[81] The deputation had the younger generation very much in mind. Bilgrami's first draft of the address to the Viceroy, revised at the suggestion of Aligarh's British principal, contained a warning about the strong feelings of English-educated Muslim youth, who felt that Muslims were losing out because they did not know how

[81] Syed Sharifuddin Pirzada, ed., *Foundations of Pakistan*, I (Karachi: National Publishing House, n.d. [1969]), xxxiii-xxxviii.

to agitate. The Simla Deputation was in part an effort to keep this new generation in line.[82]

Simla was the catalyst for the formation of the Muslim League, one of a series of efforts to establish a national Muslim political association, which now at last took root. The proposal drawn up by the Navab of Dacca stated that one of the aims of the new organization would be to enlarge Aligarh and "establish institutions on the lines of the Aligarh College in each Presidency or Chief Province in the country." Aligarh had been founded over a quarter century ago, "but to keep up *its utility and usefulness* we have to enter the next stage of political life." The League would seek "to enable our young men of education . . . to find scope . . . for public life" without falling into the arms of the Indian National Congress. "Many of our young educated Mahomedans find themselves shoved off the line of official preferment and promotion unless they join or at least show simpathy [*sic*] with the Congress Party."[83]

Aftab Ahmad Khan and Mushtaq Husain arranged the first meeting of the Muslim League in December 1906, just after the meetings of the Educational Conference, in Dacca. Muhammad Ali wrote the official account of the meeting and was otherwise very much present—at one point he successfully suppressed a minor resolution made by Aftab and seconded by Shaikh Abdullah. There was a provisional governing body under the leadership of Mahdi Ali and Mushtaq Husain. The fifty-six members of this committee included fifteen young Aligarh alumni, including Aftab Ahmad Khan, Shaikh Abdullah, Ghulam us-Saqlain, Zafar Ali Khan, and Muhammad Ali. (Shaukat Ali was still in the Opium Department and therefore disqualified.) Over the next two years, meetings were held in Karachi, Aligarh, and Amritsar,

82 "Revised Draft Memorial," printed with editorial revisions by Archbold and accompanying correspondence in file marked "Simla Delegation," AA.

83 K. Salimoolah, *The Moslem All-India Confederacy*, printed pamphlet, n.p., dated Dacca, November 9, 1906 (in Simla Delegation file, AA).

but only at the latter, in December 1908, did the organization get down to substantive political issues—in particular, the forthcoming Morley-Minto reforms. Aftab spoke against the reforms as being contrary to Muslim interests. Muhammad Ali gave a lengthy speech in their favor. In passing, he noted that the style of the League stood in marked contrast to the hurly-burly of the Congress, recently torn apart by shoe-throwing factions of its own. "This is no mass meeting, no demonstration. . . . We speak to each other not to a gallery." Muhammad Ali's polished and highly parliamentary oration, impressively decked out with discussions of current British politics, argued that "the lines of cleavage" in India were primarily according to religion, and that these divisions were political as well as spiritual. No matter how good the faith of some of the Hindu leaders, the basic conditions of India could not be changed, and an effort must be made through the new political system to secure the protection of specific Muslim interests.[84]

Until 1910, the Muslim League remained an appendage of the Muslim Educational Conference, but in 1909 the decision was made to separate the two organizations and move the League headquarters from Aligarh to Lucknow, with Aziz Mirza, leader of the 1887 student strike, as secretary. The shift to Lucknow coincided with a revival of the Muslim university movement, with Aftab and the Ali brothers vying with each other in fund raising and schemes for community control of the university. Shaukat Ali finally became secretary of the Old Boys' Association in 1912, while Aftab & Co. withdrew from the organization and ensconced themselves in the Muslim Educational Conference. As the Muslim League moved toward an alliance with the Congress, Aftab's group reverted rather uncomfortably to the old-style brand of Aligarh "loyalty" to the British raj.[85]

[84] Pirzada, *Foundations of Pakistan*, pp. 68-76.

[85] For a full account of the politics of this period see Robinson, *Separatism*; see also Gail Minault, "The Khilafat Movement" (Ph.D. dissertation, University of Pennsylvania, 1972).

In 1912, the Ali brothers met Maulana Abdul Bari of Fanangi Mahal in Lucknow; soon they were both his religious disciples and political allies. Previously men of fashionable British attire, they now appeared in flowing robes, at the same time growing beards and giving up "Mister" and "B.A." in favor of "Maulana" as title to their names. Shaukat Ali resigned from government service and became secretary of Abdul Bari's new organization for the protection of the holy places of Islam now threatened by war, the Anjuman-i Khud-dām-i Kaʿbah. Over the following years the Ali brothers became famous figures in Indian politics, but their political actions were now informed by a heavy commitment to Islamic devotionalism based on their Sufi discipleship to Abdul Bari. Though they were operating on a wider political arena and in an altered ideological spirit, they maintained their overriding concern in Aligarh affairs. Now, however, they were seeking student support for the Ottoman empire and Sultan against the British in the war.[86] By the end of the war, the Ali brothers had been interned in central India and were using words like "boycott" and "revolution."[87] In the Non-Cooperation movement of 1920, they returned to Aligarh in the company of Mahatma Gandhi, organized a student boycott, seized the Old Boys' Lodge and set up a break-away "national university," the Jāmiʿah Millīyah Islāmīyah, in opposition to the government-sponsored institution. Only thus could they fulfill their inheritance as what Muhammad Ali had earlier called "the first-born of Sir Syed and Aligarh."[88] Then, finally, the British government allowed the loyalists to have their Muslim university, a unitary establishment no different from the college except that it could grant degrees.

86 Minault, "The Khilafat Movement."

87 Letter from Muhammad Ali, printed in *Rūʾidād-i Auld Boiz Asōsīaishan*, 1916 (Old Boys' Lodge, Aligarh).

88 Muhammad Ali to the Raja of Mahmudabad, April 6, 1917, Muhammad Ali papers, Jāmiʿah Millīyah Islāmīyah, New Delhi, cited in Minault and Lelyveld, "Campaign for a Muslim University," p. 181 (this being part of the Minault contribution).

The alliance that the Ali brothers forged with ʿulama such as Abdul Bari pointed up what had been notably absent from the Muslim politics of Aligarh: Islam. The idea of the Ottoman empire and the claim of the Sultan to the status of Caliph went to the heart of the notion of Islamic political society as the ummah, the international society of believers. Aligarh leaders had ignored the idea of a society organized on the basis of God's revelation to man through the prophet Muhammad; they had rejected the leadership of the ʿulama in favor of those learned in some version of European studies. The New Light was preferable to following the wisdom of the past, though Sayyid Ahmad had tried to show that the two were ultimately compatible. His teachings, however, had not been a part of Aligarh's education, and thus there was no attempt to struggle through the emotional and intellectual conflicts that lay beneath the attempt to combine current British intellectual culture with loyalty to Islam. It was enough to pray, fast, and call oneself a Muslim. "Our communal consciousness," wrote Muhammad Ali recalling from jail his student days, "was far more secular than religious."[89] The distinction in his understanding of Islam was not a legitimate one.

In 1904, at the outset of his public career, Muhammad Ali attempted to translate the Mughal concept of pluralism into the language of European politics by projecting a bold notion of India as a "federation of religions."[90] He wanted to see educational systems and political constituencies organized along religious lines. Perhaps what he had in mind were sectors of religious autonomy so extensive that they

[89] Mohamed Ali, *My Life*, p. 22.

[90] Mohamed Ali, *The Proposed Mahomedan University* (Bombay: Caxton Printing Works, 1904). Muhammad Ali returned to this theme in his great summation of his own career and the significance of Aligarh in the political history of India: his presidential address to the Indian National Congress at Cocanada in 1923, *Select Writings and Speeches of Maulana Mohamed Ali*, ed. Afzal Iqbal (Lahore: Sh. Muhammad Ashraf, 1944), pp. 247-316.

could operate like the Ottoman *millet* system, each conceived of as a civil society unto itself. That might be a way of resolving, at least in theory, the notion of religious community within a pluralistic society, but it certainly left no room for the kind of parliamentary government and popular political participation that Muhammad Ali helped to bring to life in modern India. Muhammad Ali himself never bothered to spell out how such a federation of religions would work amidst party competition and the day-to-day activities of a modern government responsible for a wide range of economic and social functions.

Until the Ali brothers rediscovered the inspiration of Islam as a living guide to a total social order, Aligarh politics remained a rearguard action on behalf of kacahri-linked family groups, who acted as Muslims largely as a defensive action against anti-Muslim initiatives among various competitors. The college was effective in inculcating political skills, but intellectually Aligarh did not develop a well-formulated understanding of the relationship between religious loyalties and the changing political institutions of Indian society. The emotion of team loyalty, as in the ethos of cricket, often seemed more relevant than divine revelation: one was a Muslim by party spirit. Muhammad Ali and, more fully, Muhammad Iqbal—he was linked to Aligarh through T. W. Arnold's teaching in Lahore—attempted to challenge this bifurcation of religion and the social order. In both cases, they looked beyond India to an international Islamic order, and sought some vague system of loose confederation that would make it possible to develop Islamic political autonomy within the Indian subcontinent. Ultimately they felt that God had told man how to order his society, and it was the duty of man to obey.

The rise of popular electoral politics and mass techniques of protest decisively undercut Sayyid Ahmad's notion of an overarching authority that would mediate among opposing groups. In the battle between Aftab Ahmad Khan and the Ali brothers, the Ali brothers discovered the power of religious appeal in popular mobilization; in the process they were carried far beyond Aligarh itself. This rivalry was not the whole of Aligarh politics, and Aligarh was by no means the whole of Muslim politics in India. But in many respects politics was what Aligarh was all about. Though Sayyid Ahmad had founded the college with ideas of reformulating Islamic theology and introducing empirical investigation and careful scholarship into the world of Indian-English education, the social establishment that came into being taught a very different lesson. The college became a biradari, a brotherhood, to make "the qaum really a qaum," as Sayyid Ahmad himself said. Whether the qaum then was a religious confession, a political interest group, or an independent national entity was a matter left to the momentum of political competition, of leaders seeking constituencies in its name. Aligarh itself became a highly charged symbol, but exactly what it symbolized remained a matter of unresolved debate.

To be a Muslim in British India could be construed in several ways. Muslims, like other Indians, could think of themselves as colonial subjects, ruled by one of the great industrial powers of modern Europe. In the last, unhappy year of his life, Sayyid Ahmad had fallen back on this counsel of despair: "India is a conquered country held by force of arms and people have no right to complain of taxes demanded to keep them in submission."[91] "The well-being of the people of India, and especially of the Musalmans, lies in leading a quiet life under the benign rule of the English government."[92] Aligarh, then, would be a lesson in submission, in "loyalty" as it was called, teaching its students and the Muslims of India how to accept their permanent subordination. "Since . . . the Musalmans can never hope (even if they wished) to change the existing order of things," Theodore Morison told the Brotherhood, "they must be content to excel in those walks of life which are open to them."[93]

The British colonial view of India as composed of separate

[91] AIG, February 6, 1897. [92] *Ibid.*, September 18, 1897.
[93] *Ibid.*, April 3, 1894.

societies with no hope for integration except by subordination to British power was often bolstered with racial theories to justify the permanent subjugation of the indigenous people. But Sayyid Ahmad Khan, while he might accept the superior power and even to some extent the superior culture of the British as justifying their rule, was not about to admit that there was something innate in his biological origins that made him irrevocably inferior to an Englishman. The basic thrust of his political thinking was a theory of universal empire that had its origins in the Mughal concept of society. The sultanat now belonged to Queen Victoria, but Muslims as a qaum could participate in the system of rule. Muslims would eventually qualify to sit beside Englishmen in the highest positions of power, and to carve out enclaves of autonomous action. India would never be united on the principle of shared citizenship, but it could achieve some form of integration as a hierarchy of distinct social groups, each reconciled to its proper share of deference and subordination. From this point of view, it was the task of Aligarh to train Muslims to be worthy of prestige and power in a cosmopolitan empire.

What Sayyid Ahmad did not anticipate when he founded the college at Aligarh was the notion of India as a nation-state. Starting in the 1880s, an increasingly attractive response to colonial subjugation was the ideal of uniting the indigenous people on the basis of an overriding identification with "India" as a territorial, cultural, and ultimately political unity. Responding in large measure to an English prototype of a liberal social order, the formulators of the concept of Indian nationality did not develop a comfortable accommodation with the idea of society as a hierarchy of separate social groups. All would be Indians, and it would be difficult to justify the assignment of power and prestige in the new society simply on the basis of what would now be no more than inherited subcultures. From the outset Indian nationalism was couched in terms of making the prized positions in society accessible on the basis of individual achievement, as defined by the shared values of the nation as a whole. Being Muslim, then, would not in itself qualify anybody for special consideration. The widespread idea, true or false, that Muslims as such had once been the rulers of India could only inspire resentment: there were now no grounds for allowing them a privileged status. And to the extent that Muslims failed to devote their primary loyalty to the Indian nation-state, they would not be entitled to the privileges of citizenship.

Sayyid Ahmad fully understood the challenge of this competing concept of Indian society, but Aligarh was hardly in a position to control the flow of events in India as a whole. The ideal of a cosmopolitan empire rapidly lost ground in Britain as well as in India: too many people saw it as a disguise for exploitation. What then were the former students of Aligarh to make of the idea so powerfully inculcated into them that being Muslim entailed a special relationship to the political order? The concepts of Muslims as a qaum justified such aspirations in terms of inherited culture and even biology: Muslims had peculiar moral attributes that made them a ruling people. The concept of Muslims as an ummah, the community of believers, entitled Muslims to rule because they had accepted God's revelations. Neither view was compatible with the idea of a nation-state, particularly in a society where Muslims were a relatively small and powerless minority. If India were to be thought of as a whole, a political identity conceived in terms of Muslims as a ruling class would eventually lead to exclusion and even oppression. Against this there could be several lines of defense: to reach out beyond India to the international community of Islam in the hopes of creating a new world empire; to lie low and quietly hope to convert the people of India to the acceptance of God's word; or in some way, as part of an Indian confederation or independent of India altogether, to create a separate territorial entity just for Muslims. Otherwise Muslims would have to accept a political role that claimed something less than dominance, or even redefine their Muslim identity so as to divorce it from the realm of politics.

Ever since Sayyid Ahmad started his movement to found a special educational establishment for Indian Muslims, Aligarh has summoned up in both friend and foe an image of Muslim participation—as Muslims—in India's new political institutions. A large part of Aligarh's significance, its meaning, lies in this image and in the imaginations of those who created it, quite aside from any assessment of how influential they were in the society at large. But even such a cultural account must go beyond the realm of pure ideas into an examination of social experience, the experience of Aligarh's founders and first students, for example, in order to understand how being Muslim could be so salient as a political identity.

It was conceivable, of course, that "the lines of cleavage," as Muhammad Ali called them, could have been construed on some other basis than those that were posited on the category "Muslim." In the twentieth century, Indian nationalists called, on the one hand, for a political identity based on a sense of Indian nationality, and, on the other, for a social system built on competing class interests. There were efforts to project some of the features of sharīf culture on to a "national culture of India," a democratic extension of the cosmopolitan Mughal heritage.[94] Similarly, it was possible to interpret the kacahri milieu in terms of class consciousness. Aligarh students were sufficiently homogeneous from the point of view of class analysis; their economc motivations were not particularly disguised.

Did loyalty to "the Muslim community" inhibit the consolidation of class awareness? Or did it stimulate the ability to transcend narrow interests in the direction of more universal sympathies? No simple answer is ready to hand, for different people acted together or in opposition according to a complicated variety of motivations, sometimes reinforcing,

[94] S. Abid Husain, *The National Culture of India*, reprint ed. (Bombay: Jaico Publishing House, 1956).

sometimes conflicting. Despite the wishes of Sayyid Ahmad, Aligarh students did not represent a united phalanx, and the tensions among them reveal inconsistencies at the heart of the Aligarh movement. For some, recalling the conflicts of old Union debates, identity as Muslims stood in opposition to ideas of sharāfat and impelled them to a solicitude for the vast multitude of Muslims, who were in fact poor peasants and artisans—and women. The belief that political power was their destiny encouraged some to join forces with the nationalist movement against British rule, and later Aligarh generations were to include notable advocates of Indian socialism. Jawaharlal Nehru said of Aligarh College that "a feudal spirit reigned over it, and the goal of the average student was government service."[95] Others portrayed Aligarh's first generation as a rising bourgeoisie.[96] Such interpretations indicate, at least, the transitional role of Aligarh's students, the complexity and conflict of motivations that their experience embodied.

Meanwhile, being Muslim continued to be crucially important in the formation of political loyalties. Not all Muslim "separatism" was Aligarh's doing. Much of it was a response to how the British government defined political constituencies in India. A good deal was defence against anti-Muslim actions on the part of various political and religious groups. Even among Muslims, there were many important sources of leadership outside of Aligarh. Nevertheless, Aligarh was frequently the focus of efforts to formulate a new Muslim political consciousness. Nehru complained that the college failed to inspire its students with the kind of intellectual struggle that forces people to break out of the mold of past categories of thought, to develop new sensibilities and dif-

[95] Jawaharlal Nehru, *An Autobiography*, reprint ed. (Bombay: Allied Publishers, 1962), p. 464.

[96] Wilfred Cantwell Smith, *Modern Islām in India*, reprint ed. (Lahore: Sh. Muhammad Ashraf, 1963); Muhammad Ashraf, "'Alīgaṛh kī siyāsī zindigī," *'Alīgaṛh Megzīn*, Aligarh Number, Part 1, p. 157; cf. Louis Dumont, "Nationalism and Communalism," *Contributions to Indian Sociology*, VIII (1964), 30-70.

ferent social loyalties. For a nationalist and a socialist, the ideology that Aligarh stood for served only to frustrate a multitude of glorious aspirations. For many, religious Muslims as well as Indian nationalists, Muslim identity as construed at Aligarh seemed shallow: by oversimplifying the compatibility of this identity with the institutions of a large-scale, plural society, the founders and alumni of the college failed to discover the basis of a new social order or the full inspiration of an ancient ideal. What they did discover, however, was something of immense emotional power, a reaffirmation in a world of changing circumstances of the bond between religious and family feelings as a basis for political solidarity. In the face of colonial domination and new institutions of social competition, such solidarity could inspire considerable devotion as an end in itself.

Bibliography

UNPUBLISHED SOURCES

THE major manuscript collection for the history of the Aligarh College is in the Archives of Aligarh Muslim University at the Maulana Azad Library, Aligarh, Uttar Pradesh, India. In particular, I used the correspondence of the Honorary Secretary's Office, 1875-1897. The archives also contain "The Diary of Sahibzada Aftab Ahmad Khan Ahmadi, 1892-93." There is a smaller manuscript collection at the National Museum of Pakistan in Karachi. The Papers of T. W. Arnold are at the Library of the School of Oriental and African Studies, University of London. Some relevant letters are to be found in the official correspondence of the Government of Hyderabad, Deccan, from 1870 to 1910, in the Archives of the Government of Andhra Pradesh in Hyderabad.

Printed and manuscript proceedings of the Government of India, Home Department (Education Branch and Establishment Branch), Public Department, Judicial Department, and Foreign Department are to be found in the National Archives of India, New Delhi. A partial selection of these proceedings is available at the India Office Library, London, which also has Sir James Meston's "Correspondence in Connection with Muhammadan Affairs from 1912-14." Proceedings of the Government of the North-Western Provinces and Oudh, Education Department, 1860-1900, are in the Archives of the Government of Uttar Pradesh, Council House, Lucknow.

REPORTS, PROCEEDINGS, AND OTHER OFFICIAL PUBLICATIONS OF THE ALIGARH MOVEMENT

Aligarh Muslim University. *Calendar, 1921-1925*. Aligarh: Muslim University Press, 1926.

Husain, Yusuf, ed. *Selected Documents from the Aligarh Archives.* Bombay: Asia Publishing House, 1967.

Mohsin ul-Mulk, ed. *Addresses and Speeches Relating to the Mahomedan Anglo-Oriental College in Aligarh.* Aligarh: Institute Press, 1898.

Muhammadan Anglo-Oriental College, Aligarh. *Calendar, 1911-12.* Allahabad: The Indian Press, 1911.

———. *Code of Rules for the Muhammadan Anglo-Oriental College at Aligarh.* Calcutta: n.p., 1883.

———. *Report of the Progress of Education at the Muhammadan Anglo-Oriental College, Aligarh.* 1875-1886, 1891-1897. [Published annually in English or Urdu.]

———. *Rīporṭ-i sālānah kāravā'ī borḍing haus* [boarding house], *Madrasat ul-'ulūm.* 1879-1883. [Annual.]

———. *Rules and Regulations for the Appointment of the Trustees of the Mahomean Anglo-Oriental College, Aligarh.* [As amended January 31, 1899.]

———. Board of Management. *Proceedings.* 1896-1897.

———. Life Honorary Secretary [Sayyid Ahmad Khan]. *The Report of the M.A.-O. College Embezzlement.* Allahabad: Pioneer Press, 1896.

———. Principal. *Annual Report.* 1891-1903.

———. Trustees. *Rū'idād-i ijlās-i ṭrastiyān Muḥammadan Kālij 'Alīgaṛh.* 1890-1899.

Muhammadan Educational Conference. *Muhammaḍan Aijūkaishanal Kānfrans kā āṭhvān sālānah jalsah.* Agra: Mufīd-i 'Ām Press, 1894.

Old Boys' Association, M.A.-O. College. *Rū'idād-i jalsah-i sālānah o ḍinar* [dinner]. 1908-1921.

Report of the Select Committee for the Better Diffusion and Advancement of Learning among the Muhammadans of India. Benares: Medical Hall Press, 1873. [English and Urdu.]

Report of the Committee of Enquiry at Aligarh. Allahabad: Pioneer Press, 1907.

Rīporṭ-i kamiṭī-i taḥqīqāt muṭ'aliq ba Aulḍ Boiz Āsōsīashan [Old Boys' Association], *Madrasat ul-'ulūm, 'Alīgaṛh.* Aligarh: Institute Press, 1917.

Scientific Society. *Proceedings.* Nos. 1-9. 1864-1865.

Ṭarīqah-i intizām o silsilah-i ta'līm o tarbīyat jo mujvazah-i Madrasat ul-'ulūm Musalmānān kē liye tajvīz hūā. [Lucknow]: Nawal Kishore, 1873.

Ṭufail Aḥmad. *Muḥammadan Kālij Ḍairakṭarī* [Muhammadan College Directory]. Aligarh: Muhammadan Press, [1895].
———. *Muḥammadan Kālij Ḍairakṭarī*. 2 vols. and supplement. Badaun: Nizami Press, 1914.

CONTEMPORARY GOVERNMENT PUBLICATIONS

Allahabad University. *Calendar*. 1889-1900. [Annual.]
Hyderabad State. *The Classified List of Officers of the Civil Departments of H. E. H. the Nizam's Government*. 1910 and 1921.
India. *Correspondence on the Subject of the Education of the Muhammadan Community in British India and Their Employment in the Public Service Generally*. Selections from the Records of the Government of India. Vol. CCV. Calcutta: Superintendent of Government Printing, 1886.
———. *Selections from the Educational Records of the Government of India*. 2 vols. New Delhi: Government Publications, 1860 and 1963.
———. *Selections from the Vernacular Press of the Provinces of India: North-Western Provinces, Oudh, Punjab*. 1870-1900.
———. Census Commissioner. *Census of India, 1872: North-Western Provinces*. 2 vols. Calcutta: Superintendent of Government Printing, 1873.
———. Census Commissioner. *Census of India, 1881: North-Western Provinces of Agra and Oudh*. 2 vols. Calcutta: Superintendent of Government Printing, 1883.
———. Census Commissioner. *Report on the Census of British India, 1881*. 3 vols. London: Eyre and Spottiswoode, 1883.
———. Census Commissioner. Ibbetson. Denzil Charles Jelf. *Report on the Census of the Punjab, 1881*. Calcutta: Superintendent of Government Printing, 1883.
———. Education Commission. *Report of the Indian Education Commission*. Calcutta: Superintendent of Government Printing, 1883.
———. Education Commission. *Report of the North-Western Provinces and Oudh Provincial Committee*. Calcutta: Superintendent of Government Printing, 1884.
———. Education Commission. *Report of the Punjab Provincial Committee*. Calcutta: Superintendent of Government Printing, 1884.

India. Education Department. *Educational Buildings in India.* Calcutta: Superintendent of Government Printing, 1911.
North-Western Provinces. *Gazette.* 1862-1877.
———. *Selections from the Records of the Government of the North-Western Provinces.* 1868-1874.
———. Director of Public Instruction. *Report.* 1869-1876. [Annual.]
North-Western Provinces and Oudh. *Gazette.* 1877-1900.
———. *History of Services of Gazetted Officers.* 1880-1900.
———. *The Official Quarterly Civil List.* 1880-1900.
———. [Report on an Enquiry, District Establishments, N.-W.P. and Oudh, 1892.]
———. Director of Public Instruction. *Report.* 1877-1900. [Annual.]
United Provinces. *Report on the Re-organization of the Judicial Staff of the United Provinces of Agra and Oudh.* 2 vols. Allahabad: Superintendent of Government Printing, 1908.

CONTEMPORARY SERIAL PUBLICATIONS

Aligarh Institute Gazette. 1866-1885, 1897.
Aligarh Monthly. 1903-1914.
Allahabad Review. 1890-1895.
Cambridge Review. 1879-1885.
Muhammadan Anglo-Oriental College Magazine, published as supplement to *Aligarh Institute Gazette* 1891-1894 and independently printed 1894-1902; nominally combined with the defunct *Aligarh Institute Gazette*, 1899-1901.
Old Boy. Scattered issues, 1911-1913, 1928.
Tahẕīb ul-Akẖlāq. 1287-1289 H.

URDU BOOKS AND ARTICLES USED AS PRIMARY SOURCES

Asghar ʿAbbās. "Sar Sayyid kē nām mushāhīr kē khutūṭ." *Urdū Adab,* No. 2 (1971), 45-76.
———. "Sar Sayyid kē nām rafqāʾī Sar Sayyid kē ghair maṭbūʿah khutūṭ." *Urdū Adab,* No. 4 (1971), 5-52.
ʿAbdullāh, Shaikh Muḥammad. *Savāniḥ ʿumrī-i ʿAbdullāh Begam.* 2d ed. Aligarh: Muḥammad Muqtada Khān Shervānī, 1954.

———. *Mushāhadāt o ta'assurāt*. Aligarh: Female Education Association, 1969.

Ahmad Khān, Sayyid. *Āsār us-ṣanādīd*. Reprint ed. Delhi: Central Book Depot, 1965.

———. *Khuṭūṭ-i Sar Sayyid*. Edited by Sayyid Rās Mas'ūd. Badaun: Nizami Press, 1931.

———. *Makātīb-i Sar Sayyid Aḥmad Khān*. Edited by Mushtāq Ḥusain. Lahore: Star Book Depot, n.d.

———. *Maktūbāt-i Sar Sayyid*. Edited by Shaikh Muḥammad Ismā'īl Panīpatī. Lahore: Majlis-i Ṭaraqqī-i Adab, 1959.

———. *Maqālāt-i Sar Sayyid*. Edited by Muḥammad Ismā'īl Panīpatī. 16 vols. Lahore: Majlis-i Taraqqī-i Adab, 1962-1965.

———. *Mukammal majmū'ah lekcharz o ispīcaz*. Edited by Muḥammad Imāmud-dīn Gujrātī. Lahore: Muṣṭafā'ī Press, 1900.

———. *Sīrat-i Farīdiyah*. Reprint ed. Karachi: Pāk Academy, 1964.

'Alī "Maḥvī," Mas'ūd. *Kitāb-i Makhdūm Zādgān-i Fateḥpūr*. 2 vols. [Hyderabad, 1946?].

'Alī, Muḥammad. *Dīvān-i Jauhar*. Edited by Nūr ur-Raḥmān. Lahore: Shaikh Ghulām 'Alī and Sons, 1962.

Ashūb, Piarē Lāl. *Rasūm-i Hind*. Reprint ed. Lahore: Majlis-i Ṭaraqqī-i Adab, 1961.

Ghālib, Asadullāh Khan. *Divān-i Ghālib*. Edited by Mālik Rām. Delhi: Azād Kitāb Shar, n.d.

Ḥālī, Khvājah Alṭāf Ḥusain. *Divān-i Ḥālī*. Reprint ed. Delhi: 'Ilmi Kitāb Khānah, 1956.

———. *Kulliyāt-i Naṣr-i Ḥālī*. Edited by Muḥammad Ismā'īl Panīpatī. Vol. I. Lahore: Majlis-i Taraqqī-i Adab, 1967.

Ḥusain, Mīr Vilāyat. *Āp bītī*. Aligarh: privately printed by Sayyid Ḥādī Ḥusain Zaidī, 1970.

Imdād 'Alī, Sayyid. *Imdād al-āfāq binjām ahl-i vifāq ba javāb parcah-i Tahzīb ul-Akhlāq*. Kanpur: n.p., 1290 H.

Khān, Hākīm Ajmal. *Javāb-i maimōranḍam*. N.p.: published by the author, 1899.

Khān, Muḥammad Sa'īd (Navāb of Chatārī). *Yād-i ayyām*. 2 vols. Aligarh: Muslim Educational Press, n.d.

Khān, Sulṭān Aḥmad and Khān, Aftāb Aḥmad. *Savāniḥ 'umrī musūmah ḥayāt-i Aḥmadī*. Badaun: Nizami Press, n.d.

Khvājah Muḥammad Yūṣuf. *Izālat ul-auhām*. Aligarh: Muhammadan Press, 1897.
Mīrzā, Muḥammad ʿAzīz. *Khayālāt-i ʿAzīz*. Reprint ed. Karachi: Anjuman-i Taraqqī-i Urdū, 1961.
Nazīr Aḥmad. *Mirāt ul-ʿarūs*. Reprint ed. Delhi: Kutb Khānah Naẓariyah, n.d.
Rizā ʿAlī, Sayyid. *Aʿmāl nāmah*. Delhi: Hindustan Publishers, 1943.
Sarvar ul-Mulk (Aghā Mīrzā Beg). *Kārnāmah-i Sarvarī*. Aligarh: Muslim University, 1933.
Ṭufail Aḥmad, Sayyid. *ʿAligaṛh Kālij kē sarbāstah rāz kā afshā*. Badaun: Nizami Press, 1916.
———. *Musalmānōn kā raushan mustaqbil*. Delhi: ʿAlīmi, 1945.
Shiblī Nuʿmānī, Muḥammad. *Khuṭbāt-i Shiblī*. Azamgarh: Maʿārif, 1965.
———. *Maqālāt-i Shiblī*. Vol. I. Azamgarh: Maʿarif, 1954.

ENGLISH BOOKS AND TRANSLATIONS USED AS PRIMARY SOURCES

Abū'l-Faẓl ʿAllāmī. *The Ā'īn-i Akbarī*. Translated by H. Blochmann. Reprint ed. Delhi: Aadiesh Book Depot, 1965.
Adam, William. *Reports on Vernacular Education in Bengal and Behar*. Reprint ed. Calcutta: Home Secretariat Press, 1968.
Ahmad Khan, Sayyid. *Essays on the Life of Muhammad*. Reprint ed. Lahore: Premier Book House, 1968.
———. *Review on Dr. Hunter's Indian Musalmans*. Reprint ed. Lahore: Premier Book House, n.d.
———. *Sir Sayyid Ahmad Khan's History of the Bijnor Rebellion*. Edited and translated by Hafeez Malik and Morris Dembo. East Lansing, Michigan: Asia Studies Center, Michigan State University, n.d.
———. *Sir Sayyid Speaks to You*. [Edited and translated by K. A. Nizami.] Aligarh: Sir Syed Hall, 1968.
———. *Strictures on the Present State of English Education in India*. London: n.p., 1869.
———. *Writings and Speeches of Sir Syed Ahmad Khan*. Edited by Shan Mohammad. Bombay: Nackiketa Publications, 1972.
Ali, Mrs. Meer Hasan. *Observations of the Mussulmauns of India*. 2 vols. London: Parbury, Allen and Co., 1832.

Ali, Mohamed. *My Life: A Fragment*. Lahore: Sh. Muhammad Ashraf, 1942.

———. *The Proposed Mahomedan University*. Bombay: Caxton Printing Works, 1904.

———. *Selections from Maulana Mohammad Ali's Comrade*. Edited by Syed Rais Ahmad Jafri. Lahore: Mohammad Ali Academy, 1965.

———. *Select Writings and Speeches of Maulana Mohammad Ali*. Edited by Afzal Iqbal. Lahore: Sh. Muhammad Ashraf, 1944.

Ahmad, Bashir. *Justice Shah Din*. Lahore: by the author, 1962.

Arnold, T. W. *The Preaching of Islām*. Reprint ed. Lahore: Sh. Muhammad Ashraf, 1961.

Bain, Alexander. *Mental and Moral Science*. 3d ed. London: Longmans & Co., 1872.

Beck, Theodore. *Essays on Indian Topics*. Allahabad: Pioneer Press, 1888.

[Bilgrami, Sayyid Husain]. *Addresses, Poems, and Other Writings of Nawab Imadul-Mulk Bahadur (Sayyid Husain Bilgrami, C. S. I.)*. Hyderabad: Government Central Press, 1925.

Blunt, Wilfred Scawen. *India under Ripon: A Private Diary*. London: T. Fisher Unwin, 1909.

Congress Presidential Addresses. First Series (1885-1910). Madras: G. A. Natesan, 1935.

Disraeli, Benjamin. *Sybil, or The Two Nations*. London: World Classics Edition, 1956.

Elliot, H. M. *Memoirs on the History, Folk-Lore, and Distribution of the Races of the North-Western Provinces of India*. Revised by John Beames. 2 vols. London: Trübner & Co., 1869.

Hunter, W. W. *The Inaian Empire*. London: Trübner & Co., 1882.

———. *The Indian Musalmans: Are They Bound in Conscience to Rebel against the Queen?* London: Trübner & Co., 1871.

Irving, Miles, ed. *A List of Inscriptions on Christian Tombs or Monuments in the Punjab, North-West Frontier Province, Kashmir and Afghanistan*. Vol. 2, Part 1. Lahore: Government Printing Press, 1910.

Khan, Mustapha. *An Apology for the "New Light,"* Allahabad: Pioneer Press, 1891.

Khan, Paunchkouree (pseud.). *Revelations of an Orderly.* Benares: E. J. Lazarus & Co., 1866.

Kipling, Rudyard. *Kim.* Reprint ed. New York: Modern Library, n.d.

Lane-Poole, Stanley. *The Moors of Spain.* London: T. Fisher Unwin, 1885.

Lyall, Alfred C. *Asiatic Studies, Religious and Social.* 2d ed. London: J. Murray, 1884.

Mahmood, Syed. *A History of English Education in India.* Aligarh: M.A.-O. College, 1895.

Morison, Theodore. *The History of the M.A.-O. College.* Allahabad: The Pioneer Press, 1903.

———. *Imperial Rule in India.* Westminster: Archibald Constable & Co., 1899.

Naẕīr Ahmad. *The Bride's Mirror or Mir-Ātu l-Arūs.* Translated by G. E. Ward. London: Henry Frowde, 1899.

———. *The Taubau-n-Nasûh.* Translated by M. Kempson. London: W. H. Allen & Co., 1886.

Nesfield, John C. *A Brief View of the Caste System of the North-Western Provinces and Oudh.* Allahabad: N.W.P. and Oudh Government Press, 1885.

Pirzada, Syed Sharfuddin, ed. *Foundations of Pakistan.* Vol. I. Karachi: National Publishing House, n.d.

Pratap, Mahendra. *My Life Story of Fiftyfive Years.* Dehra Dun: World Federation, 1947.

Raleigh, Walter. *Laughter from a Cloud.* London: Constable & Co., 1923.

———. *The Letters of Sir Walter Raleigh.* Edited by Lady Raleigh. Vol. I. New York: Macmillan, 1926.

Rattigan, William Henry. *A Digest of Civil Law for the Punjab.* Ed. H.A.B. Rattigan. 7th ed. Lahore: Civil and Military Gazette, 1909.

Riza Ali, Syed. *Essays on Moslem Questions.* Allahabad: Standard Press, 1912.

Roberts, Lord. *Forty-One Years in India.* 2 vols. London: Richard Bently and Son, 1897.

Selkirk, George H. *Guide to the Cricket Ground.* London: Macmillan, 1867.

Server-ul-Mulk. *My Life.* Translated by Niwab Jivan Yar Jung Bahadur. London: Arthur H. Stockwell, n.d.

Shibli Numani, Muhammad. *Sirat al-Nabi*. Translated by Fazlur Rahman. Karachi: Pakistan Historical Society, 1970.

Shureef, Jaffur. *Qanoon-e-Islam*. 2d ed. Madras: J. Higginbotham, 1863.

Sidgwick, Henry. *The Methods of Ethics*. Reprint ed. Chicago: University of Chicago Press, 1962.

[Sita Ram]. *From Sepoy to Subahdar*. Translated from Hindi by Lieutenant-Colonel Norgate. Edited by D. C. Phillot. 8th ed. Calcutta: Thacker Spink & Co., 1933.

Sleeman, W. H. *Rambles and Reflections of an Indian Official*. 2 vols. London: J. Hatchard and Son, 1844.

Strachey, John. *Hastings and the Rohilla War*. Oxford: Clarendon Press, 1892.

———. *India*. 2d ed. London: Kegan, Paul, Trench, Trübner & Co., 1894.

Watson, J. Forbes and Kaye, John Wilson, eds. *The People of India*. 10 vols. London: India Museum, 1868-1875.

Whitehead, Alfred North. *The Aims of Education*. New York: Mentor Books, 1949.

Wright, W. H. *The Muir College, Allahabad*. Allahabad: Government Press, N.W.P. and Oudh, 1886.

SECONDARY WORKS IN URDU (SELECTED LIST)

ʿAbd ul-Ḥaq. *Cand Ham ʿAṣr*. Reprint ed. Karachi: Urdu Academy, 1959.

———. *Marḥūm Dehlī Kālij*. Delhi: Anjuman-i Taraqqī-i Urdū, n.d.

———. *Sar Sayyid Aḥmad K͟hān*. Delhi: Urdū Markaz, 1960.

ʿAbd ul-Karan, Sayyid. *Taẕkirah-i Maulvī Samīʿ Ullāh K͟hān marḥūm*. Agra: Shamsi Machine Press, n.d.

ʿAbd ul-Shakūr. *Ḥasrat Mohānī*. Lucknow: Anvar Book Depot, 1953.

ʿAbd ur-Raḥmān, ed. *Ḥayāt-i Ḥamīd*. Azamgarh: Maʿārif, 1973.

ʿĀbid Ḥusain, Ṣālḥah. *Yādgār-i Ḥālī*. 2d ed. Aligarh: Anjuman-i Taraqqī-i Urdū, [1955].

Aḥmad K͟hān, Mushtāq. *Ḥayāt-i Fak͟hr*. Lahore: Nuqūsh Press, 1966.

ʿAṭā, Ashraf. *Maulānah Ẓafar ʿAlī Khān*. Lahore: Caravan [1962].

ʿAlīgaṛh Megzīn: ʿAlīgaṛh Number. 1953-1954, 1954-1955.

———: *Shakhṣīyat Number*. January 1939.

ʿAzmī, ʿAbd ul-Laṭīf. *Bābā-i Urdū Maulvī ʿAbd ul-Ḥaq*. Luck now: Idarah-i Farogh-i Urdū, 1962.

Badāyūnī, Niẓāmi. *Qāmūs al-Mushāhīr*. 2 vols. Badaun: Nizami Press, 1926.

Badāyūnī, Ahīduddīn Niẓāmā, ed. *Yādgār-i Ṭufail*. Badaun: Nizami Press, 1946.

Badāyūnī, Qamruddīn Aḥmad. *Maḥfil-i ʿAzīz*. Hyderbad: Aʿjāz Printing Press, 1962.

Cishtī, Sirāj Aḥmad Usmānī. "Bābā-i Urdū kē baṛē bhā'ī." *Qaumī Zubān*, August 16, 1964.

Dehlvī, Sayyid Aḥmad. *Rasūm-i Dehlī*. Reprint ed. Rampur: Kitābkār Publications, 1965.

Ḥālī, Khvājah Alṭāf Ḥusain. *Ḥayāt-i jāvīd*. Reprint ed. Lahore: Aʿīnah-i Adab, 1966.

Iftikhār ʿĀlam (Bilgrāmī), Sayyid. *Ḥayāt un-Naẕīr*. Delhi: Shamsi Press, 1912.

———. *Muḥammadan Kālij Histaṛī*. Agra: Mufīd-i ʿĀm Press, 1901.

Ikrām, Shaikh Muḥammad. "Maulānā Muḥammad Fārūq Ciryākōṭī aur un kā naẓriyah-i 'ulūm aur ta'līm." *Al-Ma'ārif* (Lahore, 1969), pp. 3-13.

Ikrāmullāh Khān, Muḥammad. *Viqār-i Ḥayāt*. Aligarh: Muslim University, 1925.

Ja'frī, Sayyid Ra'īs Aḥmad, ed. *'Alī birādarān*. Lahore: Muhammad Ali Academy, 1963.

———. *Sīrat-i Muḥammad 'Alī*. Delhi: Maktūbah-i Jāmiʿah Milliyah Islāmiyah, 1932.

Khān, Ghulām Samdānī. *Tuzuk-i Maḥbūbiyah*. Hyderabad: Niẓām ul-Muṭābaḥ Press, n.d.

Khān, Ḥabībullāh. *Ḥayāt-i Aftāb*. Allahabad: Asrār Karīmī Press [1947].

Nadvī, Sayyid Sulaimān. *Ḥayāt-i Shiblī*. Azamgarh: Maṭbūʿah Ma'ārif, 1943.

Naim, C. M. *Readings in Urdu Prose and Poetry*. Honolulu: East-West Center Press, 1965.

Qureshī, Nasīm, ed. *'Alīgarh tahrīk: aghāz tā imrōz*. Aligarh: Aligarh Muslim University, 1960.

Raḥmān 'Alī. *Tazkīrah-i 'ulamā-i Hind*. Revised and translated from Persian to Urdu by Muḥammad Ayyūb Qādrī. Karachi: Pakistan Historical Society, 1961.

Sharār, 'Abd ul-Ḥalīm. *Guzashtah Lakhnau*. Reprint ed. Lucknow: Nasīm Book Depot, 1965.

Shervāniyah, Anīsah Hārūn Begam. *Ḥayāt-i Z. Kh. Sh.* Hyderabad. A'jāz Printing Machine, n.d.

Ṣiddīqī, Muḥammad 'Atīq. *Hindūstānī akhbār navīsī*. Aligarh: Anjuman-i Taraqqī-i Urdū (Hind), 1957.

Ṣiddīqī, Rashīd Aḥmad. *Ashuftah bayānī mērī*. Delhi: Maktūbah-i Jāmī'ah Ltd., 1966.

Surūr, Āl-i Aḥmad. *Naē aur purānē cirāgh*. Lucknow: Idārah-i Farōgh-i Urdū, 1963.

Ṭayyib, Muḥammad. *Dār ul-'ulūm Deoband*. Deoband: Daftar-i Ahtimām, Dār ul-'ulūm, Deoband, 1965.

Zakā' Ullāh. *Savāniḥ-i 'umrī Ḥājī Maulvī Muḥammad Samī' Ullāh Khān Bahādur*. Hyderabad: Nūr ul-Islām, 1909.

Zuberī, Anvār Aḥmad, ed. *Khuṭbāt-i 'Āliyah*. 3 vols. Aligarh: Muslim University Press, 1927-1928.

Zuberī, Muḥammad Amīn. [Untitled ms. history of the M.A.O. College and Muslim University, Aligarh, in 3 vols. at the Pakistan Historical Society, Karachi.]

———. *Ḥayāt-i Muḥsin*. Aligarh: Muslim University Press, 1934.

———. *Tazkirah-i Sar Sayyid*. Lahore: Publishers United, 1964.

———. *Tazkirah-i Sayyid Maḥmud marḥūm*. Bashīr Pāshah Series, Islamia High School, Etawah. Aligarh: Muslim University Press, n.d.

———. *Tazkirah-i Viqār*. Agra: 'Azīzī Press, 1938.

———. *Ziyā-i Ḥayāt*. Karachi: Maṭbū'ah Dīn Muḥammadīn, n.d.

———. *Zikr-i Shiblī*. Lucknow: Dānish Mahal, 1946.

Zūlfiqār, Ghulām Husain. *Zafar 'Alī Khān*. Lahore: Maktubah-i Khayābān-i Adab, 1967.

Zulqarnain: Ṭūfail Number. Badaun: Nizami Press, 1946.

SECONDARY WORKS IN EUROPEAN LANGUAGES (SELECTED LIST)

Abdul Hamid. *Muslim Separatism in India.* 2d ed. Lahore: Oxford University Press, 1971.

'Abdu'l-Laṭīf, Sayyid. *The Influence of English Literature on Urdu Literature.* London: Forster Groom & Co., 1924.

Abdul Qadir. *Famous Urdu Poets and Writers.* Lahore: New Book Society, 1947.

Abid Husain, S. *The Destiny of India's Muslims.* Bombay: Asia Publishing House, 1965.

———. *The National Culture of India.* Reprint ed. Bombay: Jaico Publishing House, 1956.

Ahmad, Jamil-ud-din. *The Early Phase of the Muslim Political Movement.* Lahore: Publishers United Ltd. [1967].

Ahmad, Qeyyumuddin. *The Wahabi Movement in India.* Calcutta: Firma K. L. Mukhopadhyay, 1966.

Ahmadali, S. Abid and Umaruddin, M. *Aligarh Muslim University Handbook.* Aligarh: Aligarh Muslim University Press, 1931.

Ahmad Khan, Muin-ud-din. *A Bibliographical Introduction to Modern Islamic Development in India and Pakistan, 1700-1955.* Dacca: Journal of the Asiatic Society of Pakistan, 1959.

Ali, Ahmed. *Twilight in Delhi.* Reprint ed. Bombay: Oxford University Press, 1966.

Andrews, C. F. *Zaka Ullah of Delhi.* Cambridge: W. Heffer & Sons, 1929.

Apter, David E., ed. *Ideology and Discontent.* London: Free Press of Glencoe, 1964.

Arendt, Hannah. *The Origins of Totalitarianism.* 3d ed. New York: Harcourt, Brace & World, 1966.

Ashby, Eric. *Universities: British, Indian, African.* London: Weidenfeld & Nicholson, 1966.

Athar Ali, M. *The Mughal Nobility under Aurangzeb.* Bombay: Asia Publishing House, 1966.

Aziz, K. K. *Ameer Ali: His Life and Work.* Lahore: Publishers United, Ltd., 1968.

———. *Britain and Muslim India, 1857-1947.* London: Heinemann, 1963.

———. *The Making of Pakistan*. London: Chatto & Windus, 1967.

Aziz Ahmad. *Islamic Modernism in India and Pakistan, 1857-1964*. London: Oxford University Press, 1967.

———. *Studies in Islamic Culture in the Indian Environment*. Oxford: Clarendon Press, 1964.

———, and von Grunebaum, G. E. *Muslim Self-Statement in India and Pakistan, 1857-1968*. Wiesenbaden: Otto Harrassowitz, 1970.

Bamford, T. W. *The Rise of the Public School*. London: Nelson, 1967.

Baljon, Jr., J.M.S. *The Reforms and Religious Ideas of Sir Sayyid Ahmad Khan*. 3d ed. Lahore: Sh. Muhammad Ashraf, 1964.

Berger, Peter L., and Luckmann, Thomas. *The Social Construction of Reality*. 2d ed. Garden City: Anchor Books, 1967.

Bhargava, Moti Lal. *History of Secondary Education in Uttar Pradesh*. Lucknow: Superintendent, Printing and Stationery, Uttar. Pradesh, 1958.

Bhatnagar, S. K. *History of the M.A.O. College Aligarh*. Bombay: Asia Publishing House for Sir Syed Hall, Aligarh Muslim University, 1969.

Blunt, E.A.H. *The Caste System of Northern India*. Reprint ed. Delhi: S. Chand, 1969.

Bouet, Marcel. *Signification du sport*. 4th ed. Paris: Editions Universitaires, 1968.

Buckland, C. E. *Dictionary of Indian Biography*. London: Swan Sonnenschien & Co., 1906.

Buckler, F. W. "The Political Theory of the Indian Mutiny," *Transactions of the Royal Historical Society*, Series 4, V (1922), 71-100.

Brass, Paul R. "Muslim Separatism in the United Provinces: Social Context and Political Strategy before Partition," *Economic and Political Weekly*, V (Annual Number, 1970), 167-186.

———. *Religion, Language and Politics in Northern India*. Cambridge: Cambridge University Press, 1974.

Campbell, A. Claude. *Glimpses of the Nizam's Dominions*. Bombay: C. B. Burrows, 1898.

Case, Margaret Harrison. "The Aligarh Era: Muslim Politics in North India, 1860-1910." Ph.D. dissertation, University of Chicago, 1970.

Chaudhuri, Nirad C. "The 'Martial Races' of India," *Modern Review*, LXVIII (1931), 41-51, 295-307.

Churchill, Edward D., Jr. "The Muhammadan Education Conference and the Aligarh Movement." Paper read at the Association for Asian Studies Annual Meeting, New York City, March 1972.

Cohn, Bernard S. "The Census, Social Structure and Objectification in South Asia." Paper read at the Second European Conference on Modern South Asia, Elsinore, Denmark, June 1970.

———. "The Initial British Impact on India: A Case Study of the Benares Region," *Journal of Asian Studies*, XIX (1960), 418-431.

Dar, Bashir Ahmad. *The Religious Thought of Sayyid Ahmad Khan*. Lahore: Institute of Islamic Culture, 1957.

Davison, Roderic H. *Reform in the Ottoman Empire, 1856-1876*. Princeton: Princeton University Press, 1963.

de Bary, William Theodore, ed. *Sources of Indian Tradition*. Paperback ed. 2 vols. New York: Columbia University Press, 1970.

The Dictionary of National Biography. Reprint and Supplements. 28 vols. London: Oxford University Press, 1921-1971.

Dumont, Louis. "Nationalism and Communalism," *Contributions to Indian Sociology*, VIII (1964), 30-70.

———. *Homo Hierarchicus*. 2d ed. of English translation. London: Paladin, 1972.

Durkheim, Emile. *Moral Education*. New York: Free Press, 1961.

Dutt, K. Iswara. *Congress Cyclopaedia*. New Delhi: by the author [1967].

Eisenstadt, S. N. *From Generation to Generation*. Glencoe: Free Press, 1956.

———. *The Political System of Empires*. Paperback ed. New York: Free Press, 1969.

Embree, Ainslee T. *India's Search for National Identity*. New York: Alfred A. Knopf, 1972.

Eminent Musalmans. Madras: G. A. Natesan & Co., 1926.

The Encyclopaedia of Islām. 4 vols. Leiden: E. J. Brill, 1908-1934.

———. New ed. 4 vols. and fascicles. Leiden: E. J. Brill, 1960-1974.

Erikson, Erik H. *Childhood and Society.* 2d ed. New York: W. W. Norton, 1963.

———. *Identity: Youth and Crisis.* New York: W. W. Norton, 1968.

Fanon, Frantz. *Black Skins, White Masks.* New York: Grove Press, 1967.

Faruqi, Ziya-ul-Hasan. *The Deoband School and the Demand for Pakistan.* Bombay: Asia Publishing House, 1963.

Forster, E. M. *Abinger Harvest.* Reprint ed. New York: Harcourt, Brace & World, n.d.

Foster, Joseph. *Alumni Orienses.* Vol. IV. Oxford: Oxford University Press, 1888.

Fox, Richard G. *Kin, Clan, Raja and Rule.* Berkeley and Los Angeles: University of California Press, 1971.

Futehally, Zeenuth. *Zohra.* Bombay: Hind Kitabs, Ltd., 1951.

Gallagher, John; Johnson, Gordon; and Seal, Anil, eds. *Locality, Province and Nation.* Cambridge: Cambridge University Press, 1973.

Garcin de Tassy, J.H.S.V. *Memoire sur des particularités de la religion musalmane dans l'Inde d'après les ouvrages hindustani.* Paris: Nouveau Journal Asiatique, 1831.

Garett, H.L.O., and Abdul Hamid. *A History of Government College Lahore.* Lahore: Government College Lahore, 1964.

Geertz, Clifford, ed. *Old Societies and New States.* New York: Free Press, 1963.

Gibb, H.A.R. "Some Considerations on the Sunni Theory of the Caliphate," *Archives d'histoire du droit oriental,* III (1947), 401-410.

Gilbert, Irene Adele. "The Men Who Taught India: A Study of the Indian Education Service, 1864-1924." Ph.D. dissertation, University of Chicago, 1972.

Goffman, Erving. *Asylums.* Garden City: Anchor Books, 1961.

Gopal, Ram. *The Indian Muslims: A Political History.* Bombay: Asia Publishing House, n.d.

Gopal, Madan. *The Punjab Land Revenue Act (XVII of 1887).* 2d ed. Lahore: Punjab Christian Press, 1911.

Gopal, S. *British Policy in India, 1858-1905*. Cambridge: Cambridge University Press, 1965.

Gordon, Michael, ed. *The American Family in Social-Historical Perspective*. New York: St. Martin's Press, 1973.

Graham, G.F.I. *The Life and Work of Syed Ahmed Khan, C. S. I.* Edinburgh: William Blackwood and Sons, 1885. 2d ed. London: Hodder & Stoughton, 1909.

Graham, Gail Minault. "The Khilafat Movement: A Study of Indian Muslim Leadership, 1919-1924." Ph.D. dissertation, University of Pennsylvania, 1972.

Grierson, George Abraham. *The Linguistic Survey of India*. Vol. I, Part 1. Calcutta: Government of India, 1927.

Gumperz, Ellen M[cDonald]. "English Education and Social Change in Late Nineteenth Century Bombay, 1858-1898." Ph.D. dissertation, University of California, Berkeley, 1965.

Habib, Irfan. *The Agrarian System of Mughal India*. Bombay: Asia Publishing House, 1963

———. "The Social Distribution of Landed Property in Pre-British India," *Enquiry*, New Series II, No. 3 (Winter 1965), 21-75.

Haq, Mushir U. *Muslim Politics in Modern India, 1857-1947*. Meerut: Meenakshi Prakashan, 1970.

Hardy, P. *The Muslims of British India*. Cambridge: Cambridge University Press, 1972.

Hassan, Rahmani Begum Mohammad Ruknuddin. "The Educational Movement of Sir Syed Ahmed Khan." Ph.D. dissertation, School of Oriental and African Studies, University of London, 1959.

Hirt, H. F. "Aligarh, U.P.: A Geographical Study of Urban Growth." Ph.D. dissertation, Syracuse University, 1955.

Hodgson, Marshall G. S. *The Venture of Islam*. 3 vols. Chicago: University of Chicago Press, 1975.

Holroyd, Michael. *Lytton Strachey*. Paperback ed. Harmondsworth: Penguin Books, Ltd., 1971.

Hosain, Attiya. *Phoenix Fled*. London: Chatto and Windus, 1953.

Hughes, Thomas. *Tom Brown's Schooldays*. Reprint ed. Baltimore: Penguin Books, 1972.

Huizinga, J. *Homo Ludens*. Boston: Beacon Press, 1950.

Hussain, M. Hadi. *Syed Ahmed Khan: Pioneer of Muslim Resurgence*. Lahore: Institute of Islamic Culture, 1970.

Ikram, S. M. *Modern Muslim India and the Birth of Pakistan.* 2d ed. Lahore: Sh. M. Ashraf, 1965.

Iqbal, Afzal. *The Life and Times of Mohamed Ali.* Lahore: Institute of Islamic Culture, 1974.

Iyer, Rahgavan, ed. *South Asian Affairs*, No. 1 (1960); *St. Antony's Papers*, No. 8. Carbondale: Southern Illinois University Press, 1960.

Jain, M. S. *The Aligarh Movement.* Agra: Sri Mehra & Co., 1965.

Jamil, S. M., ed. *The Muslim Year Book of India and Who's Who . . . 1948-49.* Bombay: Bombay Newspaper Co., 1948.

Kabadi, Waman P. *Indian Who's Who, 1937-38.* Bombay: Yeshanand & Co., n.d.

Karandikar, M. A. *Islam in India's Transition to Modernity.* Bombay: Orient Longmanns, 1968.

Kennedy, J. "Personal Reminiscences of Sir Syad Ahmad," *Asiatic Quarterly Review*, VI (1898), 145-151.

Kessinger, Tom G. *Vilayatpur, 1848-1968.* Berkeley and Los Angeles: University of California Press, 1974.

Khan, Iqtidar Alam. "The Nobility under Akbar and the Development of His Religious Policy, 1560-80," *Journal of the Royal Asiatic Society of Great Britain and Ireland* (1968), pp. 29-36.

Khwaja, A. M. *The Early Life of the First Student of the M.A.O. College.* Allahabad: Allahabad Law Journal Press, 1916.

Kipling, Rudyard, *Stalky & Company.* Reprint ed. New York: Macmillan, 1962.

Kraemer, H. "Islam in India Today," *Moslem World*, XXI (1931), 151-176.

Kuhn, Thomas S. *The Structure of Scientific Revolutions.* Chicago: University of Chicago Press, 1962.

Lal Bahadur. *The Muslim League.* Agra: Agra Book Store, 1962.

Lelyveld, David. "Three Aligarh Students: Aftab Ahmad Khan, Ziauddin Ahmad and Muhammad Ali," *Modern Asian Studies*, IX (1975), 103-116.

Leonard, Karen Bush. "The Kayasths of Hyderabad City: Their Internal History and Their Role in Politics and Society, from 1850 to 1900." Ph.D. dissertation, University of Wisconsin, 1969.

Lewis, Bernard. *The Emergence of Modern Turkey.* London: Oxford University Press, 1961.

Low, D. A., ed. *Soundings in Modern South Asian History*. London: Weidenfeld & Nicholson, 1968.

Malik, Hafeez. *Moslem Nationalism in India and Pakistan*. Washington: Public Affairs Press, 1963.

———. "Sir Sayyid Ahmad Khan's Contribution to the Development of Muslim Nationalism in India," *Modern Asian Studies*, IV (1970), 129-147.

———. "Sir Sayyid Ahmad Khan's Doctrines of Muslim Nationalism and National Progress," *Modern Asian Studies*, II (1968), 221-244.

———. "Sir Sayyid Ahmad Khan's Role in the Development of Muslim Nationalism in the Indo-Pakistan Sub-Continent," *Islamic Studies*, V (1966), 385-410.

McCully, Bruce Tiebout. *English Education and the Origins of Indian Nationalism*. Reprint ed. Gloucester, Mass.: Peter Smith, 1966.

McDonald, Ellen E. "English Education and Social Reform in Late Nineteenth Century Bombay: A Case Study in the Transmission of a Cultural Ideal," *Journal of Asian Studies*, XXV (1966), 453-470.

———. "The Modernizing of Communication: Vernacular Publishing in Nineteenth Century Maharashtra," *Asian Survey*, VIII (1968), 589-606.

———, and Stark, Craig M. *English Education, Nationalist Politics and Elite Groups in Maharashtra, 1885-1915*. Occasional Paper No. 5. Berkeley: Center for South and South-East Asian Studies, University of California, 1969.

Mehta, H. R. *A History of the Growth and Development of Western Education in the Punjab (1846-1884)*. Lahore: Punjab Government Records Office Publications, 1929.

Metcalf, Barbara Daly. "The Reformist ʿUlamā: Muslim Religious Leadership in India, 1860-1900." Ph.D. dissertation, University of California, Berkeley, 1974.

Metcalf, Thomas R. *The Aftermath of Revolt*. Princeton: Princeton University Press, 1965.

Minault, Gail, and Lelyveld, David. "The Campaign for a Muslim University, 1898-1920," *Modern Asian Studies*, VIII (1974), 145-189.

Misra, B. B. *The Indian Middle Classes*. London: Oxford University Press, 1961.

Mudiraj, K. Krishnaswamy. *Pictorial Hyderabad.* Vol. II. Hyderabad: Chanda Kanth Press, 1934.

Mujeeb, M. *The Indian Muslims.* London: George Allen & Unwin, 1967.

Nanda, B. R. *The Nehrus.* New York: John Day Company, 1963.

Nehru, Jawaharlal. *An Autobiography.* Reprint ed. Bombay: Allied Publishers, 1962.

Nevill, H. R. *Aligarh: A Gazetter.* Allahabad: Government Press, United Provinces, 1909.

Newsome, David. *Godliness and Good Learning.* London: Murray, 1961.

Nizami, K. A. *Sayyid Ahmad Khan.* New Delhi: Publications Division, 1966.

Nizami, Taufiq Ahmad. *Moslem Political Thought and Activity in India During the Nineteenth Century.* Aligarh: Three Men's Publications, 1969.

Nagar, R. N. "The Tahsildar in the Ceded and Conquered Provinces (1801-1833)," *Journal of the Uttar Pradesh Historical Society,* New Series, II (1954), 26-34.

Nurullah, Syed, and Naik, J. P. *A History of Education in India.* Bombay: Macmillan, 1951.

Pakistan Historical Society. *A History of the Freedom Movement.* 3 vols. in 4. Karachi: Pakistan Historical Society, 1957-1963.

Papanek, Hanna. "Purdah: Separate Worlds and Symbolic Shelter," *Comparative Studies in Society and History,* XV (1973), 289-325.

Patterson, H. Orlando. "The Ritual of Cricket," *Jamaica Journal,* III, 1 (March 1969), 23-25.

Peters, Thomas, ed. *Who's Who in India.* Poona: Sun Publishing Co., n.d.

Philips, C. H., ed. *Historians of India, Pakistan, and Ceylon.* London: Oxford University Press, 1961.

Pradhan, M. C. *The Political System of the Jats of Northern India.* Bombay: Oxford University Press, 1966.

Prasad, Beni. *The Hindu-Muslim Question.* 2d ed. Lahore: Minerva Book Shop, 1943.

Previté-Orton, C. W. *Index to Tripos List, 1748-1910.* Cambridge: Cambridge University Press, 1923.

Rahbar, Muhammad Daud. "Sir Sayyid Ahmad Khan's Principles of Exigesis." *Muslim World*, XLVI (1956), 104-112, 324-325.

Raleigh, Thomas. *Annals of the Church of Scotland*. London: Oxford University Press, 1921.

Reany, Mabel Jane. *The Psychology of the Organized Group Game*. Monograph Supplement IV, *British Journal of Psychology*. Cambridge: University Press, 1916.

Robinson, Francis. *Separatism among Indian Muslims*. Cambridge: Cambridge University Press, 1974.

Rothblatt, Sheldon. *The Revolution of the Dons*. London: Faber and Faber, 1968.

Russell, Ralph, and Khurshidul Islam. *Ghalib: Life and Letters*. London: George Allen and Unwin, 1969.

———. "The Satirical Verse of Akbar Ilāhābādī," *Modern Asian Studies*, VIII (1974), 1-58.

———. *Three Mughal Poets*. Cambridge: Harvard University Press, 1968.

Sadiq, Muhammad. *A History of Urdu Literature*. London: Oxford University Press, 1964.

Saran, P. *The Provincial Government of the Mughals*. Allahabad: Kitabistan, 1941.

Sarda, Har Bilas. *Life of Dayanand Saraswati*. Ajmere: P. Bhagwan Swarup, 1946.

Sarkar, Jadunath. *The Mughal Administration*. Calcutta: M. C. Sarkar, 1920.

Seal, Anil. *The Emergence of Indian Nationalism*. Cambridge: Cambridge University Press, 1968.

Shan Muhammad. *Sir Syed Ahmad Khan: A Political Biography*. Meerut: Meenakshi Prakashan, 1969.

S[idgwick], A. S., and E. M. *Henry Sidgwick*. London: Macmillan, 1906.

Smith, Wilfred Cantwell. *Islam in Modern History*. Paperback ed. New York: Mentor Books, 1959.

———. *Modern Islām in India*. Reprint ed. Lahore: Sh. Muhammad Ashraf, 1963.

Stokes, Adrian. "Psycho-Analytic Reflections on the Development of Ball Games, Particularly Cricket," *International Journal of Psycho-Analysis*, XXXVII (1956), 185-192.

Sufi, G.D.M. *All-Minhāj: Being the Evolution of Curriculum in the Muslim Educational Institutions of India.* Lahore: Shaikh Muhammad Ashraf, 1941.

Suhrawardy, Shāista Akhtar Banu. *A Critical Survey of the Development of the Urdu Novel and Short Story.* London: Longmanns, Green & Co., 1945.

Tandon, Prakash. *Punjabi Century, 1857-1947.* Paperback ed. Berkeley and Los Angeles: University of California Press, n.d.

Tyabji, Husain B. *Badruddin Tyabji.* Bombay: Thacker & Co., [1952].

Venn, J. A. *Alumni Cantabrigienses.* Part II, 6 vols. Cambridge: Cambridge University Press, 1922-1940.

Von Grunebaum, G. E. *Medieval Islam.* Chicago: University of Chicago Press, 1953.

———. *Modern Islam: The Search for Cultural Identity.* Berkeley and Los Angeles: University of California Press, 1962.

Vreede-de Stuers, Cora. *Parda.* Assen, The Netherlands: Van Gorcum, 1968.

Wallerstein, Immanel, ed. *Social Change: The Colonial Situation.* New York: John Wiley & Sons, 1966.

Watt, W. Montgomery. *Islam and the Integration of Society.* London: Routledge and Kegan Paul, 1961.

Weinberg, Ian. *The English Public Schools.* New York: Atherton Press, 1967.

Wilkenson, Rupert. *The Prefects.* London: Oxford University Press, 1964.

Wise, James. "The Muhammadans of Eastern Bengal," *The Journal of the Asiatic Society of Bengal,* LXIII (1894), Part III, 28-63.

Wright, W. H. *The Muir Central College, Allahabad.* Allahabad: Government Press, North-Western Provinces and Oudh, 1-86.

Yasin, Mohammad. *A Social History of Islamic India.* 2d ed. Delhi: Munshiram Manoharlal, 1974.

Young, G. M. *Victorian England: Portrait of an Age.* London: Oxford University Press, 1960.

Yusufi, Allah Bakhsh. *Life of Maulana Mohamed Ali Jauhar.* Karachi: Mohamed Ali Educational Society, 1970.

Zakaria, Rafiq. *The Rise of Muslims in Indian Politics.* 2d ed. Bombay: Somaiya Publications, 1971.

Ziaul Haque. "Muslim Religious Education in Indo-Pakistan: An Annotated Bibliography." Occasional Papers Series, Muslim Studies Sub-Committee, Committee on South Asian Studies, University of Chicago, 1972.

INTERVIEWS

Maulana Abdur Rahman, Sarai Mir, Azamgarh District, 1969.
Mrs. Hamiduddin Ahmad, St. Paul, Minnesota, 1973.
Mr. Mushtaq Ahmad, Aligarh, 1968-1969.
Dr. S. Abid Ahmedali, Lahore, 1969.
Maulvi Muzammil Abbasi, Azamgarh, 1969.
Mr. M. A. Abbasi, Hyderabad (India), 1969.
Justice Sharfuddin Ahmad, Hyderabad (India), 1969.
Mr. Hashim Muhamad Ali, Karachi, 1969.
Mr. Mahboob Ali, Hyderabad (India), 1969.
Begam Habibullah, Lucknow, 1968-1969.
Mrs. Mumtaz Haidar, Aligarh, 1969.
Mrs. Quraitualain Haidar, Bombay, 1969.
Dr. K. Sarwar Hasan, Karachi, 1969.
Justice Mushtaq Husain, Lahore, 1969.
Mr. Haleem Jang, Delhi, 1969.
Mr. Abad Ahmad Khan, Lahore, 1969.
Mr. Mujahid Kazmi, Karachi, 1969.
Professor Hamid Ahmad Khan, Lahore, 1969.
Mr. Mukhtar Ali Khan, Hyderabad (India), 1969.
Mrs. Najf Ali Khan, Hyderabad (India), 1969.
Mrs. Shakir Ali Khan, Lahore, 1969.
Khwaja Muhammad Yunus and Khwaja Muhammad Masud, Aligarh, 1968.
Professor and Mrs. Jamil Khwaja, Aligarh, 1968.
Professor A. M. Kureshy, Karachi, 1969.
Maulana Abdul Malik, Karachi, 1969.
Mr. Akbar Masood, Karachi, 1969.
Mr. Sajjad Mirza, Hyderabad (India), 1968.
Mr. Ahmad Rafiq, Delhi, 1969.
Professor Shaikh Abdur Rashid, Lahore, 1967.
Professor Haroon Khan Sherwani, Hyderabad (India), 1968.
Mr. Shaukat Sultan, Azamgarh, 1969.
Sayyid Hadi Husain Zaidi, Aligarh, 1969.
Mr. Masud Zaidi, Lahore, 1969.

Index